PE

PRINCIPLES OF POLITICAL ECONOMY

John Stuart Mill was born in London in 1806. A child of precocious intelligence, he was systematically educated by his father, James Mill, to follow in his footsteps as champion of the utilitarian philosophy. By the age of twenty he had achieved this aim: he was leader of the younger philosophical radicals, active as a propagandist in their intellectual and reforming pursuits. In 1826, however, he endured his first period of mental crisis and found he no longer believed in many aspects of the Benthamite creed. He then began a systematic examination of the alternative positions offered by Coleridge, Carlyle, the St Simonians, Comte and Tocqueville, while keeping his links with the utilitarian circle and contributing to their journal, the *London and Westminster Review*.

By the 1840s Mill was able to put forward a mature reinterpretation of his philosophical position; his *System of Logic* (1843) and the *Principles of Political Economy* (1848) formed the basis for his dominant position in Victorian intellectual life. During the years 1859–65 he wrote the other works for which he is now famous: *On Liberty, Representative Government, Utilitarianism, Examination of Sir William Hamilton's Philosophy*, and *Auguste Comte and Positivism*.

After working for thirty-five years in the East India Company, Mill was a Member of Parliament from 1865 to 1868, voting with the Radical party and strongly advocating women's suffrage. He was also concerned with such issues as the Irish land question, slavery and the American Civil War, income and property taxation, tenure reform, and trade unionism. He died at Avignon in 1873, having finished his *Autobiography* in the same year.

•

Donald Winch was educated at the London School of Economics and Princeton. He is Professor of the History of Economics in the School of Social Sciences at the University of Sussex. Among his books are *Economics and Policy* (1969); (with Susan Howson), *The Economic Advisory Council, 1930–39* (1976); *Adam Smith's Politics* (1978); and (with Stefan Collini and John Burrow), *That Noble Science of Politics* (1983).

JOHN STUART MILL

PRINCIPLES OF
POLITICAL ECONOMY

WITH SOME OF THEIR
APPLICATIONS TO SOCIAL
PHILOSOPHY

BOOKS IV AND V

———————

EDITED WITH AN INTRODUCTION
BY DONALD WINCH

PENGUIN BOOKS

Penguin Books Ltd, Harmondsworth, Middlesex, England
Viking Penguin Inc., 40 West 23rd Street, New York, New York 10010, U.S.A.
Penguin Books Australia Ltd, Ringwood, Victoria, Australia
Penguin Books Canada Ltd, 2801 John Street, Markham, Ontario, Canada L3R 1B4
Penguin Books (N.Z.) Ltd, 182–190 Wairau Road, Auckland 10, New Zealand

—

First published 1848
First published in Pelican Books 1970
Reprinted in Penguin Classics 1985

—

—

Made and printed in Great Britain by
Cox & Wyman Ltd, Reading
Set in Linotype Granjon

Contents

CONTENTS

BOOK V

ON THE INFLUENCE OF GOVERNMENT

CONTENTS

CONTENTS

APPENDIX

BOOK II

DISTRIBUTION

CONTENTS

Introduction

FROM the moment of its first publication in 1848, John Stuart Mill's *Principles of Political Economy, with Some of Their Applications to Social Philosophy* established itself as a classic. For almost half a century, and long after many of its component ideas had been controverted, it had no equal in terms of scope and stature. Considered simply as an economics textbook, it enjoyed a longer active life than any comparable work either before or since. Unlike its successors, including the work which replaced it as the bible of English economics, Alfred Marshall's *Principle of Economics*, published in 1890, it was read by the serious-minded general public as well as by dedicated students and those who merely wished to pass examinations. Indeed, it was the last work of its kind to combine broad appeal with authoritative exposition – a fact which sheds light equally on Mill's position in Victorian intellectual life, his audience, and the change which has occurred in the nature of economics since the end of the nineteenth century. As the subtitle of the book implies, the work was far from being merely a textbook of economic principles. It rapidly became part of the staple diet of progressive-minded Victorians, a common point of departure for those anxious to come to terms with the problems of the new industrial society.

For these reasons alone Mill's *Principles* remains a valuable document to those interested in Victorian economic thought and intellectual debate. But the true significance of the work lies in its author rather than its readers. It is the mature product of one who has strong claims to be at once the best as well as the most influential nineteenth-century representative of the liberal rationalist tradition in social and political thought. As a recent commentator seeking to explain the revival of interest in Mill's writings has said, he is 'perhaps the last major English thinker whose attempt to apply philosophical principles to current issues is still worth examining'.[1]

1. J. B. Schneewind (ed.), *Mill: A Collection of Critical Essays* (Anchor Books: 1968), p. xiii.

Any understanding of Mill's *Principles* must begin with some account of his intellectual career before 1848. As Mill recognized when he wrote his *Autobiography*, our chief interest in his life centres on his early education and the later influences which went to make up his mature position. Like so many of his contemporaries, Mill believed himself to be living in an 'age of transition'. As a guide to the intellectual trends and tensions to which such an age gave rise, Mill has few equals. No other English thinker in the nineteenth century made such a conscientious effort to weld together the most durable elements in the disparate responses produced by an era of unprecedented industrial and social disruption.

*

The rigours of Mill's childhood and education are well known. Greek at three, Latin at eight, Logic at twelve, Political Economy at thirteen, and History, ancient and modern, as a constant accompaniment – these are only the prominent land-marks in a conscious educational experiment carried out by his father, James Mill, designed to produce the consummate utilitarian reasoner. The pupil responded well to this severe regimen. For, at the cost of isolation from other children, he believed that his education gave him 'an advantage of a quarter of a century over my contemporaries'.[2] By the age of fifteen, when he read Bentham's *Treatise on Legislation*, Mill had accepted completely the utilitarian theory of morals and principles of reform. It provided him with 'a creed, a doctrine, a philosophy; in the best sense of the word, a religion; the inculcation and diffusion of which could be made the principal outward purpose of life'.[3] For the next four years or so Mill was at the centre of the group of young philosophical radicals which formed around his father in the 1820s. The characteristic beliefs of this group, modelled on the French *philosophes* of the eighteenth century, are described in detail by Mill in the chapter of his *Autobiography* entitled 'Youthful Propagandism'. In brief, they consisted of an amalgam

2. *Autobiography* (Columbia University Press: 1924), p. 21.
3. ibid., p. 47.

of Benthamite ideas on morals, legal reform and legislation, supplemented by Ricardian political economy and Hartleian metaphysics. The principle of the greatest happiness of the greatest number furnished them with an external, impartial and objective standard by means of which all existing institutions and policies and their alternatives could be judged. Their self-imposed duty was to expose sham, pretence, fallacious reasoning, sentimentality, mysticism, and the disguised dogma of intuitive understanding – all of which posed a barrier to the cause of legal, political, educational, and economic reform. In politics they advocated representative government on the quasi-Hobbesian grounds that only by this means could the individuals comprising the Many be protected from the depredations of the aristocratic Few. The basic freedoms for which they argued were freedom of discussion, freedom from religious constraints and influence, and freedom of trade and association – leaving the maximum sphere for individual responsibility. Since they believed that individual character was formed by circumstance, education was an essential pre-condition of this programme; it opened up the 'unlimited possibility of improving the moral and intellectual condition of mankind'.[4]

During these years Mill was content to live and work within the circle of philosophic radical speculation, proudly conscious of the fact that it separated him from other modes of thought. His writings were those of a convinced Benthamite radical, vigorous, committed, analytically skilful, but otherwise unoriginal. In 1826, however, at the age of twenty, Mill underwent his first 'mental crisis', when none of the objects in life for which he had been prepared seemed capable of giving him personal fulfilment and happiness. As a result of this crisis he came to believe that his upbringing had neglected – or even been at the expense of – 'feeling' and 'the internal culture of the individual'. From this time on Mill began to move away from his Benthamite origins, acquaintances, and opinions. He undertook an intellectual odyssey which brought him in touch with a number of schools of thought, each of which represented an alternative to his earlier

4. ibid., p. 75.

views. In place of his former sectarianism he adopted a many-sided, eclectic approach to life and to social and political questions.

The works of Wordsworth and other Romantic poets gave him comfort during his mental crisis; he drew closer to Frederick Maurice and John Sterling, two ardent representatives of the point of view associated mainly with the name of Coleridge. From the Coleridgeans Mill acquired a deeper appreciation of the 'passive susceptibilities' as opposed to the 'active capacities', of complex internal states of consciousness and feeling rather than external causes and results. They increased his awareness of the possibility of conflict between 'culture' and the progress of commercial civilization; of the need to consider political and other social institutions from a historical or relativist point of view – to ask what functions they served within a given culture rather than judge them simply as 'survivals', or the result of folly, blind custom and malign influence. In this they prepared the way for the ideas of the St Simonians and other Continental writers, under whose influence he came to believe that society was passing through a period of transition in which negative and destructive criticism of the type practised by the philosophical radicals would eventually give way to a new, organic, and more advanced way of thinking and organizing society. Having discovered, or re-discovered, these paths, Mill went on to explore the work of Carlyle, Comte and Tocqueville, all of whom in varying degrees represented new, and frequently antagonistic, positions to those inculcated by his father. On top of this, in 1830, Mill met the woman whom he eventually married eleven years later: until her death in 1858 Harriet Taylor was Mill's companion, guide and collaborator.

A good deal of Mill scholarship in recent years has been devoted to the task of unravelling and assessing these influences on Mill's mature position: the position upheld in such works as *A System of Logic* (1843), *Principles of Political Economy* (1848), *On Liberty* (1859), and *Considerations on Representative Government* (1861). How far, and in what respects, did they lead Mill to abandon or modify the views acquired from his father? Here we shall consider a few of these strands as they affected the development of Mill's views on political economy and his restatement of them in the *Principles*.

*

Mill was brought up in the very heart of classical political economy as it was undergoing an important transition from the urbane, discursive pattern established by Adam Smith's *Wealth of Nations* at the end of the eighteenth century, towards the more urgent, rigorous and narrowly gauged type of inquiry associated with the name of David Ricardo. The new science which Adam Smith had inaugurated developed rapidly in the first three decades of the nineteenth century, partly as a result of the impetus provided by the pressing economic questions thrown up by the Napoleonic Wars and their aftermath, and partly as a result of the strains connected with the early stages of Britain's transformation from being a predominantly agricultural to an industrial society. The problems of a war economy gave rise to a voluminous pamphlet literature on such issues as the suspension of cash payments by the Bank of England, the rise in the National Debt, and the increasing burden of direct and indirect taxation. Napoleon's attempted economic blockade was responsible for a renewal of the debate started by Adam Smith on the value of the mercantile system, and a preliminary discussion of the relative contributions of agriculture, commerce, and manufacturing to Britain's prosperity. The population problem which nad been placed squarely on the agenda by Thomas Malthus's *Essay on the Principle of Population* in 1798 was further highlighted by the rising cost of poor relief under the Speenhamland system during and after the war; and the means of support for Britain's growing population was brought into dramatic focus by the Corn Law debates of 1814–16. The successful attempt by landowners to gain increased protection from foreign suppliers of grain products, the connexion between food prices and wages, and the evidence gathered during the war which underlined the possibility of diminishing returns in domestic food production – these were the issues which exercised a formative influence on the train of economic speculation in this period.

Several of James Mill's earliest writings were contributions to the debate on these questions.[5] One of these, *Commerce Defended* (1807), brought him into contact with David Ricardo. Almost from the beginning of their close friendship James Mill saw his main task as that of encouraging Ricardo to publish his views on topical questions, and eventually to write a full-scale treatise on political economy. It was indeed largely as a result of James Mill's constant badgering and support that Ricardo produced his *Principles of Political Economy and Taxation* in 1817;[6] and it was this work that furnished the main characteristics and style of reasoning of orthodox political economy for the next ten years or so.

It is not easy to describe the distinctive characteristics of Ricardian economics in a few words; there is in fact considerable debate among scholars on the subject.[7] At the highest level of generality the main preoccupation of Ricardian economics was with the preconditions for the maintenance of economic growth. This would also apply to Adam Smith's work, from which Ricardo, like all other economists writing in this period, took over his most general presumptions and categories concerning the nature of economic processes; the importance of capital accumulation to a 'progressive state'; a belief in the efficacy of competitive market mechanisms; a distrust of government intervention; and the view that consumption was the true end of economic activity. But Ricardo was responsible for drawing together the looser ideas of Adam Smith on the questions of growth and value, and forming them into a strict, deductive model. In essence, the Ricardian system demonstrated that an economy facing rising food costs and experiencing capital accumulation and population growth would eventually approach a stationary state as a result of the downward pressure on profits – the source and motive for further accumulation – caused by higher wage costs and the rising share of total product passing

5. See Donald Winch (ed.), *James Mill, Selected Economic Writings* (Oliver & Boyd: 1966), pp. 23 ff.

6. See ibid., pp. 179–202, for an account of the relationship between Mill and Ricardo.

7. For a complete and convincing treatment of the subject see Mark Blaug's *Ricardian Economics* (Yale University Press: 1958).

into the hands of landowners in the form of rent. The main analytical contribution consisted in the linkage between growth and the theorems determining the shares going to land, labour and capital, the three main factors of production. In the course of designing the model Ricardo also made a distinctive contribution to the labour theory of value and the theory of comparative costs, the former providing an explanation and a means of measuring changes in relative prices, while the latter clarified the gains to be made from international specialization and trade.

Ricardian economics represented a genuine scientific impulse. But it also had the essential practical value of placing at the disposal of the economist a means of showing the advantages of free trade, particularly in foodstuffs; the effects of various taxes and other forms of governmental intervention; and the necessity for curbing the rate of increase in population as a means of raising living standards. Very few economists in the first third of the nineteenth century were Ricardians in the strict sense of the term; but expansions or attempted refutations of Ricardo provided the paradigm for economic inquiry. Similarly, very few economists were Benthamite radicals on matters of legal and political reform. But the union of Benthamism with Ricardianism, absent in Bentham himself, was amply present in James Mill, and to a lesser extent in Ricardo. It was this potent mixture that was passed on to John Stuart Mill.

James Mill had hardly finished acting as schoolmaster to Ricardo when he turned his attention to his son's education in political economy. John's induction into the rigours of Ricardian economics began at the tender age of thirteen, while his father was engaged in writing a 'school-book' on the subject, his *Elements of Political Economy* (1821). The pupil's progress was rapid: by the age of sixteen he was defending his father's views on the labour theory of value in the press. During the next seven years or so Mill wrote a number of articles on economic topics in which he upheld rather dogmatically all of the central tenets and policy conclusions of Ricardo and his father.[8] It was not until 1830–31, when he wrote the essays later published as *Essays on*

8. See *Essays on Economics and Society, Collected Works of John Stuart Mill* (University of Toronto Press: 1967), Vol. IV.

Some Unsettled Questions of Political Economy, that Mill showed he had developed a voice of his own on economic questions by arguing with a subtlety and penetration that his father could never have matched. These essays contain some of his most original contributions to economic analysis, notably on the theory of international values and on the influence of consumption on production; they represent a climax in his interest in economic theory. During the thirties and early forties there was a sharp falling-off in his economic writings. One of the reasons for this undoubtedly was his reaction against his upbringing and his growing involvement with the ideas of those who looked with disfavour on political economy.

The antagonism of the Romantic poets to political economy is legendary; the first wave of critics – Southey, Wordsworth and Coleridge – was quickly followed by another from the literary camp in the shape of Carlyle, Dickens, and, later, Ruskin. It is impossible to do justice here to what was an extremely wide-ranging dispute, albeit a peculiarly lop-sided one in which all the vituperation, frequently bordering on hysteria and scurrility, came from the 'humanist' side. With the partial exception of Malthus's *Essay*, there is little evidence that the poets read the works of the leading economists; they preferred to rely on popularized accounts and personal distillations of what they took to be the 'mood' created by political economy. As for the economists, with one significant exception, they rarely noticed or attempted to reply to their critics. The significant exception, of course, is John Stuart Mill; and even he was more interested in what lay behind the attack than in the actual economic ideas of the poets.[9]

In brief, the poets were reacting partly against their own youthful espousal of extreme perfectibility doctrines, and partly against disturbing features of the contemporary scene: materialism and a growing belief in the power of machines and mechanistic thinking; the 'aggressive individualism of the period'; the decline of benevolence and paternalism associated with the 'old order'; and the dissolution of 'common humanity'

9. For a sympathetic account of one side of this debate see R. Williams, *Culture and Society, 1780–1950* (Penguin Books: 1961).

or the 'social affections' of man. The source of this disruption of the organic order which they yearned for, and sometimes professed to see in medieval society, the causes of the deterioration in the quality of life, were clearly to be found in industrialism and the new commercial spirit. Political economy was seen as the intellectual epitome of these social changes.

Behind the poets' criticisms was a far more fundamental challenge to the position which Mill's education had been designed to foster. It was a challenge to the Enlightenment, indeed to the entire empirical tradition in English thought going back to Locke. The Romantics claimed to be custodians of a way of knowing which transcended all others. Wordsworth put it as follows in his *Preface to Lyrical Ballads*:

... Poetry is the most philosophic of all writing ... its object is truth, not individual and local, but general and operative; not standing upon external testimony, but carried alive into the heart by passion; truth which is its own testimony, which gives competence and confidence to the tribunal to which it appeals ...[10]

It is not difficult to see that this would strike anyone of James Mill's temper as rank mysticism. The distinction between 'is' and 'ought' statements is essential, though difficult to sustain, in any scientific discourse which concerns men in society. In Wordsworth the two levels of discourse are fused. No wonder then that the poets failed to see that in seeking to explain social events the economists were not necessarily giving their approval. The poets were denying the possibility of any alternative and objective way of reaching conclusions about society; they were resisting the whole idea of studying man in society from a scientific point of view.

This was certainly not the position of Comte and the St Simonians, the other main influences on Mill during his period of estrangement from utilitarianism. Having deep roots of their own in the French Enlightenment, they did not doubt the possibility of a science of man. But they were disturbed by the emerging shape of society, and were not satisfied with the English science of political economy as a means of explaining it.

10. *Wordsworth's Poetical Works* (Oxford University Press, 1908), p. 938.

Like the poets they longed for harmony; but unlike the poets they looked forward rather than backward to the emergence of a new organic order. The historical relativism of the St Simonians ran counter to the implicit universalism of the deductive approach embodied in Ricardian political economy; there was also friction between the St Simonian vision of drastic social reorganization, leading ultimately to Socialism, and the concentration of political economists on the workings of the existing state of society. For Comte political economy belonged to the metaphysical and destructive stage of human thought. In the final, positive stage it would no longer exist; it would be completely subsumed in the all-embracing science of sociology, a science which would cover both 'social statics' and 'social dynamics'. Comte, therefore, attacked political economy for its negative character, its failure to take account of the consensus of different social functions, as well as its lack of historical relativity.

One further influence on Mill's train of thought in the period of revolt against his upbringing must be mentioned briefly, namely Macaulay's attack in 1829 on the methodology of his father's *Essay on Government*. The brunt of the attack fell on the use of the deductive method to proceed from rigid and untested assumptions about human motivation to sweeping conclusions as to the best form of government, regardless of time, place, and specific experience. If there was to be a science of politics, Macaulay argued, it would have to be one based on induction and concrete historical experience. Coming as it did when many of Mill's earlier opinions were giving way, Macaulay's strictures made considerable impact; especially as Mill found his father's response unsatisfactory and off-hand. Furthermore, any attack on the 'philosophical' as opposed to 'the empirical mode of treating political phenomena' was bound to raise questions as to the adequacy or appropriateness of the deductive method as applied to the related subject of political economy.

*

Faced with the erosion of many of the opinions that had sustained him earlier, there was only one course open to a man of

Mill's temper: to return to fundamentals, which in this case meant reconstructing the philosophical and methodological basis of his position. It was Mill's firm belief that

in whatever science there are systematic differences of opinion ... the cause will be found to be, a difference in their conceptions of the philosophic method of the science. The parties who differ are guided, either knowingly or unconsciously, by different views concerning the nature of the evidence appropriate to the subject. They differ not solely in what they believe themselves to see, but in the quarter whence they obtained the light by which they think they see it.[11]

Accordingly, in 1830, he began work on the book which thirteen years later was to be published as *A System of Logic, Ratiocinative and Inductive, Being a Connected View of the Principles of Evidence and the Methods of Scientific Investigation*.

Mill's *Logic* and the *Principles* are linked on several different levels. They both belong to the mature and most original phase of his life; and together they form the solid foundation of Mill's reputation as a thinker. The *Logic* was the result of an effort to construct a more capacious system that would contain opinions, new and old, which Mill considered worth preserving. It provided a ground-plan and scaffolding for the mansion he now wished to inhabit; the *Principles* represents a completed example of the architectural style of one of its most serviceable wings. It has been pointed out by Schumpeter that the prefaces to the two works are practically interchangeable; they both insist on the need to harmonize the best ideas to be found in discordant theories; they both eschew claims to originality. In their different ways they were both an attempt to fulfil Mill's intention, as expressed in a letter to John Sterling in 1831, 'to forward that alliance among the most advanced intellects and characters of the age, which is the only definite object I ever have in literature or philosophy so far as I have any general object at all'.[12]

For our purposes, Book VI of the *Logic* – 'On the Logic of the

11. 'On the Definition and Method of Political Economy', as reprinted in *Essays on Economics and Society*, p. 324.

12. F. E. Mineka (ed.), *Earlier Letters of J. S. Mill, 1812–1848, Collected Works* (University of Toronto Press: 1963), Vol. XII, p. 79.

Moral Sciences' – is the most relevant. It is also true to say that this was one of the earliest books to be written, being based on an essay 'On the Definition and Method of Political Economy', written not long after Macaulay's critique. Much of the rest of the work on the methodology of the natural sciences was undertaken in an effort to discredit the foundations of the *a priori* or intuitive view of knowledge, which he believed was 'the great intellectual support of false doctrines and bad institutions';[13] and to re-establish the 'true' experiential method of the natural sciences as the basis for knowledge in the moral or social sciences. In so doing Mill was rejecting the 'intuitional metaphysics' at the root of the conservative reaction against the Enlightenment. As one committed to reform through the agency of scientific knowledge of man, it was essential for Mill to combat the idea that there were certain feelings or qualities of human nature that were indelible or impervious to reason, change, circumstance, and evidence.[14] However important 'feeling' and imagination might be to personal cultivation and the statement of ultimate human objectives, they could never serve as the means for discovering new knowledge. This was to provide one of Mill's reasons for distinguishing between 'science' and 'art', and was based on the distinction between positive 'is' questions and normative 'ought' questions.

This does not mean, of course, that Mill was content to accept either his father's or Bentham's interpretation of human nature, or indeed their views on method. On the contrary, one of the enduring results of his interest in the work of Coleridge and Carlyle was that he acquired a richer appreciation of human motivation and purposes than was contained in the Benthamite conception of 'interests' and 'happiness'. In accepting a more complex picture of man Mill found it necessary to re-draw the map of the social sciences, and to modify his views on the way in which man could be studied. Book VI of the *Logic* represents the culmination of Mill's efforts in this field, and constitutes one of his more lasting contributions. It is a monument to the fact that whatever else Mill may have been – philosopher, economist,

13. *Autobiography*, pp. 157–9.
14. ibid., pp. 191–2.

political scientist and radical – he was above all, and self-consciously, a social scientist, perhaps one of the first to acknowledge himself as such, and use the collective term 'social sciences'.

Mill never wavered in his conviction that the social sciences belonged on the same spectrum and should be cultivated by similar methods to those used in the natural sciences. The main issue was *which* natural scientific methods could be applied to *which* branches of the social sciences, and with what likelihood of success in terms of precise explanation and prediction. The most basic of the social sciences was psychology, or the study of the laws of the individual human mind. Closely related to this was a new science which Mill called ethology, or the study of the laws of the formation of character in different societies or nations. The nearest modern equivalent seems to be social psychology. After these sciences of individual man came those dealing with 'the actions of collective masses of mankind, and the various phenomena which constitute social life'.[15] Mill put forward several collective terms to describe these sciences – social economy, speculative politics, and the natural history of society – but eventually settled for sociology, Comte's 'convenient barbarism'. Again borrowing from Comte, sociology was divided into social statics and social dynamics; the former concerned with 'uniformities of coexistence' in social states, the theory of social consensus, and the latter with the historical laws of succession or social progress.

On the question of method Mill rejected Macaulay's strictures on the deductive method as such. The alternative – reliance on an inductive or experimental method – was not possible when applied to social phenomena, where the causes are complex and not capable of being separated by experiment, and where effects are not easily distinguishable from one another. But he also saw the error of his father's ways. Deduction was needed to avoid the common errors of casual empiricism; but his father had erred in using the analogy with deduction in geometry – a subject in which the results flowing from a single principle are incapable of being modified by any other principle. Sociology

15. *On the Logic of the Moral Sciences* (Library of Liberal Arts: 1965) – a reprint of Book VI of *A System of Logic*, p. 54.

required to be studied as a deductive science according to the model of the physical sciences, namely 'by considering all the causes which conjunctly influence the effect, and compounding their laws with one another.'[16] Using the *a priori*, or direct deductive method, it would be possible to build a positive science of sociology dealing with tendencies if not firm predictions. The *a postereiori* method using concrete observations would then take its place as the means of verifying *a priori* reasoning. With regard to the study of social dynamics, however, Mill gave his blessing to Comte's historical method, which he dubbed, rather quaintly, the inverse deductive method.

One of the results of this process of re-thinking was that Mill abandoned the Benthamite science of government as a separate entity capable of being deduced *à la* Euclid from the single elementary principle of self-interest. In modern terms, he abandoned the narrower science of government and legislation in favour of a science of political sociology. He also recognized that political economy was only one branch of sociology, and that before its principles were applied in practice, many 'disturbing causes', and the laws which governed them, would have to be brought into the reckoning. But there is a difference between Mill's attitude to the Benthamite science of government and his attitude to Ricardian political economy. While he came to believe that the former suffered from grave defects in theory, and therefore ought to be rejected as a separate inquiry, he considered that the latter merely suffered from defects in the application of the theory – a type of defect which could more easily be remedied. This explains Mill's unwillingness, in spite of Comte's influence, to deny the claims of political economy to separate existence. It was, as he said later, 'the only systematic attempt yet made by any body of thinkers, to constitute a science, not indeed of social phenomena generally, but of one great class or division of them'.[17] There was in effect a large and important category of social behaviour which depended on the desire for wealth and could be abstracted from the social consensus. Its deductions on the basis of an *assumed* state of affairs would only be strictly

16. ibid., p. 79.
17. *Auguste Comte and Positivism* (Ann Arbor Paperback: 1961), p. 80.

true in the abstract. But in practice it would be possible to make the proper allowances, especially when the other, as yet embryonic, branches of social science provided greater knowledge of the limiting circumstances.[18] It will be obvious that if Mill had yielded to new influences, with regard to political economy he had not so far yielded much.

Having laid the ground-work for a new synthesis Mill at first decided that the primary task was to begin work on the new science of ethology, and notably political ethology, 'or the theory of the causes which determine the type of character belonging to a people or to an age'.[19] This science would, in Mill's view, provide a necessary foundation for further developments in the science of society as a whole because it would furnish the intermediate links with the basic psychological laws of the human mind. Mill's emphasis on 'psychologism' was to become an important further source of divergence from the holistic approach of Comte. Ethology would serve another useful purpose in demonstrating the influence of laws, customs, and public sentiment on forms of government, and in showing the precise limitations of assumptions, like those made in political economy, concerning human motivation. In this respect ethology was closer to the modern subject of cultural anthropology than to social psychology. After a few years, however, Mill was forced to concede that he was unable to make much progress with the new science. It was at this stage he decided to write a treatise on political economy.

*

In view of his earlier training in the subject Mill felt that the project would take him a matter of months. In this he was substantially correct: the whole book of some 450,000 words took him only eighteen months to complete. The success of the *Logic* as a publishing venture was an important factor in Mill's decision to write the *Principles*. In the wake of his success he had

18. See 'On the Definition and Method of Political Economy', in *Essays on Economics and Society*, pp. 309–19, and *A System of Logic*, Book VI, Ch. IX, §3.

19. *On the Logic of the Moral Sciences*, p. 91.

already been able to publish his *Essays on Some Unsettled Questions in Political Economy* (1844), which had been turned down earlier as being too abstract and esoteric. The *Logic* had secured him a non-sectarian audience which he was anxious to educate, and, if necessary, shock. For as he said at the time,

I fully expect to offend and scandalize ten times as many people as I shall please, but that is 'all in a day's work', and I always intended to make use of any standing I might get among publicists. I have got a certain capital of that sort by the *Logic*, and I cannot too soon use it up in useful investments.[20]

In his preface to the first edition Mill claimed that his object was merely to re-survey the entire field of political economy, incorporating recent speculations 'and bringing them into harmony with the principles previously laid down by the best thinkers on the subject'. Adam Smith's *Wealth of Nations* was to provide the model: an exposition of scientific principles combined with applications of those principles to contemporary problems. But since 'for practical purposes, Political Economy is inseparably intertwined with many other branches of social philosophy', it would also be necessary 'to exhibit the economic phenomena of society in the relation in which they stand to the best social ideas of the present time'. In other words, it was to cover the abstract deductive science, while at the same time, and in accordance with the methodological writings and new intellectual influences of the period following his mental crisis, showing how its findings would need to be modified and supplemented by other branches of knowledge in practice.

The two concluding books of the *Principles* which are reprinted here deal mainly with Mill's applications of the science as expounded in the earlier books on Production (Book I), Distribution (Book II), and Exchange (Book III). The latter book included a treatment of the theory of value, the theory of international trade, and Mill's views on money. Although Books IV and V have a definite unity of their own, they represent a part only of Mill's achievement in the *Principles*. Nevertheless, they

20. Letter to H. S. Chapman, 9 March 1847, in *Earlier Letters*, Vol. XIII, p. 708–9.

contain ample evidence of the new emphases Mill wished to introduce into the subject. As he once wrote to a friend, 'I regard the purely abstract investigations of political economy ... as of very minor importance compared with the great practical questions which the progress of democracy and the spread of socialist opinions are pressing on'.[21] Once the *Principles* was published Mill chiefly confined his writings on political economy to these great practical questions, many of which are prefigured in Books IV and V. Moreover, since these books deal with questions of government intervention they are closely linked with his other writings on politics, notably the essay *On Liberty*.

At the beginning of Book IV Mill speaks of the earlier parts of the work as having established 'the economical laws of a stationary and unchanging society'. What is to follow, he says, deals with the laws of change, 'thereby adding a theory of motion to our theory of equilibrium'. The use of Comte's distinction between statics and dynamics is misleading: it may give the impression that the earlier parts exclude dynamics, and that economic theory was chiefly concerned with static equilibrium questions. Fortunately, for our purposes, Mill's distinction is not a very helpful one. Fortunately, because the opening chapters of Book IV provide an excellent summary of the main characteristics of the classical approach to secular economic change as first enunciated by Adam Smith and later modified by Ricardo. Mill's chief innovations here are to be found in the stress laid on the human factor – the 'improvement in the business capacities of the general mass of mankind' and 'the continual growth of the principle and practice of co-operation' – in determining economic progress.

Since there is relatively little of Mill's work as a pure theorist in these books, it is necessary to say something about this side of the *Principles* before considering further the wider questions which Mill set out to resolve. For Mill, Ricardo was still 'the true-founder of the abstract science of political economy'; he assured one of his more knowledgeable correspondents that the book would not require him to change his views because 'I

21. *Letters of J. S. Mill* (ed. Hugh S. R. Elliot), Vol. I (Longmans Green: 1910), p. 170.

doubt if there will be a single opinion [on pure political economy] in the book, which may not be exhibited as a corollary from [Ricardo's] doctrines'.[22] The defensive aspect of Mill's restatement of principles comes out more clearly in a review of De Quincey's *Logic of Political Economy*, which he wrote in 1845.

We dissent from the opinion that political economy does not advance. We think it is in a state of most rapid progression. But, as with other sciences in certain of their stages, the superstructure seems to be outgrowing the foundation. The science is growing at the extremities, without a proportional and suitable enlargement of the main trunk. Many important new views ... have dawned upon political economy during the last twenty years. But for want of sufficiently careful habits of systematic thought, these new views have been too frequently promulgated as contradictions of the doctrines previously received as fundamental; instead of being, what they almost always are, *developments* of them; corollaries flowing from these fundamental principles, certain conditions of fact being supposed.[23]

Many commentators have taken Mill's modesty at face-value and judged him to be little more than an unoriginal expositor of Ricardian economics. This view, as well as the idea that Mill had read virtually no economics since he wrote his *Essays on Unsettled Questions* in 1830, can be decisively refuted. Mill not only made a number of original analytical contributions to the abstract science, but even where he believed himself to be restating Ricardo's position there were major shifts of emphasis.[24] Mill's stated intention is still interesting in its own right: it shows how important it was for him not to lose contact with what was valuable and systematic in his earlier training. Throughout the *Principles* Mill performs a delicate balancing act, reaffirming and expanding the Ricardian framework, while at the same time generously incorporating new ideas and taking

22. Letter to J. Austin, 22 February 1848, in *Earlier Letters*, Vol XIII, p. 731.

23. *Essays in Economics and Society*, p. 394.

24. On this see G. J. Stigler, 'The Nature and Role of Originality in Scientific Progress', in his *Essays in the History of Economics* (University of Chicago Press: 1965) and M. Blaug, *Ricardian Economics*, pp. 168 ff.

account of evidence which others considered to be antagonistic or damaging to the Ricardian system. It is the kind of performance that invites attention to possible inconsistencies and raises questions as to whether the mixture of deference and innovation was the correct one.

Mill saw his task primarily as that of an educator. A textbook was not the place to rehearse technical anomalies. In some cases, notably on the question of Say's Law, brought into prominence by the Keynesian revolution of the 1930s, he was more dogmatic than he had been in *Unsettled Questions*, a work destined for a more specialist audience. A later generation of economic theorists could only regard with amazement Mill's complacent statement that 'happily, there is nothing in the laws of Value which remains for the present or any future writer to clear up'. They felt the same later when, with what many regard as unnecessary chivalry, Mill formally acknowledged error on the wages-fund and trade union issue, yet refused to incorporate the new speculations in a revised edition of the *Principles* in 1871. Here Mill's new-found concern with the role of what Coleridge called the 'clerisy' in a period of diverse popular opinions combined with his respect for the founding fathers of political economy. He regretted that, compared with the natural sciences, there was no 'imposing unanimity' in the social sciences. It was all too easy for dabblers and so-called 'practical men' to pronounce loudly without giving thought to these matters. Caution was needed to avoid placing weapons for crude, partial and popular use in the hands of the uninitiated. The Ricardian theoretical questions were still, for the most part, the important ones. No alternative system of equivalent power and usefulness existed; it was still worth expanding the system from within.

In spite of the lip-service Mill had paid to inductive evidence as a method of testing theory in his *Logic*, this was not where he wished to make his effort in the *Principles*. In fact, Mill showed remarkable ingenuity in admitting evidence adverse to Ricardo's predictions while preserving the essential position embodied in the theory. Nevertheless, the *Principles* reflects in a pervasive way both new intellectual influences outside political economy, and changes which had taken place in the economic and political environment since Ricardo, and indeed since Mill himself, had first written on the subject.

Although classical political economy is frequently depicted as an industrial creed, in its formative stages it was chiefly addressed to the study of agricultural, mercantile, and financial problems. The questions posed by the advent of machine and factory production, technological change, and the growth of industrial towns were either peripheral or ignored. The main emphasis in policy recommendation was on negative expedients designed to eliminate abuses, anachronisms, and restrictions: free trade in foodstuffs and other goods; abolition of encouragements to population increase; reduction of government expenditure and of taxes that either tended to encroach on the sources of capital accumulation or prevent investment from going into the economically most advantageous channels.

By the forties some of the measures which political economists advocated had been achieved – though not necessarily as a result of their efforts or for the reasons they proposed. A number of steps towards free trade were taken in the 1820s; and these were carried to their logical conclusion in 1846 when the Corn Laws were abolished. In 1834 the old Poor Law was amended along lines which received the approval of most economists of the day, including that of Mill. (See p. 334 below.) In other respects the Ricardian system had either become outdated or had proved erroneous in the light of further experience. Although population had continued to grow, it became clear that technical improvements in British agriculture had overcome any tendency towards diminishing returns. Even before the repeal of the Corn Laws the prices of many foodstuffs had started to fall. The gloomier side of the Malthusian position had never been fully accepted by all economists. After two decades of rapid, though uneven, economic growth during the thirties and forties, when *per capita* incomes (if not the standard of living of all) rose, there were few left to uphold the Malthusian view in its original stark simplicity. The earlier Ricardians, writing in the shadow of a long and expensive war, had laid great stress on the need to protect the sources of capital accumulation and prevent its dissipation. By the forties, after several minor and one major commercial crisis connected with speculation and excessive or misdirected capital accumulation, the capacity of the British economy to generate sufficient savings to maintain its rate of growth became a matter of decreased urgency.

But while some Ricardian forebodings had proved unfounded, several new or heightened problems connected with industrialization and technical change had either made their appearance or become acute. These problems were in many respects more complex, less easy to solve by means of negative expedients. Beneath the surface pessimism of the Ricardian system there lay considerable optimism concerning the prospects for an improvement in standards of living once free trade, free competition, and basic improvements in government and education had been achieved. Those, like Mill, who survived into the more complex industrial world of the mid-century, had seen trusted panaceas crumble in the face of new problems. It was possible for aggregate wealth and average standards of living to rise, 'while yet the great class at the base of the whole might increase in numbers only, and not in comfort or cultivation' (see p. 60 below). It could not be assumed, as Adam Smith did, that economic liberty and economic equality necessarily went hand in hand. Furthermore, to Mill, writing in 1848, it seemed questionable 'if all the mechanical inventions yet made have lightened the day's toil of any human being' (see p. 116 below).

The political background to economic debate had also altered sharply. Mill himself dated the change from the popular agitation which eventually resulted in the passage of the first Reform Bill in 1832. He believed that it had 'brought home for the first time to the existing generation the practical consciousness of living in a world of change. By making it evident to the public that they were on a new sea, it destroyed the force of the instinctive objection to new courses.' Coincident with this series of events was the Chartist movement, which Mill described as 'the revolt of nearly all the active talent, and a great part of the physical force, of the working classes, against their whole relation to society'.[25] Followed closely by the debates on the amend-

25. *Essays on Economics and Society*, p. 369.

ment of the Poor Laws and the opening shots in the renewed campaign to abolish the Corn Laws, Chartism aroused the conscience and fears of the ruling and middle classes; it focused their attention on the physical and moral condition of the labouring poor, and made them more receptive to new remedies. Hardly had victories for the *lasser-faire* position been scored, therefore, when new forms of intervention by the state, as typified by the Factory Acts, were being pioneered.

Even during the brief period of composition Mill found himself overtaken by events in the form of the Irish potato famine during the winter of 1846–7. He took six months off from writing the *Principles* to devote to his campaign in favour of peasant proprietorship as a solution to Ireland's grave ills. Although his efforts were in vain, the chapters on this subject in Book II provide ample testimony to his interest and concern. Anxious though he was to be relevant to the circumstances of the day, even Mill was in some respects overtaken by the change of public mood. One of the ideas with which he hoped to shock his contemporaries were his proposals – an expansion of his father's – for radical change in the laws of inheritance and property-ownership. They would, he hoped, 'pull down all large fortunes in two generations.' To his surprise, however, this part of the book made no sensation.[26] Not long after the first edition appeared the French revolution of 1848 occurred. According to Mill, after this event 'the public mind became more open to the reception of novelties in opinion, and doctrines appeared moderate which would have been thought very startling a short time before'.[27] It was this, together with Harriet Taylor's urging, that encouraged him to strengthen his chapters on socialism in the second and third editions of the *Principles*.

The revival of social conscience on the part of the middle and upper classes in the forties was accompanied by a fresh outbreak of attacks on political economy for its supposed approval of 'do-nothingism' and industrialism. Although Mill's contact with Coleridge and Carlyle had made him more tolerant of conserva-

26. As reported by his friend Alexander Bain in his *John Stuart Mill* (Longmans Green : 1882), p. 89.

27. *Autobiography*, p. 164.

tive ideas on the prior importance of moral regeneration to social reform, and on the responsibilities of government and leadership, he had no hesitation in rejecting the attempt to revive paternalism which lay behind much of the new philanthropy. This can be seen in the eloquent passages which open the justly famous chapter 'On the Probable Futurity of the Labouring Classes' reprinted below. This chapter was undertaken, Mill stated, at Harriet's request, and should be accounted a 'joint production'. Her hand can probably be seen in those parts dealing with the degrading aspects of the 'theory of dependence' as they affect the position of women – an enduring interest of Mill's which earned him much ridicule in Victorian England. This chapter, with its insistence that the future of the working classes lay with them alone, was a decisive and sensitive answer to his conservative mentors – and, incidentally, to certain lingering romantic elements still to be found in the work of present-day historians of this period.

Of greater concern to Mill was the fact that many radicals, socialists, and other representatives of working-class opinion looked upon political economy as an insulting and negative body of doctrines which attempted to place insuperable barriers in the way of social reorganization. Without giving way on any of the important points of doctrine – in fact, as we shall see in the case of Malthusianism, by stressing them – Mill placed greater emphasis than earlier economists on positive solutions, and on possible future goals, notably socialism and radical changes in the system of private property. In terms of *political* economy Ricardo and James Mill had portrayed the basic economic problem as one involving a clash between the land-owning (and governing) classes and the interests of the community at large as represented by the wage-paying and wage-earning classes. While retaining his father's anti-land-owner bias, Mill shifted attention towards the conflict between labour and capital and the means by which it could be resolved (see e.g. pp. 126 ff. below).

Of all the doctrines associated with political economy none aroused more indignation and ire than Malthus's population theory – the view that population exhibited a constant tendency to grow faster than the means of subsistence. This doctrine outraged not only the conservative Romantics and Tory radicals like William Cobbett, but many proponents of radical and socialistic change in the organization of society. It appeared to give the *quietus* to all forms of social improvement; to proclaim the permanent hegemony of Nature over Culture; and to invite heartless complacency towards the poor on the part of those traditionally entrusted with their care. There is a substantial amount of truth in this charge, though Malthus himself must be absolved from most, if not all, of the consequences which followed from the promulgation of his views. It is worth repeating that none of the leading economists of the period accepted Malthus's ideas in the precise form in which he presented them; or interpreted them in the way that Malthus did, as a result of his personal need to reconcile his population views with his religious beliefs. Among the many short-term expedients which other economists, but not Malthus himself, were willing to entertain was the important one of birth control. Mill, who was brought before the magistrates as a youth for distributing birth-control literature, was fairly typical in this respect. For as he said of the Malthusian doctrine in his *Autobiography*,

This great doctrine, originally brought forward as an argument against the indefinite improvability of human affairs, we took up with ardent zeal in the contrary sense, as indicating the sole means of realizing that improvability by securing full employment at high wages to the whole labouring population through a voluntary restriction of the increase of their numbers.[28]

This was to remain Mill's position throughout his life. Indeed, so pervasive was the emphasis on the Malthusian danger in the *Principles* that he must be considered a zealot on population matters. He admitted in 1862 that over the previous forty years subsistence and employment had increased faster than population; he constantly hoped and believed that 'the increase of intelligence, of education, and of love of independence among the working classes' would encourage self-restraint (see p. 125 below); and he acknowledged that improvements in agriculture

28. op. cit., p. 74.

in Britain had 'temporarily' overcome the tendency to diminishing returns, so that food prices had fallen in spite of population increase and the continued existence of the Corn Laws until 1846 (see p. 65 below). These conclusions ran counter to any meaningful statement of Ricardian predictions, and to the Malthusian propositions which were one of the pillars of the Ricardian theoretical system. Nevertheless, Mill continued to uphold the system, and to maintain that control over population growth was vital to any permanent prospect of improvement in standards of living. So important was it, that Mill, the opponent of the 'tyranny of mass opinion', believed it was acceptable to create a climate of opinion which would make it a disgrace to bring more children into the world than a family's circumstances allowed. In *On Liberty* he suggested that it was legitimate for governments to 'forbid marriage unless the parties can show that they have the means of supporting a family'.[29] Some idea of the moral fervour with which Mill held these views can be gained from the following statement, also from *On Liberty*.

The fact itself, of causing the existence of a human being, is one of the most responsible actions in the range of human life. To undertake this responsibility – to bestow life which may be either a curse or a blessing – unless the being on whom it is bestowed will have at least the ordinary chances of a desirable existence, is a crime against that being. And in a country either overpeopled, or threatened with being so, to produce children, beyond a very small number, with the effect of reducing the reward of labour by their competition, is a serious offence against all who live by the remuneration of their labours.[30]

Several reasons have been given to explain what some regard as an obsession on Mill's part. Mill was aware of the effect of excessive family size on his own family. Nine children had placed a great burden on his father's time, energies and patience, and had turned his mother into a drudge. It was not a happy home. Later, when his interest in female emancipation

29. *Utilitarianism, Liberty and Representative Government* (Everyman's Library: 1910), p. 163.
30. op. cit.

developed, he looked upon family limitation as an essential pre-requisite for the social independence of women. For the children of the poor it might be the only way of ensuring that they received a minimum education. In any event, and in the light of Mill's platonic relationship with Harriet, it seems unlikely that the sexual act came high on his list of priorities or even sympathies.

But these are either personal reasons or arguments based on the poverty – in the widest sense – attributable to excessive family size. Mill had other compelling reasons for being attached to the neo-Malthusian position. He believed that until Malthus had brought out the connexion between population and low wages it was impossible to give serious, and therefore realistic and hopeful, attention to the poverty of the masses. Mill the social scientist felt that while the problem of poverty was treated either as an act of God or as part of 'human destiny' to be treated by individual acts of charity, the true nature of the problem could not even be investigated. In modern jargon, the macro-nature of a problem which affected a whole class was obscured by concentration on its purely micro-social characteristics. The charges of pessimism and hard-heartedness should rightly have been laid at the door of Malthus's 'sentimental' opponents. Moreover, Mill was aware that without the Malthusian principle the Ricardian system was indeterminate, and that some of the other practical implications to which Mill was attached would be undermined. The negative form of this proposition may be more revealing, namely that he wished to combat dangerous conclusions which might be drawn from the rejection of Ricardian ideas. Malthusianism also harmonized with Mill's views on individualism and self-dependence, while not being incompatible with his socialist sympathies.

One of the most important influences of Comte and the St Simonian writers on Mill, later reinforced by Harriet Taylor, was that they opened his eyes 'to the very limited and temporary value of the old political economy, which assumes private property and inheritance as indefeasible facts, and freedom of production and exchange as the *dernier mot* of social improvement'.[31] He came to feel that the main fault of his teachers lay in the

attempt to construct a permanent fabric out of transitory materials; that they take for granted the immutability of arrangements of society, many of which are in their nature fluctuating or progressive; and enunciate with as little qualification as if they were universal and absolute truths, propositions which are perhaps applicable to no state of society except the particular one in which the writer happened to live.[32]

In the *Principles* Mill attempted to accommodate himself to this point of view by invoking the distinction between the laws of production and the laws governing distribution. While the former 'partake of the character of physical truths' the latter were almost entirely a matter of human will and institutions. This did not mean that they were arbitrary; rather that full scientific investigation of their content and consequences lay outside the narrow province of political economy; the answers were to be found partly in ethology, and partly in the historical laws which underlie human progress. For this reason, in addition to the traditional analysis of wages, profits, and rent, Mill gave extended treatment to 'different modes of distributing the produce of land and labour, which have been adopted in practice, or may be conceived in theory'. This included a chapter on socialism and one on societies in which custom rather than competition dominated economic arrangements. The chapter on socialism as it appeared in later editions is so important to an understanding of Mill's views in Book IV that an extract from it is reprinted here as an appendix. It was the first of its kind to appear in a major work on political economy, and is partly responsible for Mill's inclusion in any history of the socialist - notably the Fabian socialist - movement in this country. What precisely Mill meant when he said that he and Harriet should be classed 'decidedly under the general designation of socialists', however, continues to be the subject of debate.[33]

31. *Autobiography*, p. 117 and pp. 161-4.

32. *Essays on Economics and Society*, p. 225.

33. For a review of the evidence see L. Robbins, *The Theory of Economic Policy* (Macmillan : 1953), Ch. V.

The custom/competition distinction was introduced by Mill in support of his other distinction between the laws of production and distribution.

... only through the principle of competition has political economy any pretension to the character of a science. So far as rents, profits, wages, prices, are determined by competition, laws may be assigned for them. Assume competition to be their exclusive regulator, and principles of broad generality and scientific precision may be laid down according to which they will be regulated.[34]

Wherever competition was absent or abridged, or in communities where the desire for wealth could not be presumed to operate, conclusions derived from political economy would either be in abeyance or require to be supplemented by other evidence drawn from other social sciences – perhaps not yet in existence.

This restriction goes too far – further than Mill on other occasions was prepared to take it. In his essay on method he had claimed that the deductive method was the only appropriate one on the grounds that

though its conclusions are only locally true, its method of investigation is applicable universally; and as he who has solved a certain number of algebraic equations, can without difficulty solve others, so he who knows the political economy of England, or even Yorkshire, knows that of all nations actual or possible: provided he have sense enough not to expect the same conclusion to issue from varying premises.[35]

It was for this reason presumably that Mill, even at the height of his involvement with the St Simonians, criticized them for their lack of knowledge 'of the stricter deductions of the English school of political economy'.[36] As Edgeworth pointed out though, it was inconsistent of Mill to argue the universal applicability of the deductive method once 'he began to doubt the universality of the principle of self-interest, which he once had regarded as the foundation of economic reasoning'.[37]

34. Book II, Ch. I.   35. *Essays on Economics and Society*, p. 226.
36. Letter to A. de Tocqueville, 30 December 1840, and to G. D'Eichtal and C. Duveyrier, 30 May 1832, *Earlier Letters*, Vol. XIII, p. 458. Vol. XII, p. 109.
37. See his essay on Mill in Palgrave's *Dictionary of Political Economy*, p. 757.

A similar tension underlies Mill's relations with Comte over the publication of the *Principles*. That Mill was aware of the possibility of conflict between his resolve to write a treatise on political economy and the interest he had expressed in furthering Comte's plan of studies is apparent from letters he wrote to Comte at the time. He reassured Comte that he would never lose sight of the purely 'provisional' nature of conclusions drawn from political economy; and that he would stress the distinction between universal laws of production and the laws of distribution and exchange, which presuppose a particular, but not necessarily permanent, state of society. Although he intended to follow the plan of Adam Smith – the one economist of whom Comte approved – he would combine his exposition of political economy with the new positivist philosophy rather than the 'negative metaphysics' employed by Smith. Presented in these terms, Comte gave his approval. But, as W. J. Ashley pointed out, Mill and Comte were seriously at cross-purposes. For Comte 'provisional' meant until a positive sociology could be created, while Mill meant so long as the present system of private property lasted – a system which he thought capable of extensive improvement.[38]

This difference of opinion, and the issue of competition and the pursuit of individual self-interest *versus* its alternatives, was more than methodological in character: it enters into many of Mill's most important ideas on the future reorganization of society, and illustrates the conflict created by his concern for future improvement while wishing to be realistic about the contemporary state of society and human improvement. This can be seen to advantage in some of the most characteristic chapters reprinted here. Political economy was still useful under present conditions.

That the energies of mankind should be kept in employment by the struggle for riches, as they were formerly by the struggle of war, until the better minds succeed in educating the others into better

38. See Ashley's introduction to his edition of the *Principles* (1909), p. xxiii. The difference of opinion was made more explicit later when relations between Comte and Mill deteriorated; see J. S. Mill's *Auguste Comte and Positivism* (Ann Arbor: 1961).

things, is undoubtedly more desirable than that they should rust and stagnate. While minds are coarse they require coarse stimuli, and let them have them. (p. 114 below.)

For the same reason Mill warned socialists not to underestimate the virtues of competition (see pp. 141 ff. below).

But the future could and should be different: this is made clear in Mill's famous discussion of the stationary state. For Ricardo this state was merely an analytical construct, at most a distant prospect but mainly important as a means of illustrating the possible outcome of theoretical propositions. Mill uses it in two, possibly inconsistent, ways – both of which mark a radical departure from Ricardo. In the chapters on 'the tendency of profits to a minimum' (Bk IV, Chs. IV and V), while claiming to follow a Ricardian train of speculation, Mill actually arrives at a non-, if not anti-Ricardian destination. He concurs with an argument advanced by Wakefield and others to the effect that owing to the rapid rate of capital accumulation now possible in an advanced economy like Britain, 'the rate of profit is habitually within, as it were, a hand's breadth of the minimum, and the country is therefore on the very verge of the stationary state'. The adoption of this view – an important instance of the effect of changes in British economic circumstances since Ricardo first wrote – led to some radical departures from Ricardian policy priorities which are spelled out in the next chapter. True to his general stance throughout, Mill does not concede that his conclusions are at variance with 'the best school of preceding political economists'; but his acceptance of Wakefield's point of view led him to abandon Ricardian fears concerning the export of capital from Britain, especially to colonies; and to rescind one of the fundamental objections raised by earlier economists against extensive schemes of public expenditure for 'non-productive' purposes.[39]

The second and more famous use of the concept of the station-

39. See below, Bk IV, Ch. V, §1; the theoretical and other implications of this change of emphasis by Mill are discussed in my *Classical Political Economy and Colonies* (London School of Economics: 1965), pp. 135–43.

ary state is to be found in Chapter VI. Here Mill moves away, almost entirely, from the original use of the concept as an analytical device towards the idea of the stationary state as a kind of Utopia. This chapter is more in the nature of an espousal of non-market values, an attack on economic striving for the sake of striving. While Malthusian pressures prevented the standard of living of the masses from rising, even in the progressive state, Mill could see little point in the kind of economic progress which simply made the middle and upper classes richer. 'It is only in the backward countries of the world that increased production is still an important object: in those most advanced, what is economically needed is a better distribution, of which one indispensable means is a stricter restraint on population.' (Seee p. 114 below.) If the latter condition could be met the stationary state would become one in which it was possible to concentrate on equity in the distribution of incomes, freedom from drudgery, education, and the cultivation of the arts of living. Mill was also clearly worried by the destruction of natural amenity and solitude which living in a more populous country would entail. Economic 'stationariness', but not stagnation, was to be the pre-condition for the social diversity and dynamism Mill hoped for in *On Liberty*.

It is not difficult to understand why this chapter has attracted so much attention, and why Mill's position continues to be relevant today to the debate in advanced countries on the social and economic consequences of living in an age of affluence, increased leisure, and growing consciousness of the destruction of amenity. Mill's disillusionment with economic growth and technological progress as harbingers of improvement in the standard and quality of living of the masses has been widely echoed by today's critics of 'mere growth', and by exponents of welfare and amenity legislation.[40]

In putting forward his ideas on the stationary state Mill regarded himself as making a departure from the ideas of his

---

40. The most vocal exponent of this position has been J. K. Galbraith, *The Affluent Society* (Penguin: 1962). See also E. J. Mishan, *The Costs of Economic Growth* (Staples Press: 1968; Penguin Books: 1969).

mentors. Most commentators have accepted this interpretation. In economic terms, they have treated Mill as one who marks the transition from classical growth economics to neo-classical concern with the properties of static equilibrium and distribution. Alternatively, the chapter on the stationary state can be adduced as further evidence of Mill's movement away from the more robust individualism of his Benthamite upbringing. Neither of these interpretations can be dismissed; but it is worth pointing out some of the elements of continuity. When dealing with John Stuart Mill it is all too easy to exaggerate the extent to which, say, his father and Ricardo were concerned only with negative economic freedoms within the existing framework of private property. On the important questions of inheritance and property taxation Mill was deeply indebted to Bentham and his father. Even on the stationary state a clear link with the views of James Mill can be established. James Mill showed no interest in, and would probably have been opposed to large-scale schemes of *income* redistribution, but he cannot be accused of having a high regard for the accumulation of *wealth* as an end in itself. He believed that beyond a certain minimum of comforts material enjoyments were 'in a great measure fancy'.[41] Indeed, the ascetic tradition has predominated in economics ever since Adam Smith wrote the *Wealth of Nations*. None of the leading writers in this tradition have needed to be reminded of the purely instrumental value, and possible distorting effects, of material pursuits and pleasures. In the depths of the Great Depression in 1930 Keynes looked forward to the not-too-distant prospect when the economic problem would be solved.[42] Like Mill's plea nearly one hundred years earlier, the announcement may prove to be premature. It is as well to be reminded occasionally though that the 'realm of necessity' does not preclude choice.

Book V 'On the Influence of Government' carries further Mill's intention of applying economic principles, as modified by

41. *See Elements of Political Economy* as reprinted in Donald Winch (ed.) *James Mill, Selected Economic Writings*, pp. 234–43. See also J. S. Mill's comments on his father's character in *Autobiography*, pp. 33–5.

42. 'Economic Possibilities for Our Grandchildren', in *Essays in Persuasion* (Hart-Davis: 1952).

political, administrative and philosophical considerations, to concrete problems of policy. The discussion proceeds on two levels: how should governments discharge those functions which are either inseparable from the idea of government, or are exercised habitually and without objection by all governments: and what extra functions could or should governments undertake. Finally, Mill attempts to lay down general guidelines for state intervention. It was his intention to show in fact that no simple rule of non-interference or interference was applicable, for as he said in a letter to John Austin while he was writing the *Principles*:

I suspect there are [no *axiomata media*] which do not vary with time, place and circumstance. I doubt if much more can be done in a scientific treatment of the question than to point out a certain number of *pro's* and a certain number of *con's* of a more or less general application, and with some attempt at an estimation of the comparative importance of each, leaving the balance to be struck in each particular case as it arises.[43]

Nevertheless, as would be expected of the future author of *On Liberty*, he had strong views on these matters which derive from his enhanced concept of 'individuality' – an area where he felt there should be no authoritative intrusion by the state, and which he was anxious to protect from the insidious pressure of public opinion. Even outside this guarded sphere, where an individual's actions affected others, he felt that the onus of proof should be placed on the proponents of restriction or interference. Here we see the influence of Tocqueville in Mill's concern to safeguard the educative aspects of participatory democracy from the inertia of highly centralized, bureaucratic control. For similar reasons Mill was willing to waive the general presumption in favour of non-interference in the case of permissive or advisory action designed to help individuals and and voluntary associations to pursue their own interests more effectively.

There are many interesting features in this book of a historical

43. 13 April 1847, in *Earlier Letters*, Vol. XIII, p. 501.

and permanent kind, too many in fact to do justice to them here. Among the more interesting are Mill's views on income and property taxation; his support (later regretted) for the infant-industry argument for tariffs (pp. 283–4); and the treatment of such questions as trade unions (pp. 256–302), state education (pp. 317–21), legislation to regulate hours of work (pp. 329–30), and the problem of public-utility management (pp. 327–8). The main interest lies in the fact that we see here one of the clearest minds of the nineteenth century handling the details of these issues in the light of fundamental principles. It was during this period that the agenda of the modern industrial state was being worked out for the first time. The state and its ramifications are now so extensive that it has become more difficult to disentangle precedent from principle. The task performed by Mill for his generation may still help us to think more clearly on these matters.

This can be illustrated partially by taking the case of income and property taxation. In contrast to Ricardo, Mill's primary concern was with the problem of equity. No tax system could be perfect in this regard, but Mill clearly felt that it was essential to know what a perfect system would look like. He rejected first of all the benefit principle as a guide to tax equity: the idea that taxes should approximate to value received from the existence of government in the form of protection to persons and property. Even if this could be estimated precisely – which Mill doubted – it would entail acceptance of a faulty and narrow theory of government: 'The ends of government are as comprehensive as those of the social union.' Moreover, it was open to the *reductio ad absurdum* that the weakest, those least able to protect themselves, should pay most for protection. Those who received least benefit from the social union should not have their cause dismissed simply by being asked to pay less taxes. In modern terms, Mill was claiming that government as a whole, as well as some individual services provided by the government, should be treated as a 'public good', the benefits of which are indivisible. If it was genuinely the concern of all then it should be financed by compulsory contribution.

The next stage of the argument may at first appear strange to the modern reader: Mill was opposed to the idea of progressive or graduated income taxation on grounds of equity as well as its effect on incentives. Provided that all income below the minimum necessary for 'the requisites of life and health, and with protection against habitual bodily suffering' was exempt from taxation, the surplus should be taxed at a uniform proportionate rate. Mill rejected the theory of diminishing marginal utility of income supplied by a later, more thoroughgoing utilitarian and mathematician, Edgeworth, which was to reconcile many to the progressive principle. He did not think that a flat rate would bear more heavily on moderate than on large incomes because he believed this objection to be based on the false assumption that governments should do nothing likely 'to reduce the payer to a lower grade of social rank'. To accept this idea would be to accept as sacrosanct the existing pattern of expenditure associated with social class. Beyond the minimum exemption, Mill felt that taxation would merely involve 'sacrifices of imaginary dignity'. His contempt for the propensity of the English upper and middle classes to base their expenditure on 'regard for opinion' and the accepted 'appendages of station' could not be more clearly expressed. This uncompromising position accounts also for his support for compulsory public disclosure of incomes: it might help to discourage the pitiful habit of 'attempting to maintain the appearance to the world of a larger income than is possessed'.

Proportionate taxation would not, therefore, offend against the principle of equality of treatment. On the other side, Mill argued that progressive income taxation was not the best means of mitigating inequalities: to tax larger incomes at a higher rate would be 'to impose a penalty on people for having worked harder and saved more than their neighbours'. The problem of equality should be tackled by discriminating in favour of earned as opposed to unearned income, and terminable and uncertain as opposed to perpetual incomes. The object should be to ensure that everybody started from a fair position, 'and not in hanging a weight upon the swift to diminish the distance between them and the slow'. Hence Mill's desire to encourage saving by seeking ways of exempting it from taxation, or more specifically, double taxation; and his emphasis on gift and inheritance taxation as the proper means of equalizing wealth and opportunities. In the latter case the application of the progressive principle was both just and expedient. In so far as the end in view was the optimal balance between various means of raising a given revenue, Mill would have ranged taxes in a decreasing order of desirability as follows: taxes on the increase in income from land due to 'natural causes'; taxes on legacies and inheritances; house-taxes or rates; and finally, and preferably only in times of national emergency, proportionate taxes on incomes. It will be clear from this list how little our present tax system conforms to Mill's ideal pattern. Nevertheless, his intervention in the early debates on the principles which ought to underlie the British tax system was an important one in his day.[44] And modern readers, even those who have an interest in ways of reducing the large inequalities of wealth that persist to this day, will be surprised by the extent to which Mill was prepared to go in demanding state interference in the rights of private property in the interests of equity.

*

Mill's recognition that he was living in an 'age of transition', that it was necessary to provide a new synthesis capable of sustaining belief and action in the second half of the nineteenth century, was, paradoxically, one of the reasons for the decline in his reputation in the latter years of the century. To those taking part in the intellectual movements of this period – the neo-classical revolution in economic theory, the overwhelming interest in questions involving the history and evolution of society, the concern over socialism of one type or another – Mill's efforts to come to terms with new currents of opinion and experience seemed partial and incomplete. Thus Foxwell surveying the economic movement in England in 1887 said that while Mill was 'susceptible to all the new influences', he was 'drawn by his over-regard for the authority of a narrow though

---

44. Mill's expert evidence before the 1852 and 1861 Select Committees on Income and Property Taxes is reprinted in *Collected Works*, Vol. V. For a full account of the debate and Mill's contribution see F. Shehab, *Progressive Taxation* (Oxford University Press: 1953).

able clique to adhere to older forms of expression.'[45] Sidney
Webb regarded the *Principles* as marking a turning point in the
history of socialism, but Foxwell claimed that Mill 'does not
seem to have been quick to appreciate really original or profound conceptions, either in metaphysics or sociology', and concluded that Mill's influence was on the whole 'distinctly
soporific'.[46] Foxwell was an extreme case, but many English
Comtists and those to whom social science meant the application
of Darwinian or Spencerian ideas on evolution to society, were
apt to be patronizing towards Mill. They failed to appreciate the
extent to which their own passage towards new views had been
smoothed by Mill's earlier struggles. All they could see were his
inadequacies when judged by their newly-acquired wisdom. In
spite of the fact that his own work clearly started from and was
aided by Mill's treatment of the problem of value, even Alfred
Marshall denied Mill the status of being 'classical' or 'architec-
tonic'.[47] Mill's sustained dominance over those who came to
maturity later in the century was also cause for resentment. This
was certainly true in the case of Stanley Jevons, who inveighed
against 'the noxious influence of authority' in scientific matters.
Perhaps Sidgwick's comment was saner: 'Mill will have to be
destroyed, as he is becoming as intolerable as Aristeides, but
when he is destroyed, we shall have to build him a mausoleum
as big as his present temple of fame.[48] Much of the confidence
of intellectuals in the eighties and nineties in feeling able to
discard Mill has proved unfounded: his questions have proved
more durable than their answers.

A recurrent criticism of Mill is that he welded together incompatible positions, that he was forced into inconsistencies by
his many-sidedness and by his attempt to reconcile the claims of
individualism and socialism, science and morals, economic progress and 'culture', democracy and the values capable only of

45. *Quarterly Journal of Economics*, September 1887, p. 85.

46. S. Webb, *Socialism in England* (Swan Sonnenschein: 1893), pp. 19
and 83; and W. J. Foxwell's introduction to A. Menger, *The Right to the
Whole Produce of Labour* (MacMillan: 1899), pp. lxxviii.

47. A. C. Pigou (ed.), *Memorials of A. Marshall* (Macmillan: 1925), p.
374.

48. *Henry Sidgwick: A Memoir* (Macmillan: 1906), pp. 133–4.

being shared by an élite. That there were inconsistencies cannot be disputed. When Mill said that the 'social problem of the future' would be 'how to unite the greatest individual liberty of action with a common ownership of the raw materials of the globe, and an equal participation of all in the benefits of combined labour', he was not claiming to have solved this problem for all time or even for his own time. Like all liberal theorists, he took the individual as the basic unit of discourse. His contact with traditions antagonistic to the one in which he was brought up merely served to strengthen his attachment to individualism by enlarging his conception of what individuality should comprise. Institutional arrangements, in society should be judged basically in terms of whether they enhanced this individuality by widening the sphere of independence and choice. In so far as social, political and economic conditions inhibited or prevented individuals, or groups of individuals such as the working classes, from partaking fully in the benefits of the social union, these should be removed by direct intervention or negative prohibition. Although Mill cannot be accused of glib optimism on this score, he hoped that the necessary changes would come about by education and by means which, though involving extensive alteration in the framework of property, would nevertheless fall short of a revolutionary leap into the unknown: the test of improvement would be experiment rather than revelation.

It would be proper to reject this programme if its ideals were found to be lacking in breadth, or if some alternative path could be shown to be more effective while still meeting Mill's criteria. Those committed to the inevitability of cataclysm as a means of social change will scorn Mill's reformism. But until some society can be shown to have reconciled the claims of respect for individuality *and* socialism, his statement of the problem will command respect.

Note on the Text

The text printed here is taken from the 1871 edition of the *Principles*, the last to appear in Mill's lifetime. A complete *variorum* edition has recently appeared in the *Collected Works of J. S. Mill* (Toronto University Press, and Routledge & Kegan Paul : 1965). Volumes II and III, with an introduction by V. W. Bladen and textual editing by J. M. Robson. Books IV and V of the *Principles* are reprinted here without significant change, except for the fact that some of the lengthy citations from works illustrating the success of contemporary experiments in co-operation in Book IV, Chapter VII have been left out. Mill's chapters on Property (Book II, Chapters I and II) have been added as an appendix. The editor's footnotes are distinguished from Mill's by being placed within square brackets.

Notes on Further Reading

OTHER RELEVANT WORKS BY MILL

To complement the picture of Mill's position as put forward in the *Principles,* the most important of his other writings are:

Essays on Economics and Society, in *Collected Works* (Toronto University Press: 1967), Volumes IV and V. Volume IV contains his earlier writings, including the *Essays on Unsettled Questions in Political Economy.* Volume V mostly contains essays written on policy questions after the *Principles* was first published; it includes, for example, his review of 'Thornton on Labour and Its Claims' and the 'Chapters on Socialism', published posthumously in 1879.

Autobiography of John Stuart Mill (Columbia University Press: 1924).

On the Logic of the Moral Sciences, (Library of Liberal Arts: 1965) a reprint of Book VI of *A System of Logic.*

Utilitarianism, Liberty and Representative Government, (Everyman: 1910).

Auguste Comte and Positivism (Ann Arbor: 1961).

'Centralisation', *Edinburgh Review* (Vol. CXV, 1862).

SECONDARY WORKS AND INTERPRETATIONS

General

M. St J. Packe, *The Life of John Stuart Mill* (Secker & Warburg: 1954) is still the standard work.

L. Stephen, *The English Utilitarians* (Duckworth: 1900) in three volumes, the last of which deals with J. S. Mill. A classic late-Victorian view of Mill.

J. M. Robson, *The Improvement of Mankind* (Toronto University Press: 1968). A recent interpretation of Mill's social and political views stressing the unity of his life and thought.

J. B. Schneewind (ed.), *Mill: A Collection of Critical Essays* (Anchor Books: 1968). A varied and interesting collection mainly on Mill as a social and political philosopher.

A. Ryan, *John Stuart Mill* (Routledge & Kegan Paul: 1974). An excellent general account of Mill's position.

E. Halévy, *The Growth of Philosophic Radicalism* (Faber & Faber: 1952). Still the best study of the ideas and activities of the school taken as a whole.

G. Duncan, *Marx and Mill: Two Views of Social Conflict and Social Harmony* (Cambridge University Press: 1973). Makes good the comparative claim of the subtitle.

The following works deal with various non–Benthamite influences on Mill:

I. W. Mueller, *John Stuart Mill and French Thought* (Illinois University Press: 1956).

E. Neff, *Carlyle and Mill* (Columbia University: 1926).

H. O. Pappé, *John Stuart Mill and the Harriet Taylor Mythe* (Melbourne University Press: 1960).

Mainly Economic

M. Blaug, *Ricardian Economics* (Yale University Press: 1958). An excellent treatment of the school, its doctrines, opponents, and adherents.

M. Blaug, 'The Empirical Content of Ricardian Economics', in *Journal of Political Economy*, February 1956. An important article exploring the gap between evidence and theory. Good on Mill's balancing act.

L. Robbins, *The Theory of Economic Policy in English Classical Political Economy* (Macmillan: 1953). A survey of the views of the classical school on policy with special attention paid to Mill on socialism.

J. Viner, 'Bentham and J. S. Mill: the Utilitarian Background', reprinted in his *The Long View and the Short* (The Free Press: 1958). Exactly what its title suggests – and more.

G. J. Stigler, 'The Nature and Role of Originality in Scientific Progress', reprinted in *Essays in the History of Economics* (Chicago University Press: 1965). Identifies Mill's analytical innovations.

F. Y. Edgeworth, 'J. S. Mill', in *Palgrave's Dictionary of Political Economy* (Macmillan, 1893–9). A late-Victorian view of the *Principles* by a master theorist.

A. Harris, *Economics and Social Reform* (Harper: 1958). Devotes considerable attention to Books IV and V of Mill's *Principles*.

R. D. C. Black, *Economic Thought and the Irish Question, 1817–1870* (Cambridge University Press: 1960). A thorough study of a long debate to which Mill made an interesting contribution.

P. Schwarz, *The New Political Economy of J. S. Mill* Weidenfeld & Nicolson: 1968). A comprehensive study of Mill's economics with valuable treatments of his views on trade unions, *laissez-faire,* socialism and the future of society.

E. G. West, 'Private and Public Education, A Classical Economic Dispute', in *Journal of Political Economy,* October 1964. Mill's solution to a Victorian dilemma, still not resolved, by a present-day partisan of private education.

D. N. Winch, *Classical Political Economy and Colonies* (London School of Economics: 1965). Considers Mill's involvement with the case for 'systematic colonization' which figures prominently in Books IV and V of the *Principles*.

Facsimile of the title page of the first edition of
Principles of Political Economy *(1848)*

PRINCIPLES

OF

POLITICAL ECONOMY

WITH

SOME OF THEIR APPLICATIONS TO SOCIAL PHILOSOPHY.

BY

JOHN STUART MILL.

IN TWO VOLUMES.

VOL. I.

LONDON.

JOHN W. PARKER, WEST STRAND.

M.DCCC.XLVIII.

BOOK IV

INFLUENCE OF THE PROGRESS OF SOCIETY ON PRODUCTION AND DISTRIBUTION

CHAPTER I

General Characteristics of a Progressive State of Wealth

§1. THE three preceding Parts include as detailed a view as our limits permit, of what, by a happy generalization of a mathematical phrase, has been called the Statics of the subject. We have surveyed the field of economical facts, and have examined how they stand related to one another as causes and effects; what circumstances determine the amount of production, of employment for labour, of capital and population; what laws regulate rent, profits, and wages; under what conditions and in what proportions commodities are interchanged between individuals and between countries. We have thus obtained a collective view of the economical phenomena of society, considered as existing simultaneously. We have ascertained, to a certain extent, the principles of their interdependence; and when the state of some of the elements is known, we should now be able to infer, in a general way, the contemporaneous state of most of the others. All this, however, has only put us in possession of the economical laws of a stationary and unchanging society. We have still to consider the economical condition of mankind as liable to change, and indeed (in the more advanced portions of the race, and in all regions to which their influence reaches) as at all times undergoing progressive changes. We have to consider what these changes are, what are their laws, and what their ultimate tendencies; thereby adding a theory of motion to our theory of equilibrium – the Dynamics of political economy to the Statics.

In this inquiry, it is natural to commence by tracing the operation of known and acknowledged agencies. Whatever may be the other changes which the economy of society is destined to undergo, there is one actually in progress, concerning which there can be no dispute. In the leading countries of the world, and in all others as they come within the influence of those leading countries, there is at least one progressive movement which continues with little interruption from year to year and from generation to generation; a progress in wealth; an advancement of what is called material prosperity. All the nations which we are accustomed to call civilized, increase gradually in production and in population: and there is no reason to doubt, that not only these nations will for some time continue so to increase, but that most of the other nations of the world, including some not yet founded, will successively enter upon the same career. It will, therefore, be our first object to examine the nature and consequences of this progressive change; the elements which constitute it, and the effects it produces on the various economical facts of which we have been tracing the laws, and especially on wages, profits, rents, values, and prices.

§2. Of the features which characterize this progressive economical movement of civilized nations, that which first excites attention, through its intimate connexion with the phenomena of Production, is the perpetual, and so far as human foresight can extend, the unlimited, growth of man's power over nature. Our knowledge of the properties and laws of physical objects shows no sign of approaching its ultimate boundaries: it is advancing more rapidly, and in a greater number of directions at once, than in any previous age or generation, and affording such frequent glimpses of unexplored fields beyond, as to justify the belief that our acquaintance with nature is still almost in its infancy. This increasing physical knowledge is now, too, more rapidly than at any former period, converted, by practical ingenuity, into physical power. The most marvellous of modern inventions, one which realizes the imaginary feats of the magician, not metaphorically but literally – the electro-magnetic telegraph – sprang into existence but a few years after the establishment of the scientific theory which it realizes and exemplifies. Lastly, the manual part of these great scientific operations is now never wanting to the intellectual: there is no difficulty in finding or forming, in a sufficient number of the working hands of the community, the skill requisite for executing the most delicate processes of the application of science to practical uses. From this union of conditions, it is impossible not to look forward to a vast multiplication and long succession of contrivances for economizing labour and increasing its produce; and to an ever wider diffusion of the use and benefit of those contrivances.

Another change, which has always hitherto characterized, and will assuredly continue to characterize, the progress of civilized society, is a continual increase of the security of person and property. The people of every country in Europe, the most backward as well as the most advanced, are, in each generation, better protected against the violence and rapacity of one another, both by a more efficient judicature and police for the suppression of private crime, and by the decay and destruction of those mischievous privileges which enabled certain classes of the community to prey with impunity upon the rest. They are also, in every generation, better protected, either by institutions or by manners and opinion, against arbitrary exercise of the power of government. Even in semi-barbarous Russia, acts of spoliation directed against individuals, who have not made themselves politically obnoxious, are not supposed to be now so frequent as much to affect any person's feelings of security. Taxation, in all European countries, grows less arbitrary and oppressive, both in itself and in the manner of levying it. Wars, and the destruction they cause, are now usually confined, in almost every country, to those distant and outlying possessions at which it comes into contact with savages. Even the vicissitudes of fortune which arise from inevitable natural calamities, are more and more softened to those on whom they fall, by the continual extension of the salutary practice of insurance.

Of this increased security, one of the most unfailing effects is a great increase both of production and of accumulation. Industry and frugality cannot exist, where there is not a preponderant probability that those who labour and spare will be permitted to enjoy. And the nearer this probability approaches to certainty, the more do industry and frugality become pervading qualities in a people. Experience has shown that a large proportion of the results of labour and abstinence may be taken away by fixed taxation, without impairing, and sometimes even with the effect of stimulating, the qualities from which a great production and an abundant capital take their rise. But those qualities are not proof against a high degree of uncertainty. The Government may carry off a part; but there must be assurance that it will not interfere, nor suffer any one to interfere, with the remainder.

One of the changes which most infallibly attend the progress of modern society, is an improvement in the business capacities of the general mass of mankind. I do not mean that the practical sagacity of an individual human being is greater than formerly. I am inclined to believe that economical progress has hitherto had even a contrary effect. A person of good natural endowments, in a rude state of society, can do a great number of things tolerably well, has a greater power of adapting means to ends, is more capable of extricating himself and others from an unforeseen embarrassment, than ninety-nine in a hundred of those who have known only what is called the civilized form of life. How far these points of inferiority of faculties are compensated, and by what means they might be compensated still more completely, to the civilized man as an individual being, is a question belonging to a different inquiry from the present. But to civilized human beings collectively considered, the compensation is ample. What is lost in the separate efficiency of each, is far more than made up by the greater capacity of united action. In proportion as they put off the qualities of the savage, they become amenable to discipline; capable of adhering to plans concerted beforehand, and about which they may not have been consulted; of subordinating their individual caprice to a preconceived determination, and performing severally the parts allotted to them in a combined undertaking. Works of all sorts, impracticable to the savage or the half-civilized, are daily accomplished by civilized nations, not by any greatness of faculties in the actual agents, but through the fact that each is able to rely with certainty on the others for the portion of the work which they respectively undertake. The peculiar characteristic, in short, of civilized beings, is the capacity of co-operation; and this, like other faculties, tends to improve by practice, and becomes capable of assuming a constantly wider sphere of action.

Accordingly there is no more certain incident of the progressive change taking place in society, than the continual growth of the principle and practice of co-operation. Associations of individuals voluntarily combining their small contributions, now perform works, both of an industrial and of many other characters, which no one person or small number of persons are rich enough to accomplish, or for the performance of which the few persons capable of accomplishing them were formerly enabled to exact the most inordinate remuneration. As wealth increases and business capacity improves, we may look forward to a great extension of establishments, both for industrial and other purposes, formed by the collective contributions of large numbers; establishments like those called by the technical name of joint-stock companies, or the associations less formally constituted, which are so numerous in England, to raise funds for public or philanthropic objects, or, lastly, those associations of workpeople either for production, or to buy goods for their common consumption, which are now specially known by the name of co-operative societies.

The progress which is to be expected in the physical sciences and arts, combined with the greater security of property, and greater freedom in disposing of it, which are obvious features in the civilization of modern nations, and with the more extensive and more skilful employment of the joint-stock principle, afford space and scope for an indefinite increase of capital and production, and for the increase of population which is its ordinary accompaniment. That the growth of population will overpass the increase of production, there is not much reason to apprehend; and that it should even keep pace with it, is inconsistent with the supposition of any real improvement in the poorest classes of the people. It is, however, quite possible that there might be a great progress in industrial improvement, and in the signs of what is commonly called national prosperity; a great increase of aggregate wealth, and even, in some respects, a better distribution of it; that not only the rich might grow richer, but many of the poor might grow rich, that the intermediate classes might become more numerous and powerful, and the means of enjoyable existence be more and more largely diffused, while yet the great class at the base of the whole might increase in numbers only, and not in comfort nor in cultivation. We must, therefore, in considering the effects of the progress of industry, admit as a supposition, however greatly we deprecate as a fact, an increase of population as long-continued, as indefinite, and possibly even as rapid, as the increase of production and accumulation.

With these preliminary observations on the causes of change at work in a society which is in a state of economical progress, I proceed to a more detailed examination of the changes themselves.

CHAPTER II

Influence of the Progress of Industry and Population on Values and Prices

§1. THE changes which the progress of industry causes or presupposes in the circumstances of production, are necessarily attended with changes in the values of commodities.

The permanent values of all things which are neither under a natural nor under an artificial monopoly, depend, as we have seen, on their cost of production. But the increasing power which mankind are constantly acquiring over nature, increases more and more the efficiency of human exertion, or in other words, diminishes cost of production. All inventions by which a greater quantity of any commodity can be produced with the same labour, or the same quantity with less labour, or which abridge the process, so that the capital employed needs not be advanced for so long a time, lessen the cost of production of the commodity. As, however, value is relative; if inventions and improvements in production were made in all commodities, and all in the same degree, there would be no alteration in values. Things would continue to exchange for each other at the same rates as before; and mankind would obtain a greater quantity of all things in return for their labour and abstinence, without having that greater abundance measured and declared (as it is when it affects only one thing) by the diminished exchange value of the commodity.

As for prices, in these circumstances they would be affected or not, according as the improvements in production did or did not extend to the precious metals. If the materials of money were an exception to the general diminution of cost of production, the values of all other things would fall in relation to money, that is, there would be a fall of general prices throughout the world. But if money, like other things, and in the same degree as other things, were obtained in greater abundance and cheapness, prices would be no more affected than values would: and there would be no visible sign in the state of the markets, of any of the changes which had taken place; except that there would be (if people continued to labour as much as before) a greater quantity of all sorts of commodities, circulated at the same prices by a greater quantity of money.

Improvements in production are not the only circumstance accompanying the progress of industry, which tends to diminish the cost of producing, or at least of obtaining, commodities. Another circumstance is the increase of intercourse between different parts of the world. As commerce extends, and the ignorant attempts to restrain it by tariffs become obsolete, commodities tend more and more to be produced in the places in which their production can be carried on at the least expense of labour and capital to mankind. As civilization spreads, and security of person and property becomes established, in parts of the world which have not hitherto had that advantage, the productive capabilities of those places are called into fuller activity, for the benefit both of their own inhabitants and of foreigners. The ignorance and misgovernment in which many of the regions most favoured by nature are still grovelling, afford work, probably, for many generations before those countries will be raised even to the present level of the most civilized parts of Europe. Much will also depend on the increasing migration of labour and capital to unoccupied parts of the earth, of which the soil, climate, and situation are found, by the ample means of exploration now possessed, to promise not only a large return to industry, but great facilities of producing commodities suited to the markets of old countries. Much as the collective industry of the earth is likely to be increased in efficiency by the extension of science and of the industrial arts, a still more active source of increased cheapness of production will be found, probably, for some time to come, in the gradually unfolding consequences of Free Trade, and in the increasing scale on which Emigration and Colonization will be carried on.

From the causes now enumerated, unless counteracted by others, the progress of things enables a country to obtain at less and less of real cost, not only its own productions but those of foreign countries. Indeed, whatever diminishes the cost of its own productions, when of an exportable character, enables it, as we have already seen, to obtain its imports at less real cost.

§2. But is it the fact, that these tendencies are not counteracted? Has the progress of wealth and industry no effect in regard to cost of production, but to diminish it? Are no causes of an opposite character brought into operation by the same progress, sufficient in some cases not only to neutralize, but to overcome the former, and convert the descending movement of cost of production into an ascending movement? We are already aware that there are such causes, and that, in the case of the most important classes of commodities, food and materials, there is a tendency diametrically opposite to that of which we have been speaking. The cost of production of these commodities tends to increase.

This is not a property inherent in the commodities themselves. If population were stationary, and the produce of the earth never needed to be augmented in quantity, there would be no cause for greater cost of production. Mankind would, on the contrary, have the full benefit of all improvements in agriculture, or in the arts subsidiary to it, and there would be no difference, in this respect, between the products of agriculture and those of manufactures. The only products of industry, which, if population did not increase, would be liable to a real increase of cost of production, are those which, depending on a material which is not renewed, are either wholly or partially exhaustible; such as coal, and most if not all metals; for even iron, the most abundant as well as most useful of metallic products, which forms an ingredient of most minerals and of almost all rocks, is susceptible of exhaustion so far as regards its richest and most tractable ores.

When, however, population increases, as it has never yet failed to do when the increase of industry and of the means of subsistence made room for it, the demand for most of the productions of the earth, and particularly for food, increases in a corresponding proportion. And then comes into effect that fundamental law of production from the soil, on which we have so frequently had occasion to expatiate; the law, that increased labour, in any given state of agricultural skill, is attended with a less than proportional increase of produce. The cost of production of the fruits of the earth increases, *caeteris paribus*, with every increase of the demand.

No tendency of a like kind exists with respect to manufactured articles. The tendency is in the contrary direction. The larger the scale on which manufacturing operations are carried on, the more cheaply they can in general be performed. Mr Senior has gone the length of enunciating as an inherent law of manufacturing industry, that in it increased production takes place at a smaller cost, while in agricultural industry increased production takes place at a greater cost. I cannot think, however, that even in manufactures, increased cheapness follows increased production by anything amounting to a law. It is a probable and usual, but not a necessary, consequence.

As manufactures, however, depend for their materials either upon agriculture, or mining, or the spontaneous produce of the earth, manufacturing industry is subject, in respect of one of its essentials, to the same law as agriculture. But the crude material generally forms so small a portion of the total cost, that any tendency which may exist to a progressive increase in that single item, is much over-balanced by the diminution continually taking place in all the other elements; to which diminution it is impossible at present to assign any limit.

The tendency, then, being to a perpetual increase of the productive power of labour in manufactures, while in agriculture and mining there is a conflict between two tendencies, the one towards an increase of productive power, the other towards a diminution of it, the cost of production being lessened by every improvement in the processes, and augmented by every addition to population; it follows that the exchange values of manufactured articles, compared with the products of agriculture and of mines, have, as population and industry advance, a certain and decided tendency to fall. Money being a product of mines, it may also be laid down as a rule, that manufactured articles tend, as society advances, to fall in money price. The industrial history of modern nations, especially during the last hundred years, fully bears out this assertion.

§3. Whether agricultural produce increases in absolute as well as comparative cost of production, depends on the conflict of the two antagonist agencies, increase of population, and improvement in agricultural skill. In some, perhaps in most, states of society, (looking at the whole surface of the earth,) both agricultural skill and population are either stationary, or increase very slowly, and the cost of production of food, therefore, is nearly stationary. In a society which is advancing in wealth, population generally increases faster than agricultural skill, and food consequently tends to become more costly; but there are times when a strong impulse sets in towards agricultural improvement. Such an impulse has shown itself in Great Britain during the last twenty or thirty years. In England and Scotland agricultural skill has of late increased considerably faster than population, insomuch that food and other agricultural produce, notwithstanding the increase of people, can be grown at less cost than they were thirty years ago: and the abolition of the Corn Laws has given an additional stimulus to the spirit of improvement. In some other countries, and particularly in France, the improvement of agriculture gains ground still more decidedly upon population, because though agriculture, except in a few provinces, advances slowly, population advances still more slowly, and even with increasing slowness; its growth being kept down, not by poverty, which is diminishing, but by prudence.

Which of the two conflicting agencies is gaining upon the other at any particular time, might be conjectured with tolerable accuracy from the money price of agricultural produce (supposing bullion not to vary materially in value), provided a sufficient number of years could be taken, to form an average independent of the fluctuations of seasons. This, however, is hardly practicable, since Mr Tooke has shown that even so long a period as half a century may include a much greater proportion of abundant and a smaller of deficient seasons than is properly due to it. A mere average, therefore, might lead to conclusions only the more misleading, for their deceptive semblance of accuracy. There would be less danger of error in taking the average of only a small number of years, and correcting it by a conjectural allowance for the character of the seasons, than in trusting to a longer average without any such correction. It is hardly necessary to add, that in founding conclusions on quoted prices, allowance must also be made as far as possible for any changes in the general exchange value of the precious metals.[1]

§4. Thus far, of the effect of the progress of society on the permanent or average values and prices of commodities. It remains to be considered, in what manner the same progress affects their fluctuations. Concerning the answer to this question there can be no doubt. It tends in a very high degree to diminish them.

In poor and backward societies, as in the East, and in Europe during the Middle Ages, extraordinary differences in the price of the same commodity might exist in places not very distant from each other, because the want of roads and canals, the imperfection of marine navigation, and the insecurity of communications generally, prevented things from being transported from the places where they were cheap to those where they were dear. The things most liable to fluctuations in value, those directly influenced by the seasons, and especially food, were seldom carried to any great distances. Each locality depended, as a general rule, on its own produce and that of its immediate neighbourhood. In most years, accordingly, there was, in some part or other of any large country, a real dearth. Almost every season must be unpropitious to some among the many soils and climates to be found in an extensive tract of country; but as the same season is also in general more than ordinarily favourable to others, it is only occasionally that the aggregate produce of the whole country is deficient, and even then in a less degree than that of many separate portions; while a deficiency at all considerable, extending to the whole world, is a thing almost unknown. In modern times, therefore, there is only dearth, where there formerly would have been famine, and sufficiency every-

1. A still better criterion, perhaps, than that suggested in the text, would be the increase or diminution of the amount of the labourer's wages estimated in agricultural produce.

where when anciently there would have been scarcity in some places and superfluity in others.

The same change has taken place with respect to all other articles of commerce. The safety and cheapness of communications, which enable a deficiency in one place to be supplied from the surplus of another, at a moderate or even a small advance on the ordinary price, render the fluctuations of prices much less extreme than formerly. This effect is much promoted by the existence of large capitals, belonging to what are called speculative merchants, whose business it is to buy goods in order to resell them at a profit. These dealers naturally buying things when they are cheapest, and storing them up to be brought again into the market when the price has become unusually high; the tendency of their operations is to equalize price, or at least to moderate its inequalities. The prices of things are neither so much depressed at one time, nor so much raised at another, as they would be if speculative dealers did not exist.

Speculators, therefore, have a highly useful office in the economy of society; and (contrary to common opinion) the most useful portion of the class are those who speculate in commodities affected by the vicissitudes of seasons. If there were no corn-dealers, not only would the price of corn be liable to variations much more extreme than at present, but in a deficient season the necessary supplies might not be forthcoming at all. Unless there were speculators in corn, or unless, in default of dealers, the farmers became speculators, the price in a season of abundance would fall without any limit or check, except the wasteful consumption that would invariably follow. That any part of the surplus of one year remains to supply the deficiency of another, is owing either to farmers who withhold corn from the market, or to dealers who buy it when at the cheapest and lay it up in store.

§5. Among persons who have not much considered the subject, there is a notion that the gains of speculators are often made by causing an artificial scarcity; that they create a high price by their own purchases, and then profit by it. This may easily be shown to be fallacious. If a corn-dealer makes purchases on speculation, and produces a rise, when there is neither at the time nor afterwards any cause for a rise of price except his own proceedings; he no doubt appears to grow richer as long as his purchases continue, because he is a holder of an article which is quoted at a higher and higher price: but this apparent gain only seems within his reach so long as he does not attempt to realize it. If he has bought, for instance, a million of quarters, and by withholding them from the market, has raised the price ten shillings a quarter; just so much as the price has been raised by withdrawing a million quarters, will it be lowered by bringing them back, and the best that he can hope is that he will lose nothing except interest and his expenses. If by a gradual and cautious sale he is able to realize, on some portion of his stores, a part of the increased price, so also he will undoubtedly have had to pay a part of that price on some portion of his purchases. He runs considerable risk of incurring a still greater loss; for the temporary high price is very likely to have tempted others, who had no share in causing it, and who might otherwise not have found their way to his market at all, to bring their corn there, and intercept a part of the advantage. So that instead of profiting by a scarcity caused by himself, he is by no means unlikely, after buying in an average market, to be forced to sell in a superabundant one.

As an individual speculator cannot gain by a rise of price solely of his own creating, so neither can a number of speculators gain collectively by a rise which their operations have artificially produced. Some among a number of speculators may gain, by superior judgment or good fortune in selecting the time for realizing, but they make this gain at the expense, not of the consumer, but of the other speculators who are less judicious. They, in fact, convert to their own benefit the high price produced by the speculations of the others, leaving to these the loss resulting from the recoil. It is not to be denied, therefore, that speculators may enrich themselves by other people's loss. But it is by the losses of other speculators. As much must have been lost by one set of dealers as is gained by another set.

When a speculation in a commmodity proves profitable to the

speculators as a body, it is because, in the interval between their buying and reselling, the price rises from some cause independent of them, their only connexion with it consisting in having foreseen it. In this case, their purchases make the price begin to rise sooner than it otherwise would do, thus spreading the privation of the consumers over a longer period, but mitigating it at the time of its greatest height: evidently to the general advantage. In this, however, it is assumed that they have not overrated the rise which they looked forward to. For it often happens that speculative purchases are made in the expectation of some increase of demand, or deficiency of supply, which after all does not occur, or not to the extent which the speculator expected. In that case the speculation, instead of moderating fluctuation, has caused a fluctuation of price which otherwise would not have happened, or aggravated one which would. But in that case, the speculation is a losing one, to the speculators collectively, however much some individuals may gain by it. All that part of the rise of price by which it exceeds what there are independent grounds for, cannot give to the speculators as a body any benefit, since the price is as much depressed by their sales as it was raised by their purchases; and while they gain nothing by it, they lose, not only their trouble and expenses, but almost always much more, through the effects incident to the artificial rise of price, in checking consumption, and bringing forward supplies from unforeseen quarters. The operations, therefore, of speculative dealers, are useful to the public whenever profitable to themselves; and though they are sometimes injurious to the public, by heightening the fluctuations which their more usual office is to alleviate, yet whenever this happens the speculators are the greatest losers. The interest, in short, of the speculators as a body, coincides with the interest of the public; and as they can only fail to serve the public interest in proportion as they miss their own, the best way to promote the one is to leave them to pursue the other in perfect freedom.

I do not deny that speculators may aggravate a *local* scarcity. In collecting corn from the villages to supply the towns, they make the dearth penetrate into nooks and corners which might otherwise have escaped from bearing their share of it. To buy and resell in the same place, tends to alleviate scarcity; to buy in one place and resell in another, may increase it in the former of the two places, but relieves it in the latter, where the price is higher, and which, therefore, by the very supposition, is likely to be suffering more. And these sufferings always fall hardest on the poorest consumers, since the rich, by outbidding, can obtain their accustomed supply undiminished if they choose. To no persons, therefore, are the operations of corn-dealers on the whole so beneficial as to the poor. Accidentally and exceptionally, the poor may suffer from them: it might sometimes be more advantageous to the rural poor to have corn cheap in winter, when they are entirely dependent on it, even if the consequence were a dearth in spring, when they can perhaps obtain partial substitutes. But there are no substitutes, procurable at that season, which serve in any great degree to replace bread-corn as the chief article of food: if there were, its price would fall in the spring, instead of continuing, as it always does, to rise till the approach of harvest.

There is an opposition of immediate interest, at the moment of sale, between the dealer in corn and the consumer, as there always is between the seller and the buyer: and a time of dearth being that in which the speculator makes his largest profits, he is an object of dislike and jealousy at that time, to those who are suffering while he is gaining. It is an error, however, to suppose that the corn-dealer's business affords him any extraordinary profit: he makes his gains not constantly, but at particular times, and they must therefore occasionally be great, but the chances of profit in a business in which there is so much competition, cannot on the whole be greater than in other employments. A year of scarcity, in which great gains are made by corn-dealers, rarely comes to an end without a recoil which places many of them in the list of bankrupts. There have been few more promising seasons for corn-dealers than the year 1847, and seldom was there a greater break-up among the speculators than in the autumn of that year. The chances of failure, in this most precarious trade, are a set off against great occasional profits. If the corn-dealer were to sell his stores, during a dearth, at a lower price than that which the competition of the consumers assigns to him, he would make a sacrifice, to charity or philanthropy, of the fair profits of his employment, which may be quite as reasonably required from any other person of equal means. His business being a useful one, it is the interest of the public that the ordinary motives should exist for carrying it on, and that neither law nor opinion should prevent an operation beneficial to the public from being attended with as much private advantage as is compatible with full and free competition.

It appears, then, that the fluctuations of values and prices arising from variations of supply, or from alterations in real (as distinguished from speculative) demand, may be expected to become more moderate as society advances. With regard to those which arise from miscalculation, and especially from the alterations of undue expansion and excessive contraction of credit, which occupy so conspicuous a place among commercial phenomena, the same thing cannot be affirmed with equal confidence. Such vicissitudes, beginning with irrational speculation and ending with a commercial crisis, have not hitherto become either less frequent or less violent with the growth of capital and extension of industry. Rather they may be said to have become more so: in consequence, as is often said, of increased competition; but, as I prefer to say, of a low rate of profits and interest, which makes capitalists dissatisfied with the ordinary course of safe mercantile gains. The connexion of this low rate of profit with the advance of population and accumulation, is one of the points to be illustrated in the ensuing chapters.

Influence of the Progress of Industry and Population on Rents, Profits, and Wages

§1. CONTINUING the inquiry into the nature of the economical changes taking place in a society which is in a state of industrial progress, we shall next consider what is the effect of that progress on the distribution of the produce among the various classes who share in it. We may confine our attention to the system of distribution which is the most complex, and which virtually includes all others – that in which the produce of manufactures is shared between two classes, labourers and capitalists, and the produce of agriculture among three, labourers, capitalists, and landlords.

The characteristic features of what is commonly meant by industrial progress, resolve themselves mainly into three, increase of capital, increase of population, and improvements in production; understanding the last expression in its widest sense, to include the process of procuring commodities from a distance, as well as that of producing them. The other changes which take place are chiefly consequences of these; as, for example, the tendency to a progressive increase of the cost of production of food; arising from an increased demand, which may be occasioned either by increased population, or by an increase of capital and wages, enabling the poorer classes to increase their consumption. It will be convenient to set out by considering each of the three causes, as operating separately; after which we can suppose them combined in any manner we think fit.

Let us first suppose that population increases, capital and the arts of production remaining stationary. One of the effects of this change of circumstances is sufficiently obvious: wages will fall; the labouring class will be reduced to an inferior condition. The state of the capitalist, on the contrary, will be improved. With the same capital, he can purchase more labour, and obtain more produce. His rate of profit is increased. The dependence of the rate of profits on the cost of labour is here verified; for the labourer obtaining a diminished quantity of commodities, and no alteration being supposed in the circumstances of their production, the diminished quantity represents a diminished cost. The labourer obtains not only a smaller real reward, but the product of a smaller quantity of labour. The first circumstance is the important one to himself, the last to his employer.

Nothing has occurred, thus far, to affect in any way the value of any commodity; and no reason, therefore, has yet shown itself, why rent should be either raised or lowered. But if we look forward another stage in the series of effects, we may see our way to such a consequence. The labourers have increased in numbers: their condition is reduced in the same proportion; the increased numbers divide among them only the produce of the same amount of labour as before. But they may economize in their other comforts, and not in their food: each may consume as much food, and of as costly a quality as previously; or they may submit to a reduction, but not in proportion to the increase of numbers. On this supposition, notwithstanding the diminution of real wages, the increased population will require an increased quantity of food. But since industrial skill and knowledge are supposed to be stationary, more food can only be obtained by resorting to worse land, or to methods of cultivation which are less productive in proportion to the outlay. Capital for this extension of agriculture will not be wanting; for though, by hypothesis, no addition takes place to the capital in existence, a sufficient amount can be spared from the industry which previously supplied the other and less pressing wants which the labourers have been obliged to curtail. The additional supply of food, therefore, will be produced, but produced at a greater cost; and the exchange value of agricultural produce must rise. It may be objected, that profits having risen, the extra cost of producing food can be defrayed from profits, without any increase of price. It could, undoubtedly, but it will not; because if it did, the agriculturist would be placed in an inferior position to other capitalists. The increase of profits, being the effect of diminished wages, is common to all employers of labour. The increased expenses arising from the necessity of a more costly cultivation, affect the agriculturist alone. For this peculiar burthen he must be peculiarly compensated, whether the general rate of profit be high or low. He will not submit indefinitely to a deduction from his profits, to which other capitalists are not subject. He will not extend his cultivation by laying out fresh capital, unless for a return sufficient to yield him as high a profit as could be obtained by the same capital in other investments. The value, therefore, of his commodity will rise, and rise in proportion to the increased cost. The farmer will thus be indemnified for the burthen which is peculiar to himself, and will also enjoy the augmented rate of profit which is common to all capitalists.

It follows, from principles with which we are already familiar, that in these circumstances rent will rise. Any land can afford to pay, and under free competition will pay, a rent equal to the excess of its produce above the return to an equal capital on the worst land, or under the least favourable conditions. Whenever, therefore, agriculture is driven to descend to worse land, or more onerous processes, rent rises. Its rise will be twofold, for, in the first place, rent in kind, or corn rent, will rise; and in the second, since the value of agricultural produce has also risen, rent, estimated in manufactured or foreign commodities (which is represented, *caeteris paribus*, by money rent) will rise still more.

The steps of the process (if, after what has been formerly said, it is necessary to retrace them) are as follows. Corn rises in price, to repay with the ordinary profit the capital required for producing additional corn on worse land or by more costly processes. So far as regards this additional corn, the increased price is but an equivalent for the additional expense; but the rise, extending to all corn, affords on all, except the last produced, an extra profit. If the farmer was accustomed to produce 100 quarters of wheat at 40s., and 120 quarters are now required, of which the last twenty cannot be produced under 45s., he obtains the extra five shillings on the entire 120 quarters, and not on the last twenty alone. He has thus an extra 25l. beyond the ordinary profits, and this, in a state of free competition, he will not be able to retain. He cannot however be compelled to give it up to the consumer, since a less price than 45s. would be inconsistent with the production of the last twenty quarters. The price, then, will remain at 45s., and the 25l. will be transferred by competition not to the consumer but to the landlord. A rise of rents is therefore inevitably consequent on an increased demand for agricultural produce, when unaccompanied by increased facilities for its production. A truth which, after this final illustration, we may henceforth take for granted.

The new element now introduced – an increased demand for food – besides occasioning an increase of rent, still further disturbs the distribution of the produce between capitalists and labourers. The increase of population will have diminished the reward of labour: and if its cost is diminished as greatly as its real remuneration, profits will be increased by the full amount. If, however, the increase of population leads to an increased production of food, which cannot be supplied but at an enhanced cost of production, the cost of labour will not be so much diminished as the real reward of it, and profits, therefore, will not be so much raised. It is even possible that they might not be raised at all. The labourers may previously have been so well provided for, that the whole of what they now lose may be struck off from their other indulgences, and they may not, either by necessity or choice, undergo any reduction in the quantity or quality of their food. To produce the food for the increased number may be attended with such an increase of expense, that wages, though reduced in quantity, may represent as great a cost, may be the product of as much labour, as before, and the capitalist may not be at all benefited. On this supposition the loss to the labourer is partly absorbed in the additional labour required for producing the last instalment of agricultural produce; and the remainder is gained by the landlord, the only sharer who always benefits by an increase of population.

§2. Let us now reverse our hypothesis, and instead of supposing capital stationary and population advancing, let us suppose capital advancing and population stationary; the facilities of production, both natural and acquired, being, as before, unaltered. The real wages of labour, instead of falling, will now rise; and since the cost of production of the things consumed by the labourer is not diminished, this rise of wages implies an equivalent increase of the cost of labour, and diminution of profits. To state the same deduction in other terms; the labourers not being more numerous, and the productive power of their labour being only the same as before, there is no increase of the produce; the increase of wages, therefore, must be at the charge of the capitalist. It is not impossible that the cost of labour might be increased in even a greater ratio than its real remuneration. The improved condition of the labourers may increase the demand for food. The labourers may have been so ill off before, as not to have food enough; and may now consume more: or they may choose to expend their increased means partly or wholly in a more costly quality of food, requiring more labour and more land; wheat, for example, instead of oats, or potatoes. This extension of agriculture implies, as usual, a greater cost of production and a higher price, so that besides the increase of the cost of labour arising from the increase of its reward, there will be a further increase (and an additional fall of profits) from the increased costliness of the commodities of which that reward consists. The same causes will produce a rise of rent. What the capitalists lose, above what the labourers gain, is partly transferred to the landlord, and partly swallowed up in the cost of growing food on worse land or by a less productive process.

§3. Having disposed of the two simple cases, an increasing population and stationary capital, and an increasing capital and stationary population, we are prepared to take into consideration the mixed case, in which the two elements of expansion are combined, both population and capital increasing. If either element increases faster than the other, the case is so far assimilated with one or other of the two preceding: we shall suppose them, therefore, to increase with equal rapidity; the test of equality being, that each labourer obtains the same commodities as before, and the same quantity of those commodities. Let us examine what will be the effect, on rent and profits, of this double progress.

Population having increased, without any falling off in the labourer's condition, there is of course a demand for more food. The arts of production being supposed stationary, this food must be produced at an increased cost. To compensate for this greater cost of the additional food, the price of agricultural produce must rise. The rise extending over the whole amount of food produced, though the increased expenses only apply to a part, there is a greatly increased extra profit, which, by competition, is transferred to the landlord. Rent will rise both in quantity of produce and in cost; while wages, being supposed to be the same in quantity, will be greater in cost. The labourer obtaining the same amount of necessaries, money wages have risen; and as the rise is common to all branches of production, the capitalist cannot indemnify himself by changing his employment, and the loss must be borne by profits.

It appears, then, that the tendency of an increase of capital and population is to add to rent at the expense of profits: though rent does not gain all that profits lose, a part being absorbed in increased expenses of production, that is, in hiring or feeding a greater number of labourers to obtain a given amount of agricultural produce. By profits, must of course be understood the *rate* of profit; for a lower rate of profit on a larger capital may yield a larger gross profit, considered absolutely, though a smaller in proportion to the entire produce.

This tendency of profits to fall, is from time to time counteracted by improvements in production: whether arising from increase of knowledge, or from an increased use of the knowledge already possessed. This is the third of the three elements, the effects of which on the distribution of the produce we undertook to investigate; and the investigation will be facilitated by supposing, as in the case of the other two elements, that it operates, in the first instance, alone.

§4. Let us then suppose capital and population stationary, and a sudden improvement made in the arts of production; by the invention of more efficient machines, or less costly processes, or by obtaining access to cheaper commodities through foreign trade.

The improvement may either be in some of the necessaries or indulgences which enter into the habitual consumption of the labouring class; or it may be applicable only to luxuries consumed exclusively by richer people. Very few, however, of the great industrial improvements are altogether of this last description. Agricultural improvements, except such as specially relate to some of the rarer and more peculiar products, act directly upon the principal objects of the labourer's expenditure. The steam-engine and every other invention which affords a manageable power, are applicable to all things, and of course to those consumed by the labourer. Even the power-loom and the spinning-jenny, though applied to the most delicate fabrics, are available no less for the coarse cottons and woollens worn by the labouring class. All improvements in locomotion cheapen the transport of necessaries as well as of luxuries. Seldom is a new branch of trade opened, without, either directly or in some indirect way, causing some of the articles which the mass of the people consume to be either produced or imported at smaller cost. It may safely be affirmed, therefore, that improvements in production generally tend to cheapen the commodities on which the wages of the labouring class are expended.

In so far as the commodities affected by an improvement are those which the labourers generally do not consume, the improvement has no effect in altering the distribution of the produce. Those particular commodities, indeed, are cheapened; being produced at less cost, they fall in value and in price, and all who consume them, whether landlords, capitalists, or skilled and privileged labourers, obtain increased means of enjoyment. The rate of profits, however, is not raised. There is a larger gross profit, reckoned in quantity of commodities. But the capital also, if estimated in those commodities, has risen in value. The profit is the same percentage on the capital that it was before. The capitalists are not benefited as capitalists, but as consumers. The landlords and the privileged classes of labourers, if they are consumers of the same commodities, share the same benefit.

The case is different with improvements which diminish the cost of production of the necessaries of life, or of commodities which enter habitually into the consumption of the great mass of labourers. The play of the different forces being here rather complex, it is necessary to analyse it with some minuteness.

As formerly observed, there are two kinds of agricultural improvements. Some consist in a mere saving of labour, and enable a given quantity of food to be produced at less cost, but not on a smaller surface of land than before. Others enable a given extent of land to yield not only the same produce with less labour, but a greater produce; so that if no greater produce is required, a part of the land already under culture may be dispensed with. As the part rejected will be the least productive portion, the market will thenceforth be regulated by a better description of land than what was previously the worst under cultivation.

To place the effect of the improvement in a clear light, we must suppose it to take place suddenly, so as to leave no time during its introduction, for any increase of capital or of population. Its first effect will be a fall of the value and price of agricultural produce. This is a necessary consequence of either kind of improvement, but especially of the last.

An improvement of the first kind, not increasing the produce, does not dispense with any portion of the land; the margin of cultivation (as Dr Chalmers terms it) remains where it was; agriculture does not recede, either in extent of cultivated land, or in elaborateness of method: and the price continues to be regarded by the same land, and by the same capital, as before. But since that land or capital, and all other land or capital which produces food, now yields its produce at smaller cost, the price of food will fall proportionally. If one-tenth of the expense of production has been saved, the price of produce will fall one-tenth.

But suppose the improvement to be of the second kind; enabling the land to produce, not only the same corn with one-tenth less labour, but a tenth more corn with the same labour. Here the effect is still more decided. Cultivation can now be contracted, and the market supplied from a smaller quantity of land. Even if this smaller surface of land were of the same average quality as the larger surface, the price would fall one-tenth, because the same produce would be obtained with a tenth less labour. But since the portion of land abandoned will be the least fertile portion, the price of produce will thenceforth be regulated by a better quality of land than before. In addition, therefore, to the original diminution of one-tenth in the cost of production, there will be a further diminution, corresponding with the recession of the 'margin' of agriculture to land of greater fertility. There will thus be a twofold fall of price.

Let us now examine the effect of the improvements, thus suddenly made, on the division of the produce; and in the first place, on rent. By the former of the two kinds of improvement, rent would be diminished. By the second, it would be diminished still more.

Suppose that the demand for food requires the cultivation of three qualities of land, yielding, on an equal surface, and at an equal expense, 100, 80, and 60 bushels of wheat. The price of wheat will, on the average, be just sufficient to enable the third quality to be cultivated with the ordinary profit. The first quality therefore will yield forty and the second twenty bushels of extra profit, constituting the rent of the landlord. And first, let an improvement be made, which, without enabling more corn to be grown, enables the same corn to be grown with one-fourth less labour. The price of wheat will fall one-fourth, and 80 bushels will be sold for the price for which 60 were sold before. But the produce of the land which produces 60 bushels is still required, and the expenses being as much reduced as the price, that land can still be cultivated with the ordinary profit. The first and second qualities will therefore continue to yield a surplus of 40 and 20 bushels, and corn rent will remain the same as before. But corn having fallen in price one-fourth, the same corn rent is equivalent to a fourth less of money and of all other commodities. So far, therefore, as the landlord expends his income in manufactured or foreign products, he is one-fourth worse off than before. His income as landlord is reduced to three-quarters of its amount: it is only as a consumer of corn that he is as well off.

If the improvement is of the other kind, rent will fall in a still greater ratio. Suppose that the amount of produce which the market requires, can be grown not only with a fourth less labour, but on a fourth less land. If all the land already in cultivation continued to be cultivated, it would yield a produce much larger than necessary. Land, equivalent to a fourth of the produce, must now be abandoned; and as the third quality yielded exactly one-fourth, (being 60 out of 240,) that quality will go out of cultivation. The 240 bushels can now be grown on land of the first and second qualities only; being, on the first, 100 bushels plus one-third, or $133\frac{1}{3}$ bushels; on the second, 80 bushels plus one-third, or $106\frac{2}{3}$ bushels; together 240. The second quality of land, instead of the third, is now the lowest, and regulates the price. Instead of 60, it is sufficient if $106\frac{2}{3}$ bushels repay the capital with the ordinary profit. The price of wheat will consequently fall, not in the ratio of 60 to 80, as in the other case, but in the ratio of 60 to $106\frac{2}{3}$. Even this gives an insufficient idea of the degree in which rent will be affected. The whole produce of the second quality of land will now be required to repay the expenses of production. That land, being the worst in cultivation, will pay no rent. And the first quality will only yield the difference between $133\frac{1}{3}$ bushels and $106\frac{2}{3}$, being $26\frac{2}{3}$ bushels instead of 40. The landlords collectively will have lost $33\frac{1}{3}$ out of 60 bushels in corn rent alone, while the value and price of what is left will have been diminished in the ratio of 60 to $106\frac{2}{3}$.

It thus appears, that the interest of the landlord is decidedly hostile to the sudden and general introduction of agricultural improvements. This assertion has been called a paradox, and made a ground for accusing its first promulgator, Ricardo, of great intellectual perverseness, to say nothing worse. I cannot discern in what the paradox consists; and the obliquity of vision seems to me to be on the side of his assailants. The opinion is only made to appear absurd by stating it unfairly. If the assertion were that a landlord is injured by the improvement of his estate, it would certainly be indefensible; but what is asserted is, that he is injured by the improvement of the estates of other people, although his own is included. Nobody doubts that he would gain greatly by the improvement if he could keep it to himself, and unite the two benefits, an increased produce from his land, and a price as high as before. But if the increase of produce took place simultaneously on all lands, the price would not be as high as before; and there is nothing unreasonable in supposing that the landlords would be, not benefited, but injured. It is admitted that whatever permanently reduces the price of produce diminishes rent: and it is quite in accordance with common notions to suppose that if, by the increased productiveness of land, less land were required for cultivation, its value, like that of other articles for which the demand had diminished, would fall.

I am quite willing to admit that rents have not really been lowered by the progress of agricultural improvement; but why? Because improvement has never in reality been sudden, but always slow; at no time much outstripping, and often falling far short of, the growth of capital and population, which tends as much to raise rent, as the other to lower it, and which is enabled as we shall presently see, to raise it much higher, by means of the additional margin afforded by improvements in agriculture. First, however, we must examine in what manner the sudden cheapening of agricultural produce would affect profits and wages.

In the beginning, money wages would probably remain the same as before, and the labourers would have the full benefit of the cheapness. They would be enabled to increase their consumption either of food or of other articles, and would receive the same cost, and a greater quantity. So far, profits would be unaffected. But the permanent remuneration of the labourers essentially depends on what we have called their habitual standard; the extent of the requirements which, as a class, they insist on satisfying before they choose to have children. If their tastes and requirements receive a durable impress from the sudden improvement in their condition, the benefit to the class will be permanent. But the same cause which enables them to purchase greater comforts and indulgences with the same wages, would enable them to purchase the same amount of comforts and indulgences with lower wages; and a greater population may now exist, without reducing the labourers below the condition to which they are accustomed. Hitherto this and no other has been the use which the labourers have commonly made of any increase of their means of living; they have treated it simply as convertible into food for a greater number of children. It is probable, therefore, that population would be stimulated, and that after the lapse of a generation the real wages of labour would be no higher than before the improvement: the reduction being partly brought about by a fall of money wages, and partly through the price of food, the cost of which, from the demand occasioned by the increase of population, would be increased. To the extent to which money wages fell, profits would rise: the capitalist obtaining a greater quantity of equally efficient labour by the same outlay of capital. We thus see that a diminution of the cost of living, whether arising from agricultural improvements or from the importation of foreign produce, if the habits and requirements of the labourers are not raised, usually lowers money wages and rent, and raises the general rate of profit.

What is true of improvements which cheapen the production of food, is true also of the substitution of a cheaper for a more costly variety of it. The same land yields to the same labour a much greater quantity of human nutriment in the form of maize or potatoes, than in the form of wheat. If the labourers were to give up bread, and feed only on those cheaper products, taking as their compensation not a greater quantity of other consumable commodities, but earlier marriages and larger families, the cost of labour would be much diminished, and if labour continued equally efficient, profits would rise; while rent would be much lowered, since food for the whole population could be raised on half or a third part of the land now sown with corn. At the same time, it being evident that land too barren to be cultivated for wheat might be made in case of necessity to yield potatoes sufficient to support the little labour necessary for producing them, cultivation might ultimately descend lower, and rent eventually rise higher, on a potato or maize system, than on a corn system; because the land would be capable of feeding a much larger population before reaching the limit of its powers.

If the improvement, which we suppose to take place, is not in the production of food, but of some manufactured article consumed by the labouring class, the effect on wages and profits will at first be the same; but the effect on rent very different. It will not be lowered; it will even, if the ultimate effect of the improvement is an increase of population, be raised: in which last case profits will be lowered. The reasons are too evident to require statement.

§5. We have considered, on the one hand, the manner in which the distribution of the produce into rent, profits, and wages, is affected by the ordinary increase of population and capital, and on the other, how it is affected by improvements in production, and more especially in agriculture. We have found that the former cause lowers profits, and raises rent and the cost of labour: while the tendency of agricultural improvements is to diminish rent; and all improvements which cheapen any article of the labourer's consumption, tend to diminish the cost of labour and to raise profits. The tendency of each cause in its separate state being thus ascertained, it is easy to determine the tendency of the actual course of things, in which the two movements are going on simultaneously, capital and population increasing with tolerable steadiness, while improvements in agriculture are made from time to time, and the knowledge and practice of improved methods become diffused gradually through the community.

The habits and requirements of the labouring classes being given (which determine their real wages), rents, profits, and money wages at any given time, are the result of the composition of these rival forces. If during any period agricultural improvement advances faster than population, rent and money wages during that period will tend downward, and profits upward. If population advances more rapidly than agricultural improvement, either the labourers will submit to a reduction in the quantity or quality of their food, or if not, rent and money wages will progressively rise, and profits will fall.

Agricultural skill and knowledge are of slow growth, and still slower diffusion. Inventions and discoveries, too, occur only occasionally, while the increase of population and capital are continuous agencies. It therefore seldom happens that improvement, even during a short time, has so much the start of population and capital as actually to lower rent, or raise the rate of profits. There are many countries in which the growth of population and capital is not rapid, but in these agricultural improvement is less active still. Population almost everywhere treads close on the heels of agricultural improvement, and effaces its effects as fast as they are produced.

The reason why agricultural improvement seldom lowers rent, is that it seldom cheapens food, but only prevents it from growing dearer; and seldom, if ever, throws lands out of cultivation, but only enables worse and worse land to be taken in for the supply of an increasing demand. What is sometimes called the natural state of a country which is but half cultivated, namely, that the land is highly productive, and food obtained in great abundance by little labour, is only true of unoccupied countries colonized by a civilized people. In the United States the worst land in cultivation is of a high quality (except sometimes in the immediate vicinity of markets or means of conveyance, where a bad quality is compensated by a good situation); and even if no further improvements were made in agriculture or locomotion, cultivation would have many steps yet to descend, before the increase of population and capital would be brought to a stand; but in Europe five hundred years ago, though so thinly peopled in comparison to the present population, it is probable that the worst land under the plough was, from the rude state of agriculture, quite as unproductive as the worst land now cultivated; and that cultivation had approached as near to the ultimate limit of profitable tillage, in those times as in the present. What the agricultural improvements since made have really done is, by increasing the capacity of production of land in general, to enable tillage to extend downwards to a much worse natural quality of land than the worst which at that time would have admitted of cultivation by a capitalist for profit; thus rendering a much greater increase of capital and population possible, and removing always a little and a little further off, the barrier which restrains them; population meanwhile always pressing so hard against the barrier, that there is never any visible margin left for it to seize, every inch of ground made vacant for it by improvement being at once filled up by its advancing columns. Agricultural improvement may thus be considered to be not so much a counterforce conflicting with increase of population, as a partial relaxation of the bonds which confine that increase.

The effects produced on the division of the produce by an increase of production, under the joint influence of increase of population and capital and improvements of agriculture, are very different from those deduced from the hypothetical cases previously discussed. In particular, the effect on rent is most materially different. We remarked that – while a great agricultural improvement made suddenly and universally would in the first instance inevitably lower rent – such improvements enable rent, in the progress of society, to rise gradually to a much higher limit than it could otherwise attain, since they enable a much lower quality of land to be ultimately cultivated. But in the case we are now supposing, which nearly corresponds to the usual course of things, this ultimate effect becomes the immediate effect. Suppose cultivation to have reached, or almost reached, the utmost limit permitted by the state of the industrial arts, and rent, therefore, to have attained nearly the highest point to which it can be carried by the progress of population and capital, with the existing amount of skill and knowledge. If a great agricultural improvement were suddenly introduced, it might throw back rent for a considerable space, leaving it to regain its lost ground by the progress of population and capital, and afterwards to go on further. But, taking place, as such improvement always does, very gradually, it causes no retrograde movement of either rent or cultivation; it merely enables the one to go on rising, and the other extending, long after they must otherwise have stopped. It would do this even without the necessity of resorting to a worse quality of land; simply by enabling the lands already in cultivation to yield a greater produce, with no increase of the proportional cost. If by improvements of agriculture all the lands in cultivation could be made, even with double labour and capital, to yield a double produce, (supposing that in the meantime population increased so as to require this double quantity) all rents would be doubled.

To illustrate the point, let us revert to the numerical example in a former page. Three qualities of land yield respectively 100, 80, and 60 bushels to the same outlay on the same extent of surface. If No. 1 could be made to yield 200, No. 2, 160, and No. 3, 120 bushels, at only double the expense, and therefore without any increase of the cost of production, and if the population, having doubled, required all this increased quantity, the rent of No. 1 would be 80 bushels instead of 40, and of No. 2, 40 instead of 20, while the price and value per bushel would be the same as before: so that corn rent and money rent would both be doubled. I need not point out the difference between this result, and what we have shown would take place if there were an improvement in production without the accompaniment of an increased demand for food.

Agricultural improvement, then, is always ultimately, and in the manner in which it generally takes place also immediately, beneficial to the landlord. We may add, that when it takes place in that manner, it is beneficial to no one else. When the demand for produce fully keeps pace with the increased capacity of production, food is not cheapened; the labourers are not, even temporarily, benefited; the cost of labour is not diminished, nor profits raised. There is a greater aggregate production, a greater produce divided among the labourers, and a larger gross profit; but the wages being shared among a larger population, and the profits spread over a larger capital, no labourer is better off, nor does any capitalist derive from the same amount of capital a larger income.

The result of this long investigation may be summed up as follows. The economical progress of a society constituted of landlords, capitalists, and labourers, tends to the progressive enrichment of the landlord class; while the cost of the labourer's subsistence tends on the whole to increase, and profits to fall. Agricultural improvements are a counteracting force to the two last effects; but the first, though a case is conceivable in which it would be temporarily checked, is ultimately in a high degree promoted by those improvements; and the increase of population tends to transfer all the benefits derived from agricultural improvement to the landlords alone. What other consequences, in addition to these, or in modification of them, arise from the industrial progress of a society thus constituted, I shall endeavour to show in the succeeding chapter.

CHAPTER IV

Of the Tendency of Profits to a Minimum

§1. THE tendency of profits to fall as society advances, which has been brought to notice in the preceding chapter, was early recognized by writers on industry and commerce; but the laws which govern profits not being then understood, the phenomenon was ascribed to a wrong cause. Adam Smith considered profits to be determined by what he called the competition of capital; and concluded that when capital increased, this competition must likewise increase, and profits must fall. It is not quite certain what sort of competition Adam Smith had here in view. His words in the chapter on Profits of Stock[1] are, 'When the stocks of many rich merchants are turned into the same trade, their mutual competition naturally tends to lower its profits; and when there is a like increase of stock in all the different trades carried on in the same society, the same competition must produce the same effect in them all.' This passage would lead us to infer that, in Adam Smith's opinion, the manner in which the competition of capital lowers profits is by lowering prices; that being usually the mode in which an increased investment of capital in any particular trade, lowers the profits of that trade. But if this was his meaning, he overlooked the circumstance, that the fall of price, which if confined to one commodity really does lower the profits of the producer, ceases to have that effect as soon as it extends to all commodities; because, when all things have fallen, nothing has really fallen, except nominally; and even computed in money, the expenses of every producer have diminished as much as his returns. Unless indeed labour be the one commodity which has not fallen in money price, when all other things have: if so, what has really taken place is a rise of wages; and it is that, and not the fall of prices, which has lowered the profits of capital. There is another thing which escaped the notice of Adam Smith; that the supposed universal fall of

1. *Wealth of Nations*, Bk I, Ch. 9.

prices, through increased competition of capitals, is a thing which cannot take place. Prices are not determined by the competition of the sellers only, but also by that of the buyers; by demand as well as supply. The demand which affects money prices consists of all the money in the hands of the community, destined to be laid out in commodities; and as long as the proportion of this to the commodities is not diminished, there is no fall of general prices. Now, howsoever capital may increase, and give rise to an increased production of commodities, a full share of the capital will be drawn to the business of producing or importing money, and the quantity of money will be augmented in an equal ratio with the quantity of commodities. For if this were not the case, and if money, therefore, were, as the theory supposes, perpetually acquiring increased purchasing power, those who produced or imported it would obtain constantly increasing profits; and this could not happen without attracting labour and capital to that occupation from other employments. If a general fall of prices, and increased value of money, were really to occur, it could only be as a consequence of increased cost of production, from the gradual exhaustion of the mines.

It is not tenable, therefore, in theory, that the increase of capital produces, or tends to produce, a general decline of money prices. Neither is it true, that any general decline of prices, as capital increased, has manifested itself in fact. The only things observed to fall in price with the progress of society, are those in which there have been improvements in production, greater than have taken place in the production of the precious metals; as for example, all spun and woven fabrics. Other things, again, instead of falling, have risen in price, because their cost of production, compared with that of gold and silver, has increased. Among these are all kinds of food, comparison being made with a much earlier period of history. The doctrine, therefore, that competition of capital lowers profits by lowering prices, is incorrect in fact, as well as unsound in principle.

But it is not certain that Adam Smith really held that doctrine; for his language on the subject is wavering and unsteady, denoting the absence of a definite and well-digested opinion. Occasionally he seems to think that the mode in which the competition of capital lowers profits, is by raising wages. And when speaking of the rate of profit in new colonies, he seems on the very verge of grasping the complete theory of the subject. 'As the colony increases, the profits of stock gradually diminish. When the most fertile and best situated lands have been all occupied, less profit can be made by the cultivators of what is inferior both in soil and situation.' Had Adam Smith meditated longer on the subject, and systematized his view of it by harmonizing with each other the various glimpses which he caught of it from different points, he would have perceived that this last is the true cause of the fall of profits usually consequent upon increase of capital.

§2. Mr Wakefield, in his Commentary on Adam Smith, and his important writings on Colonization, takes a much clearer view of the subject, and arrives, through a substantially correct series of deductions, at practical conclusions which appear to me just and important; but he is not equally happy in incorporating his valuable speculations with the results of previous thought, and reconciling them with other truths. Some of the theories of Dr Chalmers, in his chapter 'On the Increase and Limits of Capital', and the two chapters which follow it, coincide in their tendency and spirit with those of Mr Wakefield; but Dr Chalmers' ideas, though delivered, as is his custom, with a most attractive semblance of clearness, are really on this subject much more confused than even those of Adam Smith, and more decidedly infected with the often refuted notion that the competition of capital lowers general prices; the subject of Money apparently not having been included among the parts of Political Economy which this acute and vigorous writer had carefully studied.

Mr Wakefield's explanation of the fall of profits is briefly this. Production is limited not solely by the quantity of capital and of labour, but also by the extent of the 'field of employment'. The field of employment for capital is twofold; the land of the country, and the capacity of foreign markets to take its manufactured commodities. On a limited extent of land, only a limited quantity of capital can find employment at a profit. As the quantity of capital approaches this limit, profit falls; when the limit is attained, profit is annihilated; and can only be restored through an extension of the field of employment, either by the acquisition of fertile land, or by opening new markets in foreign countries, from which food and materials can be purchased with the products of domestic capital. These propositions are, in my opinion, substantially true; and, even to the phraseology in which they are expressed, considered as adapted to popular and practical rather than scientific uses, I have nothing to object. The error which seems to me imputable to Mr Wakefield is that of supposing his doctrines to be in contradiction to the principles of the best school of preceding political economists, instead of being, as they really are, corollaries from those principles; though corollaries which, perhaps, would not always have been admitted by those political economists themselves.

The most scientific treatment of the subject which I have met with, is in an essay on the effects of Machinery, published in the *Westminster Review* for January 1826, by Mr William Ellis;[2] which was doubtless unknown to Mr Wakefield, but which had preceded him, though by a different path, in several of his leading conclusions. This essay excited little notice, partly from being published anonymously in a periodical, and partly because it was much in advance of the state of political economy at the time. In Mr Ellis's view of the subject, the questions and difficulties raised by Mr Wakefield's speculations and by those of Dr Chalmers, find a solution consistent with the principles of political economy laid down in the present treatise.

§3. There is at every time and place some particular rate of profit, which is the lowest that will induce the people of that country and time to accumulate savings, and to employ those savings productively. This minimum rate of profit varies according to circumstances. It depends on two elements. One is, the strength

2. Now so much better known through his apostolic exertions, by pen, purse, and person, for the improvement of popular education, and especially for the introduction into it of the elements of practical Political Economy.

of the effective desire of accumulation; the comparative estimate made by the people of that place and era, of future interests when weighed against present. This element chiefly affects the inclination to save. The other element, which affects not so much the willingness to save as the disposition to employ savings productively, is the degree of security of capital engaged in industrial operations. A state of general insecurity, no doubt affects also the disposition to save. A hoard may be a source of additional danger to its reputed possessor. But as it may also be a powerful means of averting dangers, the effects in this respect may perhaps be looked upon as balanced. But in employing any funds which a person may possess as capital on his own account, or in lending it to others to be so employed, there is always some additional risk, over and above that incurred by keeping it idle in his own custody. This extra risk is great in proportion as the general state of society is insecure: it may be equivalent to twenty, thirty, or fifty per cent, or to no more than one or two; something, however, it must always be: and for this, the expectation of profit must be sufficient to compensate.

There would be adequate motives for a certain amount of saving, even if capital yielded no profit. There would be an inducement to lay by in good times a provision for bad; to reserve something for sickness and infirmity, or as a means of leisure and independence in the latter part of life, or a help to children in the outset of it. Savings, however, which have only these ends in view, have not much tendency to increase the amount of capital permanently in existence. These motives only prompt persons to save at one period of life what they purpose to consume at another, or what will be consumed by their children before they can completely provide for themselves. The savings by which an addition is made to the national capital, usually emanate from the desire of persons to improve what is termed their condition in life, or to make a provision for children or others, independent of their exertions. Now, to the strength of these inclinations it makes a very material difference how much of the desired object can be effected by a given amount and duration of self-denial; which again depends on the rate of profit. And there is in every country some rate of profit, below which persons in general will not find sufficient motive to save for the mere purpose of growing richer, or of leaving others better off than themselves. Any accumulation, therefore, by which the general capital is increased, requires as its necessary condition a certain rate of profit; a rate which an average person will deem to be an equivalent for abstinence, with the addition of a sufficient insurance against risk. There are always some persons in whom the effective desire of accumulation is above the average, and to whom less than this rate of profit is a sufficient inducement to save; but these merely step into the place of others whose taste for expense and indulgence is beyond the average, and who, instead of saving, perhaps even dissipate what they have received.

I have already observed that this minimum rate of profit, less than which is not consistent with the further increase of capital, is lower in some states of society than in others; and I may add, that the kind of social progress characteristic of our present civilization tends to diminish it. In the first place, one of the acknowledged effects of that progress is an increase of general security. Destruction by wars, and spoliation by private or public violence, are less and less to be apprehended; and the improvements which may be looked for in education and in the administration of justice, or, in their default, increased regard for opinion, afford a growing protection against fraud and reckless mismanagement. The risks attending the investment of savings in productive employment require, therefore, a smaller rate of profit to compensate for them than was required a century ago, and will hereafter require less than at present. In the second place, it is also one of the consequences of civilization that mankind become less the slaves of the moment, and more habituated to carry their desires and purposes forward into a distant future. This increase of providence is a natural result of the increased assurance with which futurity can be looked forward to; and is, besides, favoured by most of the influences which an industrial life exercises over the passions and inclinations of human nature. In proportion as life has fewer vicissitudes, as habits become more fixed, and great prizes are less and less to be hoped for by any other means than long perseverance, mankind become more willing to sacrifice present indulgence for future objects. This increased capacity of forethought and self-control may assuredly find other things to exercise itself upon than increase of riches, and some considerations connected with this topic will shortly be touched upon. The present kind of social progress, however, decidedly tends, though not perhaps to increase the desire of accumulation, yet to weaken the obstacles to it, and to diminish the amount of profit which people absolutely require as an inducement to save and accumulate. For these two reasons, diminution of risk and increase of providence, a profit or interest of three or four per cent is as sufficient a motive to the increase of capital in England at the present day, as thirty or forty per cent in the Burmese Empire, or in England at the time of King John. In Holland during the last century a return of two per cent, on government security, was consistent with an undiminished, if not with an increasing capital. But though the minimum rate of profit is thus liable to vary, and though to specify exactly what it is would at any given time be impossible, such a minimum always exists; and whether it be high or low, when once it is reached, no further increase of capital can for the present take place. The country has then attained what is known to political economists under the name of the stationary state.

§4. We now arrive at the fundamental proposition which this chapter is intended to inculcate. When a country has long possessed a large production, and a large net income to make savings from, and when, therefore, the means have long existed of making a great annual addition to capital; (the country not having, like America, a large reserve of fertile land still unused;) it is one of the characteristics of such a country, that the rate of profit is habitually within, as it were, a hand's breadth of the minimum, and the country therefore on the very verge of the stationary state. By this I do not mean that this state is likely, in any of the great countries of Europe, to be soon actually reached, or that capital does not still yield a profit considerably greater than what is barely sufficient to induce the people of those countries to save and accumulate. My meaning is, that it would require but a short time to reduce profits to the minimum, if capital continued to increase at its present rate, and no circumstances having a tendency to raise the rate of profit occurred in the meantime. The expansion of capital would soon reach its ultimate boundary, if the boundary itself did not continually open and leave more space.

In England, the ordinary rate of interest on government securities, in which the risk is next to nothing, may be estimated at a little more than three per cent: in all other investments, therefore, the interest or profit calculated upon (exclusively of what is properly a remuneration for talent or exertion) must be as much more than this amount, as is equivalent to the degree of risk to which the capital is thought to be exposed. Let us suppose that in England even so small a net profit as one per cent, exclusive of insurance against risk, would constitute a sufficient inducement to save, but that less than this would not be a sufficient inducement. I now say, that the mere continuance of the present annual increase of capital, if no circumstance occurred to counteract its effect, would suffice in a small number of years to reduce the rate of net profit to one per cent.

To fulfil the conditions of the hypothesis, we must suppose an entire cessation of the exportation of capital for foreign investment. No more capital sent abroad for railways or loans; no more emigrants taking capital with them, to the colonies, or to other countries; no fresh advances made, or credits given, by bankers or merchants to their foreign correspondents. We must also assume that there are no fresh loans for unproductive expenditure, by the government, or on mortgage, or otherwise; and none of the waste of capital which now takes place by the failure of undertaking, which people are tempted to engage in by the hope of a better income than can be obtained in safe paths at the present habitually low rate of profit. We must suppose the entire savings of the community to be annually invested in really productive employment within the country itself; and no new channels opened by industrial inventions, or by a more extensive substitution of the best known processes for inferior ones.

Few persons would hesitate to say, that there would be great difficulty in finding remunerative employment every year for so much new capital, and most would conclude that there would be what used to be termed a general glut; that commodities would be produced, and remain unsold, or be sold only at a loss. But the full examination which we have already given to this question,[3] has shown that this is not the mode in which the inconvenience would be experienced. The difficulty would not consist in any want of a market. If the new capital were duly shared among many varieties of employment, it would raise up a demand for its own produce, and there would be no cause why any part of that produce should remain longer on hand than formerly. What would really be, not merely difficult, but impossible, would be to employ this capital without submitting to a rapid reduction of the rate of profit.

As capital increased, population either would also increase, or it would not. If it did not, wages would rise, and a greater capital would be distributed in wages among the same number of labourers. There being no more labour than before, and no improvements to render the labour more efficient, there would not be any increase of the produce; and as the capital, however largely increased, would only obtain the same gross return, the whole savings of each year would be exactly so much subtracted from the profits of the next and of every following year. It is hardly necessary to say that in such circumstances profits would very soon fall to the point at which further increase of capital would cease. An augmentation of capital, much more rapid than that of population, must soon reach its extreme limit, unless accompanied by increased efficiency of labour (through inventions and discoveries, or improved mental and physical education), or unless some of the idle people, or of the unproductive labourers, became productive.

If population did increase with the increase of capital, and in proportion to it, the fall of profits would still be inevitable. Increased population implies increased demand for agricultural produce. In the absence of industrial improvements, this demand can only be supplied at an increased cost of production, either by cultivating worse land, or by a more elaborate and costly cultivation of the land already under tillage. The cost of the labourer's subsistence is therefore increased; and unless the labourer sub-

3. Bk III, Ch. XIV.

mits to a deterioration of his condition, profits must fall. In an old country like England, if, in addition to supposing all improvement in domestic agriculture suspended, we suppose that there is no increased production in foreign countries for the English market, the fall of profits would be very rapid. If both these avenues to an increased supply of food were closed, and population continued to increase, as it is said to do, at the rate of a thousand a day, all waste land which admits of cultivation in the existing state of knowledge would soon be cultivated, and the cost of production and price of food would be so increased, that, if the labourers received the increased money wages necessary to compensate for their increased expenses, profits would very soon reach the minimum. The fall of profits would be retarded if money wages did not rise, or rose in a less degree; but the margin which can be gained by a deterioration of the labourers' condition is a very narrow one : in general they cannot bear much reduction; when they can, they have also a higher standard of necessary requirements, and *will* not. On the whole, therefore, we may assume that in such a country as England, if the present annual amount of savings were to continue, without any of the counteracting circumstances which now keep in check the natural influence of those savings in reducing profit, the rate of profit would speedily attain the minimum, and all further accumulation of capital would for the present cease.

§5. What, then, are these counteracting circumstances, which, in the existing state of things, maintain a tolerably equal struggle against the downward tendency of profits, and prevent the great annual savings which take place in this country, from depressing the rate of profit much nearer to that lowest point to which it is always tending, and which, left to itself, it would so promptly attain? The resisting agencies are of several kinds.

First among them, we may notice one which is so simple and so conspicuous, that some political economists, especially M. de Sismondi and Dr Chalmers, have attended to it almost to the exclusion of all others. This is, the waste of capital in periods of over-trading and rash speculation, and in the commercial revulsions by which such times are always followed. It is true that a great part of what is lost at such periods is not destroyed, but merely transferred, like a gambler's losses, to more successful speculators. But even of these mere transfers, a large portion is always to foreigners, by the hasty purchase of unusual quantities of foreign goods at advanced prices. And much also is absolutely wasted. Mines are opened, railways or bridges made, and many other works of uncertain profit commenced, and in these enterprises much capital is sunk which yields either no return, or none adequate to the outlay. Factories are built and machinery erected beyond what the market requires, or can keep in employment. Even if they are kept in employment, the capital is no less sunk; it has been converted from circulating into fixed capital, and has ceased to have any influence on wages or profits. Besides this, there is a great unproductive consumption of capital, during the stagnation which follows a period of general overtrading. Establishments are shut up, or kept working without any profit, hands are discharged, and numbers of persons in all ranks, being deprived of their income, and thrown for support on their savings, find themselves, after the crisis has passed away, in a condition of more or less impoverishment. Such are the effects of a commercial revulsion: and that such revulsions are almost periodical, is a consequence of the very tendency of profits which we are considering. By the time a few years have passed over without a crisis, so much additional capital has been accumulated, that it is no longer possible to invest it at the accustomed profit: all public securities rise to a high price, the rate of interest on the best mercantile security falls very low, and the complaint is general among persons in business that no money is to be made. Does not this demonstrate how speedily profit would be at the minimum, and the stationary condition of capital would be attained, if these accumulations went on without any counteracting principle? But the diminished scale of all safe gains, inclines persons to give a ready ear to any projects which hold out, though at the risk of loss, the hope of a higher rate of profit; and speculations ensue, which, with the subsequent revulsions, destroy, or transfer to foreigners, a considerable amount of capital, produce a temporary rise of interest and profit, make room for fresh accumulations, and the same round is recommenced.

This, doubtless, is one considerable cause which arrests profits in their descent to the minimum, by sweeping away from time to time a part of the accumulated mass by which they are forced down. But this is not, as might be inferred from the language of some writers, the principal cause. If it were, the capital of the country would not increase; but in England it does increase greatly and rapidly. This is shown by the increasing productiveness of almost all taxes, by the continual growth of all the signs of national wealth, and by the rapid increase of population, while the condition of the labourers is certainly not declining, but on the whole improving. These things prove that each commercial revulsion, however disastrous, is very far from destroying all the capital which has been added to the accumulations of the country since the last revulsion preceding it, and that, invariably, room is either found or made for the profitable employment of a perpetually increasing capital, consistently with not forcing down profits to a lower rate.

§6. This brings us to the second of the counter-agencies, namely, improvements in production. These evidently have the effect of extending what Mr Wakefield terms the field of employment, that is, they enable a greater amount of capital to be accumulated and employed without depressing the rate of profit: provided always that they do not raise, to a proportional extent, the habits and requirements of the labourer. If the labouring class gain the full advantage of the increased cheapness, in other words, if money wages do not fall, profits are not raised, nor their fall retarded. But if the labourers people up to the improvement in their condition, and so relapse to their previous state, profits will rise. All inventions which cheapen any of the things consumed by the labourers, unless their requirements are raised in an equivalent degree, in time lower money wages: and by doing so, enable a greater capital to be accumulated and employed, before profits fall back to what they were previously.

Improvements which only affect things consumed exclusively

by the richer classes, do not operate precisely in the same manner. The cheapening of lace or velvet has no effect in diminishing the cost of labour; and no mode can be pointed out in which it can raise the rate of profit, so as to make room for a larger capital before the minimum is attained. It, however, produces an effect which is virtually equivalent; it lowers, or tends to lower, the minimum itself. In the first place, increased cheapness of articles of consumption promotes the inclination to save, by affording to all consumers a surplus which they may lay by, consistently with their accustomed manner of living; and unless they were previously suffering actual hardships, it will require little self-denial to save some part at least of this surplus. In the next place, whatever enables people to live equally well on a smaller income, inclines them to lay by capital for a lower rate of profit. If people can live on an independence of 500*l.* a year in the same manner as they formerly could on one of 1000*l.*, some persons will be induced to save in hopes of the one, who would have been deterred by the more remote prospect of the other. All improvements, therefore, in the production of almost any commodity, tend in some degree to widen the interval which has to be passed before arriving at the stationary state: but this effect belongs in a much greater degree to the improvements which affect the articles consumed by the labourer, since these conduce to it in two ways; they induce people to accumulate for a lower profit, and they also raise the rate of profit itself.

§7. Equivalent in effect to improvements in production, is the acquisition of any new power of obtaining cheap commodities from foreign countries. If necessaries are cheapened, whether they are so by improvements at home or importation from abroad, is exactly the same thing to wages and profits. Unless the labourer obtains, and by an improvement of his habitual standard, keeps, the whole benefit, the cost of labour is lowered, and the rate of profit raised. As long as food can continue to be imported for an increasing population without any diminution of cheapness, so long the declension of profits through the increase of population and capital is arrested, and accumulation may go on without making the rate of profit draw nearer to the minimum. And on this ground it is believed by some, that the repeal of the corn laws has opened to this country a long era of rapid increase of capital with an undiminished rate of profit.

Before inquiring whether this expectation is reasonable, one remark must be made, which is much at variance with commonly received notions. Foreign trade does not necessarily increase the field of employment for capital. It is not the mere opening of a market for a country's productions, that tends to raise the rate of profits. If nothing were obtained in exchange for those productions but the luxuries of the rich, the expenses of no capitalist would be diminished; profits would not be at all raised, nor room made for the accumulation of more capital without submitting to a reduction of profits: and if the attainment of the stationary state were at all retarded, it would only be because the diminished cost at which a certain degree of luxury could be enjoyed, might induce people, in that prospect, to make fresh savings for a lower profit than they formerly were willing to do. When foreign trade makes room for more capital at the same profit, it is by enabling the necessaries of life, or the habitual articles of the labourer's consumption, to be obtained at smaller cost. It may do this in two ways; by the importation either of those commodities themselves, or of the means and appliances for producing them. Cheap iron has, in a certain measure, the same effect on profits and the cost of labour as cheap corn, because cheap iron makes cheap tools for agriculture and cheap machinery for clothing. But a foreign trade which neither directly, nor by any indirect consequence, increases the cheapness of anything consumed by the labourers, does not, any more than an invention or discovery in the like case, tend to raise profits or retard their fall; it merely substitutes the production of goods for foreign markets, in the room of the home production of luxuries, leaving the employment for capital neither greater nor less than before. It is true, that there is scarcely any export trade which, in a country that already imports necessaries or materials, comes within these conditions: for every increase of exports enables the country to obtain all its imports on cheaper terms than before.

A country which, as is now the case with England, admits food of all kinds, and all necessaries and the materials of necessaries, to be freely imported from all parts of the world, no longer depends on the fertility of her own soil to keep up her rate of profits, but on the soil of the whole world. It remains to consider how far this resource can be counted upon, for making head during a very long period against the tendency of profits to decline as capital increases.

It must, of course, be supposed that with the increase of capital, population also increases; for if it did not, the consequent rise of wages would bring down profits, in spite of any cheapness of food. Suppose then that the population of Great Britain goes on increasing at its present rate, and demands every year a supply of imported food considerably beyond that of the year preceding. This annual increase in the food demanded from the exporting countries, can only be obtained either by great improvements in their agriculture, or by the application of a great additional capital to the growth of food. The former is likely to be a very slow process, from the rudeness and ignorance of the agricultural classes in the food-exporting countries of Europe, while the British colonies and the United States are already in possession of most of the improvements yet made, so far as suitable to their circumstances. There remains as a resource, the extension of cultivation. And on this it is to be remarked, that the capital by which any such extension can take place, is mostly still to be created. In Poland, Russia, Hungary, Spain, the increase of capital is extremely slow. In America it is rapid, but not more rapid than the population. The principal fund at present available for supplying this country with a yearly increasing importation of food, is that portion of the annual savings of America which has heretofore been applied to increasing the manufacturing establishments of the United States, and which free trade in corn may possibly divert from that purpose to growing food for our market. This limited source of supply, unless great improvements take place in agriculture, cannot be expected to keep pace with the growing demand of so rapidly increasing a population as that of Great Britain; and if our population and capital continue to increase with their present rapidity, the only mode in which food can continue to be supplied cheaply to the one, is by sending the other abroad to produce it.

*8. This brings us to the last of the counter-forces which check the downward tendency of profits, in a country whose capital increases faster than that of its neighbours, and whose profits are therefore nearer to the minimum. This is, the perpetual overflow of capital into colonies or foreign countries, to seek higher profits than can be obtained at home. I believe this to have been for many years one of the principal causes by which the decline of profits in England has been arrested. It has a twofold operation. In the first place, it does what a fire, or an inundation, or a commercial crisis would have done: it carries off a part of the increase of capital from which the reduction of profits proceeds. Secondly, the capital so carried off is not lost, but is chiefly employed either in founding colonies, which become large exporters of cheap agricultural produce, or in extending and perhaps improving the agriculture of older communities. It is to the emigration of English capital, that we have chiefly to look for keeping up a supply of cheap food and cheap materials of clothing, proportional to the increase of our population; thus enabling an increasing capital to find employment in the country, without reduction of profit, in producing manufactured articles with which to pay for this supply of raw produce. Thus, the exportation of capital is an agent of great efficacy in extending the field of employment for that which remains: and it may be said truly that, up to a certain point, the more capital we send away, the more we shall possess and be able to retain at home.

In countries which are further advanced in industry and population, and have therefore a lower rate of profit, than others, there is always, long before the actual minimum is reached, a practical minimum, viz. when profits have fallen to much below what they are elsewhere, that, were they to fall lower, all further accumulations would go abroad. In the present state of the industry of the world, when there is occasion, in any rich and improving country, to take the minimum of profits at all into consideration for practical purposes, it is only this practical minimum that needs be considered. As long as there are old countries where capital increases very rapidly, and new countries where profit is still high, profits in the old countries will not sink to the rate which would put a stop to accumulation; the fall is stopped at the point which sends capital abroad. It is only, however, by improvements in production, and even in the production of things consumed by labourers, that the capital of a country like England is prevented from speedily reaching that degree of lowness of profit, which would cause all further savings to be sent to find employment in the colonies, or in foreign countries.

CHAPTER V

Consequences of the Tendency of Profits to a Minimum

§1. THE theory of the effect of accumulation on profits, laid down in the preceding chapter, materially alters many of the practical conclusions which might otherwise be supposed to follow from the general principles of Political Economy, and which were, indeed, long admitted as true by the highest authorities on the subject.

It must greatly abate, or rather, altogether destroy, in countries where profits are low, the immense importance which used to be attached by political economists to the effects which an event or a measure of government might have in adding to or subtracting from the capital of the country. We have now seen that the lowness of profits is a proof that the spirit of accumulation is so active, and that the increase of capital has proceeded at so rapid a rate, as to outstrip the two counter-agencies, improvements in production, and increased supply of cheap necessaries from abroad: and that unless a considerable portion of the annual increase of capital were either periodically destroyed, or exported for foreign investment, the country would speedily attain the point at which further accumulation would cease, or at least spontaneously slacken, so as no longer to overpass the march of invention in the arts which produce the necessaries of life. In such a state of things as this, a sudden addition to the capital of the country, unaccompanied by any increase of productive power, would be but of transitory duration; since by depressing profits and interest, it would either diminish by a corresponding amount the savings which would be made from income in the year or two following, or it would cause an equivalent amount to be sent abroad, or to be wasted in rash speculations. Neither, on the other hand, would a sudden abstraction of capital, unless of inordinate amount, have any real effect in impoverishing the country. After a few months or years, there would exist in the country just as much capital as if none had been taken away. The abstraction, by raising profits and interest, would give a fresh stimulus to the accumulative principle, which would speedily fill up the vacuum. Probably, indeed, the only effect that would ensue, would be that for some time afterwards less capital would be exported, and less thrown away in hazardous speculation.

In the first place, then, this view of things greatly weakens, in a wealthy and industrious country, the force of the economical argument against the expenditure of public money for really valuable, even though industriously unproductive, purposes. If for any great object of justice or philanthropic policy, such as the industrial regeneration of Ireland, or a comprehensive measure of colonization or of public education, it were proposed to raise a large sum by way of loan, politicians need not demur to the abstraction of so much capital, as tending to dry up the permanent sources of the country's wealth, and diminish the fund which supplies the subsistence of the labouring population. The utmost expense which could be requisite for any of these purposes, would not in all probability deprive one labourer of employment, or diminish the next year's production by one ell of cloth or one bushel of grain. In poor countries, the capital of the country requires the legislator's sedulous care; he is bound to be most cautious of encroaching upon it, and should favour to the utmost its accumulation at home, and its introduction from abroad. But in rich, populous, and highly cultivated countries, it is not capital which is the deficient element, but fertile land; and what the legislator should desire and promote, is not a greater aggregate saving, but a greater return to savings, either by improved cultivation, or by access to the produce of more fertile lands in other parts of the globe. In such countries, the government may take any moderate portion of the capital of the country and expend it as revenue, without affecting the national wealth: the whole being either drawn from that portion of the annual savings which would otherwise be sent abroad, or being subtracted from the unproductive expenditure of individuals for the next year or two, since every million spent makes room for another million to be saved before reaching the overflowing point. When the object in view is worth the sacrifice of such an amount of the expenditure that furnishes the daily enjoyments of the people, the only well-grounded economical objection against taking the necessary funds directly from capital, consists of the inconveniences attending the process of raising a revenue by taxation, to pay the interest of a debt.

The same considerations enable us to throw aside as unworthy of regard, one of the common arguments against emigration as a means of relief for the labouring class. Emigration, it is said, can do no good to the labourers, if, in order to defray the cost, as much must be taken away from the capital of the country as from its population. That anything like this proportion could require to be abstracted from capital for the purpose even of the most extensive colonization, few, I should think, would now assert: but even on that untenable supposition, it is an error to suppose that no benefit would be conferred on the labouring class. If one-tenth of the labouring people of England were transferred to the colonies, and along with them one-tenth of the circulating capital of the country, either wages, or profits, or both, would be greatly benefited, by the diminished pressure of capital and population upon the fertility of the land. There would be a reduced demand for food: the inferior arable lands would be thrown out of cultivation, and would become pasture; the superior would be cultivated less highly, but with a greater proportional return; food would be lowered in price, and though money wages would not rise, every labourer would be considerably improved in circumstances, an improvement which, if no increased stimulus to population and fall of wages ensued, would be permanent; while if there did, profits would rise, and accumulation start forward so as to repair the loss of capital. The landlords alone would sustain some loss of income; and even they, only if colonization went to the length of actually diminishing capital and population, but not if it merely carried off the annual increase.

§2. From the same principles we are now able to arrive at a final conclusion respecting the effects which machinery, and generally the sinking of capital for a productive purpose, produce upon

the immediate and ultimate interests of the labouring class. The
characteristic property of this class of industrial improvements
is the conversion of circulating capital into fixed: and it was
shown in the first Book, that in a country where capital accumulates slowly, the introduction of machinery, permanent improvements of land, and the like, might be, for the time, extremely
injurious; since the capital so employed might be directly taken
from the wages fund, the subsistence of the people and the
employment for labour curtailed, and the gross annual produce
of the country actually diminished. But in a country of great
annual savings and low profits, no such effects need be apprehended. Since even the emigration of capital, or its unproductive
expenditure, or its absolute waste, do not in such a country, if
confined within any moderate bounds, at all diminish the
aggregate amount of the wages fund – still less can the mere
conversion of a like sum into fixed capital, which continues to be
productive, have that effect. It merely draws off at one orifice
what was already flowing out at another; or if not, the greater
vacant space left in the reservoir does but cause a greater quantity to flow in. Accordingly, in spite of the mischievous derange-
ments of the money-market which were at one time occasioned
by the sinking of great sums in railways, I was never able to
agree with those who apprehended mischief, from this source,
to the productive resources of the country. Not on the absurd
ground (which to any one acquainted with the elements of the
subject needs no confutation) that railway expenditure is a mere
transfer of capital from hand to hand, by which nothing is lost
or destroyed. This is true of what is spent in the purchase of the
land; a portion too of what is paid to parliamentary agents,
counsel, engineers, and surveyors, is saved by those who receive
it, and becomes capital again: but what is laid out in the *bona
fide* construction of the railway itself, is lost and gone; when
once expended, it is incapable of ever being paid in wages or
applied to the maintenance of labourers again; as a matter of
account, the result is that so much food and clothing and tools
have been consumed, and the country has got a railway instead.
But what I would urge is, that sums so applied are mostly a
mere appropriation of the annual overflowing which would

otherwise have gone abroad, or been thrown away unprofitably, leaving neither a railway nor any other tangible result. The railway gambling of 1844 and 1845 probably saved the country from a depression of profits and interest, and a rise of all public and private securities, which would have engendered still wilder speculations, and when the effects came afterwards to be complicated by the scarcity of food, would have ended in a still more formidable crisis than was experienced in the years immediately following. In the poorer countries of Europe, the rage for railway construction might have had worse consequences than in England, were it not that in those countries such enterprises are in a great measure carried on by foreign capital. The railway operations of the various nations of the world may be looked upon as a sort of competition for the overflowing capital of the countries where profit is low and capital abundant, as England and Holland. The English railway speculations are a struggle to keep our annual increase of capital at home; those of foreign countries are an effort to obtain it.[1]

It already appears from these considerations, that the conversion of circulating capital into fixed, whether by railways, or manufactories, or ships, or machinery, or canals, or mines, or works of drainage and irrigation, is not likely, in any rich country, to diminish the gross produce or the amount of employment for labour. How much then is the case strengthened, when we consider that these transformations of capital are of the nature of improvements in production, which, instead of ultimately diminishing circulating capital, are the necessary conditions of its increase, since they alone enable a country to possess a constantly augmenting capital without reducing profits to the rate which would cause accumulation to stop. There is hardly any increase of fixed capital which does not enable the country to contain eventually a larger circulating capital, than it otherwise could possess and employ within its own limits; for there is hardly any creation of fixed capital which, when it proves suc-

1. It is hardly needful to point out how fully the remarks in the text have been verified by subsequent facts. The capital of the country, far from having been in any degree impaired by the large amount sunk in railway construction, was soon again overflowing.

cessful, does not cheapen the articles on which wages are habitually expended. All capital sunk in the permanent improvement of land, lessens the cost of food and materials; almost all improvements in machinery cheapen the labourer's clothing or lodging, or the tools with which these are made; improvements in locomotion, such as railways, cheapen to the consumer all things which are brought from a distance. All these improvements make the labourers better off with the same money wages, better off if they do not increase their rate of multiplication. But if they do, and wages consequently fall, at least profits rise, and, while accumulation receives an immediate stimulus, room is made for a greater amount of capital before a sufficient motive arises for sending it abroad. Even the improvements which do not cheapen the things consumed by the labourer, and which, therefore, do not raise profits nor retain capital in the country, nevertheless, as we have seen, by lowering the minimum of profit for which people will ultimately consent to save, leave an ampler margin than previously for eventual accumulation, before arriving at the stationary state.

We may conclude, then, that improvements in production, and emigration of capital to the more fertile soils and unworked mines of the uninhabited or thinly peopled parts of the globe, do not, as appears to a superficial view, diminish the gross produce and the demand for labour at home; but, on the contrary, are what we have chiefly to depend on for increasing both, and are even the necessary conditions of any great or prolonged augmentation of either. Nor is it any exaggeration to say, that within certain, and not very narrow, limits, the more capital a country like England expends in these two ways, the more she will have left.

CHAPTER VI

Of the Stationary State

§1. THE preceding chapters comprise the general theory of the economical progress of society, in the sense in which those terms are commonly understood; the progress of capital, of population, and of the productive arts. But in contemplating any progressive movement, not in its nature unlimited, the mind is not satisfied with merely tracing the laws of the movement; it cannot but ask the further question, to what goal? Towards what ultimate point is society tending by its industrial progress? When the progress ceases, in what condition are we to expect that it will leave mankind?

It must always have been seen, more or less distinctly, by political economists, that the increase of wealth is not boundless: that at the end of what they term the progressive state lies the stationary state, that all progress in wealth is but a postponement of this, and that each step in advance is an approach to it. We have now been led to recognize that this ultimate goal is at all times near enough to be fully in view; that we are always on the verge of it, and that if we have not reached it long ago, it is because the goal itself flies before us. The richest and most prosperous countries would very soon attain the stationary state, if no further improvements were made in the productive arts, and if there were a suspension of the overflow of capital from those countries into the uncultivated or ill-cultivated regions of the earth.

This impossibility of ultimately avoiding the stationary state – this irresistible necessity that the stream of human industry should finally spread itself out into an apparently stagnant sea – must have been, to the political economists of the last two generations, an unpleasing and discouraging prospect; for the tone and tendency of their speculations goes completely to identify all that is economically desirable with the progressive state, and with that alone. With Mr M'Culloch, for example, prosperity does not mean a large production and a good distribution of wealth, but a rapid increase of it; his test of prosperity is high profits; and as the tendency of that very increase of wealth, which he calls prosperity, is towards low profits, economical progress, according to him, must tend to the extinction of prosperity. Adam Smith always assumes that the condition of the mass of the people, though it may not be positively distressed, must be pinched and stinted in a stationary condition of wealth, and can only be satisfactory in a progressive state. The doctrine that, to however distant a time incessant struggling may put off our doom, the progress of society must 'end in shallows and in miseries', far from being, as many people still believe, a wicked invention of Mr Malthus, was either expressly or tacitly affirmed by his most distinguished predecessors, and can only be successfully combated on his principles. Before attention had been directed to the principle of population as the active force in determining the remuneration of labour, the increase of mankind was virtually treated as a constant quantity; it was, at all events, assumed that in the natural and normal state of human affairs population must constantly increase, from which it followed that a constant increase of the means of support was essential to the physical comfort of the mass of mankind. The publication of Mr Malthus' Essay is the era from which better views of this subject must be dated; and notwithstanding the acknowledged errors of his first edition, few writers have done more than himself, in the subsequent editions, to promote these juster and more hopeful anticipations.

Even in a progressive state of capital, in old countries, a conscientious or prudential restraint on population is indispensable, to prevent the increase of numbers from outstripping the increase of capital, and the condition of the classes who are at the bottom of society from being deteriorated. Where there is not, in the people, or in some very large proportion of them, a resolute resistance to this deterioration – a determination to preserve an established standard of comfort – the condition of the poorest class sinks, even in a progressive state, to the lowest point which they will consent to endure. The same determination would be equally effectual to keep up their condition in the stationary state, and would be quite as likely to exist. Indeed, even now, the countries in which the greatest prudence is manifested in the regulating of population, are often those in which capital increases least rapidly. Where there is an indefinite prospect of employment for increased numbers, there is apt to appear less necessity for prudential restraint. If it were evident that a new hand could not obtain employment but by displacing, or succeeding to, one already employed, the combined influences of prudence and public opinion might in some measure be relied on for restricting the coming generation within the numbers necessary for replacing the present.

§2. I cannot, therefore, regard the stationary state of capital and wealth with the unaffected aversion so generally manifested towards it by political economists of the old school. I am inclined to believe that it would be, on the whole, a very considerable improvement on our present condition. I confess I am not charmed with the ideal of life held out by those who think that the normal state of human beings is that of struggling to get on; that the trampling, crushing, elbowing, and treading on each other's heels, which form the existing type of social life, are the most desirable lot of human kind, or anything but the disagreeable symptoms of one of the phases of industrial progress. It may be a necessary stage in the progress of civilization, and those European nations which have hitherto been so fortunate as to be preserved from it, may have it yet to undergo. It is an incident of growth, not a mark of decline, for it is not necessarily destructive of the higher aspirations and the heroic virtues; as America, in her great civil war, has proved to the world, both by her conduct as a people and by numerous splendid individual examples, and as England, it is to be hoped, would also prove, on an equally trying and exciting occasion.[1] But it is not a kind of social perfection which philanthropists to come will feel any very

1. [In the 1848 edition the preceding passage ran as follows: The northern and middle states of America are a specimen of this stage of civilization in very favourable circumstances; having, apparently, got rid of all social injustices and inequalities that affect persons of Caucasian race and of the male sex, while the proportion of population to capital and land is such as

eager desire to assist in realizing. Most fitting, indeed, is it, that while riches are power, and to grow as rich as possible the universal object of ambition, the path to its attainment should be open to all, without favour or partiality. But the best state for human nature is that in which, while no one is poor, no one desires to be richer, nor has any reason to fear being thrust back, by the efforts of others to push themselves forward.

That the energies of mankind should be kept in employment by the struggle for riches, as they were formerly by the struggle of war, until the better minds succeed in educating the others into better things, is undoubtedly more desirable than that they should rust and stagnate. While minds are coarse they require coarse stimuli, and let them have them. In the meantime, those who do not accept the present very early stage of human improvement as its ultimate type, may be excused for being comparatively indifferent to the kind of economical progress which excites the congratulations of ordinary politicians; the mere increase of production and accumulation. For the safety of national independence it is essential that a country should not fall much behind its neighbours in these things. But in themselves they are of little importance, so long as either the increase of population or anything else prevents the mass of the people from reaping any part of the benefit of them. I know not why it should be matter of congratulation that persons who are already richer than any one needs to be, should have doubled their means of consuming things which give little or no pleasure except as representative of wealth; or that numbers of individuals should pass over, every year, from the middle classes into a richer class, or from the class of the occupied rich to that of the unoccupied. It is only in the backward countries of the world that increased production is still an important object: in those most advanced, what is economically needed is a better distribution, of which one indispensable means is a stricter

---

to ensure abundance to every able-bodied member of the community who does not forfeit it by misconduct. They have the six points of Chartism, and they have no poverty: and all that these advantages seem to have done for them is that the life of the whole of one sex is devoted to dollar-hunting, and of the other to breeding dollar-hunters.]

restraint on population. Levelling institutions, either of a just or of an unjust kind, cannot alone accomplish it; they may lower the heights of society, but they cannot, of themselves, permanently raise the depths.

On the other hand, we may suppose this better distribution of property attained, by the joint effect of the prudence and frugality of individuals, and of a system of legislation favouring equality of fortunes, so far as is consistent with the just claim of the individual to the fruits, whether great or small, of his or her own industry. We may suppose, for instance (according to the suggestion thrown out in a former chapter[2]), a limitation of the sum which any one person may acquire by gift or inheritance, to the amount sufficient to constitute a moderate independence. Under this twofold influence, society would exhibit these leading features: a well-paid and affluent body of labourers; no enormous fortunes, except what were earned and accumulated during a single lifetime; but a much larger body of persons than at present, not only exempt from the coarser toils, but with sufficient leisure, both physical and mental, from mechanical details, to cultivate freely the graces of life, and afford examples of them to the classes less favourably circumstanced for their growth. This condition of society, so greatly preferable to the present, is not only perfectly compatible with the stationary state, but, it would seem, more naturally allied with that state than with any other.

There is room in the world, no doubt, and even in old countries, for a great increase of population, supposing the arts of life to go on improving, and capital to increase. But even if innocuous, I confess I see very little reason for desiring it. The density of population necessary to enable mankind to obtain, in the greatest degree, all the advantages both of co-operation and of social intercourse, has, in all the most populous countries, been attained. A population may be too crowded, though all be amply supplied with food and raiment. It is not good for man to be kept perforce at all times in the presence of his species. A world from which solitude is extirpated, is a very poor ideal. Solitude, in the sense of being often alone, is essential to any

2. [See below pp. 376-80.]

depth of meditation or of character; and solitude in the presence of natural beauty and grandeur, is the cradle of thoughts and aspirations which are not only good for the individual, but which society could ill do without. Nor is there much satisfaction in contemplating the world with nothing left to the spontaneous activity of nature; with every rood of land brought into cultivation, which is capable of growing food for human beings; every flowery waste or natural pasture ploughed up, all quadrupeds or birds which are not domesticated for man's use exterminated as his rivals for food, every hedgerow or superfluous tree rooted out, and scarcely a place left where a wild shrub or flower could grow without being eradicated as a weed in the name of improved agriculture. If the earth must lose that great portion of its pleasantness which it owes to things that the unlimited increase of wealth and population would extirpate from it, for the mere purpose of enabling it to support a larger, but not a better or a happier population, I sincerely hope, for the sake of posterity, that they will be content to be stationary, long before necessity compels them to it.

It is scarcely necessary to remark that a stationary condition of capital and population implies no stationary state of human improvement. There would be as much scope as ever for all kinds of mental culture, and moral and social progress; as much room for improving the Art of Living, and much more likelihood of its being improved, when minds ceased to be engrossed by the art of getting on. Even the industrial arts might be as earnestly and as successfully cultivated, with this sole difference, that instead of serving no purpose but the increase of wealth, industrial improvements would produce their legitimate effect, that of abridging labour. Hitherto it is questionable if all the mechanical inventions yet made have lightened the day's toil of any human being. They have enabled a greater population to live the same life of drudgery and imprisonment, and an increased number of manufacturers and others to make fortunes. They have increased the comforts of the middle classes. But they have not yet begun to effect those great changes in human destiny, which it is in their nature and in their futurity to accomplish. Only when, in addition to just institutions, the increase of mankind shall be under the deliberate guidance of judicious foresight, can the conquests made from the powers of nature by the intellect and energy of scientific discoverers, become the common property of the species, and the means of improving and elevating the universal lot.

CHAPTER VII

On the Probable Futurity of the
Labouring Classes

§1. THE observations in the preceding chapter had for their principal object to deprecate a false ideal of human society. Their applicability to the practical purposes of present times, consists in moderating the inordinate importance attached to the mere increase of production, and fixing attention upon improved distribution, and a large remuneration of labour, as the two desiderata. Whether the aggregate produce increases absolutely or not, is a thing in which, after a certain amount has been obtained, neither the legislator nor the philanthropist need feel any strong interest: but, that it should increase relatively to the number of those who share in it, is of the utmost possible importance; and this, (whether the wealth of mankind be stationary, or increasing at the most rapid rate ever known in an old country), must depend on the opinions and habits of the most numerous class, the class of manual labourers.

When I speak, either in this place or elsewhere, of 'the labouring classes', or of labourers as a 'class', I use those phrases in compliance with custom, and as descriptive of an existing, but by no means a necessary or permanent, state of social relations. I do not recognize as either just or salutary, a state of society in which there is any 'class' which is not labouring; any human beings, exempt from bearing their share of the necessary labours of human life, except those unable to labour, or who have fairly earned rest by previous toil. So long, however, as the great social evil exists of a non-labouring class, labourers also constitute a class, and may be spoken of, though only provisionally, in that character.

Considered in its moral and social aspect, the state of the labouring people has latterly been a subject of much more speculation and discussion than formerly; and the opinion that it is not now what it ought to be, has become very general. The suggestions which have been promulgated, and the controversies which have been excited, on detached points rather than on the foundations of the subject, have put in evidence the existence of two conflicting theories, respecting the social position desirable for manual labourers. The one may be called the theory of dependence and protection, the other that of self-dependence.

According to the former theory, the lot of the poor, in all things which affect them collectively, should be regulated *for* them, not *by* them. They should not be required or encouraged to think for themselves, or give to their own reflection or forecast an influential voice in the determination of their destiny. It is supposed to be the duty of the higher classes to think for them, and to take the responsibility of their lot, as the commander and officers of an army take that of the soldiers composing it. This function, it is contended, the higher classes should prepare themselves to perform conscientiously, and their whole demeanour should impress the poor with a reliance on it, in order that, while yielding passive and active obedience to the rules prescribed for them, they may resign themselves in all other respects to a trustful *insouciance*, and repose under the shadow of their protectors. The relation between rich and poor, according to this theory (a theory also applied to the relation between men and women) should be only partly authoritative; it should be amiable, moral, and sentimental: affectionate tutelage on the one side, respectful and grateful deference on the other. The rich should be *in loco parentis* to the poor, guiding and restraining them like children. Of spontaneous action on their part there should be no need. They should be called on for nothing but to do their day's work, and to be moral and religious. Their morality and religion should be provided for them by their superiors, who should see them properly taught it, and should do all that is necessary to ensure their being, in return for labour and attachment, properly fed, clothed, housed, spiritually edified, and innocently amused.

This is the ideal of the future, in the minds of those whose dissatisfaction with the present assumes the form of affection and regret towards the past. Like other ideals, it exercises an unconscious influence on the opinions and sentiments of numbers who never consciously guide themselves by any ideal. It has also this in common with other ideals, that it has never been historically realized. It makes its appeal to our imaginative sympathies in the character of a restoration of the good times of our forefathers. But no times can be pointed out in which the higher classes of this or any other country performed a part even distantly resembling the one assigned to them in this theory. It is an idealization, grounded on the conduct and character of here and there an individual. All privileged and powerful classes, as such, have used their power in the interest of their own selfishness, and have indulged their self-importance in despising, and not in lovingly caring for, those who were, in their estimation, degraded by being under the necessity of working for their benefit. I do not affirm that what has always been must always be, or that human improvement has no tendency to correct the intensely selfish feelings engendered by power; but though the evil may be lessened, it cannot be eradicated, until the power itself is withdrawn. This, at least, seems to me undeniable, that long before the superior classes could be sufficiently improved to govern in the tutelary manner supposed, the inferior classes would be too much improved to be so governed.

I am quite sensible of all that is seductive in the picture of society which this theory presents. Though the facts of it have no prototype in the past, the feelings have. In them lies all that there is of reality in the conception. As the idea is essentially repulsive of a society only held together by the relations and feelings arising out of pecuniary interests, so there is something naturally attractive in a form of society abounding in strong personal attachments and disinterested self-devotion. Of such feelings it must be admitted that the relation of protector and protected has hitherto been the richest source. The strongest attachments of human beings in general, are towards the things or the persons that stand between them and some dreaded evil. Hence, in an age of lawless violence and insecurity, and general hardness and roughness of manners, in which life is beset with dangers and sufferings at every step, to those who have neither a commanding position of their own, nor a claim on the protection of some one who has – a generous giving of protection, and a grateful receiving of it, are the strongest ties which connect human beings; the feelings arising from that relation are their warmest feelings; all the enthusiasm and tenderness of the most sensitive natures gather round it; loyalty on the one part and chivalry on the other are principles exalted into passions. I do not desire to depreciate these qualities. The error lies in not perceiving, that these virtues and sentiments, like the clanship and the hospitality of the wandering Arab, belong emphatically to a rude and imperfect state of the social union; and that the feelings between protector and protected, whether between kings and subjects, rich and poor, or men and women, can no longer have this beautiful and endearing character, where there are no longer any serious dangers from which to protect. What is there in the present state of society to make it natural that human beings, of ordinary strength and courage, should glow with the warmest gratitude and devotion in return for protection? The laws protect them, wherever the laws do not criminally fail in their duty. To be under the power of some one, instead of being as formerly the sole condition of safety, is now, speaking generally, the only situation which exposes to grievous wrong. The so-called protectors are now the only persons against whom, in any ordinary circumstances, protection is needed. The brutality and tyranny with which every police report is filled, are those of husbands to wives, of parents to children. That the law does not prevent these atrocities, that it is only now making a first timid attempt to repress and punish them, is no matter of necessity, but the deep disgrace of those by whom the laws are made and administered. No man or woman who either possesses or is able to earn an independent livelihood, requires any other protection than that which the law could and ought to give. This being the case, it argues great ignorance of human nature to continue taking for granted that relations founded on protection must always subsist, and not to see that the assumption of the part of protector, and of the power which belongs to it, without any of the necessities which justify it, must engender feelings opposite to loyalty.

Of the working men, at least in the more advanced countries of Europe, it may be pronounced certain, that the patriarchal or paternal system of government is one to which they will not again be subject. That question was decided, when they were taught to read, and allowed access to newspapers and political tracts; when dissenting preachers were suffered to go among them, and appeal to their faculties and feelings in opposition to the creeds professed and countenanced by their superiors; when they were brought together in numbers, to work socially under the same roof; when railways enabled them to shift from place to place, and change their patrons and employers as easily as their coats; when they were encouraged to seek a share in the government, by means of the electoral franchise. The working classes have taken their interests into their own hands, and are perpetually showing that they think the interests of their employers not identical with their own, but opposite to them. Some among the higher classes flatter themselves that these tendencies may be counteracted by moral and religious education: but they have let the time go by for giving an education which can serve their purpose. The principles of the Reformation have reached as low down in society as reading and writing, and the poor will not much longer accept morals and religion of other people's prescribing. I speak more particularly of this country, especially the town population, and the districts of the most scientific agriculture or the highest wages, Scotland and the north of England. Among the more inert and less modernized agricultural population of the southern counties, it might be possible for the gentry to retain, for some time longer, something of the ancient deference and submission of the poor, by bribing them with high wages and constant employment; by insuring them support, and never requiring them to do anything which they do not like. But these are two conditions which never have been combined, and never can be, for long together. A guarantee of subsistence can only be practically kept up, when work is enforced and superfluous multiplication restrained by at least a moral compulsion. It is then, that the would-be revivers of old times which they do not understand, would feel practically in how hopeless a task they were engaged. The whole fabric of patriarchal or seignorial influence, attempted to be raised on the foundation of caressing the poor, would be shattered against the necessity of enforcing a stringent Poor-law.

§2. It is on a far other basis that the well-being and well-doing of the labouring people must henceforth rest. The poor have come out of leading-strings, and cannot any longer be governed or treated like children. To their own qualities must now be commended the care of their destiny. Modern nations will have to learn the lesson, that the well-being of a people must exist by means of the justice and self-government, the δικαιοσύνη and σωφροσύνη, of the individual citizens. The theory of dependence attempts to dispense with the necessity of these qualities in the dependent classes. But now, when even in position they are becoming less and less dependent, and their minds less and less acquiescent in the degree of dependence which remains, the virtues of independence are those which they stand in need of. Whatever advice, exhortation, or guidance is held out to the labouring classes, must henceforth be tendered to them as equals, and accepted by them with their eyes open. The prospect of the future depends on the degree in which they can be made rational beings.

There is no reason to believe that prospect other than hopeful. The progress indeed has hitherto been, and still is, slow. But there is a spontaneous education going on in the minds of the multitude, which may be greatly accelerated and improved by artificial aids. The instruction obtained from newspapers and political tracts may not be the most solid kind of instruction, but it is an immense improvement upon none at all. What it does for a people, has been admirably exemplified during the cotton crisis,[1] in the case of the Lancashire spinners and weavers, who have acted with the consistent good sense and forbearance so justly applauded, simply because, being readers of newspapers, they understood the causes of the calamity which had befallen them, and knew that it was in no way imputable either to their employers or to the Government. It is not certain that their conduct would have been as rational and exemplary, if the distress had preceded the salutary measure of fiscal eman-

1. [Added in 1865 edition: the crisis was the result of the American Civil War.]

cipation which gave existence to the penny press. The institutions for lectures and discussion, the collective deliberations on questions of common interest, the trades unions, the political agitation, all serve to awaken public spirit, to diffuse variety of ideas among the mass, and to excite thought and reflection in the more intelligent. Although the too early attainment of political franchises by the least educated class might retard, instead of promoting, their improvement, there can be little doubt that it has been greatly stimulated by the attempt to acquire them. In the meantime, the working classes are now part of the public; in all discussions on matters of general interest they, or a portion of them, are now partakers; all who use the press as an instrument may, if it so happens, have them for an audience; the avenues of instruction through which the middle classes acquire such ideas as they have, are accessible to, at least, the operatives in the towns. With these resources, it cannot be doubted that they will increase in intelligence, even by their own unaided efforts; while there is reason to hope that great improvements both in the quality and quantity of school education will be effected by the exertions either of government or of individuals, and that the progress of the mass of the people in mental cultivation, and in the virtues which are dependent on it, will take place more rapidly, and with fewer intermittences and aberrations, than if left to itself.

From this increase of intelligence, several effects may be confidently anticipated. First: that they will become even less willing than at present to be led and governed, and directed into the way they should go, by the mere authority and *prestige* of superiors. If they have not now, still less will they have hereafter, any deferential awe, or religious principle of obedience, holding them in mental subjection to a class above them. The theory of dependence and protection will be more and more intolerable to them, and they will require that their conduct and condition shall be essentially self-governed. It is, at the same time, quite possible that they may demand, in many cases, the intervention of the legislature in their affairs, and the regulation by law of various things which concern them, often under very mistaken ideas and suggestions, to which they will demand that effect should be given, and not rules laid down for them by other people. It is quite consistent with this, that they should feel respect for superiority of intellect and knowledge, and defer much to the opinions, on any subject, of those whom they think well acquainted with it. Such deference is deeply grounded in human nature; but they will judge for themselves of the persons who are and are not entitled to it.

§3. It appears to me impossible but that the increase of intelligence, of education, and of the love of independence among the working classes, must be attended with a corresponding growth of the good sense which manifests itself in provident habits of conduct, and that population, therefore, will bear a gradually diminishing ratio to capital and employment. This most desirable result would be much accelerated by another change, which lies in the direct line of the best tendencies of the time; the opening of industrial occupations freely to both sexes. The same reasons which make it no longer necessary that the poor should depend on the rich, make it equally unnecessary that women should depend on men; and the least which justice requires is that law and custom should not enforce dependence (when the correlative protection has become superfluous) by ordaining that a woman, who does not happen to have a provision by inheritance, shall have scarely any means open to her of gaining a livelihood, except as a wife and mother. Let women who prefer that occupation, adopt it; but that there should be no option, no other *carrière* possible for the great majority of women, except in the humbler departments of life, is a flagrant social injustice. The ideas and institutions by which the accident of sex is made the groundwork of an inequality of legal rights, and a forced dissimilarity of social functions, must ere long be recognized as the greatest hindrance to moral, social, and even intellectual improvement. On the present occasion I shall only indicate, among the probable consequences of the industrial and social independence of women, a great diminution of the evil of over-population. It is by devoting one-half of the human species to that exclusive function, by making it fill the entire life of one sex, and interweave itself with almost all the objects of the other, that the animal instinct in question is nursed into the disproportionate preponderance which it has hitherto exercised in human life.

§4. The political consequences of the increasing power and importance of the operative classes, and of the growing ascendancy of numbers, which, even in England and under the present institutions, is rapidly giving to the will of the majority at least a negative voice in the acts of government, are too wide a subject to be discussed in this place. But, confining ourselves to economical considerations, and notwithstanding the effect which improved intelligence in the working classes, together with just laws, may have in altering the distribution of the produce to their advantage, I cannot think that they will be permanently contented with the condition of labouring for wages as their ultimate state. They may be willing to pass through the class of servants in their way to that of employers; but not to remain in it all their lives. To begin as hired labourers, then after a few years to work on their own account, and finally employ others, is the normal condition of labourers in a new country, rapidly increasing in wealth and population, like America or Australia. But in an old and fully peopled country, those who begin life as labourers for hire, as a general rule, continue such to the end, unless they sink into the still lower grade of recipients of public charity. In the present stage of human progress, when ideas of equality are daily spreading more widely among the poorer classes, and can no longer be checked by anything short of the entire suppression of printed discussion and even of freedom of speech, it is not to be expected that the division of the human race into two hereditary classes, employers and employed, can be permanently maintained. The relation is nearly as unsatisfactory to the payer of wages as to the receiver. If the rich regard the poor as, by a kind of natural law, their servants and dependents, the rich in their turn are regarded as a mere prey and pasture for the poor; the subject of demands and expectations wholly indefinite, increasing in extent with every concession made to them. The total absence of regard for justice or fairness in the relations between the two, is as marked on the side of the employed as on that of the employers. We look in vain among the working classes in general for the just pride which will choose to give good work for good wages; for the most part, their sole endeavour is to receive as much, and return as little in the shape of service, as possible. It will sooner or later become insupportable to the employing classes, to live in close and hourly contact with persons whose interests and feelings are in hostility to them. Capitalists are almost as much interested as labourers in placing the operations of industry on such a footing, that those who labour for them may feel the same interest in the work, which is felt by those who labour on their own account.

The opinion expressed in a former part of this treatise respecting small landed properties and peasant proprietors, may have made the reader anticipate that a wide diffusion of property in land is the resource on which I rely for exempting at least the agricultural labourers from exclusive dependence on labour for hire. Such, however, is not my opinion. I indeed deem that form of agricultural economy to be most groundlessly cried down, and to be greatly preferable, in its aggregate effects on human happiness, to hired labour in any form in which it exists at present; because the prudential check to population acts more directly, and is shown by experience to be more efficacious; and because, in point of security, of independence, of exercise of any other than the animal faculties, the state of a peasant proprietor is far superior to that of an agricultural labourer in this or any other old country. Where the former system already exists, and works on the whole satisfactorily, I should regret, in the present state of human intelligence, to see it abolished in order to make way for the other, under a pedantic notion of agricultural improvement as a thing necessarily the same in every diversity of circumstances. In a backward state of industrial improvement, as in Ireland, I should urge its introduction, in preference to an exclusive system of hired labour; as a more powerful instrument for raising a population from semi-savage listlessness and recklessness, to persevering industry and prudent calculation.

But a people who have once adopted the large system of production, either in manufactures or in agriculture, are not likely to recede from it; and when population is kept in due proportion to the means of support, it is not desirable that they should. Labour is unquestionably more productive on the system of large industrial enterprises; the produce, if not greater absolutely, is greater in proportion to the labour employed: the same number of persons can be supported equally well with less toil and greater leisure; which will be wholly an advantage, as soon as civilization and improvement have so far advanced, that what is a benefit to the whole shall be a benefit to each individual composing it. And in the moral aspect of the question, which is still more important than the economical, something better should be aimed at as the goal of industrial improvement, than to disperse mankind over the earth in single families, each ruled internally, as families now are, by a patriarchal despot, and having scarcely any community of interest, or necessary mental communion, with other human beings. The domination of the head of the family over the other members, in this state of things, is absolute; while the effect on his own mind tends towards concentration of all interests in the family, considered as an expansion of self, and absorption of all passions in that of exclusive possession, of all cares in those of preservation and acquisition. As a step out of the merely animal state into the human, out of reckless abandonment to brute instincts into prudential foresight and self-government, this moral condition may be seen without displeasure. But if public spirit, generous sentiments, or true justice and equality are desired, association, not isolation, of interests, is the school in which these excellences are nurtured. The aim of improvement should be not solely to place human beings in a condition in which they will be able to do without one another, but to enable them to work with or for one another in relations not involving dependence. Hitherto there has been no alternative for those who lived by their labour, but that of labouring either each for himself alone, or for a master. But the civilizing and improving influences of association, and the efficiency and economy of production on a large scale, may be obtained without dividing the producers into two parties with hostile interests and feelings, the many who do the work being mere servants under the command of the one who supplies the funds, and having no interest of their own in the enterprise except to earn their wages with as little labour as possible. The speculations and discussions of the last fifty years, and the events of the last thirty, are abundantly conclusive on this point. If the improvement which even triumphant military despotism has only retarded, not stopped, shall continue its course, there can be little doubt that the *status* of hired labourers will gradually tend to confine itself to the description of workpeople whose low moral qualities render them unfit for anything more independent: and that the relation of masters and workpeople will be gradually superseded by partnership, in one of two forms: in some cases, association of the labourers with the capitalist; in others, and perhaps finally in all, association of labourers among themselves.

§5. The first of these forms of association has long been practised, not indeed as a rule, but as an exception. In several departments of industry there are already cases in which every one who contributes to the work, either by labour or by pecuniary resources, has a partner's interest in it, proportional to the value of his contribution. It is already a common practice to remunerate those in whom peculiar trust is reposed, by means of a percentage on the profits: and cases exist in which the principle is, with excellent success, carried down to the class of mere manual labourers.

In the American ships trading to China, it has long been the custom for every sailor to have an interest in the profits of the voyage; and to this has been ascribed the general good conduct of those seamen, and the extreme rarity of any collision between them and the government or people of the country. An instance in England, not so well known as it deserves to be, is that of the Cornish miners. 'In Cornwall the mines are worked strictly on the system of joint adventure; gangs of miners contracting with the agent, who represents the owner of the mine, to execute a certain portion of a vein and fit the ore for market, at the price of so much in the pound of the sum for which the ore is sold. These contracts are put up at certain regular periods, generally every two months, and taken by a voluntary partnership of men accustomed to the mine. This system has its disadvantages, in consequence of the uncertainty and irregularity of the earnings, and consequent necessity of living for long periods on credit; but it has advantages which more than counterbalance these drawbacks. It produces a degree of intelligence, independence, and moral elevation, which raise the condition and character of the Cornish miner far above that of the generality of the labouring class. We are told by Dr Barham, that "they are not only, as a class, intelligent for labourers, but men of considerable knowledge". Also, that "they have a character of independence, something American, the system by which the contracts are let giving the takers entire freedom to make arrangements among themselves; so that each man feels, as a partner in his little firm, that he meets his employers on nearly equal terms". .. With this basis of intelligence and independence in their character, we are not surprised when we hear that "a very great number of miners are now located on possessions of their own, leased for three lives or ninety-nine years, on which they have built houses"; or that "281,541*l*. are deposited in saving banks in Cornwall, of which two-thirds are estimated to belong to miners".'[2]

Mr Babbage, who also gives an account of this system, observes that the payment to the crews of whaling ships is governed by a similar principle; and that 'the profits arising from fishing with nets on the south coast of England are thus divided: one-half the produce belongs to the owner of the boat and net; the other half is divided in equal portions between the persons using it, who are also bound to assist in repairing the net when required.' Mr Babbage has the great merit of having pointed out the practicability, and the advantage, of extending the principle to manufacturing industry generally.[3]

Some attention has been excited by an experiment of this

2. This passage is from the Prize Essay on the Causes and Remedies of National Distress, by Mr Samuel Laing. The extracts which it includes are from the Appendix to the Report of the Children's Employment Commission.

3. *Economy of Machinery and Manufactures*, 3rd edition, Ch. 26.

nature, commenced above thirty years ago by a Paris tradesman, a house-painter, M. Leclaire,[4] and described by him in a pamphlet published in the year 1842. M. Leclaire, according to his statement, employs on an average two hundred workmen, whom he pays in the usual manner, by fixed wages or salaries. He assigns to himself, besides interest for his capital, a fixed allowance for his labour and responsibility as manager. At the end of the year, the surplus profits are divided among the body, himself included, in the proportion of their salaries.[5] The reasons by which M. Leclaire was led to adopt this system are highly instructive. Finding the conduct of his workmen unsatisfactory, he first tried the effect of giving higher wages, and by this he managed to obtain a body of excellent workmen, who would not quit his service for any other. 'Having thus succeeded' (I quote from an abstract of the pamphlet in Chambers' Journal,[6]) 'in producing some sort of stability in the arrangement of his establishment, M. Leclaire expected, he says, to enjoy greater peace of mind. In this, however, he was disappointed. So long as he was able to superintend everything himself, from the general concerns of his business down to its minutest details, he did enjoy a certain satisfaction; but from the moment that, owing to the increase of his business, he found that he could be nothing more than the centre from which orders were issued, and to which reports were brought in, his former anxiety and discomfort returned upon him.' He speaks lightly of the other sources of anxiety to which a tradesman is subject, but describes as an incessant cause of vexation the losses arising from the misconduct of workmen. An employer 'will find workmen whose indifference to his interests is such that they do not perform two-thirds of the

4. His establishment is 11, Rue Saint Georges.

5. It appears, however, that the workmen whom M. Leclaire had admitted to this participation of profits, were only a portion (rather less than half) of the whole number whom he employed. This is explained by another part of his system. M. Leclaire pays the full market rate of wages to all his workmen. The share of profit assigned to them is, therefore, a clear addition to the ordinary gains of their class, which he very laudably uses as an instrument of improvement, by making it the reward of desert, or the recompense for peculiar trust.

6. For 27 September, 1845.

amount of work which they are capable of; hence the continual fretting of masters, who, seeing their interests neglected, believe themselves entitled to suppose that workmen are constantly conspiring to ruin those from whom they derive their livelihood. If the journeyman were sure of constant employment, his position would in some respects be more enviable than that of the master, because he is assured of a certain amount of day's wages, which he will get whether he works much or little. He runs no risk, and has no other motive to stimulate him to do his best than his own sense of duty. The master, on the other hand, depends greatly on chance for his returns: his position is one of continual irritation and anxiety. This would no longer be the case to the same extent, if the interests of the master and those of the workmen were bound up with each other, connected by some bond of mutual security, such as that which would be obtained by the plan of a yearly division of profits.'

Until the passing of the Limited Liability Act, it was held that an arrangement similar to M. Leclaire's would have been impossible in England, as the workmen could not, in the previous state of the law, have been associated in the profits, without being liable for losses. One of the many benefits of that great legislative improvement has been to render partnerships of this description possible, and we may now expect to see them carried into practice. Messrs Briggs, of the Whitwood and Methley collieries, near Normanton in Yorkshire, have taken the first step. They now work these mines by a company, two-thirds of the capital of which they themselves continue to hold, but undertake, in the allotment of the remaining third, to give the preference to the 'officials and operatives employed in the concern'; and, what is of still greater importance, whenever the annual profit exceeds 10 per cent, one-half the excess is divided among the workpeople and employés, whether shareholders or not, in proportion to their earnings during the year. It is highly honourable to these important employers of labour to have initiated a system so full of benefit both to the operatives employed and to the general interest of social improvement: and they express no more than a just confidence in the principle when they say, that 'the adoption of the mode of appropriation thus recommended would, it is believed, add so great an element of success to the undertaking as to increase rather than diminish the dividend to the shareholders.'

§6. The form of association, however, which if mankind continue to improve, must be expected in the end to predominate, is not that which can exist between a capitalist as chief, and work-people without a voice in the management, but the association of the labourers themselves on terms of equality, collectively owning the capital with which they carry on their operations, and working under managers elected and removable by themselves. So long as this idea remained in a state of theory, in the writings of Owen or of Louis Blanc, it may have appeared, to the common modes of judgment, incapable of being realized, and not likely to be tried unless by seizing on the existing capital, and confiscating it for the benefit of the labourers; which is even now imagined by many persons, and pretended by more, both in England and on the Continent, to be the meaning and purpose of Socialism. But there is a capacity of exertion and self-denial in the masses of mankind, which is never known but on the rare occasions on which it is appealed to in the name of some great idea or elevated sentiment. Such an appeal was made by the French Revolution of 1848. For the first time it then seemed to the intelligent and generous of the working classes of a great nation, that they had obtained a government who sincerely desired the freedom and dignity of the many, and who did not look upon it as their natural and legitimate state to be instruments of production, worked for the benefit of the possessors of capital. Under this encouragement, the ideas sown by Socialist writers, of an emancipation of labour to be effected by means of association, throve and fructified; and many working people came to the resolution, not only that they would work for one another, instead of working for a master tradesman or manufacturer, but that they would also free themselves, at whatever cost of labour or privation, from the necessity of paying, out of the produce of their industry, a heavy tribute for the use of capital; that they would extinguish this tax, not by robbing the capitalists of what they or their predecessors had acquired by labour and preserved by economy, but by honestly acquiring capital for themselves. If only a few operatives had attempted this arduous task, or if, while many attempted it, a few only had succeeded, their success might have been deemed to furnish no argument for their system as a permanent mode of industrial organization. But, excluding all the instances of failure, there exist, or existed a short time ago, upwards of a hundred successful, and many eminently prosperous, associations of operatives in Paris alone, besides a considerable number in the departments.

The same admirable qualities by which the associations were carried through their early struggles, maintained them in their increasing prosperity. Their rules of discipline, instead of being more lax, are stricter than those of ordinary workshops; but being rules self-imposed, for the manifest good of the community, and not for the convenience of an employer regarded as having an opposite interest, they are far more scrupulously obeyed, and the voluntary obedience carries with it a sense of personal worth and dignity. With wonderful rapidity the associated workpeople have learnt to correct those of the ideas they set out with, which are in opposition to the teaching of reason and experience. Almost all the associations, at first, excluded piece-work, and gave equal wages whether the work done was more or less. Almost all have abandoned this system, and after allowing to every one a fixed minimum, sufficient for subsistence, they apportion all further remuneration according to the work done: most of them even dividing the profits at the end of the year, in the same proportion as the earnings.

It is the declared principle of most of these associations, that they do not exist for the mere private benefit of the individual members, but for the promotion of the co-operative cause. With every extension, therefore, of their business, they take in additional members, not (when they remain faithful to their original plan) to receive wages from them as hired labourers, but to enter at once into the full benefits of the association, without being required to bring anything in, except their labour: the only condition imposed is that of receiving during a few years a smaller share in the annual division of profits, as some equivalent for the sacrifices of the founders. When members quit the association, which they are always at liberty to do, they carry none of the capital with them: it remains an indivisible property, of which the members for the time being have the use, but not the arbitrary disposal: by the stipulations of most of the contracts, even if the association breaks up, the capital cannot be divided, but must be devoted entire to some work of beneficence or of public utility. A fixed, and generally a considerable, proportion of the annual profits is not shared among the members, but added to the capital of the association, or devoted to the repayment of advances previously made to it: another portion is set aside to provide for the sick and disabled, and another to form a fund for extending the practice of association, or aiding other associations in their need. The managers are paid, like other members, for the time which is occupied in management, usually at the rate of the highest paid labour: but the rule is adhered to, that the exercise of power shall never be an occasion of profit.

Of the ability of the associations to compete successfully with individual capitalists, even at an early period of their existence, M. Feugueray[7] said, 'Les associations qui ont été fondées depuis deux années, avaient bien des obstacles à vaincre; la plupart manquaient presque absolument de capital; toutes marchaient dans une voie encore inexplorée; elles bravaient les périls qui menacent toujours les novateurs et les débutants. Et néanmoins, dans beaucoup d'industries où elles se sont établies, elles constituent déjà pour les anciennes maisons une rivalité redoutable, qui suscite même des plaintes nombreuses dans une partie de la bourgeoisie, non pas seulement chez les traiteurs, les limonadiers et les coiffeurs, c'est-à-dire dans les industries où la nature des produits permet aux associations de compter sur la clientèle démocratique, mais dans d'autres industries où elles n'ont pas les mêmes avantages. On n'a qu'à consulter par exemple les fabricants de fauteuils, de chaises, de limes, et l'on saura d'eux si les établissements les plus importants en leurs genres de fabrication ne sont pas les établissements des associés.'

The vitality of these associations must indeed be great, to have enabled about twenty of them to survive not only the anti-socialist reaction, which for the time discredited all attempts to

7. *L'Association Ouvrière Industrielle et Agricole*, pp. 37-8.

enable workpeople to be their own employers – not only the *tracasseries* of the police, and the hostile policy of the government since the usurpation – but in addition to these obstacles, all the difficulties arising from the trying condition of financial and commercial affairs from 1854 to 1858. Of the prosperity attained by some of them even while passing through this difficult period, I have given examples which must be conclusive to all minds as to the brilliant future reserved for the principle of co-operation.

It is not in France alone that these associations have commenced a career of prosperity. To say nothing at present of Germany, Piedmont, and Switzerland (where the Konsum-Verein of Zürich is one of the most prosperous co-operative associations in Europe), England can produce cases of success rivalling even those which I have cited from France. Under the impulse commenced by Mr Owen, and more recently propagated by the writings and personal efforts of a band of friends, chiefly clergymen and barristers, to whose noble exertions too much praise can scarcely be given, the good seed was widely sown; the necessary alterations in the English law of partnership were obtained from Parliament, on the benevolent and public-spirited initiative of Mr Slaney; many industrial associations, and a still greater number of co-operative stores for retail purchases, were founded. Among these are already many instances of remarkable prosperity, the most signal of which are the Leeds Flour Mill, and the Rochdale Society of Equitable Pioneers. Of this last association, the most successful of all, the history has been written in a very interesting manner by Mr Holyoake;[8] and the notoriety which by this and other means has been given to facts so encouraging, is causing a rapid extension of associations with similar objects in Lancashire, Yorkshire, London, and elsewhere.

It is not necessary to enter into any details respecting the subsequent history of English Co-operation; the less so, as it is now

8. 'Self-help by the People – History of Co-operation in Rochdale.' An instructive account of this and other co-operative associations has also been written in the 'Companion to the Almanack' for 1862, by Mr John Plummer, of Kettering; himself one of the most inspiring examples of mental cultivation and high principle in a self-instructed working man.

one of the recognized elements in the progressive movement of the age, and, as such, has latterly been the subject of elaborate articles in most of our leading periodicals, one of the most recent and best of which was in the *Edinburgh Review* for October 1864: and the progress of Co-operation from month to month is regularly chronicled in the *Co-operator*. I must not, however, omit to mention the last great step in advance in reference to the Co-operative Stores, the formation in the North of England (and another is in course of formation in London) of a Wholesale Society, to dispense with the services of the wholesale merchant as well as of the retail dealer, and extend to the Societies the advantage which each society gives to its own members, by an agency for co-operative purchases, of foreign as well as domestic commodities, direct from the producers.

It is hardly possible to take any but a hopeful view of the prospects of mankind, when, in two leading countries of the world, the obscure depths of society contain simple working men whose integrity, good sense, self-command, and honourable confidence in one another, have enabled them to carry these noble experiments to the triumphant issue which the facts recorded in the preceding pages[9] attest.

From the progressive advance of the co-operative movement, a great increase may be looked for even in the aggregate productiveness of industry. The sources of the increase are twofold. In the first place, the class of mere distributors, who are not producers but auxiliaries of production, and whose inordinate numbers, far more than the gains of capitalists, are the cause why so great a portion of the wealth produced does not reach the producers – will be reduced to more modest dimensions. Distributors differ from producers in this, that when producers increase, even though in any given department of industry they may be too numerous, they actually produce more: but the multiplication of distributors does not make more distribution to be done, more wealth to be distributed; it does but divide the same work among a greater number of persons, seldom even cheapening the process. By limiting the distributors to the number really required for making the commodities accessible to the consumers

9. [Not printed in this edition.]

– which is the direct effect of the co-operative system – a vast number of hands will be set free for production, and the capital which feeds and the gains which remunerate them will be applied to feed and remunerate producers. This great economy of the world's resources would be realized even if co-operation stopped at associations for purchase and consumption, without extending to production.

The other mode in which co-operation tends, still more efficaciously, to increase the productiveness of labour, consists in the vast stimulus given to productive energies, by placing the labourers, as a mass, in a relation to their work which would make it their principle and their interest – at present it is neither – to do the utmost, instead of the least possible, in exchange for their remuneration. It is scarcely possible to rate too highly this material benefit, which yet is as nothing compared with the moral revolution in society that would accompany it: the healing of the standing feud between capital and labour; the transformation of human life, from a conflict of classes struggling for opposite interests, to a friendly rivalry in the pursuit of a good common to all; the elevation of the dignity of labour; a new sense of security and independence in the labouring class; and the conversion of each human being's daily occupation into a school of the social sympathies and the practical intelligence.

Such is the noble idea which the promoters of Co-operation should have before them. But to attain, in any degree, these objects, it is indispensable that all, and not some only, of those who do the work should be identified in interest with the prosperity of the undertaking. Associations which, when they have been successful, renounce the essential principle of the system, and become joint-stock companies of a limited number of shareholders, who differ from those of other companies only in being working men; associations which employ hired labourers without any interest in the profits (and I grieve to say that the Manufacturing Society even of Rochdale has thus degenerated) are, no doubt, exercising a lawful right in honestly employing the existing system of society to improve their position as individuals, but it is not from them that anything need be expected towards replacing that system by a better. Neither will such societies, in the long run, succeed in keeping their ground against individual competition. Individual management, by the one person principally interested, has great advantages over every description of collective management. Co-operation has but one thing to oppose to those advantages – the common interest of all the workers in the work. When individual capitalists, as they will certainly do, add this to their other points of advantage; when, even if only to increase their gains, they take up the practice which these co-operative societies have dropped, and connect the pecuniary interest of every person in their employment with the most efficient and most economical management of the concern; they are likely to gain an easy victory over societies which retain the defects, while they cannot possess the full advantages, of the old system.

Under the most favourable supposition, it will be desirable, and perhaps for a considerable length of time, that individual capitalists, associating their work-people in the profits, should coexist with even those co-operative societies which are faithful to the co-operative principle. Unity of authority makes many things possible, which could not or would not be undertaken subject to the chance of divided councils or changes in the management. A private capitalist, exempt from the control of a body, if he is a person of capacity, is considerably more likely than almost any association to run judicious risks, and originate costly improvements. Co-operative societies may be depended on for adopting improvements after they have been tested by success, but individuals are more likely to commence things previously untried. Even in ordinary business, the competition of capable persons who in the event of failure are to have all the loss, and in the case of success the greater part of the gain, will be very useful in keeping the managers of co-operative societies up to the due pitch of activity and vigilance.

When, however, co-operative societies shall have sufficiently multiplied, it is not probable that any but the least valuable work-people will any longer consent to work all their lives for wages merely; both private capitalists and associations will gradually find it necessary to make the entire body of labourers participants in profits. Eventually, and in perhaps a less remote future than may be supposed, we may, through the co-operative principle, see our way to a change in society, which would combine the freedom and independence of the individual, with the moral, intellectual, and economical advantages of aggregate production; and which, without violence or spoliation, or even any sudden disturbance of existing habits and expectations, would realize, at least in the industrial department, the best aspirations of the democratic spirit, by putting an end to the division of society into the industrious and the idle, and effacing all social distinctions but those fairly earned by personal services and exertions. Associations like those which we have described, by the very process of their success, are a course of education in those moral and active qualities by which alone success can be either deserved or attained. As associations multiplied, they would tend more and more to absorb all work-people, except those who have too little understanding, or too little virtue, to be capable of learning to act on any other system than that of narrow selfishness. As this change proceeded, owners of capital would gradually find it to their advantage, instead of maintaining the struggle of the old system with work-people of only the worst description, to lend their capital to the associations; to do this at a diminishing rate of interest, and at last, perhaps, even to exchange their capital for terminable annuities. In this or some such mode, the existing accumulations of capital might honestly, and by a kind of spontaneous process, become in the end the joint property of all who participate in their productive employment: a transformation which, thus effected, (and assuming of course that both sexes participate equally in the rights and in the government of the association)[10] would be the nearest

10. In this respect also the Rochdale Society has given an example of reason and justice, worthy of the good sense and good feeling manifested in their general proceedings. 'The Rochdale Story', says Mr Holyoake, 'renders incidental but valuable aid towards realizing the civil independence of women. Women may be members of this Store, and vote in its proceedings. Single and married women join. Many married women become members because their husbands will not take the trouble, and others join in it in self-defence, to prevent the husband from spending their money in drink. The husband cannot withdraw the savings at the Store standing in the wife's name, unless she signs the order.

approach to social justice, and the most beneficial ordering of industrial affairs for the universal good, which it is possible at present to foresee.

§7. I agree, then with the Socialist writers in their conception of the form which industrial operations tend to assume in the advance of improvement; and I entirely share their opinion that the time is ripe for commencing this transformation, and that it should by all just and effectual means be aided and encouraged. But while I agree and sympathize with Socialists in this practical portion of their aims, I utterly dissent from the most conspicuous and vehement part of their teaching, their declamations against competition. With moral conceptions in many respects far ahead of the existing arrangements of society, they have in general very confused and erroneous notions of its actual working; and one of their greatest errors, as I conceive, is to charge upon competition all the economical evils which at present exist. They forget that wherever competition is not, monopoly is; and that monopoly, in all its forms, is the taxation of the industrious for the support of indolence, if not of plunder. They forget, too, that with the exception of competition among labourers, all other competition is for the benefit of the labourers, by cheapening the articles they consume; that competition even in the labour market is a source not of low but of high wages, wherever the competition *for* labour exceeds the competition *of* labour, as in America, in the colonies, and in the skilled trades; and never could be a cause of low wages, save by the overstocking of the labour market through the too great numbers of the labourers' families; while, if the supply of labourers is excessive, not even Socialism can prevent their remuneration from being low. Besides, if association were universal, there would be no competition between labourer and labourer; and that between association and association would be for the benefit of the consumers, that is, of the associations; of the industrious classes generally.

I do not pretend that there are no inconveniences in competition, or that the moral objections urged against it by Socialist writers, as a source of jealousy and hostility among those engaged in the same occupation, are altogether groundless. But if competition has its evils, it prevents greater evils. As M. Feugueray well says, 'La racine la plus profonde des maux et des iniquités qui couvrent le monde industriel, n'est pas la concurrence, mais bien l'exploitation due travail par le capital, et la part énorme que les possesseurs des instruments de travail prélèvent sur les produits ... Si la concurrence a beaucoup de puissance pour le mal, elle n'a pas moins de fécondité pour le bien, surtout en ce qui concerne le devéloppement des facultés individuelles, et le succés des innovations.' It is the common error of Socialists to overlook the natural indolence of mankind; their tendency to be passive, to be the slaves of habit, to persist indefinitely in a course once chosen. Let them once attain any state of existence which they consider tolerable, and the danger to be apprehended is that they will thenceforth stagnate; will not exert themselves to improve, and by letting their faculties rust, will lose even the energy required to preserve them from deterioration. Competition may not be the best conceivable stimulus, but it is at present a necessary one, and no one can foresee the time when it will not be indispensable to progress. Even confining ourselves to the industrial department, in which, more than in any other, the majority may be supposed to be competent judges of improvements; it would be difficult to induce the general assembly of an association to submit to the trouble and inconvenience of altering their habits by adopting some new and promising invention, unless their knowledge of the existence of rival associations made them apprehend that what they would not consent to do, others would, and that they would be left behind in the race.

Instead of looking upon competition as the baneful and antisocial principle which it is held to be by the generality of Socialists, I conceive that, even in the present state of society and industry, every restriction of it is an evil, and every extension of it, even if for the time injuriously affecting some class of labourers, is always an ultimate good. To be protected against competition is to be protected in idleness, in mental dulness; to be saved the necessity of being as active and as intelligent as other people; and if it is also to be protected against being underbid for employment by a less highly paid class of labourers, this is only where old custom, or local and partial monopoly, has placed some particular class of artisans in a privileged position as compared with the rest; and the time has come when the interest of universal improvement is no longer promoted by prolonging the privileges of a few. If the slopsellers and others of their class have lowered the wages of tailors, and some other artisans, by making them an affair of competition instead of custom, so much the better in the end. What is now required is not to bolster up old customs, whereby limited classes of labouring people obtain partial gains which interest them in keeping up the present organization of society, but to introduce new general practices beneficial to all; and there is reason to rejoice at whatever makes the privileged classes of skilled artisans feel that they have the same interests, and depend for their remuneration on the same general causes, and must resort for the improvement of their condition to the same remedies, as the less fortunately circumstanced and comparatively helpless multitude.

BOOK V

ON THE INFLUENCE OF
GOVERNMENT

---

CHAPTER I

*Of the Functions of Government
in General*

§1. One of the most disputed questions both in political science
and in practical statesmanship at this particular period, relates
to the proper limits of the functions and agency of governments.
At other times it has been a subject of controversy how governments should be constituted, and according to what principles
and rules they should exercise their authority; but it is now almost equally a question, to what departments of human affairs
that authority should extend. And when the tide sets so strongly
towards changes in government and legislation, as a means of
improving the condition of mankind, this discussion is more
likely to increase than to diminish in interest. On the one hand,
impatient reformers, thinking it easier and shorter to get possession of the government than of the intellects and dispositions
of the public, are under a constant temptation to stretch the
province of government beyond due bounds: while, on the
other, mankind have been so much accustomed by their rulers
to interference for purposes other than the public good, or under
an erroneous conception of what that good requires, and so
many rash proposals are made by sincere lovers of improvement,
for attempting, by compulsory regulation, the attainment of
objects which can only be effectually or only usefully compassed
by opinion and discussion, that there has grown up a spirit of
resistance *in limine* to the interference of government, merely as
such, and a disposition to restrict its sphere of action within the

narrowest bounds. From differences in the historical development of different nations, not necessary to be here dwelt upon, the former excess, that of exaggerating the province of government, prevails most, both in theory and in practice, among the Continental nations, while in England the contrary spirit has hitherto been predominant.

The general principles of the question, in so far as it is a question of principle, I shall make an attempt to determine in a later chapter of this Book: after first considering the effects produced by the conduct of government in the exercise of the functions universally acknowledged to belong to it. For this purpose, there must be a specification of the functions which are either inseparable from the idea of a government, or are exercised habitually and without objection by all governments; as distinguished from those respecting which it has been considered questionable whether governments should exercise them or not. The former may be termed the *necessary*, the latter the *optional*, functions of government. By the term optional it is not meant to imply, that it can ever be a matter of indifference, or of arbitrary choice, whether the government should or should not take upon itself the functions in question; but only that the expediency of its exercising them does not amount to necessity, and is a subject on which diversity of opinion does or may exist.

§2. In attempting to enumerate the necessary functions of government, we find them to be considerably more multifarious than most people are at first aware of, and not capable of being circumscribed by those very definite lines of demarcation, which, in the inconsiderateness of popular discussion, it is often attempted to draw round them. We sometimes, for example, hear it said that governments ought to confine themselves to affording protection against force and fraud: that, these two things apart, people should be free agents, able to take care of themselves, and that so long as a person practises no violence or deception, to the injury of others in person or property, legislatures and governments are in no way called on to concern themselves about him. But why should people be protected by their government, that is, by their own collective strength, against violence and fraud, and not against other evils, except that the expediency is more obvious? If nothing, but what people cannot possibly do for themselves, can be fit to be done for them by government, people might be required to protect themselves by their skill and courage even against force, or to beg or buy protection against it, as they actually do where the government is not capable of protecting them: and against fraud every one has the protection of his own wits. But without further anticipating the discussion of principles, it is sufficient on the present occasion to consider facts.

Under which of these heads, the repression of force or of fraud, are we to place the operation, for example, of the laws of inheritance? Some such laws must exist in all societies. It may be said, perhaps, that in this matter government has merely to give effect to the disposition which an individual makes of his own property by will. This, however, is at least extremely disputable; there is probably no country by whose laws the power of testamentary disposition is perfectly absolute. And suppose the very common case of there being no will: does not the law, that is, the government, decide on principles of general expediency, who shall take the succession? and in case the successor is in any manner incompetent, does it not appoint persons, frequently officers of its own, to collect the property and apply it to his benefit? There are many other cases in which the government undertakes the administration of property, because the public interest, or perhaps only that of the particular persons concerned, is thought to require it. This is often done in case of litigated property; and in cases of judicially declared insolvency. It has never been contended that in doing these things, a government exceeds its province.

Nor is the function of the law in defining property itself, so simple a thing as may be supposed. It may be imagined, perhaps, that the law has only to declare and protect the right of every one to what he has himself produced, or acquired by the voluntary consent, fairly obtained, of those who produced it. But is there nothing recognized as property except what has been produced? Is there not the earth itself, its forests and waters, and all other natural riches, above and below the surface? These are the inheritance of the human race, and there must be regulations for the common enjoyment of it. What rights, and under what conditions, a person shall be allowed to exercise over any portion of this common inheritance, cannot be left undecided. No function of government is less optional than the regulation of these things, or more completely involved in the idea of civilized society.

Again, the legitimacy is conceded of repressing violence or treachery; but under which of these heads are we to place the obligation imposed on people to perform their contracts? Non-performance does not necessarily imply fraud; the person who entered into the contract may have sincerely intended to fulfil it: and the term fraud, which can scarcely admit of being extended even to the case of voluntary breach of contract when no deception was practised, is certainly not applicable when the omission to perform is a case of negligence. Is it no part of the duty of governments to enforce contracts? Here the doctrine of non-interference would no doubt be stretched a little, and it would be said, that enforcing contracts is not regulating the affairs of individuals at the pleasure of government, but giving effect to their own expressed desire. Let us acquiesce in this enlargement of the restrictive theory, and take it for what it is worth. But governments do not limit their concern with contracts to a simple enforcement. They take upon themselves to determine what contracts are fit to be enforced. It is not enough that one person, not being either cheated or compelled, makes a promise to another. There are promises by which it is not for the public good that persons should have the power of binding themselves. To say nothing of engagements to do something contrary to law, there are engagements which the law refuses to enforce, for reasons connected with the interest of the promiser, or with the general policy of the state. A contract by which a person sells himself to another as a slave, would be declared void by the tribunals of this and of most other European countries. There are few nations whose laws enforce a contract for what is looked upon as prostitution, or any matrimonial engagement of which the conditions vary in any respect from those which the law has thought fit to prescribe. But when once it is admitted that there are any engagements which for reasons of expediency the law ought not to enforce, the same question is necessarily opened with respect to all engagements. Whether, for example, the law should enforce a contract to labour, when the wages are too low or the hours of work too severe: whether it should enforce a contract by which a person binds himself to remain, for more than a very limited period, in the service of a given individual: whether a contract of marriage, entered into for life, should continue to be enforced against the deliberate will of the persons, or of either of the persons, who entered into it. Every question which can possibly arise as to the policy of contracts, and of the relations which they establish among human beings, is a question for the legislator; and one which he cannot escape from considering, and in some way or other deciding.

Again, the prevention and suppression of force and fraud afford appropriate employment for soldiers, policemen, and criminal judges; but there are also civil tribunals. The punishment of wrong is one business of an administration of justice, but the decision of disputes is another. Innumerable disputes arise between persons, without *mala fides* on either side, through misconception of their legal rights, or from not being agreed about the facts, on the proof of which those rights are legally dependent. Is it not for the general interest that the State should appoint persons to clear up these uncertainties and terminate these disputes? It cannot be said to be a case of absolute necessity. People might appoint an arbitrator, and engage to submit to his decision; and they do so where there are no courts of justice, or where the courts are not trusted, or where their delays and expenses, or the irrationality of their rules of evidence, deter people from resorting to them. Still, it is universally thought right that the State should establish civil tribunals; and if their defects often drive people to have recourse to substitutes, even then the power held in reserve of carrying the case before a legally constituted court, gives to the substitutes their principal efficacy.

Not only does the State undertake to decide disputes, it takes precautions beforehand that disputes may not arise. The laws of most countries lay down rules for determining many things, not because it is of much consequence in what way they are determined, but in order that they may be determined somehow, and there may be no question on the subject. The law prescribes forms of words for many kinds of contract, in order that no dispute or misunderstanding may arise about their meaning: it makes provision that if a dispute does arise, evidence shall be procurable for deciding it, by requiring that the document be attested by witnesses and executed with certain formalities. The law preserves authentic evidence of facts to which legal consequences are attached, by keeping a registry of such facts; as of births, deaths, and marriages, of wills and contracts, and of judicial proceedings. In doing these things, it has never been alleged that government oversteps the proper limits of its functions.

Again, however wide a scope we may allow to the doctrine that individuals are the proper guardians of their own interests, and that government owes nothing to them but to save them from being interfered with by other people, the doctrine can never be applicable to any persons but those who are capable of acting in their own behalf. The individual may be an infant, or a lunatic, or fallen into imbecility. The law surely must look after the interests of such persons. It does not necessarily do this through officers of its own. It often devolves the trust upon some relative or connexion. But in doing so is its duty ended? Can it make over the interests of one person to the control of another, and be excused from supervision, or from holding the person thus trusted, responsible for the discharge of the trust?

There is a multitude of cases in which governments, with general approbation, assume powers and execute functions for which no reason can be assigned except the simple one, that they conduce to general convenience. We may take as an example, the function (which is a monopoly too) of coining money. This is assumed for no more recondite purpose than that of saving to individuals the trouble, delay, and expense of weighing and assaying. No one, however, even of those most jealous of state interference, has objected to this as an improper exercise of the powers of government. Prescribing a set of standard weights and measures is another instance. Paving, lighting, and cleansing the streets and thoroughfares, is another; whether done by the general government, or as is more usual, and generally more advisable, by a municipal authority. Making or improving harbours, building lighthouses, making surveys in order to have accurate maps and charts, raising dykes to keep the sea out, and embankments to keep rivers in, are cases in point.

Examples might be indefinitely multiplied without intruding on any disputed ground. But enough has been said to show that the admitted functions of government embrace a much wider field than can easily be included within the ring-fence of any restrictive definition, and that it is hardly possible to find any ground of justification common to them all, except the comprehensive one of general expediency; nor to limit the interference of government by any universal rule, save the simple and vague one, that it should never be admitted but when the case of expediency is strong.

§3. Some observations, however, may be usefully bestowed on the nature of the considerations on which the question of government interference is most likely to turn, and on the mode of estimating the comparative magnitude of the expediencies involved. This will form the last of the three parts, into which our discussion of the principles and effects of government interference may conveniently be divided. The following will be our division of the subject.

We shall first consider the economical effects arising from the manner in which governments perform their necessary and acknowledged functions.

We shall then pass to certain governmental interferences of what I have termed the optional kind (i.e. overstepping the boundaries of the universally acknowledged functions) which have heretofore taken place, and in some cases still take place, under the influence of false general theories.

It will lastly remain to inquire whether, independently of any false theory, and consistently with a correct view of the laws which regulate human affairs, there be any cases of the optional class in which governmental interference is really advisable, and what are those cases.

The first of these divisions is of an extremely miscellaneous character: since the necessary functions of government, and those which are so manifestly expedient that they have never or very rarely been objected to, are, as already pointed out, too various to be brought under any very simple classification. Those, however, which are of principal importance, which alone it is necessary here to consider, may be reduced to the following general heads.

First, the means adopted by governments to raise the revenue which is the condition of their existence.

Secondly, the nature of the laws which they prescribe on the two great subjects of Property and Contracts.

Thirdly, the excellences or defects of the system of means by which they enforce generally the execution of their laws, namely, their judicature and police.

We commence with the first head, that is, with the theory of Taxation.

CHAPTER II

On the General Principles of Taxation

§1. THE qualities desirable, economically speaking, in a system of taxation, have been embodied by Adam Smith in four maxims or principles, which, having been generally concurred by subsequent writers, may be said to have become classical, and this chapter cannot be better commenced than by quoting them.[1]

'1. The subjects of every state ought to contribute to the support of the government, as nearly as possible in proportion to their respective abilities: that is, in proportion to the revenue which they respectively enjoy under the protection of the state. In the observation or neglect of this maxim consists what is called the equality or inequality of taxation.

'2. The tax which each individual is bound to pay ought to be certain, and not arbitrary. The time of payment, the manner of payment, the quantity to be paid, ought all to be clear and plain to the contributor, and to every other person. Where it is otherwise, every person subject to the tax is put more or less in the power of the tax-gatherer, who can either aggravate the tax upon any obnoxious contributor, or extort by the terror of such aggravation, some present or perquisite to himself. The uncertainty of taxation encourages the insolence and favours the corruption of an order of men who are naturally unpopular, even when they are neither insolent nor corrupt. The certainty of what each individual ought to pay is, in taxation, a matter of so great importance, that a very considerable degree of inequality, it appears, I believe, from the experience of all nations, is not near so great an evil, as a very small degree of uncertainty.

'3. Every tax ought to be levied at the time, or in the manner, in which it is most likely to be convenient for the contributor to pay it. A tax upon the rent of land or of houses, payable at the same term at which such rents are usually paid, is levied at a time when it is most likely to be convenient for the contributor to pay; or when he is most likely to have wherewithal to pay.

1. *Wealth of Nations*, Bk V, Ch. 2.

Taxes upon such consumable goods as are articles of luxury, are all finally paid by the consumer, and generally in a manner that is very convenient to him. He pays them by little and little, as he has occasion to buy the goods. As he is at liberty, too, either to buy or not to buy, as he pleases, it must be his own fault if he ever suffers any considerable inconvenience from such taxes.

'4. Every tax ought to be so contrived as both to take out and to keep out of the pockets of the people as little as possible over and above what it brings into the public treasury of the state. A tax may either take out or keep out of the pockets of the people a great deal more than it brings into the public treasury, in the four following ways. First, the levying of it may require a great number of officers, whose salaries may eat up the greater part of the produce of the tax, and whose perquisites may impose another additional tax upon the people. Secondly, it may divert a portion of the labour and capital of the community from a more to a less productive employment. Thirdly, by the forfeitures and other penalties which those unfortunate individuals incur who attempt unsuccessfully to evade the tax, it may frequently ruin them, and thereby put an end to the benefit which the community might have derived from the employment of their capitals. An injudicious tax offers a great temptation to smuggling. Fourthly, by subjecting the people to the frequent visits and the odious examination of the tax-gatherers, it may expose them to much unnecessary trouble, vexation, and oppression': to which may be added, that the restrictive regulations to which trades and manufactures are often subjected to prevent evasion of a tax, are not only in themselves troublesome and expensive, but often oppose insuperable obstacles to making improvements in the processes.

The last three of these four maxims require little other explanation or illustration than is contained in the passage itself. How far any given tax conforms to, or conflicts with them, is a matter to be considered in the discussion of particular taxes. But the first of the four points, equality of taxation, requires to be more fully examined, being a thing often imperfectly understood, and on which many false notions have become to a certain degree accredited, through the absence of any definite principles of judgment in the popular mind.

§2. For what reason ought equality to be the rule in matters of taxation? For the reason, that it ought to be so in all affairs of government. As a government ought to make no distinction of persons or classes in the strength of their claims on it, whatever sacrifices it requires from them should be made to bear as nearly as possible with the same pressure upon all, which, it must be observed, is the mode by which least sacrifice is occasioned on the whole. If any one bears less than his fair share of the burthen, some other person must suffer more than his share, and the alleviation to the one is not, *caeteris paribus*, so great a good to him, as the increased pressure upon the other is an evil. Equality of taxation, therefore, as a maxim of politics, means equality of sacrifice. It means apportioning the contribution of each person towards the expenses of government, so that he shall feel neither more nor less inconvenience from his share of the payment than every other person experiences from his. This standard, like other standards of perfection, cannot be completely realized; but the first object in every practical discussion should be to know what perfection is.

There are persons, however, who are not content with the general principles of justice as a basis to ground a rule of finance upon, but must have something, as they think, more specifically appropriate to the subject. What best pleases them is, to regard the taxes paid by each member of the community as an equivalent for value received, in the shape of service to himself; and they prefer to rest the justice of making each contribute in proportion to his means, upon the ground, that he who has twice as much property to be protected, receives, on an accurate calculation, twice as much protection, and ought, on the principles of bargain and sale, to pay twice as much for it. Since, however, the assumption that government exists solely for the protection of property, is not one to be deliberately adhered to; some consistent adherents of the *quid pro quo* principle go on to observe, that protection being required for person as well as property, and everybody's person receiving the same amount of protection, a poll-tax of a fixed sum per head is a proper equivalent for this part of the benefits of government, while the remaining part, protection to property, should be paid for in proportion to property. There is in this adjustment a false air of nice adaptation, very acceptable to some minds. But in the first place, it is not admissible that the protection of persons and that of property are the sole purposes of government. The ends of government are as comprehensive as those of the social union. They consist of all the good, and all the immunity from evil, which the existence of government can be made either directly or indirectly to bestow. In the second place, the practice of setting definite values on things essentially indefinite, and making them a ground of practical conclusions, is peculiarly fertile in false views of social questions. It cannot be admitted, that to be protected in the ownership of ten times as much property, is to be ten times as much protected. Neither can it be truly said that the protection of 1000*l.* a year costs the state ten times as much as that of 100*l.* a year, rather than twice as much, or exactly as much. The same judges, soldiers, and sailors who protect the one protect the other, and the larger income does not necessarily, though it may sometimes, require even more policemen. Whether the labour and expense of the protection, or the feelings of the protected person, or any other definite thing be made the standard, there is no such proportion as the one supposed, nor any other definable proportion. If we wanted to estimate the degrees of benefit which different persons derive from the protection of government, we should have to consider who would suffer most if that protection were withdrawn: to which question if any answer could be made, it must be, that those would suffer most who were weakest in mind or body, either by nature or by position. Indeed, such persons would almost infallibly be slaves. If there were any justice, therefore, in the theory of justice now under consideration, those who are least capable of helping or defending themselves, being those to whom the protection of government is the most indispensable, ought to pay the greatest share of its price: the reverse of the true idea of distributive justice, which consists not in imitating but in redressing the inequalities and wrongs of nature.

Government must be regarded as so pre-eminently a concern of all, that to determine who are most interested in it is of no real importance. If a person or class of persons receive so small a share of the benefit as makes it necessary to raise the question, there is something else than taxation which is amiss, and the thing to be done is to remedy the defect, instead of recognizing it and making it a ground for demanding less taxes. As, in a case of voluntary subscription for a purpose in which all are interested, all are thought to have done their part fairly when each has contributed according to his means, that is, has made an equal sacrifice for the common object; in like manner should this be the principle of compulsory contributions: and it is superfluous to look for a more ingenious or recondite ground to rest the principle upon.

§3. Setting out, then, from the maxim that equal sacrifices ought to be demanded from all, we have next to inquire whether this is in fact done, by making each contribute the same percentage on his pecuniary means. Many persons maintain the negative, saying that a tenth part taken from a small income is a heavier burthen than the same fraction deducted from one much larger: and on this is grounded the very popular scheme of what is called a graduated property tax, viz. an income tax in which the percentage rises with the amount of the income.

On the best consideration I am able to give to this question, it appears to me that the portion of truth which the doctrine contains, arises principally from the difference between a tax which can be saved from luxuries, and one which trenches, in ever so small a degree, upon the necessaries of life. To take a thousand a year from the possessor of ten thousand, would not deprive him of anything really conducive either to the support or to the comfort of existence; and if such *would* be the effect of taking five pounds from one whose income is fifty, the sacrifice required from the last is not only greater than, but entirely incommensurable with, that imposed upon the first. The mode of adjusting these inequalities of pressure, which seems to be the most equitable, is that recommended by Bentham, of leaving a certain minimum of income, sufficient to provide the necessaries of life, untaxed. Suppose 50*l.* a year to be sufficient to provide the number of persons ordinarily supported from a single income, with the requisites of life and health, and with protection against habitual bodily suffering, but not with any indulgence. This then should be made the minimum, and incomes exceeding it should pay taxes not upon their whole amount, but upon the surplus. If the tax be ten per cent, an income of 60*l.* should be considered as a net income of 10*l.*, and charged with 1*l.* a year, while an income of 1000*l.* should be charged as one of 950*l.* Each would then pay a fixed proportion, not of his whole means, but of his superfluities.[2] An income not exceeding 50*l.* should not be taxed at all, either directly or by taxes on necessaries; for as by supposition this is the smallest income which labour ought to be able to command, the government ought not to be a party to making it smaller. This arrangement however would constitute a reason, in addition to others which might be stated, for maintaining taxes on articles of luxury consumed by the poor. The immunity extended to the income required for necessaries, should depend on its being actually expended for that purpose; and the poor who, not having more than enough for necessaries, divert any part of it to indulgences, should like other people contribute their quota out of those indulgences to the expenses of the state.

The exemption in favour of the smaller incomes should not, I think, be stretched further than to the amount of income needful for life, health, and immunity from bodily pain. If 50*l.* a year is sufficient (which may be doubted) for these purposes, an income of 100*l.* a year would, as it seems to me, obtain all the relief it is entitled to, compared with one of 1000*l.*, by being taxed only on 50*l.* of its amount. It may be said, indeed, that to take 100*l.* from 1000*l.* (even giving back five pounds) is a heavier impost than 1000*l.* taken from 10,000*l.* (giving back the same

2. This principle of assessment has been partially adopted by Mr Gladstone in renewing the income-tax. From 100*l.*, at which the tax begins, up to 200*l.*, the income only pays tax on the excess above 60*l.*

five pounds). But this doctrine seems to me too disputable altogether, and even if true at all, not true to a sufficient extent, to be made the foundation of any rule of taxation. Whether the person with 10,000*l.* a year cares less for 1000*l.* than the person with only 1000*l.* a year cares for 100*l.*, and if so, how much less, does not appear to me capable of being decided with the degree of certainty on which a legislator or a financier ought to act.

Some indeed contend that the rule of proportional taxation bears harder upon the moderate than upon the large incomes, because the same proportional payment has more tendency in the former case than in the latter, to reduce the payer to a lower grade of social rank. The fact appears to me more than questionable. But even admitting it, I object to its being considered incumbent on government to shape its course by such considerations, or to recognize the notion that social importance is or can be determined by amount of expenditure. Government ought to set an example of rating all things at their true value, and riches, therefore, at the worth, for comfort or pleasure, of the things which they will buy: and ought not to sanction the vulgarity of prizing them for the pitiful vanity of being known to possess them, or the paltry shame of being suspected to be without them, the presiding motives of three-fourths of the expenditure of the middle classes. The sacrifices of real comfort or indulgence which government requires, it is bound to apportion among all persons with as much equality as possible; but their sacrifices of the imaginary dignity dependent on expense, it may spare itself the trouble of estimating.

Both in England and on the Continent a graduated property tax (*l'impôt progressif*) has been advocated, on the avowed ground that the state should use the instrument of taxation as a means of mitigating the inequalities of wealth. I am as desirous as any one, that means should be taken to diminish those inequalities, but not so as to relieve the prodigal at the expense of the prudent. To tax the larger incomes at a higher percentage than the smaller, is to lay a tax on industry and economy; to impose a penalty on people for having worked harder and saved more than their neighbours. It is not the fortunes which are earned, but those which are unearned, that it is for the public good to place under limitation. A just and wise legislation would abstain from holding out motives for dissipating rather than saving the earnings of honest exertion. Its impartiality between competitors would consist in endeavouring that they should all start fair, and not in hanging a weight upon the swift to diminish the distance between them and the slow. Many, indeed, fail with greater efforts than those with which others succeed, not from difference of merits, but difference of opportunities; but if all were done which it would be in the power of a good government to do, by instruction and by legislation, to diminish this inequality of opportunities, the differences of fortune arising from people's own earnings could not justly give umbrage. With respect to the large fortunes acquired by gift or inheritance, the power of bequeathing is one of those privileges of property which are fit subjects for regulation on grounds of general expediency; and I have already suggested,[3] as a possible mode of restraining the accumulation of large fortunes in the hands of those who have not earned them by exertion, a limitation of the amount which any one person should be permitted to acquire by gift, bequest, or inheritance. Apart from this, and from the proposal of Bentham (also discussed in a former chapter) that collateral inheritance *ab intestato* should cease, and the property escheat to the state, I conceive that inheritances and legacies, exceeding a certain amount, are highly proper subjects for taxation: and that the revenue from them should be as great as it can be made without giving rise to evasions, by donation *inter vivos* or concealment of property, such as it would be impossible adequately to check. The principle of graduation (as it is called,) that is, of levying a larger percentage on a larger sum, though its application to general taxation would be in my opinion objectionable, seems to me both just and expedient as applied to legacy and inheritance duties.

The objection to a graduated property tax applies in an aggravated degree to the proposition of an exclusive tax on what is called 'realized property', that is, property not forming a part of any capital engaged in business, or rather in business under the superintendence of the owner: as land, the public funds,

3. [See below pp. 368–88.]

money lent on mortgage, and shares (I presume) in joint-stock companies. Except the proposal of applying a sponge to the national debt, no such palpable violation of common honesty has found sufficient support in this country, during the present generation, to be regarded as within the domain of discussion. It has not the palliation of a graduated property tax, that of lay- ing the burthen on those best able to bear it; for 'realized property' includes the far larger portion of the provision made for those who are unable to work, and consists, in great part, of extremely small fractions. I can hardly conceive a more shameless pretension, than that the major part of the property of the country, that of merchants, manufacturers, farmers, and shopkeepers, should be exempted from its share of taxation; that these classes should only begin to pay their proportion after retiring from business, and if they never retire should be excused from it altogether. But even this does not give an adequate idea of the injustice of the proposition. The burthen thus exclusively thrown on the owners of the smaller portion of the wealth of the community, would not even be a burthen on that *class* of persons in perpetual succession, but would fall exclusively on those who happened to compose it when the tax was laid on. As land and those particular securities would thenceforth yield a smaller net income, relatively to the general interest of capital and to the profits of trade; the balance would rectify itself by a permanent depreciation of those kinds of property. Future buyers would acquire land and securities at a reduction of price, equivalent to the peculiar tax, which tax they would, therefore, escape from paying; while the original possessors would remain burthened with it even after parting with the property, since they would have sold their land or securities at a loss of value equivalent to the fee-simple of the tax. Its imposition would thus be tanta- mount to the confiscation for public uses of a percentage of their property, equal to the percentage laid on their income by the tax. That such a proposition should find any favour, is a striking instance of the want of conscience in matters of taxation, result- ing from the absence of any fixed principles in the public mind, and of any indication of a sense of justice on the subject in the general conduct of governments. Should the scheme ever enlist a large party in its support, the fact would indicate a laxity of pecuniary integrity in national affairs, scarcely inferior to American repudiation.

§4. Whether the profits of trade may not rightfully be taxed at a lower rate than incomes derived from interest or rent, is part of the more comprehensive question, so often mooted on the occasion of the present income tax, whether life incomes should be subjected to the same rate of taxation as perpetual incomes: whether salaries, for example, or annuities, or the gains of professions, should pay the same percentage as the income from inheritable property.

The existing tax treats all kinds of incomes exactly alike, taking its sevenpence (now fourpence) in the pound, as well from the person whose income dies with him, as from the landholder, stockholder, or mortgagee, who can transmit his fortune undiminished to his descendants. This is a visible injustice: yet it does not arithmetically violate the rule that taxation ought to be in proportion to means. When it is said that a temporary income ought to be taxed less than a permanent one, the reply is irresistible, that it is taxed less; for the income which lasts only ten years pays the tax only ten years, while that which lasts for ever pays for ever. On this point some financial reformers are guilty of a great fallacy. They contend that incomes ought to be assessed to the income tax not in proportion to their annual amount, but to their capitalized value: that, for example, if the value of a perpetual annuity of 100*l.* is 3000*l.*, and a life annuity of the same amount, being worth only half the number of years' purchase, could only be sold for 1500*l.*, the perpetual income should pay twice as much per cent income tax as the terminable income; if the one pays 10*l.* a year the other should pay only 5*l.* But in this argument there is the obvious oversight, that it values the incomes by one standard and the payments by another; it capitalizes the incomes, but forgets to capitalize the payments. An annuity worth 3000*l.* ought, it is alleged, to be taxed twice as highly as one which is only worth 1500*l.*, and no assertion can be more unquestionable; but it is forgotten that the income worth 3000*l.* pays to the supposed income tax 10*l.* a year in perpetuity, which is equivalent, by supposition, to 300*l.*, while the terminable income pays the same 10*l.* only during the life of its owner, which on the same calculation is a value of 150*l.*, and could actually be bought for that sum. Already, therefore, the income which is only half as valuable, pays only half as much to the tax; and if in addition to this its annual quota were reduced from 10*l.* to 5*l.*, it would pay, not half, but a fourth part only of the payment demanded from the perpetual income. To make it just that the one income should pay only half as much per annum as the other, it would be necessary that it should pay that half for the same period, that is, in perpetuity.

The rule of payment which this school of financial reformers contend for, would be very proper if the tax were only to be levied once, to meet some national emergency. On the principle of requiring from all payers an equal sacrifice, every person who had anything belonging to him, reversioners included, would be called on for a payment proportioned to the present value of his property. I wonder it does not occur to the reformers in question, that precisely because this principle of assessment would be just in the case of a payment made once for all, it cannot possibly be just for a permanent tax. When each pays only once, one person pays no oftener than another; and the proportion which would be just in that case, cannot also be just if one person has to make the payment only once, and the other several times. This, however, is the type of the case which actually occurs. The permanent incomes pay the tax as much oftener than the temporary ones, as a perpetuity exceeds the certain or uncertain length of time which forms the duration of the income for life or years.

All attempts to establish a claim in favour of terminable incomes on numerical grounds – to make out, in short, that a proportional tax is not a proportional tax – are manifestly absurd. The claim does not rest on grounds of arithmetic, but of human wants and feelings. It is not because the temporary annuitant has smaller means, but because he has greater necessities, that he ought to be assessed at a lower rate.

In spite of the nominal equality of income, A, an annuitant of 1000*l.* a year, cannot so well afford to pay 100*l.* out of it, as B who derives the same annual sum from heritable property; A having usually a demand on his income which B has not, namely, to provide by saving for children or others; to which, in the case of salaries or professional gains, must generally be added a provision for his own later years; while B may expend his whole income without injury to his old age, and still have it all to bestow on others after his death. If A, in order to meet these exigencies, must lay by 300*l.* of his income, to take 100*l.* from him as income tax is to take 100*l.* from 700*l.*, since it must be retrenched from that part only of his means which he can afford to spend on his own consumption. Were he to throw it rateably on what he spends and on what he saves, abating 70*l.* from his consumption and 30*l.* from his annual saving, then indeed his immediate sacrifice would be proportionately the same as B's: but then his children or his old age would be worse provided for in consequence of the tax. The capital sum which would be accumulated for them would be one-tenth less, and on the reduced income afforded by this reduced capital, they would be a second time charged with income tax; while B's heirs would only be charged once.

The principle, therefore, of equality of taxation, interpreted in its only just sense, equality of sacrifice, requires that a person who has no means of providing for old age, or for those in whom he is interested, except by saving from income, should have the tax remitted on all that part of his income which is really and *bonâ fide* applied to that purpose.

If, indeed, reliance could be placed on the conscience of the contributors, or sufficient security taken for the correctness of their statements by collateral precautions, the proper mode of assessing an income tax would be to tax only the part of income devoted to expenditure, exempting that which is saved. For when saved and invested (and all savings, speaking generally, are invested) it thenceforth pays income tax on the interest or profit which it brings, notwithstanding that it has already been taxed on the principal. Unless, therefore, savings are exempted from income tax, the contributors are twice taxed on what they save, and only once on what they spend. A person who spends all he receives, pays 7*d.* in the pound, or say three per cent, to the tax, and no more; but if he saves part of the year's income and buys stock, then in addition to the three per cent which he has paid on the principal, and which diminishes the interest in the same ratio, he pays three per cent annually on the interest itself, which is equivalent to an immediate payment of a second three per cent on the principal. So that while unproductive expenditure pays only three per cent, savings pay six per cent: or more correctly, three per cent on the whole, and another three per cent on the remaining ninety-seven. The difference thus created to the disadvantage of prudence and economy, is not only impolitic but unjust. To tax the sum invested, and afterwards tax also the proceeds of the investment, is to tax the same portion of the contributor's means twice over. The principal and the interest cannot both together form part of his resources; they are the same portion twice counted: if he has the interest, it is because he abstains from using the principal; if he spends the principal, he does not receive the interest. Yet because he can do either of the two, he is taxed as if he could do both, and could have the benefit of the saving and that of the spending, concurrently with one another.

It has been urged as an objection to exempting savings from taxation, that the law ought not to disturb, by artificial interference, the natural competition between the motives for saving and those for spending. But we have seen that the law disturbs this natural competition when it taxes savings, not when it spares them; for as the savings pay at any rate the full tax as soon as they are invested, their exemption from payment in the earlier stage is necessary to prevent them from paying twice, while money spent in unproductive consumption pays only once. It has been further objected, that since the rich have the greatest means of saving, any privilege given to savings is an advantage bestowed on the rich at the expense of the poor. I answer, that it is bestowed on them only in proportion as they abdicate the personal use of their riches; in proportion as they divert their income from the supply of their own wants, to a productive investment, through which, instead of being consumed by themselves, it is distributed in wages among the poor. If this be favouring the rich, I should like to have it pointed out, what mode of assessing taxation can deserve the name of favouring the poor.

No income tax is really just, from which savings are not exempted; and no income tax ought to be voted without that provision, if the form of the returns, and the nature of the evidence required, could be so arranged as to prevent the exemption from being taken fraudulent advantage of, by saving with one hand and getting into debt with the other, or by spending in the following year what had been passed tax-free as saving in the year preceding. If this difficulty could be surmounted, the difficulties and complexities arising from the comparative claims of temporary and permanent incomes, would disappear; for, since temporary incomes have no just claim to lighter taxation than permanent incomes, except in so far as their possessors are more called upon to save, the exemption of what they do save would fully satisfy the claim. But if no plan can be devised for the exemption of actual savings, sufficiently free from liability to fraud, it is necessary, as the next thing in point of justice, to take into account in assessing the tax, what the different classes of contributors *ought* to save. And there would probably be no other mode of doing this than the rough expedient of two different rates of assessment. There would be great difficulty in taking into account differences of duration between one terminable income and another; and in the most frequent case, that of incomes dependent on life, differences of age and health would constitute such extreme diversity as it would be impossible to take proper cognizance of. It would probably be necessary to be content with one uniform rate for all incomes of inheritance, and another uniform rate for all those which necessarily terminate with the life of the individual. In fixing the proportion between the two rates, there must inevitably be something arbitrary; perhaps a deduction of one-fourth in favour of life-incomes would be as little objectionable as any which could be made, it being thus assumed that one-fourth of a life-income is, on the average of all ages and states of health, a suitable proportion to be laid by as a provision for successors and for old age.[4]

4. Mr Hubbard, the first person who, as a practical legislator, has attempted the rectification of the income tax on principles of unimpeachable justice, and whose well-conceived plan wants little of being as near an approximation to a just assessment as it is likely that means could be

Of the net profits of persons in business, a part, as before observed, may be considered as interest on capital, and of a perpetual character, and the remaining part as remuneration for the skill and labour of superintendence. The surplus beyond interest depends on the life of the individual, and even on his

---

found of carrying into practical effect, proposes a deduction not of a fourth but of a third, in favour of industrial and professional incomes. He fixes on this ratio, on the ground that, independently of all consideration as to what the industrial and professional classes ought to save, the attainable evidence goes to prove that a third of their incomes is what on an average they do save, over and above the proportion saved by other classes. 'The savings' (Mr Hubbard observes) 'effected out of incomes derived from invested property are estimated at one-tenth. The savings effected out of industrial incomes are estimated at four-tenths. The amounts which would be assessed under these two classes being nearly equal, the adjustment is simplified by striking off one-tenth on either side, and then reducing by three-tenths, or one-third, the assessable amount of industrial incomes.' Proposed Report (p. xiv. of the Report and Evidence of the Committee of 1861). In such an estimate there must be a large element of conjecture; but in so far as it can be substantiated, it affords a valid ground for the practical conclusion which Mr Hubbard founds on it.

Several writers on the subject, including Mr Mill in his Elements of Political Economy, and Mr M'Culloch in his work on Taxation, have contended that as much should be deducted as would be sufficient to insure the possessor's life for a sum which would give to his successors for ever an income equal to what he reserves for himself; since this is what the possessor of heritable property can do without saving at all: in other words, that temporary incomes should be converted into perpetual incomes of equal present value, and taxed as such. If the owners of life-incomes actually did save this large proportion of their income, or even a still larger, I would gladly grant them an exemption from taxation on the whole amount, since, if practical means could be found of doing it, I would exempt savings altogether. But I cannot admit that they have a claim to exemption on the general assumption of their being obliged to save this amount. Owners of life-incomes are not bound to forego the enjoyment of them for the sake of leaving to a perpetual line of successors an independent provision equal to their own temporary one; and no one ever dreams of doing so. Least of all is it to be required or expected from those whose incomes are the fruits of personal exertion, that they should leave to their posterity for ever, without any necessity for exertion, the same incomes which they allow to themselves. All they are bound to do, even for their children, is to place them in circumstances in which they will have favourable chances of earning their own living. To give, however, either to children or to others, by

continuance in business, and is entitled to the full amount of exemption allowed to terminable incomes. It has also, I conceive, a just claim to a further amount of exemption in consideration of its precariousness. An income which some not unusual vicissitude may reduce to nothing, or even convert into a loss, is not the same thing to the feelings of the possessor as a permanent income of 1000*l.* a year, even though on an average of years it may yield 1000*l.* a year. If life-incomes were assessed at three-fourths of their amount, the profits of business, after deducting interest on capital, should not only be assessed at three-fourths, but should pay, on that assessment, a lower rate. Or perhaps the claims of justice in this respect might be sufficiently met by allowing the deduction of a fourth on the entire income, interest included.

These are the chief cases, of ordinary occurrence, in which any difficulty arises in interpreting the maxim of equality of taxation. The proper sense to be put upon it, as we have seen in the preceding example, is, that people should be taxed, not in proportion to what they have, but to what they can afford to spend. It is no objection to this principle that we cannot apply it consistently to all cases. A person with a life-income and precarious health, or who has many persons depending on his exertions, must, if he wishes to provide for them after his death, be more rigidly economical than one who has a life-income of equal amount, with a strong constitution, and few claims upon him; and if it be conceded that taxation cannot accommodate itself to these distinctions, it is argued that there is no use in attending to any distinctions, where the absolute amount of income is the same. But the difficulty of doing perfect justice is no reason against doing as much as we can. Though it may be a hardship to an annuitant whose life is only worth five years' purchase, to be allowed no greater abatement than is granted to

---

bequest, being a legitimate inclination, which these persons cannot indulge without laying by a part of their income, while the owners of heritable property can; this real inequality in cases where the incomes themselves are equal, should be considered, to a reasonable degree, in the adjustment of taxation, so as to require from both, as nearly as practicable, an equal sacrifice.

one whose life is worth twenty, it is better for him even so, than if neither of them were allowed any abatement at all.

§5. Before leaving the subject of Equality of Taxation, I must remark that there are cases in which exceptions may be made to it, consistently with that equal justice which is the groundwork of the rule. Suppose that there is a kind of income which constantly tends to increase, without any exertion or sacrifice on the part of the owners: those owners constituting a class in the community, whom the natural course of things progressively enriches, consistently with complete passiveness on their own part. In such a case it would be no violation of the principles on which private property is grounded, if the state should appropriate this increase of wealth, or part of it, as it arises. This would not properly be taking anything from anybody; it would merely be applying an accession of wealth, created by circumstances, to the benefit of society, instead of allowing it to become an unearned appendage to the riches of a particular class.

Now this is actually the case with rent. The ordinary progress of a society which increases in wealth, is at all times tending to augment the incomes of landlords; to give them both a greater amount and a greater proportion of the wealth of the community, independently of any trouble or outlay incurred by themselves. They grow richer, as it were in their sleep, without working, risking, or economizing. What claim have they, on the general principle of social justice, to this accession of riches? In what would they have been wronged if society had, from the beginning, reserved the right of taxing the spontaneous increase of rent, to the highest amount required by financial exigencies? I admit that it would be unjust to come upon each individual estate, and lay hold of the increase which might be found to have taken place in its rental; because there would be no means of distinguishing in individual cases, between an increase owing solely to the general circumstances of society, and one which was the effect of skill and expenditure on the part of the proprietor. The only admissible mode of proceeding would be by a general measure. The first step should be a valuation of all the land in the country. The present value of all land should be exempt from the tax; but after an interval had elapsed, during which society had increased in population and capital, a rough estimate might be made of the spontaneous increase which had accrued to rent since the valuation was made. Of this the average price of produce would be some criterion: if that had risen, it would be certain that rent had increased, and (as already shown) even in a greater ratio than the rise of price. On this and other data, an approximate estimate might be made, how much value had been added to the land of the country by natural causes; and in laying on a general land-tax, which for fear of miscalculation should be considerably within the amount thus indicated, there would be an assurance of not touching any increase of income which might be the result of capital expended or industry exerted by the proprietor.

But though there could be no question as to the justice of taxing the increase of rent, if society had avowedly reserved the right, has not society waived that right by not exercising it? In England, for example, have not all who bought land for the last century or more, given value not only for the existing income, but for the prospects of increase, under an implied assurance of being only taxed in the same proportion with other incomes? This objection, in so far as valid, has a different degree of validity in different countries; depending on the degree of desuetude into which society has allowed a right to fall, which, as no one can doubt, it once fully possessed. In most countries of Europe, the right to take by taxation, as exigency might require, an indefinite portion of the rent of land, has never been allowed to slumber. In several parts of the Continent, the land-tax forms a large proportion of the public revenues, and has always been confessedly liable to be raised or lowered without reference to other taxes. In these countries no one can pretend to have become the owner of land on the faith of never being called upon to pay an increased land-tax. In England the land-tax has not varied since the early part of the last century. The last act of the legislature in relation to its amount, was to diminish it; and though the subsequent increase in the rental of the country has been immense, not only from agriculture, but from the growth of towns and the increase of buildings, the ascendancy of landholders in the legislature has prevented any tax from being imposed, as it so justly might, upon the very large portion of this increase which was unearned, and, as it were, accidental. For the expectations thus raised, it appears to me that an amply sufficient allowance is made, if the whole increase of income which has accrued during this long period from a mere natural law, without exertion or sacrifice, is held sacred from any peculiar taxation. From the present date, or any subsequent time at which the legislature may think fit to assert the principle, I see no objection to declaring that the future increment of rent should be liable to special taxation; in doing which all injustice to the landlords would be obviated, if the present market-price of their land were secured to them; since that includes the present value of all future expectations. With reference to such a tax, perhaps a safer criterion than either a rise of rents or a rise of the price of corn, would be a general rise in the price of land. It would be easy to keep the tax within the amount which would reduce the market value of land below the original valuation: and up to that point, whatever the amount of the tax might be, no injustice would be done to the proprietors.

§6. But whatever may be thought of the legitimacy of making the State a sharer in all future increase of rent from natural causes, the existing land-tax (which in this country unfortunately is very small) ought not to be regarded as a tax, but as a rent-charge in favour of the public; a portion of the rent, reserved from the beginning by the State, which has never belonged to or formed part of the income of the landlords, and should not therefore be counted to them as part of their taxation, so as to exempt them from their fair share of every other tax. As well might the tithe be regarded as a tax on the landlords: as well, in Bengal, where the State, though entitled to the whole rent of the land, gave away one-tenth of it to individuals, retaining the other nine-tenths, might those nine-tenths be considered as an unequal and unjust tax on the grantees of the tenth. That a person owns part of the rent, does not make the rest of it his just right, injuriously withheld from him. The landlords originally held their estates subject to feudal burthens, for which the present land-tax is an exceedingly small equivalent, and for their relief from which they should have been required to pay a much higher price. All who have bought land since the tax existed have bought it subject to the tax. There is not the smallest pretence for looking upon it as a payment exacted from the existing race of landlords.

These observations are applicable to a land-tax, only in so far as it is a peculiar tax, and not when it is merely a mode of levying from the landlords the equivalent of what is taken from other classes. In France, for example, there are peculiar taxes on other kinds of property and income (the *mobilier* and the *patente*), and supposing the land-tax to be not more than equivalent to these, there would be no ground for contending that the State had reserved to itself a rent-charge on the land. But wherever and in so far as income derived from land is prescriptively subject to a deduction for public purposes, beyond the rate of taxation levied on other incomes, the surplus is not properly taxation, but a share of the property in the soil, reserved by the state. In this country there are no peculiar taxes on other classes, corresponding to, or intended to countervail, the land-tax. The whole of it, therefore, is not taxation, but a rent-charge, and is as if the state had retained, not a portion of the rent, but a portion of the land. It is no more a burthen on the landlord, than the share of one joint tenant is a burthen on the other. The landlords are entitled to no compensation for it, nor have they any claim to its being allowed for, as part of their taxes. Its continuance on the existing footing is no infringement of the principle of Equal Taxation.[5]

5. The same remarks obviously apply to those local taxes, of the peculiar pressure of which on landed property so much has been said by the remnant of the Protectionists. As much of these burthens as is of old standing, ought to be regarded as a prescriptive deduction or reservation, for public purposes, of a portion of the rent. And any recent additions have either been incurred for the benefit of the owners of landed property, or occasioned by their fault: in neither case giving them any just ground of complaint.

We shall hereafter consider, in treating of Indirect Taxation, how far, and with what modifications, the rule of equality is applicable to that department.

§7. In addition to the preceding rules, another general rule of taxation is sometimes laid down, namely, that it should fall on income, and not on capital. That taxation should not encroach upon the amount of the national capital, is indeed of the greatest importance; but this encroachment, when it occurs, is not so much a consequence of any particular mode of taxation, as of its excessive amount. Over-taxation, carried to a sufficient extent, is quite capable of ruining the most industrious community, especially when it is in any degree arbitrary, so that the payer is never certain how much or how little he shall be allowed to keep; or when it is so laid on as to render industry and economy a bad calculation. But if these errors be avoided, and the amount of taxation be not greater than it is at present even in the most heavily taxed country of Europe, there is no danger lest it should deprive the country of a portion of its capital.

To provide that taxation shall fall entirely on income, and not at all on capital, is beyond the power of any system of fiscal arrangements. There is no tax which is not partly paid from what would otherwise have been saved; no tax, the amount of which, if remitted, would be wholly employed in increased expenditure, and no part whatever laid by as an addition to capital. All taxes, therefore, are in some sense partly paid out of capital; and in a poor country it is impossible to impose any tax which will not impede the increase of the national wealth. But in a country where capital abounds, and the spirit of accumulation is strong, this effect of taxation is scarcely felt. Capital having reached the stage in which, were it not for a perpetual succession of improvements in production, any further increase would soon be stopped – and having so strong a tendency even to outrun those improvements, that profits are only kept above the minimum by emigration of capital, or by a periodical sweep called a commercial crisis; to take from capital by taxation what emigration would remove, or a commercial crisis destroy, is only to do what either of those causes would have done, namely, to make a clear space for further saving.

I cannot, therefore, attach any importance, in a wealthy country, to the objection made against taxes on legacies and inheritances, that they are taxes on capital. It is perfectly true that they are so. As Ricardo observes, if 100*l*. are taken from any one in a tax on houses or on wine, he will probably save it, or a part of it, by living in a cheaper house, consuming less wine, or retrenching from some other of his expenses; but if the same sum be taken from him because he has received a legacy of 1000*l*., he considers the legacy as only 900*l*., and feels no more inducement than at any other time (probably feels rather less inducement) to economize in his expenditure. The tax, therefore, is wholly paid out of capital: and there are countries in which this would be a serious objection. But in the first place, the argument cannot apply to any country which has a national debt, and devotes any portion of revenue to paying it off; since the produce of the tax, thus applied, still remains capital, and is merely transferred from the tax-payer to the fundholder. But the objection is never applicable in a country which increases rapidly in wealth. The amount which would be derived, even from a very high legacy duty, in each year, is but a small fraction of the annual increase of capital in such a country; and its abstraction would but make room for saving to an equivalent amount: while the effect of not taking it, is to prevent that amount of saving, or cause the savings, when made, to be sent abroad for investment. A country which, like England, accumulates capital not only for itself, but for half the world, may be said to defray the whole of its public expenses from its overflowings; and its wealth is probably at this moment as great as if it had no taxes at all. What its taxes really do is, to subtract from its means, not of production, but of enjoyment; since whatever any one pays in taxes, he could, if it were not taken for that purpose, employ in indulging his ease, or in gratifying some want or taste which at present remains unsatisfied.

CHAPTER III

Of Direct Taxes

§1. Taxes are either direct or indirect. A direct tax is one which is demanded from the very persons who, it is intended or desired, should pay it. Indirect taxes are those which are demanded from one person in the expectation and intention that he shall indemnify himself at the expense of another: such as the excise or customs. The producer or importer of a commodity is called upon to pay a tax on it, not with the intention to levy a peculiar contribution upon him, but to tax through him the consumers of the commodity, from whom it is supposed that he will recover the amount by means of an advance in price.

Direct taxes are either on income, or on expenditure. Most taxes on expenditure are indirect, but some are direct, being imposed not on the producer or seller of an article, but immediately on the consumer. A house-tax, for example, is a direct tax on expenditure, if levied, as it usually is, on the occupier of the house. If levied on the builder or owner, it would be an indirect tax. A window-tax is a direct tax on expenditure; so are the taxes on horses and carriages, and the rest of what are called the assessed taxes.

The sources of income are rent, profits, and wages. This includes every sort of income, except gift or plunder. Taxes may be laid on any one of the three kinds of income, or an uniform tax on all of them. We will consider these in their order.

§2. A tax on rent falls wholly on the landlord. There are no means by which he can shift the burthen upon any one else. It does not affect the value or price of agricultural produce, for this is determined by the cost of production in the most unfavourable circumstances, and in those circumstances, as we have so often demonstrated, no rent is paid. A tax on rent, therefore, has no effect, other than its obvious one. It merely takes so much from the landlord, and transfers it to the state.

This, however, is, in strict exactness, only true of the rent which is the result either of natural causes, or of improvements made by tenants. When the landlord makes improvements which increase the productive power of his land, he is remunerated for them by an extra payment from the tenant; and this payment, which to the landlord is properly a profit on capital, is blended and confounded with rent; which indeed it really is, to the tenant, and in respect of the economical laws which determine its amount. A tax on rent, if extending to this portion of it, would discourage landlords from making improvements: but it does not follow that it would raise the price of agricultural produce. The same improvements might be made with the tenant's capital, or even with the landlord's if lent by him to the tenant; provided he is willing to give the tenant so long a lease as will enable him to indemnify himself before it expires. But whatever hinders improvements from being made in the manner in which people prefer to make them, will often prevent them from being made at all: and on this account a tax on rent would be inexpedient, unless some means could be devised of excluding from its operation that portion of the nominal rent which may be regarded as landlord's profit. This argument, however, is not needed for the condemnation of such a tax. A peculiar tax on the income of any class, not balanced by taxes on other classes, is a violation of justice, and amounts to a partial confiscation. I have already shown grounds for excepting from this censure a tax which, sparing existing rents, should content itself with appropriating a portion of any future increase arising from the mere action of natural causes. But even this could not be justly done, without offering as an alternative the market price of the land. In the case of a tax on rent which is not peculiar, but accompanied by an equivalent tax on other incomes, the objection grounded on its reaching the profit arising from improvements is less applicable: since, profits being taxed as well as rent, the profit which assumes the form of rent is liable to its share in common with other profits; but since profits altogether ought, for reasons formerly stated, to be taxed somewhat lower than rent properly so called, the objection is only diminished, not removed.

§3. A tax on profits, like a tax on rent, must, at least in its immediate operation, fall wholly on the payer. All profits being alike affected, no relief can be obtained by a change of employment. If a tax were laid on the profits of any one branch of productive employment, the tax would be virtually an increase of the cost of production, and the value and price of the article would rise accordingly; by which the tax would be thrown upon the consumers of the commodity, and would not affect profits. But a general and equal tax on all profits would not affect general prices, and would fall, at least in the first instance, on capitalists alone.

There is, however, an ulterior effect, which, in a rich and prosperous country, requires to be taken into account. When the capital accumulated is so great and the rate of annual accumulation so rapid, that the country is only kept from attaining the stationary state by the emigration of capital, or by continual improvements in production; any circumstance which virtually lowers the rate of profit cannot be without a decided influence on these phenomena. It may operate in different ways. The curtailment of profit, and the consequent increased difficulty in making a fortune or obtaining a subsistence by the employment of capital, may act as a stimulus to inventions, and to the use of them when made. If improvements in production are much accelerated, and if these improvements cheapen, directly or indirectly, any of the things habitually consumed by the labourer, profits may rise, and rise sufficiently to make up for all that is taken from them by the tax. In that case the tax will have been realized without loss to any one, the produce of the country being increased by an equal, or what would in that case be a far greater amount. The tax, however, must even in this case be considered as paid from profits, because the receivers of profits are those who would be benefited if it were taken off.

But though the artificial abstraction of a portion of profits would have a real tendency to accelerate improvements in production, no considerable improvements might actually result, or only of such a kind as not to raise general profits at all, or not to raise them so much as the tax had diminished them. If so, the rate of profit would be brought closer to that practical minimum, to which it is constantly approaching: and this diminished return to capital would either give a decided check to further accumulation, or would cause a greater proportion than before of the annual increase to be sent abroad, or wasted in unprofitable speculations. At its first imposition the tax falls wholly on profits: but the amount of increase of capital, which the tax prevents, would, if it had been allowed to continue, have tended to reduce profits to the same level; and at every period of ten or twenty years there will be found less difference between profits as they are, and profits as they would in that case have been: until at last there is no difference, and the tax is thrown either upon the labourer or upon the landlord. The real effect of a tax on profits is to make the country possess at any given period, a smaller capital and a smaller aggregate production, and to make the stationary state be attained earlier, and with a smaller sum of national wealth. It is possible that a tax on profits might even diminish the existing capital of the country. If the rate of profit is already at the practical minimum, that is, at the point at which all that portion of the annual increment which would tend to reduce profits is carried off either by exportation or by speculation; then if a tax is imposed which reduces profits still lower, the same causes which previously carried off the increase would probably carry off a portion of the existing capital. A tax on profits is thus, in a state of capital and accumulation like that in England, extremely detrimental to the national wealth. And this effect is not confined to the case of a peculiar, and therefore intrinsically unjust, tax on profits. The mere fact that profits have to bear their share of a heavy general taxation, tends, in the same manner as a peculiar tax, to drive capital abroad, to stimulate imprudent speculations by diminishing safe gains, to discourage further accumulation, and to accelerate the attainment of the stationary state. This is thought to have been the principal cause of the decline of Holland, or rather of her having ceased to make progress.

Even in countries which do not accumulate so fast as to be always within a short interval of the stationary state, it seems impossible that, if capital is accumulating at all, its accumulation should not be in some degree retarded by the abstraction of a portion of its profit; and unless the effect in stimulating improvements be a full counter-balance, it is inevitable that a part of the burthen will be thrown off the capitalist, upon the labourer or the landlord. One or other of these is always the loser by a diminished rate of accumulation. If population continues to increase as before, the labourer suffers: if not, cultivation is checked in its advance, and the landlords lose the accession of rent which would have accrued to them. The only countries in which a tax on profits seems likely to be permanently a burthen on capitalists exclusively, are those in which capital is stationary, because there is no new accumulation. In such countries the tax might not prevent the old capital from being kept up through habit, or from unwillingness to submit to impoverishment, and so the capitalist might continue to bear the whole of the tax. It is seen from these considerations that the effects of a tax on profits are much more complex, more various, and in some points more uncertain, than writers on this subject have commonly supposed.

§4. We now turn to Taxes on Wages. The incidence of these is very different, according as the wages taxed are those of ordinary unskilled labour, or are the remuneration of such skilled or privileged employments, whether manual or intellectual, as are taken out of the sphere of competition by a natural or conferred monopoly.

I have already remarked, that in the present low state of popular education, all the higher grades of mental or educated labour are at a monopoly price; exceeding the wages of common workmen in a degree very far beyond that which is due to the expense, trouble, and loss of time required in qualifying for the employment. Any tax levied on these gains, which still leaves them above (or not below) their just proportion, falls on those who pay it; they have no means of relieving themselves at the expense of any other class. The same thing is true of ordinary wages, in cases like that of the United States, or of a new colony, where, capital increasing as rapidly as population can increase, wages are kept up by the increase of capital, and not by the adherence of the labourers to a fixed standard of comforts. In such a case some deterioration of their condition, whether by a tax or otherwise, might possibly take place without checking the increase of population. The tax would in that case fall on the labourers themselves, and would reduce them prematurely to that lower state to which, on the same supposition with regard to their habits, they would in any case have been reduced ultimately, by the inevitable diminution in the rate of increase of capital, through the occupation of all the fertile land.

Some will object that, even in this case, a tax on wages cannot be detrimental to the labourers, since the money raised by it, being expended in the country, comes back to the labourers again through the demand for labour. The fallacy, however, of this doctrine has been so completely exhibited in the First Book, that I need do little more than refer to that exposition. It was there shown that funds expended unproductively have no tendency to raise or keep up wages, unless when expended in the direct purchase of labour. If the government took a tax of a shilling a week from every labourer, and laid it all out in hiring labourers for military service, public works, or the like, it would, no doubt, indemnify the labourers as a class for all that the tax took from them. That would really be 'spending the money among the people'. But if it expended the whole in buying goods, or in adding to the salaries of employés who bought goods with it, this would not increase the demand for labour, or tend to raise wages. Without, however, reverting to general principles, we may rely on an obvious *reductio ad absurdum*. If to take money from the labourers and spend it in commodities is giving it back to the labourers, then, to take money from other classes, and spend it in the same manner, must be giving it to the labourers; consequently, the more a government takes in taxes, the greater will be the demand for labour, and the more opulent the condition of the labourers. A proposition the absurdity of which no one can fail to see.

In the condition of most communities, wages are regulated by the habitual standard of living to which the labourers adhere, and on less than which they will not multiply. Where there exists such a standard, a tax on wages will indeed for a time be borne by the labourers themselves; but unless this temporary depression has the effect of lowering the standard itself, the increase of population will receive a check, which will raise wages, and restore the labourers to their previous condition. On whom, in this case, will the tax fall? According to Adam Smith, on the community generally, in their character of consumers; since the rise of wages, he thought, would raise general prices. We have seen, however, that general prices depend on other causes, and are never raised by any circumstance which affects all kinds of productive employment in the same manner and degree. A rise of wages occasioned by a tax, must, like any other increase of the cost of labour, be defrayed from profits. To attempt to tax day-labourers, in an old country, is merely to impose an extra tax upon all employers of common labour; unless the tax has the much worse effect of permanently lowering the standard of comfortable subsistence in the minds of the poorest class.

We find in the preceding considerations an additional argument for the opinion already expressed, that direct taxation should stop short of the class of incomes which do not exceed what is necessary for healthful existence. These very small incomes are mostly derived from manual labour; and, as we now see, any tax imposed on these, either permanently degrades the habits of the labouring class, or falls on profits, and burthens capitalists with an indirect tax, in addition to their share of the direct taxes; which is doubly objectionable, both as a violation of the fundamental rule of equality, and for the reasons which, as already shown, render a peculiar tax on profits detrimental to the public wealth, and consequently to the means which society possesses of paying any taxes whatever.

§5. We now pass, from taxes on the separate kinds of income, to a tax attempted to be assessed fairly upon all kinds; in other words, an Income Tax. The discussion of the conditions necessary for making this tax consistent with justice, has been anticipated in the last chapter. We shall suppose, therefore, that these conditions are complied with. They are, first, that incomes below a certain amount should be altogether untaxed. This minimum should not be higher than the amount which suffices for the necessaries of the existing population. The exemption from the present income tax, of all incomes under 100*l.* a year, and the lower percentage formerly levied on those between 100*l.* and 150*l.*, are only defensible on the ground that almost all the indirect taxes press more heavily on incomes between 50*l.* and 150*l.* than on any others whatever. The second condition is, that incomes above the limit should be taxed only in proportion to the surplus by which they exceed the limit. Thirdly, that all sums saved from income and invested, should be exempt from the tax: or if this be found impracticable, that life incomes, and incomes from business and professions, should be less heavily taxed than inheritable incomes, in a degree as nearly as possible equivalent to the increased need of economy arising from their terminable character: allowance being also made, in the case of variable incomes, for their precariousness.

An income-tax, fairly assessed on these principles, would be, in point of justice, the least exceptionable of all taxes. The objection to it, in the present low state of public morality, is the impossibility of ascertaining the real incomes of the contributors. The supposed hardship of compelling people to disclose the amount of their incomes, ought not, in my opinion, to count for much. One of the social evils of this country is the practice, amounting to a custom, of maintaining, or attempting to maintain, the appearance to the world of a larger income than is possessed; and it would be far better for the interest of those who yield to this weakness, if the extent of their means were universally and exactly known, and the temptation removed to expending more than they can afford, or stinting real wants in order to make a false show externally. At the same time, the reason of the case, even on this point, is not so exclusively on one side of the argument as is sometimes supposed. So long as the vulgar of any country are in the debased state of mind which this national habit presupposes – so long as their respect (if such a word can be applied to it) is proportioned to what they suppose to be each person's pecuniary means – it may be doubted whether anything which would remove all uncertainty as to that point, would not considerably increase the presumption and arrogance of the vulgar rich, and their insolence towards those above them in mind and character, but below them in fortune.

Notwithstanding, too, what is called the inquisitorial nature of the tax, no amount of inquisitorial power which would be tolerated by a people the most disposed to submit to it, could enable the revenue officers to assess the tax from actual knowledge of the circumstances of contributors. Rent, salaries, annuities, and all fixed incomes, can be exactly ascertained. But the variable gains of professions, and still more the profits of business, which the person interested cannot always himself exactly ascertain, can still less be estimated with any approach to fairness by a tax-collector. The main reliance must be placed, and always has been placed, on the returns made by the person himself. No production of accounts is of much avail, except against the more flagrant cases of falsehood; and even against these the check is very imperfect, for if fraud is intended, false accounts can generally be framed which it will baffle any means of inquiry possessed by the revenue officers to detect: the easy resource of omitting entries on the credit side being often sufficient without the aid of fictitious debts or disbursements. The tax, therefore, on whatever principles of equality it may be imposed, is in practice unequal in one of the worst ways, falling heaviest on the most conscientious. The unscrupulous succeed in evading a great proportion of what they should pay; even persons of integrity in their ordinary transactions are tempted to palter with their consciences, at least to the extent of deciding in their own favour all points on which the smallest doubt or discussion could arise: while the strictly veracious may be made to pay more than the state intended, by the powers of arbitrary assessment necessarily intrusted to the Commssioners, as the last defence against the tax-payer's power of concealment.

It is to be feared, therefore, that the fairness which belongs to the principle of an income tax, cannot be made to attach to it in practice: and that this tax, while apparently the most just of all modes of raising a revenue, is in effect more unjust than many others which are *primâ facie* more objectionable. This consideration would lead us to concur in the opinion which, until of late, has usually prevailed – that direct taxes on income should be reserved as an extraordinary resource for great national emergencies, in which the necessity of a large additional revenue overrules all objections.

The difficulties of a fair income tax have elicited a proposition for a direct tax of so much per cent, not on income but on expenditure; the aggregate amount of each person's expenditure being ascertained, as the amount of income now is, from statements furnished by the contributors themselves. The author of this suggestion, Mr Revans, in a clever pamphlet on the subject,[1] contends that the returns which persons would furnish of their expenditure would be more trustworthy than those which they now make of their income, inasmuch as expenditure is in its own nature more public than income, and false representations of it more easily detected. He cannot, I think, have sufficiently considered, how few of the items in the annual expenditure of most families can be judged of with any approximation to correctness from the external signs. The only security would still be the veracity of individuals, and there is no reason for supposing that their statements would be more trustworthy on the subject of their expenses than that of their revenues; especially as, the expenditure of most persons being composed of many more items than their income, there would be more scope for concealment and suppression in the detail of expenses than even of receipts.

The taxes on expenditure at present in force, either in this or in other countries, fall only on particular kinds of expenditure, and differ no otherwise from taxes on commodities than in being paid directly by the person who consumes or uses the article, instead of being advanced by the producer or seller, and reimbursed in the price. The taxes on horses and carriages, on dogs, on servants, are all of this nature. They evidently fall on the persons from whom they are levied – those who use the commodity taxed. A tax of a similar description, and more important, is a house-tax; which must be considered at somewhat greater length.

1. 'A Percentage Tax on Domestic Expenditure to supply the whole of the Public Revenue.' By John Revans. Published by Hatchard, in 1847.

§6. The rent of a house consists of two parts, the ground-rent, and what Adam Smith calls the building-rent. The first is determined by the ordinary principles of rent. It is the remuneration given for the use of the portion of land occupied by the house and its appurtenances; and varies from a mere equivalent for the rent which the ground would afford in agriculture, to the monopoly rents paid for advantageous situations in populous thoroughfares. The rent of the house itself, as distinguished from the ground, is the equivalent given for the labour and capital expended on the building. The fact of its being received in quarterly or half-yearly payments, makes no difference in the principles by which it is regulated. It comprises the ordinary profit on the builder's capital, and an annuity, sufficient at the current rate of interest, after paying for all repairs chargeable on the proprietor, to replace the original capital by the time the house is worn out, or by the expiration of the usual term of a building lease.

A tax of so much per cent on the gross rent, falls on both those portions alike. The more highly a house is rented, the more it pays to the tax, whether the quality of the situation or that of the house itself is the cause. The incidence, however, of these two portions of the tax must be considered separately.

As much of it as is a tax on building-rent, must ultimately fall on the consumer, in other words the occupier. For as the profits of building are already not above the ordinary rate, they would, if the tax fell on the owner and not on the occupier, become lower than the profits of untaxed employments, and houses would not be built. It is probable however that for some time after the tax was first imposed, a great part of it would fall, not on the renter, but on the owner of the house. A large proportion of the consumers either could not afford, or would not choose, to pay their former rent with the tax in addition, but would content themselves with a lower scale of accommodation. Houses therefore would be for a time in excess of the demand. The consequence of such excess, in the case of most other articles, would be an almost immediate diminution of the supply: but so durable a commodity as houses does not rapidly diminish in amount. New buildings indeed, of the class for which the demand had decreased, would cease to be erected, except for special reasons; but in the meantime the temporary superfluity would lower rents, and the consumers would obtain perhaps nearly the same accommodation as formerly, for the same aggregate payment, rent and tax together. By degrees, however, as the existing houses wore out, or as increase of population demanded a greater supply, rents would again rise; until it became profitable to recommence building, which would not be until the tax was wholly transferred to the occupier. In the end, therefore, the occupier bears that portion of a tax on rent, which falls on the payment made for the house itself, exclusively of the ground it stands on.

The case is partly different with the portion which is a tax on ground-rent. As taxes on rent, properly so called, fall on the landlord, a tax on ground-rent, one would suppose, must fall on the ground-landlord, at least after the expiration of the building lease. It will not however fall wholly on the landlord, unless with the tax on ground-rent there is combined an equivalent tax on agricultural rent. The lowest rent of land let for building is very little above the rent which the same ground would yield in agriculture: since it is reasonable to suppose that land, unless in case of exceptional circumstances, is let or sold for building as soon as it is decidedly worth more for that purpose than for cultivation. If, therefore, a tax were laid on ground-rents without being also laid on agricultural rents, it would, unless of trifling amount, reduce the return from the lowest ground-rents below the ordinary return from land, and would check further building quite as effectually as if it were a tax on building-rents, until either the increased demand of a growing population, or a diminution of supply by the ordinary causes of destruction, had raised the rent by a full equivalent for the tax. But whatever raises the lowest ground-rents, raises all others, since each exceeds the lowest by the market value of its peculiar advantages. If, therefore, the tax on ground-rents were a fixed sum per square foot, the more valuable situations paying no more than those least in request, this fixed payment would ultimately fall on the occupier. Suppose the lowest ground-rent to be 10*l.* per acre, and the highest

1000*l*., a tax of 1*l*. per acre on ground-rents would ultimately raise the former to 11*l*., and the latter consequently to 1001*l*., since the difference of value between the two situations would be exactly what it was before: the annual pound, therefore, would be paid by the occupier. But a tax on ground-rent is supposed to be a portion of a house-tax, which is not a fixed payment, but a percentage on the rent. The cheapest site, therefore, being supposed as before to pay 1*l*., the dearest would pay 100*l*., of which only the 1*l*. could be thrown upon the occupier, since the rent would still be only raised to 100*l*. Consequently, 99*l*. of the 100*l*. levied from the expensive site, would fall on the ground-landlord. A house-tax thus requires to be considered in a double aspect, as a tax on all occupiers of houses, and a tax on ground-rents.

In the vast majority of houses, the ground-rent forms but a small proportion of the annual payment made for the house, and nearly all the tax falls on the occupier. It is only in exceptional cases, like that of the favourite situations in large towns, that the predominant element in the rent of the house is the ground-rent; and among the very few kinds of income which are fit subjects for peculiar taxation, these ground-rents hold the principal place, being the most gigantic example extant of enormous accessions of riches acquired rapidly, and in many cases unexpectedly, by a few families, from the mere accident of their possessing certain tracts of land, without their having themselves aided in the acquisition by the smallest exertion, outlay, or risk. So far therefore as a house-tax falls on the ground-landlord, it is liable to no valid objection.

In so far as it falls on the occupier, if justly proportioned to the value of the house, it is one of the fairest and most unobjectionable of all taxes. No part of a person's expenditure is a better criterion of his means, or bears, on the whole, more nearly the same proportion to them. A house-tax is a nearer approach to a fair income tax, than a direct assessment on income can easily be; having the great advantage, that it makes spontaneously all the allowances which it is so difficult to make, and so impracticable to make exactly, in assessing an income tax: for if what a person pays in house-rent is a test of anything, it is a test not of what he possesses, but of what he thinks he can afford to spend. The equality of this tax can only be seriously questioned on two grounds. The first is, that a miser may escape it. This objection applies to all taxes on expenditure: nothing but a direct tax on income can reach a miser. But as misers do not now hoard their treasure, but invest it in productive employments, it not only adds to the national wealth, and consequently to the general means of paying taxes, but the payment claimable from itself is only transferred from the principal sum to the income afterwards derived from it, which pays taxes as soon as it comes to be expended. The second objection is, that a person may require a larger and more expensive house, not from having greater means, but from having a larger family. Of this, however, he is not entitled to complain; since having a large family is at a person's own choice: and, so far as concerns the public interest, is a thing rather to be discouraged than promoted.[2]

A large portion of the taxation of this country is raised by a house-tax. The parochial taxation of the towns entirely, and of the rural districts partially, consists of an assessment on house-

2. Another common objection is that large and expensive accommodation is often required, not as a residence, but for business. But it is an admitted principle that buildings or portions of buildings occupied exclusively for business, such as shops, warehouses, or manufactories, ought to be exempted from house-tax. The plea that persons in business may be compelled to live in situations, such as the great thoroughfares of London, where house-rent is at a monopoly rate, seems to me unworthy of regard: since no one does so but because the extra profit which he expects to derive from the situation, is more than an equivalent to him for the extra cost. But in any case, the bulk of the tax on this extra rent will not fall on him, but on the ground-landlord.

It has been also objected that house-rent in the rural districts is much lower than in towns, and lower in some towns and in some rural districts than in others: so that a tax proportioned to it would have a corresponding inequality of pressure. To this, however, it may be answered, that in places where house-rent is low, persons of the same amount of income usually live in larger and better houses, and thus expend in house-rent more nearly the same proportion of their incomes than might at first sight appear. Or if not, the probability will be, that many of them live in those places precisely because they are too poor to live elsewhere, and have therefore the strongest claim to be taxed lightly. In some cases, it is precisely because the people are poor, that house-rent remains low.

rent. The window-tax, which was also a house-tax, but of a bad kind, operating as a tax on light, and a cause of deformity in building, was exchanged in 1851 for a house-tax properly so called, but on a much lower scale than that which existed previously to 1834. It is to be lamented that the new tax retains the unjust principle on which the old house-tax was assessed, and which contributed quite as much as the selfishness of the middle classes to produce the outcry against the tax. The public were justly scandalized on learning that residences like Chatsworth or Belvoir were only rated on an imaginary rent of perhaps 200*l.* a year, under the pretext that owing to the great expense of keeping them up, they could not be let for more. Probably, indeed, they could not be let even for that, and if the argument were a fair one, they ought not to have been taxed at all. But a house-tax is not intended as a tax on incomes derived from houses, but on expenditure incurred for them. The thing which it is wished to ascertain is what a house costs to the person who lives in it, not what it would bring in if let to some one else. When the occupier is not the owner, and does not hold on a repairing lease, the rent he pays is the measure of what the house costs him : but when he is the owner, some other measure must be sought. A valuation should be made of the house, not at what it would sell for, but at what would be the cost of rebuilding it, and this valuation might be periodically corrected by an allowance for what it had lost in value by time, or gained by repairs and improvements. The amount of the amended valuation would form a principal sum, the interest of which, at the current price of the public funds, would form the annual value at which the building should be assessed to the tax.

As incomes below a certain amount ought to be exempt from income tax, so ought houses below a certain value, from house-tax, on the universal principle of sparing from all taxation the absolute necessaries of healthful existence. In order that the occupiers of lodgings, as well as of houses, might benefit, as in justice they ought, by this exemption, it might be optional with the owners to have every portion of a house which is occupied by a separate tenant, valued and assessed separately, as is now usually the case with chambers.

CHAPTER IV

Of Taxes on Commodities

§1. By taxes on commodities are commonly meant, those which are levied either on the producers, or on the carriers or dealers who intervene between them and the final purchasers for consumption. Taxes imposed directly on the consumers of particular commodities, such as a house-tax, or the tax in this country on horses and carriages, might be called taxes on commodities, but are not; the phrase being, by custom, confined to indirect taxes—those which are advanced by one person, to be, as is expected and intended, reimbursed by another. Taxes on commodities are either on production within the country, or on importation into it, or on conveyance or sale within it; and are classed respectively as excise, customs, or tolls and transit duties. To whichever class they belong, and at whatever stage in the progress of the community they may be imposed, they are equivalent to an increase of the cost of production; using that term in its most enlarged sense, which includes the cost of transport and distribution, or, in common phrase, of bringing the commodity to market.

When the cost of production is increased artificially by a tax, the effect is the same as when it is increased by natural causes. If only one or a few commodities are affected, their value and price rise, so as to compensate the producer or dealer for the peculiar burthen; but if there were a tax on all commodities, exactly proportioned to their value, no such compensation would be obtained : there would neither be a general rise of values, which is an absurdity, nor of prices, which depend on causes entirely different. There would, however, as Mr M'Culloch has pointed out, be a disturbance of values, some falling, others rising, owing to a circumstance, the effect of which on values and prices we formerly discussed; the different durability of the capital employed in different occupations. The gross produce of industry consists of two parts; one portion serving to replace the capital consumed, while the other portion is profit. Now equal capitals in two branches of production must have equal expectations of profit; but if a greater portion of the one than of the other is fixed capital, or if that fixed capital is more durable, there will be a less consumption of capital in the year, and less will be required to replace it, so that the profit, if absolutely the same, will form a greater proportion of the annual returns. To derive from a capital of 1000*l.* a profit of 100*l.*, the one producer may have to sell produce to the value of 1100*l.*, the other only to the value of 500*l.* If on these two branches of industry a tax be imposed of five per cent *ad valorem*, the last will be charged only with 25*l.*, the first with 55*l.*; leaving to the one 75*l.* profit, to the other only 45*l.* To equalize, therefore, their expectation of profit, the one commodity must rise in price, or the other must fall, or both: commodities made chiefly by immediate labour must rise in value, as compared with those which are chiefly made by machinery. It is unnecessary to prosecute this branch of the inquiry any further.

§2. A tax on any one commodity, whether laid on its production, its importation, its carriage from place to place, or its sale, and whether the tax be a fixed sum of money for a given quantity of the commodity, or an *ad valorem* duty, will, as a general rule, raise the value and price of the commodity by at least the amount of the tax. There are few cases in which it does not raise them by more than that amount. In the first place, there are few taxes on production on account of which it is not found or deemed necessary to impose restrictive regulations on the manufacturers or dealers, in order to check evasions of the tax. These regulations are always sources of trouble and annoyance, and generally of expense, for all of which, being peculiar disadvantages, the producers or dealers must have compensation in the price of their commodity. These restrictions also frequently interfere with the processes of manufacture, requiring the producer to carry on his operations in the way most convenient to the revenue, though not the cheapest, or most efficient for purposes of production. Any regulations whatever, enforced by law, make it difficult for the producer to adopt new and improved processes. Further, the necessity of advancing the tax obliges producers and dealers to carry on their business with larger capitals than would otherwise be necessary, on the whole of which they must receive the ordinary rate of profit, though a part only is employed in defraying the real expenses of production or importation. The price of the article must be such as to afford a profit on more than its natural value, instead of a profit on only its natural value. A part of the capital of the country, in short, is not employed in production, but in advances to the state, repaid in the price of goods; and the consumers must give an indemnity to the sellers, equal to the profit which they could have made on the same capital if really employed in production.[1] Neither ought it to be forgotten, that whatever renders a larger capital necessary in any trade or business, limits the competition in that business; and by giving something like a monopoly to a few dealers, may enable them either to keep up the price beyond what would afford the ordinary rate of profit, or to obtain the ordinary rate of profit with a less degree of exertion for improving and cheapening their commodity. In these several modes, taxes on commodities often cost to the consumer, through the increased price of the article, much more than they bring into the treasury of the state. There is still another consideration. The higher price necessitated by the tax, almost always checks the demand for the commodity; and since there are many improvements in production which, to make them practicable, require a certain extent of demand, such improvements are obstructed, and many of them prevented altogether. It is a well-known fact that the branches of production in which fewest improvements are made, are those with which the revenue officer interferes; and that nothing, in general, gives a greater impulse to improvements in the production of a commodity, than taking off a tax which narrowed the market for it.

1. It is true, this does not constitute, as at first sight it appears to do, a case of taking more out of the pockets of the people than the state receives; since if the state needs the advance, and gets it in this manner, it can dispense with an equivalent amount of borrowing in stock or exchequer bills. But it is more economical that the necessities of the state should be supplied from the disposable capital in the hands of the lending class, than by an artificial addition to the expenses of one or several classes of producers or dealers.

§3. Such are the effects of taxes on commodities, considered generally; but as there are some commodities (those composing the necessaries of the labourer) of which the values have an influence on the distribution of wealth among different classes of the community, it is requisite to trace the effects of taxes on those particular articles somewhat farther. If a tax be laid, say on corn, and the price rises in proportion to the tax, the rise of price may operate in two ways. First: it may lower the condition of the labouring classes; temporarily indeed it can scarcely fail to do so. If it diminishes their consumption of the produce of the earth, or makes them resort to a food which the soil produces more abundantly, and therefore more cheaply, it to that extent contributes to throw back agriculture upon more fertile lands or less costly processes, and to lower the value and price of corn; which therefore ultimately settles at a price, increased not by the whole amount of the tax, but by only a part of its amount. Secondly, however, it may happen that the dearness of the taxed food does not lower the habitual standard of the labourer's requirements, but that wages, on the contrary, through an action on population, rise, in a shorter or longer period, so as to compensate the labourers for their portion of the tax; the compensation being of course at the expense of profits. Taxes on necessaries must thus have one of two effects. Either they lower the condition of the labouring classes; or they exact from the owners of capital, in addition to the amount due to the state on their own necessaries, the amount due on those consumed by the labourers. In the last case, the tax on necessaries, like a tax on wages, is equivalent to a peculiar tax on profits; which is, like all other partial taxation, unjust, and is specially prejudicial to the increase of the national wealth.

It remains to speak of the effect on rent. Assuming (what is usually the fact,) that the consumption of food is not diminished, the same cultivation as before will be necessary to supply the wants of the community; the margin of cultivation, to use Dr Chalmers' expression, remains where it was; and the same land or capital which, as the least productive, already regulated the value and price of the whole produce, will continue to regulate them. The effect which a tax on agricultural produce will have on rent, depends on its affecting or not affecting the difference between the return to this least productive land or capital, and the returns to other lands and capitals. Now this depends on the manner in which the tax is imposed. If it is an *ad valorem* tax, or what is the same thing, a fixed proportion of the produce, such as tithe for example, it evidently lowers corn-rents. For it takes more corn from the better lands than from the worse; and exactly in the degree in which they are better; land of twice the productiveness paying twice as much to the tithe. Whatever takes more from the greater of two quantities than from the less, diminishes the difference between them. The imposition of a tithe on corn would take a tithe also from corn-rent: for if we reduce a series of numbers by a tenth each, the differences between them are reduced one-tenth.

For example, let there be five qualities of land, which severally yield, on the same extent of ground, and with the same expenditure, 100, 90, 80, 70, and 60 bushels of wheat; the last of these being the lowest quality which the demand for food renders it necessary to cultivate. The rent of these lands will be as follows:

The land producing	100 bushels	will yield a rent of	100—60, or 40 bushels.
That producing	90 ,,	,,	90—60, or 30 ,,
,,	80 ,,	,,	80—60, or 20 ,,
,,	70 ,,	,,	70—60, or 10 ,,
,,	60 ,,	,,	no rent.

Now let a tithe be imposed, which takes from these five pieces of land 10, 9, 8, 7, and 6 bushels respectively, the fifth quality still being the one which regulates the price, but returning to the farmer, after payment of tithe, no more than 54 bushels:

The land producing	100 bushels reduced to 90,	will yield a rent of	90—54, or 36 bushels.
That producing	90 ,, ,, 81	,,	81–54, or 27 ,,
,,	80 ,, ,, 72	,,	72–54, or 18 ,,
,,	70 ,, ,, 63	,,	63–54, or 9 ,,

and that producing 60 bushels, reduced to 54, will yield, as before, no rent. So that the rent of the first quality of land has lost four bushels; of the second, three; of the third, two; and of the fourth, one: that is, each has lost exactly one-tenth. A tax, therefore, of a fixed proportion of the produce, lowers, in the same proportion, corn-rent.

But it is only corn-rent that is lowered, and not rent estimated in money, or in any other commodity. For, in the same proportion as corn-rent is reduced in quantity, the corn composing it is raised in value. Under the tithe, 54 bushels will be worth in the market what 60 were before; and nine-tenths will in all cases sell for as much as the whole ten-tenths previously sold for. The landlords will therefore be compensated in value and price for what they lose in quantity; and will suffer only so far as they consume their rent in kind, or after receiving it in money, expend it in agricultural produce: that is, they only suffer as consumers of agricultural produce, and in common with all the other consumers. Considered as landlords, they have the same income as before; the tithe, therefore, falls on the consumer, and not on the landlord.

The same effect would be produced on rent, if the tax, instead of being a fixed proportion of the produce, were a fixed sum per quarter or per bushel. A tax which takes a shilling for every bushel, takes more shillings from one field than from another, just in proportion as it produces more bushels; and operates exactly like tithe, expect that tithe is not only the same proportion on all lands, but is also the same proportion at all times, while a fixed sum of money per bushel will amount to a greater or a less proportion, according as corn is cheap or dear.

There are other modes of taxing agriculture, which would affect rent differently. A tax proportioned to the rent would fall wholly on the rent, and would not at all raise the price of corn, which is regulated by the portion of the produce that pays no rent. A fixed tax of so much per cultivated acre, without distinction of value, would have effects directly the reverse. Taking no more from the best qualities of land than from the worst, it would leave the differences the same as before, and consequently the same corn-rents, and the landlords would profit to the full extent of the rise of price. To put the thing in another manner; the price must rise sufficiently to enable the worst land to pay the tax; thus enabling all lands which produce more than the worst, to pay not only the tax, but also an increased rent to the landlords. These, however, are not so much taxes on the produce of land, as taxes on the land itself. Taxes on the produce, properly so called, whether fixed or *ad valorem*, do not affect rent, but fall on the consumer: profits, however, generally bearing either the whole or the greatest part of the portion which is levied on the consumption of the labouring classes.

§4. The preceding is, I apprehend, a correct statement of the manner in which taxes on agricultural produce operate when first laid on. When, however, they are of old standing, their effect may be different, as was first pointed out, I believe, by Mr Senior. It is, as we have seen, an almost infallible consequence of any reduction of profits, to retard the rate of accumulation. Now the effect of accumulation, when attended by its usual accompaniment, an increase of population, is to increase the value and price of food, to raise rent, and to lower profits: that is, to do precisely what is done by a tax on agricultural produce, except that this does not raise rent. The tax, therefore, merely anticipates the rise of price, and fall of profits, which would have taken place ultimately through the mere progress of accumulation; while it at the same time prevents, or at least retards, that progress. If the rate of profit was such, previous to the imposition of a tithe, that the effect of the tithe reduces it to the practical minimum, the tithe will put a stop to all further accumulation, or cause it to take place out of the country; and the only effect which the tithe will then have had on the consumer, is to make him pay earlier the price which he would have had to pay somewhat later – part of which, indeed, in the gradual progress of wealth and population, he would have almost immediately begun to pay. After a lapse of time which would have admitted of a rise of one-tenth through the natural progress of wealth, the consumer will be paying no more that he would have paid if the tithe had never existed; he will have ceased to pay any portion of it, and the person who will really pay it is the landlord, whom it deprives of the increase of rent which would by that time have accrued to him. At every successive point in this interval of time, less of the burthen will rest on the consumer, and more of it on the landlord: and in the ultimate result, the minimum of profits will be reached with a smaller capital and population, and a lower rental, than if the course of things had not been disturbed by the imposition of the tax. If, on the other hand, the tithe or other tax on agricultural produce does not reduce profits to the minimum, but to something above the minimum, accumulation will not be stopped, but only slackened: and if population also increases, the two-fold increase will continue to produce its effects – a rise of the price of corn, and an increase of rent. These consequences, however, will not take place with the same rapidity as if the higher rate of profit had continued. At the end of twenty years the country will have a smaller population and capital, than, but for the tax, it would by that time have had; the landlords will have a smaller rent; and the price of corn, having increased less rapidly than it would otherwise have done, will not be so much as a tenth higher than what, if there had been no tax, it would by that time have become. A part of the tax, therefore, will already have ceased to fall on the consumer, and devolved upon the landlord; and the proportion will become greater and greater by lapse of time.

Mr Senior illustrates this view of the subject by likening the effects of tithes, or other taxes on agricultural produce to those of natural sterility of soil. If the land of a country without access to foreign supplies, were suddenly smitten with a permanent deterioration of quality, to an extent which would make a tenth more labour necessary to raise the existing produce, the price of corn would undoubtedly rise one-tenth. But it cannot hence be inferred that if the soil of the country had from the beginning been one-tenth worse than it is, corn would at present have been one-tenth dearer than we find it. It is far more probable, that the smaller return to labour and capital, ever since the first settlement of the country, would have caused in each successive generation a less rapid increase than has taken place: that the country would now have contained less capital, and maintained a smaller population, so that notwithstanding the inferiority of the soil, the price of corn would not have been higher, nor profits lower, than at present; rent alone would certainly have been lower. We may suppose two islands, which, being alike in extent, in natural fertility, and industrial advancement, have up to a certain time been equal in population and capital, and have had equal rentals, and the same price of corn. Let us imagine a tithe imposed in one of these islands, but not in the other. There will be immediately a difference in the price of corn, and therefore probably in profits. While profits are not tending downwards in either country, that is, while improvements in the production of necessaries fully keep pace with the increase of population, this difference of prices and profits between the islands may continue. But if, in the untithed island, capital increases, and population along with it, more than enough to counterbalance any improvements which take place, the price of corn will gradually rise, profits will fall, and rent will increase; while in the tithed island capital and population will either not increase (beyond what is balanced by the improvements), or if they do, will increase in a less degree; so that rent and the price of corn will either not rise at all, or rise more slowly. Rent, therefore, will soon be higher in the untithed than in the tithed island, and profits not so much higher, nor corn so much cheaper, as they were on the first imposition of the tithe. These effects will be progressive. At the end of every ten years there will be a greater difference between the rentals and between the aggregate wealth and population of the two islands, and a less difference in profits and in the price of corn.

At what point will these last differences entirely cease, and the temporary effect of taxes on agricultural produce, in raising the price, have entirely given place to the ultimate effect, that of limiting the total produce of the country? Though the untithed island is always verging towards the point at which the price of food would overtake that in the tithed island, its progress towards that point naturally slackens as it draws nearer to attaining it; since – the difference between the two islands in the rapidity of accumulation depending upon the difference in the rates of profit – in proportion as these approximate, the movement which draws them closer together, abates of its force. The one may not actually overtake the other, until both islands reach the minimum of profits: up to that point, the tithed island may continue more or less ahead of the untithed island in the price of corn: considerably ahead if it is far from the minimum, and is therefore accumulating rapidly; very little ahead if it is near the minimum, and accumulating slowly.

But whatever is true of the tithed and untithed islands in our hypothetical case, is true of any country having a tithe, compared with the same country if it had never had a tithe.

In England the great emigration of capital, and the almost periodical occurrence of commercial crises through the speculations occasioned by the habitually low rate of profit, are indications that profit has attained the practical, though not the ultimate minimum, and that all the savings which take place (beyond what improvements, tending to the cheapening of necessaries, make room for) are either sent abroad for investment, or periodically swept away. There can therefore, I think, be little doubt that if England had never had a tithe, or any tax on agricultural produce, the price of corn would have been by this time as high, and the rate of profits as low, as at present. Independently of the more rapid accumulation which would have taken place if profits had not been prematurely lowered by these imposts; the mere saving of a part of the capital which has been wasted in unsuccessful speculations, and the keeping at home a part of that which has been sent abroad, would have been quite sufficient to produce the effect. I think, therefore, with Mr Senior, that the tithe, even before its commutation, had ceased to be a cause of high prices or low profits, and had become a mere deduction from rent; its other effects being, that it caused the country to have no greater capital, no larger production, and no more numerous population than if it had been one-tenth less fertile than it is; or let us rather say one-twentieth (considering how great a portion of the land of Great Britain was tithe-free).

But though tithes and other taxes on agricultural produce, when of long standing, either do not raise the price of food and lower profits at all, or if at all, not in proportion to the tax; yet the abrogation of such taxes, when they exist, does not the less diminish price, and, in general, raise the rate of profit. The abolition of a tithe takes one-tenth from the cost of production, and consequently from the price, of all agricultural produce; and unless it permanently raises the labourer's requirements, it lowers the cost of labour, and raises profits. Rent, estimated in money or in commodities, generally remains as before; estimated in agricultural produce, it is raised. The country adds as much by the repeal of a tithe, to the margin which intervenes between it and the stationary state, as is cut off from that margin by a tithe when first imposed. Accumulation is greatly accelerated; and if population also increases, the price of corn immediately begins to recover itself, and rent to rise; thus gradually transferring the benefit of the remission, from the consumer to the landlord.

The effects which thus result from abolishing tithe, result equally from what has been done by the arrangements under the Commutation Act for converting it into a rent-charge. When the tax, instead of being levied on the whole produce of the soil, is levied only from the portions which pay rent, and does not touch any fresh extension of cultivation, the tax no longer forms any part of the cost of production of the portion of the produce which regulates the price of all the rest. The land or capital which pays no rent, can now send its produce to market one-tenth cheaper. The commutation of tithe ought therefore to have produced a considerable fall in the average price of corn. If it had not come so gradually into operation, and if the price of corn had not during the same period been under the influence of several other causes of change, the effect would probably have been markedly conspicuous. As it is, there can be no doubt that this circumstance has had its share in the fall which has taken place in the cost of production and in the price of home-grown produce; though the effects of the great agricultural improvements which have been simultaneously advancing, and of the free admission of agricultural produce from foreign countries, have masked those of the other cause. This fall of price would not in itself have any tendency injurious to the landlord, since corn-rents are increased in the same ratio in which the price of corn is diminished. But neither does it in any way tend to increase his income. The rent-charge, therefore, which is substituted for tithe, is a dead loss to him at the expiration of existing leases: and the commutation of tithe was not a mere alteration in the mode in which the landlord bore an existing burthen, but the imposition of a new one; relief being afforded to the consumer at the expense of the landlord, who, however, begins immediately to receive progressive indemnification at the consumer's expense, by the impulse given to accumulation and population.

§5. We have hitherto inquired into the effects of taxes on commodities, on the assumption that they are levied impartially on every mode in which the commodity can be produced or brought to market. Another class of considerations is opened, if we suppose that this impartiality is not maintained, and that the tax is imposed, not on the commodity, but on some particular mode of obtaining it.

Suppose that a commodity is capable of being made by two different processes; as a manufactured commodity may be produced either by hand or by steam-power; sugar may be made either from the sugar-cane or from beet-root, cattle fattened either on hay and green crops, or on oil-cake and the refuse of breweries. It is the interest of the community, that of the two methods, producers should adopt that which produces the best article at the lowest price. This being also the interest of the producers, unless protected against competition, and shielded from the penalties of indolence; the process most advantageous to the community is that which, if not interfered with by government, they ultimately find it to their advantage to adopt. Suppose however that a tax is laid on one of the processes, and no tax at all, or one of smaller amount, on the other. If the taxed process is the one which the producers would not have adopted, the measure is simply nugatory. But if the tax falls, as it is of course intended to do, upon the one which they would have adopted, it creates an artificial motive for preferring the untaxed process, though the inferior of the two. If, therefore, it has any effect at all, it causes the commodity to be produced of worse quality, or at a greater expense of labour; it causes so much of the labour of the community to be wasted, and the capital employed in supporting and remunerating the labour to be expended as uselessly, as if it were spent in hiring men to dig holes and fill them up again. This waste of labour and capital constitutes an addition to the cost of production of the commodity, which raises its value and price in a corresponding ratio, and thus the owners of the capital are indemnified. The loss falls on the consumers; though the capital of the country is also eventually diminished, by the diminution of their means of saving, and in some degree, of their inducements to save.

The kind of tax, therefore, which comes under the general denomination of a discriminating duty, transgresses the rule that taxes should take as little as possible from the tax-payer beyond what they bring into the treasury of the state. A discriminating duty makes the consumer pay two distinct taxes, only one of which is paid to the government, and that frequently the less onerous of the two. If a tax were laid on sugar produced from the cane, leaving the sugar from beet-root untaxed, then in so far as cane sugar continued to be used, the tax on it would be paid to the treasury, and might be as objectionable as most other taxes; but if cane sugar, having previously been cheaper than beet-root sugar, was now dearer, and beet-root sugar was to any considerable amount substituted for it, and fields laid out and manufactories established in consequence, the government would gain no revenue from the beet-root sugar, while the consumers of it would pay a real tax. They would pay for beet-root sugar more than they had previously paid for cane sugar, and the difference would go to indemnify producers for a portion of the labour of the country actually thrown away, in producing by the labour of (say) three hundred men, what could be obtained by the other process with the labour of two hundred.

One of the commonest cases of discriminating duties, is that of a tax on the importation of a commodity capable of being produced at home, unaccompanied by an equivalent tax on the home production. A commodity is never permanently imported, unless it can be obtained from abroad at a smaller cost of labour and capital on the whole, than is necessary for producing it. If, therefore, by a duty on the importation, it is rendered cheaper to produce the article than to import it, an extra quantity of labour and capital is expended, without any extra result. The labour is useless, and the capital is spent in paying people for laboriously doing nothing. All custom duties which operate as an encouragement to the home production of the taxed article, are thus an eminently wasteful mode of raising a revenue.

This character belongs in a peculiar degree to custom duties on the produce of land, unless countervailed by excise duties on the home production. Such taxes bring less into the public treasury, compared with what they take from the consumers, than any other imposts to which civilized nations are usually subject. If the wheat produced in a country is twenty millions of quarters, and the consumption twenty-one millions, a million being annually imported, and if on this million a duty is laid which raises the price ten shillings per quarter, the price which is raised is not that of the million only, but of the whole twenty-one millions. Taking the most favourable, but extremely improbable supposition, that the importation is not at all checked, nor the home production enlarged, the state gains a revenue of only half a million, while the consumers are taxed ten millions and a half; the ten millions being a contribution to the home growers, who are forced by competition to resign it all to the landlords. The consumer thus pays to the owners of land an additional tax, equal to twenty times that which he pays to the state. Let us now suppose that the tax really checks importation. Suppose importation stopped altogether in ordinary years; it being found that the million of quarters can be obtained, by a more elaborate cultivation, or by breaking up inferior land, at a less advance than ten shillings upon the previous price – say, for instance, five shillings a quarter. The revenue now obtains nothing, except from the extraordinary imports which may happen to take place in a season of scarcity. But the consumers pay every year a tax of five shillings on the whole twenty-one millions of quarters, amounting to 5¼ millions sterling. Of this the odd 250,000*l.* goes to compensate the growers of the last million of quarters for the labour and capital wasted under the compulsion of the law. The remaining five millions go to enrich the landlords as before.

Such is the operation of what are technically termed Corn Laws, when first laid on; and such continues to be their operation, so long as they have any effect at all in raising the price of corn. But I am by no means of opinion that in the long run they keep up either prices or rents in the degree which these considerations might lead us to suppose. What we have said respecting the effect of tithes and other taxes on agricultural produce, applies in a great degree to corn laws: they anticipate artificially a rise of price and of rent, which would at all events have taken place through the increase of population and of production. The difference between a country without corn laws, and a country which has long had corn laws, is not so much that the last has a higher price or a larger rental, but that it has the same price and the same rental with a smaller aggregate capital and a smaller population. The imposition of corn laws raises rents, but retards that progress of accumulation which would in no long period have raised them fully as much. The repeal of corn laws tends to lower rents, but it unchains a force which, in a progressive state of capital and population, restores and even increases the former amount. There is every reason to expect that under the virtually free importation of agricultural produce, at last extorted from the ruling powers of this country, the price of food, if population goes on increasing, will gradually but steadily rise; though this effect may for a time be postponed by the strong current which in this country has set in (and the impulse is extending itself to other countries) towards the improvement of agricultural science, and its increased application to practice.

What we have said of duties on importation generally, is equally applicable to discriminating duties which favour importation from one place or in one particular manner, in contradistinction to others: such as the preference given to the produce of a colony, or of a country with which there is a commercial treaty: or the higher duties formerly imposed by our navigation laws on goods imported in other than British shipping. Whatever else may be alleged in favour of such distinctions, whenever they are not nugatory, they are economically wasteful. They induce a resort to a more costly mode of obtaining a commodity, in lieu of one less costly, and thus cause a portion of the labour which the country employs in providing itself with foreign commodities, to be sacrificed without return.

§6. There is one more point relating to the operation of taxes on commodities conveyed from one country to another, which requires notice: the influence which they exert on international exchanges. Every tax on a commodity tends to raise its price, and consequently to lessen the demand for it in the market in which it is sold. All taxes on international trade tend, therefore, to produce a disturbance and a readjustment of what we have termed the Equation of International Demand. This consideration leads to some rather curious consequences, which have been pointed out in the separate essay on International Commerce, already several times referred to in this treatise.[2]

Taxes on foreign trade are of two kinds – taxes on imports, and on exports. On the first aspect of the matter it would seem that both these taxes are paid by the consumers of the commodity; that taxes on exports consequently fall entirely on foreigners, taxes on imports wholly on the home consumer. The true state of the case, however, is much more complicated.

'By taxing exports, we may, in certain circumstances, produce a division of the advantage of the trade more favourable to ourselves. In some cases we may draw into our coffers, at the expense of foreigners, not only the whole tax, but more than the tax: in other cases, we should gain exactly the tax; in others, less than the tax. In this last case, a part of the tax is borne by ourselves: possibly the whole, possibly even, as we shall show, more than the whole.'

Reverting to the supposititious case employed in the Essay, of a trade between Germany and England in broadcloth and linen, 'suppose that England taxes her export of cloth, the tax not being supposed high enough to induce Germany to produce cloth for

2. [Mill is referring here to his essay on this topic in *Some Unsettled Questions in Political Economy*.]

herself. The price at which cloth can be sold in Germany is augmented by the tax. This will probably diminish the quantity consumed. It may diminish it so much that, even at the increased price, there will not be required so great a money value as before. Or it may not diminish it at all, or so little, that in consequence of the higher price, a greater money value will be purchased than before. In this last case, England will gain, at the expense of Germany, not only the whole amount of the duty, but more; for, the money value of her exports to Germany being increased, while her imports remain the same, money will flow into England from Germany. The price of cloth will rise in England, and consequently in Germany; but the price of linen will fall in Germany, and consequently in England. We shall export less cloth, and import more linen, till the equilibrium is restored. It thus appears (what is at first sight somewhat remarkable) that by taxing her exports, England would, in some conceivable circumstances, not only gain from her foreign customers the whole amount of the tax, but would also get her imports cheaper. She would get them cheaper in two ways; for she would obtain them for less money, and would have more money to purchase them with. Germany, on the other hand, would suffer doubly: she would have to pay for her cloth a price increased not only by the duty, but by the influx of money into England, while the same change in the distribution of the circulating medium would leave her less money to purchase it with.

'This, however, is only one of three possible cases. If, after the imposition of the duty, Germany requires so diminished a quantity of cloth, that its total value is exactly the same as before, the balance of trade would be undisturbed; England will gain the duty, Germany will lose it, and nothing more. If, again, the imposition of the duty occasions such a falling off in the demand that Germany requires a less pecuniary value than before, our exports will no longer pay for our imports; money must pass from England into Germany; and Germany's share of the advantage of the trade will be increased. By the change in the distribution of money, cloth will fall in England; and therefore it will, of course, fall in Germany. Thus Germany will not pay the whole of the tax. From the same cause, linen will rise in Germany, and consequently in England. When this alteration of prices has so adjusted the demand, that the cloth and the linen again pay for one another, the result is that Germany has paid only a part of the tax, and the remainder of what has been received into our treasury has come indirectly out of the pockets of our own consumers of linen, who pay a higher price for that imported commodity in consequence of the tax on our exports, while at the same time they, in consequence of the efflux of money and the fall of prices, have smaller money incomes wherewith to pay for the linen at that advanced price.

'It is not an impossible supposition that by taxing our exports we might not only gain nothing from the foreigner, the tax being paid out of our own pockets, but might even compel our own people to pay a second tax to the foreigner. Suppose, as before, that the demand of Germany for cloth falls off so much on the imposition of the duty, that she requires a smaller money value than before, but that the case is so different with linen in England, that when the price rises the demand either does not fall off at all, or so little that the money value required is greater than before. The first effect of laying on the duty is, as before, that the cloth exported will no longer pay for the linen imported. Money will therefore flow out of England into Germany. One effect is to raise the price of linen in Germany, and consequently in England. But this, by the supposition, instead of stopping the efflux of money, only makes it greater, because the higher the price, the greater the money value of the linen consumed. The balance, therefore, can only be restored by the other effect, which is going on at the same time, namely, the fall of cloth in the English and consequently in the German market. Even when cloth has fallen so low that its price with the duty is only equal to what its price without the duty was at first, it is not a necessary consequence that the fall will stop; for the same amount of exportation as before will not now suffice to pay the increased money value of the imports; and although the German consumers have now not only cloth at the old price, but likewise increased money incomes, it is not certain that they will be inclined to employ the increase of their incomes in increasing their purchases of cloth. The price of cloth, therefore, must perhaps fall, to restore the equilibrium, more than the whole amount of the duty; Germany may be enabled to import cloth at a lower price when it is taxed, than when it was untaxed: and this gain she will acquire at the expense of the English consumers of linen, who, in addition, will be the real payers of the whole of what is received at their own custom-house under the name of duties on the export of cloth.'

It is almost unnecessary to remark that cloth and linen are here merely representatives of exports and imports in general; and that the effect which a tax on exports might have in increasing the costs of imports, would affect the imports from all countries, and not peculiarly the articles which might be imported from the particular country to which the taxed exports were sent.

'Such are the extremely various effects which may result to ourselves and to our customers from the imposition of taxes on our exports; and the determining circumstances are of a nature so imperfectly ascertainable, that it must be almost impossible to decide with any certainty, even after the tax has been imposed, whether we have been gainers by it or losers.' In general however there could be little doubt that a country which imposed such taxes would succeed in making foreign countries contribute something to its revenue; but unless the taxed article be one for which their demand is extremely urgent, they will seldom pay the whole of the amount which the tax brings in.[3] 'In any case, whatever we gain is lost by somebody else, and there is the expense of the collection besides: if international morality, therefore, were rightly understood and acted upon, such taxes, as being contrary to the universal weal, would not exist.'

Thus far of duties on exports. We now proceed to the more ordinary case of duties on imports. 'We have had an example

3. Probably the strongest known instance of a large revenue raised from foreigners by a tax on exports, is the opium trade with China. The high price of the article under the Government monopoly (which is equivalent to a high export duty) has so little effect in discouraging its consumption, that it is said to have been occasionally sold in China for as much as its weight in silver.

of a tax on exports, that is, on foreigners, falling in part on ourselves. We shall therefore not be surprised if we find a tax on imports, that is, on ourselves, partly falling upon foreigners.

'Instead of taxing the cloth which we export, suppose that we tax the linen which we import. The duty which we are now supposing must not be what is termed a protecting duty, that is, a duty sufficiently high to induce us to produce the article at home. If it had this effect, it would destroy entirely the trade both in cloth and in linen, and both countries would lose the whole of the advantage which they previously gained by exchanging those commodiities with one another. We suppose a duty which might diminish the consumption of the article, but which would not prevent us from continuing to import, as before, whatever linen we did consume.

'The equilibrium of trade would be disturbed if the imposition of the tax diminished, in the slightest degree, the quantity of linen consumed. For, as the tax is levied at our own customhouse, the German exporter only receives the same price as formerly, though the English consumer pays a higher one. If, therefore, there be any diminution of the quantity bought, although a larger sum of money may be actually laid out in the article, a smaller one will be due from England to Germany: this sum will no longer be an equivalent for the sum due from Germany to England for cloth, the balance therefore must be paid in money. Prices will fall in Germany and rise in England; linen will fall in the German market; cloth will rise in the English. The Germans will pay a higher price for cloth, and will have smaller money incomes to buy it with; while the English will obtain linen cheaper, that is, its price will exceed what it previously was by less than the amount of the duty, while their means of purchasing it will be increased by the increase of their money incomes.

'If the imposition of the tax does not diminish the demand, it will leave the trade exactly as it was before. We shall import as much, and export as much; the whole of the tax will be paid out of our own pockets.

'But the imposition of a tax on a commodity almost always diminishes the demand more or less; and it can never, or scarcely ever, increase the demand. It may, therefore, be laid down as a principle, that a tax on imported commodities, when it really operates as a tax, and not as a prohibition either total or partial, almost always falls in part upon the foreigners who consume our goods; and that this is a mode in which a nation may appropriate to itself, at the expense of foreigners, a larger share than would otherwise belong to it of the increase in the general productiveness of the labour and capital of the world, which results from the interchange of commodities among nations.'

Those are, therefore, in the right who maintain that taxes on imports are partly paid by foreigners; but they are mistaken when they say, that is is by the foreign producer. It is not on the person from whom we buy, but on all those who buy from us, that a portion of our custom-duties spontaneously falls. It is the foreign consumer of our exported commodities, who is obliged to pay a higher price for them because we maintain revenue duties on foreign goods.

There are but two cases in which duties on commodities can in any degree, or in any manner, fall on the producer. One is, when the article is a strict monopoly, and at a scarcity price. The price in this case being only limited by the desires of the buyer; the sum obtained from the restricted supply being the utmost which the buyers would consent to give rather than go without it; if the treasury intercepts a part of this, the price cannot be further raised to compensate for the tax, and it must be paid from the monopoly profits. A tax on rare and high-priced wines will fall wholly on the growers, or rather, on the owners of the vineyards. The second case in which the producer sometimes bears a portion of the tax, is more important: the case of duties on the produce of land or of mines. These might be so high as to diminish materially the demand for the produce, and compel the abandonment of some of the inferior qualities of land or mines. Supposing this to be the effect, the consumers, both in the country itself and in those which dealt with it, would obtain the produce at smaller cost; and a part only, instead of the whole, of the duty would fall on the purchaser, who would be indemnified chiefly at the expense of the landowners or mine-owners in the producing country.

Duties on importation may, then, be divided 'into two classes: those which have the effect of encouraging some particular branch of domestic industry, and those which have not. The former are purely mischievous, both to the country imposing them, and to those with whom it trades. They prevent a saving of labour and capital, which, if permitted to be made, would be divided in some proportion or other between the importing country and the countries which buy what that country does or might export.

'The other class of duties are those which do not encourage one mode of procuring an article at the expense of another, but allow interchange to take place just as if the duty did not exist, and to produce the saving of labour which constitutes the motive to international, as to all other commerce. Of this kind are duties on the importation of any commodity which could not by any possibility be produced at home; and duties not sufficiently high to counterbalance the difference of expense between the production of the article at home and its importation. Of the money which is brought into the treasury of any country by taxes of this last description, a part only is paid by the people of that country; the remainder by the foreign consumers of their goods.

'Nevertheless, this latter kind of taxes are in principle as ineligible as the former, though not precisely on the same ground. A protecting duty can never be a cause of gain, but always and necessarily of loss, to the country imposing it, just so far as it is efficacious to its end. A non-protecting duty, on the contrary, would in most cases be a source of gain to the country imposing it, in so far as throwing part of the weight of its taxes upon other people is a gain; but it would be a means which it could seldom be advisable to adopt, being so easily counteracted by a precisely similar proceeding on the other side.

'If England, in the case already supposed, sought to obtain for herself more than her natural share of the advantage of the trade with Germany, by imposing a duty upon linen, Germany would only have to impose a duty upon cloth, sufficient to diminish the demand for that article about as much as the demand for linen had been diminished in England by the tax.

Things would then be as before, and each country would pay its own tax. Unless, indeed, the sum of the two duties exceeded the entire advantage of the trade; for in that case the trade, and its advantage, would cease entirely.

'There would be no advantage, therefore, in imposing duties of this kind, with a view to gain by them in the manner which has been pointed out. But when any part of the revenue is derived from taxes on commodities, these may often be as little objectionable as the rest. It is evident, too, that considerations of reciprocity, which are quite unessential when the matter in debate is a protecting duty, are of material importance when the repeal of duties of this other description is discussed. A country cannot be expected to renounce the power of taxing foreigners, unless foreigners will in return practise towards itself the same forbearance. The only mode in which a country can save itself from being a loser by the revenue duties imposed by other countries on its commodities, is to impose corresponding revenue duties on theirs. Only it must take care that those duties be not so high as to exceed all that remains of the advantage of the trade, and put an end to importation altogether, causing the article to be either produced at home, or imported from another and a dearer market.'

CHAPTER V

Of Some Other Taxes

§1. BESIDES direct taxes on income, and taxes on consumption, the financial systems of most countries comprise a variety of miscellaneous imposts, not strictly included in either class. The modern European systems retain many such taxes, though in much less number and variety than those semi-barbarous governments which European influence has not yet reached. In some of these, scarcely any incident of life has escaped being made an excuse for some fiscal exaction; hardly any act, not belonging to daily routine, can be performed by any one, without obtaining leave from some agent of government, which is only granted in consideration of a payment: especially when the act requires the aid or the peculiar guarantee of a public authority. In the present treatise we may confine our attention to such taxes as lately existed, or still exist, in countries usually classed as civilized.

In almost all nations a considerable revenue is drawn from taxes on contracts. These are imposed in various forms. One expedient is that of taxing the legal instrument which serves as evidence of the contract, and which is commonly the only evidence legally admissible. In England, scarcely any contract is binding unless executed on stamped paper, which has paid a tax to government; and until very lately, when the contract related to property the tax was proportionally much heavier on the smaller than on the larger transactions; which is still true of some of those taxes. There are also stamp-duties on the legal instruments which are evidence of the fulfilment of contracts; such as acknowledgments of receipt, and deeds of release. Taxes on contracts are not always levied by means of stamps. The duty on sales by auction, abrogated by Sir Robert Peel, was an instance in point. The taxes on transfers of landed property, in France, are another: in England there are stamp-duties. In some countries, contracts of many kinds are not valid unless registered, and their registration is made an occasion for a tax.

Of taxes on contracts, the most important are those on the transfer of property; chiefly on purchases and sales. Taxes on the sale of consumable commodities are simply taxes on those commodities. If they affect only some particular commodities, they raise the prices of those commodities, and are paid by the consumer. If the attempt were made to tax all purchases and sales, which, however absurd, was for centuries the law of Spain, the tax, if it could be enforced, would be equivalent to a tax on all commodities, and would not affect prices: if levied from the sellers, it would be a tax on profits, if from the buyers, a tax on consumption; and neither class could throw the burthen upon the other. If confined to some one mode of sale, as for example by auction, it discourages recourse to that mode, and if of any material amount, prevents it from being adopted at all, unless in a case of emergency; in which case as the seller is under a necessity to sell, but the buyer under no necessity to buy, the tax falls on the seller; and this was the strongest of the objections to the auction duty: it almost always fell on a necessitous person, and in the crisis of his necessities.

Taxes on the purchase and sale of land are, in most countries, liable to the same objection. Landed property in old countries is seldom parted with, except from reduced circumstances, or some urgent need: the seller, therefore, must take what he can get, while the buyer, whose object is an investment, makes his calculations on the interest which he can obtain for his money in other ways, and will not buy if he is charged with a government tax on the transaction.[1] It has indeed been objected, that this argument would not apply if all modes of permanent investment, such as the purchase of government securities, shares in joint-stock companies, mortgages, and the like, were subject to the same tax. But even then, if paid by the buyer, it would be equivalent to a tax on interest: if sufficiently heavy to be of any

---

1. The statement in the text requires modification in the case of countries where the land is owned in small portions. These, being neither a badge of importance, nor in general an object of local attachment, are readily parted with at a small advance on their original cost, with the intention of buying elsewhere; and the desire of acquiring land even on disadvantageous terms is so great, as to be little checked by even a high rate of taxation.

importance, it would disturb the established relation between interest and profit; and the disturbance would redress itself by a rise in the rate of interest, and a fall of the price of land and of all securities. It appears to me, therefore, that the seller is the person by whom such taxes, unless under peculiar circumstances, will generally be borne.

All taxes must be condemned which throw obstacles in the way of the sale of land, or other instruments of production. Such sales tend naturally to render the property more productive. The seller, whether moved by necessity or choice, is probably some one who is either without the means, or without the capacity, to make the most advantageous use of the property for productive purposes; while the buyer, on the other hand, is at any rate not needy, and is frequently both inclined and able to improve the property, since, as it is worth more to such a person than to any other, he is likely to offer the highest price for it. All taxes, therefore, and all difficulties and expenses, annexed to such contracts, are decidedly detrimental; especially in the case of land, the source of subsistence, and the original foundation of all wealth, on the improvement of which, therefore, so much depends. Too great facilities cannot be given to enable land to pass into the hands, and assume the modes of aggregation or division, most conducive to its productiveness. If landed properties are too large, alienation should be free, in order that they may be subdivided; if too small, in order that they may be united. All taxes on the transfer of landed property should be abolished; but, as the landlords have no claim to be relieved from any reservation which the state has hitherto made in its own favour from the amount of their rent, an annual impost equivalent to the average produce of these taxes should be distributed over the land generally, in the form of a land-tax.

Some of the taxes on contracts are very pernicious, imposing a virtual penalty upon transactions which it ought to be the policy of the legislator to encourage. Of this sort is the stamp-duty on leases, which in a country of large properties are an essential condition of good agriculture; and the taxes on insurances, a direct discouragement to prudence and forethought.

§2. Nearly allied to the taxes on contracts are those on communication. The principal of these is the postage tax; to which may be added taxes on advertisements, and on newspapers, which are taxes on the communication of information.

The common mode of levying a tax on the conveyance of letters, is by making the government the sole authorized carrier of them, and demanding a monopoly price. When this price is so moderate as it is in this country under the uniform penny postage, scarcely if at all exceeding what would be charged under the freest competition by any private company, it can hardly be considered as taxation, but rather as the profits of a business; whatever excess there is above the ordinary profits of stock being a fair result of the saving of expense, caused by having only one establishment and one set of arrangements for the whole country, instead of many competing ones. The business, too, being one which both can and ought to be conducted on fixed rules, is one of the few businesses which it is not unsuitable to a government to conduct. The post office, therefore, is at present one of the best of the sources from which this country derives its revenue. But a postage much exceeding what would be paid for the same service in a system of freedom, is not a desirable tax. Its chief weight falls on letters of business, and increases the expense of mercantile relations between distant places. It is like an attempt to raise a large revenue by heavy tolls: it obstructs all operations by which goods are conveyed from place to place, and discourages the production of commodities in one place for consumption in another; which is not only in itself one of the greatest sources of economy of labour, but is a necessary condition of almost all improvements in production, and one of the strongest stimulants to industry, and promoters of civilization.

The tax on advertisements was not free from the same objection, since in whatever degree advertisements are useful to business, by facilitating the coming together of the dealer or producer and the consumer, in that same degree, if the tax be high enough to be a serious discouragement to advertising, it prolongs the period during which goods remain unsold, and capital locked up in idleness.

A tax on newspapers is objectionable, not so much where it does fall as where is does not, that is, where it prevents newspapers from being used. To the generality of those who buy them, newspapers are a luxury which they can as well afford to pay for as any other indulgence, and which is as unexceptionable a source of revenue. But to that large part of the community who have been taught to read, but have received little other intellectual education, newspapers are the source of nearly all the general information which they possess, and of nearly all their acquaintance with the ideas and topics current among mankind; and an interest is more easily excited in newspapers, than in books or other more recondite sources of instruction. Newspapers contribute so little, in a direct way, to the origination of useful ideas, that many persons undervalue the importance of their office in disseminating them. They correct many prejudices and superstitions, and keep up a habit of discussion, and interest in public concerns, the absence of which is a great cause of stagnation of mind usually found in the lower and middle, if not in all, ranks, of those countries where newspapers of an important or interesting character do not exist. There ought to be no taxes (as in this country there now are not) which render this great diffuser of information, of mental excitement, and mental exercise, less accessible to that portion of the public which most needs to be carried into a region of ideas and interests beyond its own limited horizon.

§3. In the enumeration of bad taxes, a conspicuous place must be assigned to law taxes; which extract a revenue for the state from the various operations involved in an application to the tribunals. Like all needless expenses attached to law proceedings, they are a tax on redress, and therefore a premium on injury. Although such taxes have been abolished in this country as a general source of revenue, they still exist in the form of fees of court, for defraying the expense of the courts of justice; under the idea, apparently, that those may fairly be required to bear the expenses of the administration of justice, who reap the benefit of it. The fallacy of this doctrine was powerfully exposed by Bentham. As he remarked, those who are under the necessity of going to law, are those who benefit least, not most, by the law and its administration. To them the protection which the law affords has not been complete, since they have been obliged to resort to a court of justice to ascertain their rights, or maintain those rights against infringement: while the remainder of the public have enjoyed the immunity from injury conferred by the law and the tribunals, without the inconvenience of an appeal to them.

§4. Besides the general taxes of the State, there are in all or most countries local taxes, to defray any expenses of a public nature which it is thought best to place under the control or management of a local authority. Some of these expenses are incurred for purposes in which the particular locality is solely or chiefly interested; as the paving, cleansing, and lighting of the streets; or the making and repairing of roads and bridges, which may be important to people from any part of the country, but only in so far as they, or goods in which they have an interest, pass along the roads or over the bridges. In other cases again, the expenses are of a kind as nationally important as any others, but are defrayed locally because supposed more likely to be well administered by local bodies; as, in England, the relief of the poor, and the support of gaols, and in some other countries, of schools. To decide for what public objects local superintendence is best suited, and what are those which should be kept immediately under the central government, or under a mixed system of local management and central superintendence, is a question not of political economy, but of administration. It is an important principle, however, that taxes imposed by a local authority, being less amenable to publicity and discussion than the acts of the government, should always be special – laid on for some definite service, and not exceeding the expense actually incurred in rendering the service. Thus limited, it is desirable, whenever practicable, that the burthen should fall on those to whom the service is rendered; that the expense, for instance, of roads and bridges, should be defrayed by a toll on passengers and goods conveyed by them, thus dividing the cost between those who use them for pleasure or convenience, and the consumers of the goods which they enable to be brought to and from the market at a diminished expense. When, however, the tolls have repaid with interest the whole of the expenditure, the road or bridge should be thrown open free of toll, that it may be used also by those to whom, unless open gratuitously, it would be valueless; provision being made for repairs either from the funds of the state, or by a rate levied on the localities which reap the principal benefit.

In England, almost all local taxes are direct, (the coal duty of the City of London, and a few similar imposts, being the chief exceptions), though the greatest part of the taxation for general purposes is indirect. On the contrary, in France, Austria, and other countries where direct taxation is much more largely employed by the state, the local expenses of towns are principally defrayed by taxes levied on commodities when entering them. These indirect taxes are much more objectionable in towns than on the frontier, because the things which the country supplies to the towns are chiefly the necessaries of life and the materials of manufacture, while, of what a country imports from foreign countries, the greater part usually consists of luxuries. An octroi cannot produce a large revenue, without pressing severely upon the labouring classes of the towns; unless their wages rise proportionally, in which case the tax falls in a great measure on the consumers of town produce, whether residing in town or country, since capital will not remain in the towns if its profits fall below their ordinary proportion as compared with the rural districts.

CHAPTER VI

Comparison between Direct and Indirect Taxation

§1. ARE direct or indirect taxes the most eligible? This question, at all times interesting, has of late excited a considerable amount of discussion. In England there is a popular feeling, of old standing, in favour of indirect, or it should rather be said in opposition to direct, taxation. The feeling is not grounded on the merits of the case, and is of a puerile kind. An Englishman dislikes, not so much the payment, as the act of paying. He dislikes seeing the face of the tax-collector, and being subjected to his peremptory demand. Perhaps, too, the money which he is required to pay directly out of his pocket is the only taxation which he is quite sure that he pays at all. That a tax of one shilling per pound on tea, or of two shillings per bottle on wine, raises the price of each pound of tea and bottle of wine which he consumes, by that and more than that amount, cannot indeed be denied; it is the fact, and is intended to be so, and he himself, at times, is perfectly aware of it; but it makes hardly any impression on his practical feelings and associations, serving to illustrate the distinction between what is merely known to be true and what is felt to be so. The unpopularity of direct taxation, contrasted with the easy manner in which the public consent to let themselves be fleeced in the prices of commodities, has generated in many friends of improvement a directly opposite mode of thinking to the foregoing. They contend that the very reason which makes direct taxation disagreeable, makes it preferable. Under it, every one knows how much he really pays; and if he votes for a war, or any other expensive national luxury, he does so with his eyes open to what it costs him. If all taxes were direct, taxation would be much more perceived than at present; and there would be a security which now there is not, for economy in the public expenditure.

Although this argument is not without force, its weight is

likely to be constantly diminishing. The real incidence of indirect taxation is every day more generally understood and more familiarly recognized: and whatever else may be said of the changes which are taking place in the tendencies of the human mind, it can scarcely, I think, be denied, that things are more and more estimated according to their calculated value, and less according to their non-essential accompaniments. The mere distinction between paying money directly to the tax-collector, and contributing the same sum through the intervention of the tea-dealer or the wine-merchant, no longer makes the whole difference between dislike or opposition, and passive acquiescence. But further, while any such infirmity of the popular mind subsists, the argument grounded on it tells partly on the other side of the question. If our present revenue of about seventy millions were all raised by direct taxes, an extreme dissatisfaction would certainly arise at having to pay so much; but while men's minds are so little guided by reason, as such a change of feeling from so irrelevant a cause would imply, so great an aversion to taxation might not be an unqualified good. Of the seventy millions in question, nearly thirty are pledged, under the most binding obligations, to those whose property has been borrowed and spent by the state: and while this debt remains unredeemed, a greatly increased impatience of taxation would involve no little danger of a breach of faith, similar to that which, in the defaulting states of America, has been produced, and in some of them still continues, from the same cause. That part, indeed, of the public expenditure, which is devoted to the maintenance of civil and military establishments, (that is, all except the interest of the national debt,) affords, in many of its details, ample scope for retrenchment. But while much of the revenue is wasted under the mere pretence of public service, so much of the most important business of government is left undone, that whatever can be rescued from useless expenditure is urgently required for useful. Whether the object be education; a more efficient and accessible administration of justice; reforms of any kind which, like the Slave Emancipation, require compensation to individual interests; or what is as important as any of these, the entertainment of a sufficient staff of able and educated public servants, to conduct in a better than the present awkward manner the business of legislation and administration; every one of these things implies considerable expense, and many of them have again and again been prevented by the reluctance which existed to apply to Parliament for an increased grant of public money, though (besides that the existing means would probably be sufficient if applied to the proper purposes) the cost would be repaid, often a hundredfold, in mere pecuniary advantage to the community generally. If so great an addition were made to the public dislike of taxation as might be the consequence of confining it to the direct form, the classes who profit by the misapplication of public money might probably succeed in saving that by which they profit, at the expense of that which would only be useful to the public.

There is, however, a frequent plea in support of indirect taxation, which must be altogether rejected, as grounded on a fallacy. We are often told that taxes on commodities are less burthensome than other taxes, because the contributor can escape from them by ceasing to use the taxed commodity. He certainly can, if that be his object, deprive the government of the money: but he does so by a sacrifice of his own indulgences, which (if he chose to undergo it) would equally make up to him for the same amount taken from him by direct taxation. Suppose a tax laid on wine, sufficient to add five pounds to the price of the quantity of wine which he consumes in a year. He has only (we are told) to diminish his consumption of wine by 5*l.,* and he escapes the burthen. True: but if the 5*l.,* instead of being laid on wine, had been taken from him by an income tax, he could, by expending 5*l.* less in wine, equally save the amount of the tax, so that the difference between the two cases is really illusory. If the government takes from the contributor five pounds a year, whether in one way or another, exactly that amount must be retrenched from his consumption to leave him as well off as before; and in either way the same amount of sacrifice, neither more nor less, is imposed on him.

On the other hand, it is some advantage on the side of indirect taxes, that what they exact from the contributor is taken at a time and in a manner likely to be convenient to him. It is paid at a time when he has at any rate a payment to make; it causes, therefore, no additional trouble, nor (unless the tax be on necessaries) any inconvenience but what is inseparable from the payment of the amount. He can also, except in the case of very perishable articles, select his own time for laying in a stock of the commodity, and consequently for payment of the tax. The producer or dealer who advances these taxes, is, indeed, sometimes subjected to inconvenience; but, in the case of imported goods, this inconvenience is reduced to a minimum by what is called the Warehousing System, under which, instead of paying the duty at the time of importation, he is only required to do so when he takes out the goods for consumption, which is seldom done until he has either actually found, or has the prospect of immediately finding, a purchaser.

The strongest objection, however, to raising the whole or the greater part of a large revenue by direct taxes, is the impossibility of assessing them fairly without a conscientious co-operation on the part of the contributors, not to be hoped for in the present low state of public morality. In the case of an income tax, we have already seen that unless it be found practicable to exempt savings altogether from the tax, the burthen cannot be apportioned with any tolerable approach to fairness upon those whose incomes are derived from business or professions; and this is in fact admitted by most of the advocates of direct taxation, who, I am afraid, generally get over the difficulty by leaving those classes untaxed, and confining their projected income tax to 'realized property', in which form it certainly has the merit of being a very easy form of plunder. But enough has been said in condemnation of this expedient. We have seen, however, that a house-tax is a form of direct taxation not liable to the same objections as an income tax, and indeed liable to as few objections of any kind as perhaps any of our indirect taxes. But it would be impossible to raise by a house-tax alone, the greatest part of the revenue of Great Britain, without producing a very objectionable over-crowding of the population, through the strong motive which all persons would have to avoid the tax by restricting their house accommodation. Besides, even a house-tax has inequalities, and consequent injustices; no tax is exempt from them, and it is neither just nor politic to make all the inequalities fall in the same places, by calling upon one tax to defray the whole or the chief part of the public expenditure. So much of the local taxation, in this country, being already in the form of a house-tax, it is probable that ten millions a year would be fully as much as could beneficially be levied, through this medium, for general purposes.

A certain amount of revenue may, as we have seen, be obtained without injustice by a peculiar tax on rent. Besides the present land-tax, and an equivalent for the revenue now derived from stamp duties on the conveyance of land, some further taxation might, I have contended, at some future period be imposed, to enable the state to participate in the progressive increase of the incomes of landlords from natural causes. Legacies and inheritances, we have also seen, ought to be subjected to taxation sufficient to yield a considerable revenue. With these taxes, and a house-tax of suitable amount, we should, I think, have reached the prudent limits of direct taxation, save in a national emergency so urgent as to justify the government in disregarding the amount of inequality and unfairness which may ultimately be found inseparable from an income tax. The remainder of the revenue would have to be provided by taxes on consumption, and the question is, which of these are the least objectionable.

§2. There are some forms of indirect taxation which must be peremptorily excluded. Taxes on commodities, for revenue purposes, must not operate as protecting duties, but must be levied impartially on every mode in which the articles can be obtained, whether produced in the country itself, or imported. An exclusion must also be put upon all taxes on the necessaries of life, or on the materials or instruments employed in producing those necessaries. Such taxes are always liable to encroach on what should be left untaxed, the incomes barely sufficient for healthful existence; and on the most favourable supposition, namely, that wages rise to compensate the labourers for the tax, it operates as a peculiar tax on profits, which is at once unjust, and detrimental to national wealth.[1] What remain are taxes on luxuries. And these have some properties which strongly recommend them. In the first place, they can never, by any possibility, touch those whose whole income is expended on necessaries; while they do reach those by whom what is required for necessaries, is expended on indulgences. In the next place, they operate in some cases as an useful, and the only useful, kind of sumptuary law. I disclaim all asceticism, and by no means wish to see discouraged, either by law or opinion, any indulgence (consistent with the means and obligations of the person using it) which is sought from a genuine inclination for, and enjoyment of, the thing itself; but a great portion of the expenses of the higher and middle classes in most countries, and the greatest in this, is not incurred for the sake of the pleasure afforded by the things on which the money is spent, but from regard to opinion, and an idea that certain expenses are expected from them, as an appendage of station; and I cannot but think that expenditure of this sort is a most desirable subject of taxation. If taxation discourages it, some good is done, and if not, no harm; for in so far as taxes are levied on things which are desired and possessed from motives of this description, nobody is the worse for them. When a thing is bought not for its use but for its costliness, cheapness is no recommendation. As Sismondi remarks, the consequence of cheapening articles of vanity, is not that less is expended on such things, but that the buyers substitute for the cheapened article some other which is more costly, or a more elaborate quality of the same thing; and as the inferior quality answered the purpose of vanity equally well when it was equally expen-

---

1. Some argue that the materials and instruments of all production should be exempt from taxation; but these, when they do not enter into the production of necessaries, seem as proper subjects of taxation as the finished article. It is chiefly with reference to foreign trade, that such taxes have been considered injurious. Internationally speaking, they may be looked upon as export duties, and, unless in cases in which an export duty is advisable, they should be accompanied with an equivalent drawback on exportation. But there is no sufficient reason against taxing the materials and instruments used in the production of anything which is itself a fit object of taxation.

sive, a tax on the article is really paid by nobody: it is a creation of public revenue by which nobody loses.[2]

§3. In order to reduce as much as possible the inconveniences, and increase the advantages, incident to taxes on commodities, the following are the practical rules which suggest themselves. 1st. To raise as large a revenue as conveniently may be, from those classes of luxuries which have most connexion with vanity, and least with positive enjoyment; such as the more costly qualities of all kinds of personal equipment and ornament. 2ndly.

2. 'Were we to suppose that diamonds could only be procured from one particular and distant country, and pearls from another, and were the produce of the mines in the former, and of the fishery in the latter, from the operation of natural causes, to become doubly difficult to procure, the effect would merely be that in time half the quantity of diamonds and pearls would be sufficient to mark a certain opulence and rank, that it had before been necessary to employ for that purpose. The same quantity of gold, or some commodity reducible at last to labour, would be required to produce the now reduced amount, as the former larger amount. Were the difficulty interposed by the regulations of legislators ... it could make no difference to the fitness of these articles to serve the purposes of vanity.' Suppose that means were discovered whereby the physiological process which generates the pearl might be induced *ad libitum*, the result being that the amount of labour expended in procuring each pearl, came to be only the five hundredth part of what it was before. 'The ultimate effect of such a change would depend on whether the fishery were free or not. Were it free to all, as pearls could be got simply for the labour of fishing for them, a string of them might be had for a few pence. The very poorest class of society could therefore afford to decorate their persons with them. They would thus soon become extremely vulgar and unfashionable, and so at last valueless. If however we suppose that instead of the fishery being free, the legislator owns and has complete command of the place, where alone pearls are to be procured; as the progress of discovery advanced, he might impose a duty on them equal to the diminution of labour necessary to procure them. They would then be as much esteemed as they were before. What simple beauty they have would remain unchanged. The difficulty to be surmounted in order to obtain them would be different, but equally great, and they would therefore equally serve to mark the opulence of those who possessed them.' The net revenue obtained by such a tax 'would not cost the society anything. If not abused in its application, it would be a clear addition of so much to the resources of the community.' – Rae, *New Principles of Political Economy*, pp. 369–71.

Whenever possible, to demand the tax, not from the producer, but directly from the consumer, since when levied on the producer it raises the price always by more, and often by much more, than the mere amount of the tax. Most of the minor assessed taxes in this country are recommended by both these considerations. But with regard to horses and carriages, as there are many persons to whom, from health or constitution, these are not so much luxuries as necessaries, the tax paid by those who have but one riding horse, or but one carriage, especially of the cheaper descriptions, should be low; while taxation should rise very rapidly with the number of horses and carriages, and with their costliness. 3rdly. But as the only indirect taxes which yield a large revenue are those which fall on articles of universal or very general consumption, and as it is therefore necessary to have some taxes on real luxuries, that is, on things which afford pleasure in themselves, and are valued on that account rather than for their cost; these taxes should, if possible, be so adjusted as to fall with the same proportional weight on small, on moderate, and on large incomes. This is not an easy matter; since the things which are the subjects of the more productive taxes, are in proportion more largely consumed by the poorer members of the community than by the rich. Tea, coffee, sugar, tobacco, fermented drinks, can hardly be so taxed that the poor shall not bear more than their due share of the burthen. Something might be done by making the duty on the superior qualities, which are used by the richer consumers, much higher in proportion to the value (instead of much lower, as is almost universally the practice, under the present English system); but in some cases the difficulty of at all adjusting the duty to the value, so as to prevent evasion, is said, with what truth I know not, to be insuperable; so that it is thought necessary to levy the same fixed duty on all the qualities alike: a flagrant injustice to the poorer class of contributors, unless compensated by the existence of other taxes from which, as from the present income tax, they are altogether exempt. 4thly. As far as is consistent with the preceding rules, taxation should rather be concentrated on a few articles than diffused over many, in order that the expenses of collection may be smaller, and that as few employments as possible may be burthensomely and vexatiously interfered with. 5thly. Among luxuries of general consumption, taxation should by preference attach itself to stimulants, because these, though in themselves as legitimate indulgences as any others, are more liable than most others to be used in excess, so that the check to consumption, naturally arising from taxation, is on the whole better applied to them than to other things. 6thly. As far as other considerations permit, taxation should be confined to imported articles, since these can be taxed with a less degree of vexatious interference, and with fewer incidental bad effects, than when a tax is levied on the field or on the workshop. Custom-duties are, *caeteris paribus*, much less objectionable than excise: but they must be laid only on things which either cannot, or at least will not, be produced in the country itself; or else their production there must be prohibited (as in England is the case with tobacco), or subjected to an excise duty of equivalent amount. 7thly. No tax ought to be kept so high as to furnish a motive to its evasion, too strong to be counteracted by ordinary means of prevention: and especially no commodity should be taxed so highly as to raise up a class of lawless characters, smugglers, illicit distillers, and the like.

Of the excise and custom duties lately existing in this country, all which are intrinsically unfit to form part of a good system of taxation, have, since the last reforms by Mr Gladstone, been got rid of. Among these are all duties on ordinary articles of food, whether for human beings or for cattle; those on timber, as falling on the materials of lodging, which is one of the necessaries of life; all duties on the metals, and on implements made of them; taxes on soap, which is a necessary of cleanliness, and on tallow, the material both of that and of some other necessaries; the tax on paper, an indispensable instrument of almost all business and of most kinds of instruction. The duties which now yield nearly the whole of the customs and excise revenue, those on sugar, coffee, tea, wine, beer, spirits, and tobacco, are in themselves where a large amount of revenue is necessary, extremely proper taxes; but at present grossly unjust, from the disproportionate weight with which they press on the poorer classes; and some of them (those on spirits and tobacco) are so high as to cause a considerable amount of smuggling. It is probable that most of these taxes might bear a great reduction without any material loss of revenue. In what manner the finer articles of manufacture, consumed by the rich, might most advantageously be taxed, I must leave to be decided by those who have the requisite practical knowledge. The difficulty would be, to effect it without an inadmissible degree of interference with production. In countries which, like the United States, import the principal part of the finer manufactures which they consume, there is little difficulty in the matter : and even where nothing is imported but the raw material, that may be taxed, especially the qualities of it which are exclusively employed for the fabrics used by the richer class of consumers. Thus, in England a high custom-duty on raw silk would be consistent with principle; and it might perhaps be practicable to tax the finer qualities of cotton or linen yarn, whether spun in the country itself or imported.

CHAPTER VII

Of a National Debt

§1. THE question must now be considered, how far it is right or expedient to raise money for the purpose of government, not by laying on taxes to the amount required, but by taking a portion of the capital of the country in the form of a loan, and charging the public revenue with only the interest. Nothing needs be said about providing for temporary wants by taking up money; for instance, by an issue of exchequer bills, destined to be paid off, at furthest in a year or two, from the proceeds of the existing taxes. This is a convenient expedient, and when the government does not possess a treasure or hoard, is often a necessary one, on the occurrence of extraordinary expenses, or of a temporary failure in the ordinary sources of revenue. What we have to discuss is the propriety of contracting a national debt of a permanent character; defraying the expenses of a war, or of any season of difficulty, by loans, to be redeemed either very gradually and at a distant period, or not at all.

This question has already been touched upon in the First Book. We remarked, that if the capital taken in loans is abstracted from funds either engaged in production, or destined to be employed in it, their diversion from that purpose is equivalent to taking the amount from the wages of the labouring classes. Borrowing, in this case, is not a substitute for raising the supplies within the year. A government which borrows does actually take the amount within the year, and that too by a tax exclusively on the labouring classes : than which it could have done nothing worse, if it had supplied its wants by avowed taxation; and in that case the transaction, and its evils, would have ended with the emergency; while by the circuitous mode adopted, the value extracted from the labourers is gained, not by the state, but by the employers of labour, the state remaining charged with the debt besides, and with its interest in perpetuity. The system of public loans, in such circumstances, may be pronounced the very worst which, in the present state of civilization, is still included in the catalogue of financial expedients.

We however remarked that there are other circumstances in which loans are not chargeable with these pernicious consequences: namely, first, when what is borrowed is foreign capital, the overflowings of the general accumulation of the world; or, secondly, when it is capital which either would not have been saved at all unless this mode of investment had been open to it, or after being saved, would have been wasted in unproductive enterprises, or sent to seek employment in foreign countries. When the progress of accumulation has reduced profits either to the ultimate or to the practical minimum, – to the rate, less than which would either put a stop to the increase of capital, or send the whole of the new accumulations abroad; government may annually intercept these new accumulations, without trenching on the employment or wages of the labouring classes in the country itself, or perhaps in any other country. To this extent, therefore, the loan system may be carried, without being liable to the utter and peremptory condemnation which is due to it when it overpasses this limit. What is wanted is an index to determine whether, in any given series of years, as during the last great war for example, the limit has been exceeded or not.

Such an index exists, at once a certain and an obvious one. Did the government, by its loan operations, augment the rate of interest? If it only opened a channel for capital which would not otherwise have been accumulated, or which, if accumulated, would not have been employed within the country; this implies that the capital, which the government took and expended, could not have found employment at the existing rate of interest. So long as the loans do no more than absorb this surplus, they prevent any tendency to a fall of the rate of interest, but they cannot occasion any rise. When they do raise the rate of interest, as they did in a most extraordinary degree during the French war, this is positive proof that the government is a competitor for capital with the ordinary channels, of productive investment, and is carrying off, not merely funds which would not, but funds which would, have found productive employment within the country. To the full extent, therefore, to which the loans of government, during the war, caused the rate of interest to exceed what it was before, and what it has been since, those loans are chargeable with all the evils which have been described. If it be objected that interest only rose because profits rose, I reply that this does not weaken, but strengthens, the argument. If the government loans produced the rise of profits by the great amount of capital which they absorbed, by what means can they have had this effect, unless by lowering the wages of labour? It will perhaps be said, that what kept profits high during the war was not the drafts made on the national capital by the loans, but the rapid progress of industrial improvements. This, in a great measure, was the fact; and it no doubt alleviated the hardship to the labouring classes, and made the financial system which was pursued less actively mischievous, but not less contrary to principle. These very improvements in industry, made room for a larger amount of capital; and the government, by draining away a great part of the annual accumulations, did not indeed prevent that capital from existing ultimately, (for it started into existence with great rapidity after the peace), but prevented it from existing at the time, and subtracted just so much, while the war lasted, from distribution among productive labourers. If the government had abstained from taking this capital by loan, and had allowed it to reach the labourers, but had raised the supplies which it required by a direct tax on the labouring classes, it would have produced (in every respect but the expense and inconvenience of collecting the tax) the very same economical effects which it did produce, except that we should not now have had the debt. The course it actually took was therefore worse than the very worst mode which it could possibly have adopted of raising the supplies within the year : and the only excuse, or justification, which it admits of, (so far as that excuse could be truly pleaded), was hard necessity; the impossibility of raising so enormous an annual sum by taxation, without resorting to taxes which from their odiousness, or from the facility of evasion, it would have been found impracticable to enforce.

When government loans are limited to the overflowings of the national capital, or to those accumulations which would not take place at all unless suffered to overflow, they are at least not liable to this grave condemnation: they occasion no privation to any one at the time, except by the payment of the interest, and may even be beneficial to the labouring class during the term of their expenditure, by employing in the direct purchase of labour, as that of soldiers, sailors, &c., funds which might otherwise have quitted the country altogether. In this case therefore the question really is, what it is commonly supposed to be in all cases, namely, a choice between a great sacrifice at once, and a small one indefinitely prolonged. On this matter it seems rational to think, that the prudence of a nation will dictate the same conduct as the prudence of an individual; to submit to as much of the privation immediately, as can easily be borne, and only when any further burthen would distress or cripple them too much, to provide for the remainder by mortgaging their future income. It is an excellent maxim to make present resources suffice for present wants; the future will have its own wants to provide for. On the other hand, it may reasonably be taken into consideration that in a country increasing in wealth, the necessary expenses of government do not increase in the same ratio as capital or population; any burthen, therefore, is always less and less felt: and since those extraordinary expenses of government which are fit to be incurred at all, are most beneficial beyond the existing generation, there is no injustice in making posterity pay a part of the price, if the inconvenience would be extreme of defraying the whole of it by the exertions and sacrifices of the generation which first incurred it.

§2. When a country, wisely or unwisely, has burthened itself with a debt, is it expedient to take steps for redeeming that debt? In principle it is impossible not to maintain the affirmative. It is true that the payment of the interest, when the creditors are members of the same community, is no national loss, but a mere transfer. The transfer, however, being compulsory, is a serious evil, and the raising a great extra revenue by any system of taxation necessitates so much expense, vexation, disturbance of the channels of industry, and other mischiefs over and above the mere payment of the money wanted by the government, that to get rid of the necessity of such taxation is at all times worth a considerable effort. The same amount of sacrifice which would have been worth incurring to avoid contracting the debt, it is worth while to incur, at any subsequent time, for the purpose of extinguishing it.

Two modes have been contemplated of paying off a national debt: either at once by a general contribution, or gradually by a surplus revenue. The first would be incomparably the best, if it were practicable; and it would be practicable if it could justly be done by assessment on property alone. If property bore the whole interest of the debt, property might, with great advantage to itself, pay it off; since this would be merely surrendering to a creditor the principal sum, the whole annual proceeds of which were already his by law; and would be equivalent to what a land-owner does when he sells part of his estate, to free the remainder from a mortgage. But property, it needs hardly be said, does not pay, and cannot just be required to pay, the whole interest of the debt. Some indeed affirm that it can, on the plea that the existing generation is only bound to pay the debts of its predecessors from the assets it has received from them, and not from the produce of its own industry. But has no one received anything from previous generations except those who have succeeded to property? Is the whole difference between the earth as it is, with its clearings and improvements, its roads and canals, its towns and manufactories, and the earth as it was when the first human being set foot on it, of no benefit to any but those who are called the owners of the soil? Is the capital accumulated by the labour and abstinence of all former generations, of no advantage to any but those who have succeeded to the legal ownership of part of it? And have we not inherited a mass of acquired knowledge, both scientific and empirical, due to the sagacity and industry of those who preceded us, the benefits of which are the common wealth of all? Those who are born to the ownership of property have, in addition to these common benefits, a separate inheritance, and to this difference it is right that advertence should be had in regulating taxation. It belongs to the general financial system of the country to take due account of this principle, and I have indicated, as in my opinion a proper mode of taking account of it, a considerable tax on legacies and inheritances. Let it be determined directly and openly what is due from property to the state, and from the state to property, and let the institutions of the state be regulated accordingly. Whatever is the fitting contribution from property to the general expenses of the state, in the same and in no greater proportion should it contribute towards either the interest or the repayment of the national debt.

This, however, if admitted, is fatal to any scheme for the extinction of the debt by a general assessment on the community. Persons of property could pay their share of the amount by a sacrifice of property, and have the same net income as before; but if those who have no accumulations, but only incomes, were required to make up by a single payment the equivalent of the annual charge laid on them by the taxes maintained to pay the interest of the debt, they could only do so by incurring a private debt equal to their share of the public debt; while, from the insufficiency, in most cases, of the security which they could give, the interest would amount to a much larger annual sum than their share of that now paid by the state. Besides, a collective debt defrayed by taxes, has over the same debt parcelled out among individuals, the immense advantage, that it is virtually a mutual insurance among the contributors. If the fortune of a contributor diminishes, his taxes diminish; if he is ruined, they cease altogether, and his portion of the debt is wholly transferred to the solvent members of the community. If it were laid on him as a private obligation, he would still be liable to it even when penniless.

When the state possesses property, in land or otherwise, which there are not strong reasons of public utility for its retaining at its disposal, this should be employed, as far as it will go, in extinguishing debt. Any casual gain, or godsend, is naturally devoted to the same purpose. Beyond this, the only mode which is both just and feasible, of extinguishing or reducing a national debt, is by means of a surplus revenue.

§3. The desirableness, *per se*, of maintaining a surplus for this purpose, does not, I think, admit of a doubt. We sometimes, indeed, hear it said that the amount should rather be left to 'fructify in the pockets of the people'. This is a good argument, as far as it goes, against levying taxes unnecessarily for purposes of unproductive expenditure, but not against paying off a national debt. For, what is meant by the word fructify? If it means anything, it means productive employment; and as an argument against taxation, we must understand it to assert, that if the amount were left with the people they would save it, and convert it into capital. It is probable, indeed, that they would save a part, but extremely improbable that they would save the whole: while if taken by taxation, and employed in paying off debt, the whole is saved, and made productive. To the fundholder who receives the payment it is already capital, not revenue, and he will make it 'fructify', that it may continue to afford him an income. The objection, therefore, is not only groundless, but the real argument is on the other side: the amount is much more certain of fructifying if it is not 'left in the pockets of the people'.

It is not, however, advisable in all cases to maintain a surplus revenue for the extinction of debt. The advantage of paying off the national debt of Great Britain, for instance, is that it would enable us to get rid of the worse half of our taxation. But of this worse half some portions must be worse than others, and to get rid of those would be a greater benefit proportionally than to get rid of the rest. If renouncing a surplus revenue would enable us to dispense with a tax, we ought to consider the very worst of all our taxes as precisely the one which we are keeping up for the sake of ultimately abolishing taxes not so bad as itself. In a country advancing in wealth, whose increasing revenue gives it the power of ridding itself from time to time of the most inconvenient portions of its taxation, I conceive that the increase of revenue should rather be disposed of by taking off taxes, than by liquidating debt, as long as any very objectionable imposts remain. In the present state of England, therefore, I hold it to be good policy in the government, when it has a surplus of an apparently permanent character, to take off taxes, provided these are rightly selected. Even when no taxes remain but such as are not unfit to form part of a permanent system, it is wise to continue the same policy by experimental reductions of those taxes, until the point is discovered at which a given amount of revenue can be raised with the smallest pressure on the contributors. After this, such surplus revenue as might arise from any further increase of the produce of the taxes, should not, I conceive, be remitted, but applied to the redemption of debt. Eventually, it might be expedient to appropriate the entire produce of particular taxes to this purpose; since there would be more assurance that the liquidation would be persisted in, if the fund destined to it were kept apart, and not blended with the general revenues of the state. The succession duties would be peculiarly suited to such a purpose, since taxes paid as they are, out of capital, would be better employed in reimbursing capital than in defraying current expenditure. If this separate appropriation were made, any surplus afterwards arising from the increasing produce of the other taxes, and from the saving of interest on the successive portions of debt paid off, might form a ground for a remission of taxation.

It has been contended that some amount of national debt is desirable, and almost indispensable, as an investment for the savings of the poorer or more inexperienced part of the community. Its convenience in that respect is undeniable; but (besides that the progress of industry is gradually affording other modes of investment almost as safe and untroublesome, such as the shares or obligations of great public companies) the only real superiority of an investment in the funds consists in the national guarantee, and this could be afforded by other means than that of a public debt, involving compulsory taxation. One mode which would answer the purpose, would be a national bank of deposit and discount, with ramifications throughout the country; which might receive any money confided to it, and either fund it at a fixed rate of interest, or allow interest on a floating balance, like the joint-stock banks; the interest given being of course lower than the rate at which individuals can borrow, in proportion to the greater security of a government investment; and the expenses of the establishment being defrayed by the difference between the interest which the bank would pay, and that which it would obtain, by lending its deposits on mercantile, landed, or other security. There are no insuperable objections in principle, nor, I should think, in practice, to an institution of this sort, as a means of supplying the same convenient mode of investment now afforded by the public funds. It would constitute the state a great insurance company, to insure that part of the community who live on the interest of their property, against the risk of losing it by the bankruptcy of those to whom they might otherwise be under the necessity of confiding it.

CHAPTER VIII

Of the Ordinary Functions of Government, considered as to their Economical Effects

§1. Before we discuss the line of demarcation between the things with which government should, and those with which they should not, directly interfere, it is necessary to consider the economical effects, whether of a bad or of a good complexion, arising from the manner in which they acquit themselves of the duties which devolve on them in all societies, and which no one denies to be incumbent on them.

The first of these is the protection of person and property. There is no need to expatiate on the influence exercised over the economical interests of society by the degree of completeness with which this duty of government is performed. Insecurity of person and property, is as much as to say, uncertainty of the connexion between all human exertion or sacrifice, and the attainment of the ends for the sake of which they are undergone. It means, uncertainty whether they who sow shall reap, whether they who produce shall consume, and they who spare to-day shall enjoy to-morrow. It means, not only that labour and frugality are not the road to acquisition, but that violence is. When person and property are to a certain degree insecure, all the possessions of the weak are at the mercy of the strong. No one can keep what he has produced, unless he is more capable of defending it, than others who give no part of their time and exertions to useful industry are of taking it from him. The productive classes, therefore, when the insecurity surpasses a certain point, being unequal to their own protection against the predatory population, are obliged to place themselves individually in a state of dependence on some member of the predatory class, that it may be his interest to shield them from all depredation except his own. In this manner, in the Middle Ages, allodial property generally became feudal, and numbers of the poorer

239

freemen voluntarily made themselves and their posterity serfs of some military lord.

Nevertheless, in attaching to this great requisite, security of person and property, the importance which is justly due to it, we must not forget that even for economical purposes there are other things quite as indispensable, the presence of which will often make up for a very considerable degree of imperfection in the protective arrangements of government. As was observed in a previous chapter,[1] the free cities of Italy, Flanders, and the Hanseatic league, were habitually in a state of such internal turbulence, varied by such destructive external wars, that person and property enjoyed very imperfect protection; yet during several centuries they increased rapidly in wealth and prosperity, brought many of the industrial arts to a high degree of advancement, carried on distant and dangerous voyages of exploration and commerce with extraordinary success, became an overmatch in power for the greatest feudal lords, and could defend themselves even against the sovereigns of Europe: because in the midst of turmoil and violence, the citizens of those towns enjoyed a certain rude freedom, under conditions of union and co-operation, which, taken together, made them a brave, energetic, and high-spirited people, and fostered a great amount of public spirit and patriotism. The prosperity of these and other free states in a lawless age, shows that a certain degree of insecurity, in some combinations of circumstances, has good as well as bad effects, by making energy and practical ability the conditions of safety. Insecurity paralyses, only when it is such in nature and in degree, that no energy of which mankind in general are capable, affords any tolerable means of self-protection. And this is a main reason why oppression by the government, whose power is generally irresistible by any efforts that can be made by individuals, has so much more baneful an effect on the springs of national prosperity, than almost any degree of lawlessness and turbulence under free institutions. Nations have acquired some wealth, and made some progress in improvement, in states of social union so imperfect as to border on anarchy: but no countries in which the people were exposed without limit to

1. [Not printed in this edition.]

arbitrary exactions from the officers of government, ever yet continued to have industry or wealth. A few generations of such a government never fail to extinguish both. Some of the fairest, and once the most prosperous, regions of the earth, have, under the Roman and afterwards under the Turkish dominion, been reduced to a desert, solely by that cause. I say solely, because they would have recovered with the utmost rapidity, as countries always do, from the devastations of war, or any other temporary calamities. Difficulties and hardships are often but an incentive to exertion: what is fatal to it, is the belief that it will not be suffered to produce its fruits.

§2. Simple over-taxation by government, though a great evil, is not comparable in the economical part of its mischiefs to exactions much more moderate in amount, which either subject the contributor to the arbitrary mandate of government officers, or are so laid on as to place skill, industry, and frugality at a disadvantage. The burthen of taxation in our own country is very great, yet as every one knows its limit, and is seldom made to pay more than he expects and calculates on, and as the modes of taxation are not of such a kind as much to impair the motives to industry and economy, the sources of prosperity are little diminished by the pressure of taxation; they may even, as some think, be increased, by the extra exertions made to compensate for the pressure of the taxes. But in the barbarous despotisms of many countries of the East, where taxation consists in fastening upon those who have succeded in acquiring something, in order to confiscate it, unless the possessor buys its release by submitting to give some large sum as a compromise, we cannot expect to find voluntary industry, or wealth derived from any source but plunder. And even in comparatively civilized countries, bad modes of raising a revenue have had effects similar in kind, though in an inferior degree. French writers before the Revolution represented the *taille* as a main cause of the backward state of agriculture, and of the wretched condition of the rural population; not from its amount, but because, being proportioned to the visible capital of the cultivator, it gave him a motive for appearing poor, which sufficed to turn the scale in favour of indolence. The arbitrary powers also of fiscal officers, of *intendants* and *subdélégués*, were more destructive of prosperity than a far larger amount of exactions, because they destroyed security: there was a marked superiority in the condition of the *pays d'états*, which were exempt from this scourge. The universal venality ascribed to Russian functionaries, must be an immense drag on the capabilities of economical improvement possessed so abundantly by the Russian empire: since the emoluments of public officers must depend on the success with which they can multiply vexations, for the purpose of being bought off by bribes.

Yet mere excess of taxation, even when not aggravated by uncertainty, is, independently of its injustice, a serious economical evil. It may be carried so far as to discourage industry by insufficiency of reward. Very long before it reaches this point, it prevents or greatly checks accumulation, or causes the capital accumulated to be sent for investment to foreign countries. Taxes which fall on profits, even though that kind of income may not pay more than its just share, necessarily diminish the motive to any saving, except for investment in foreign countries where profits are higher. Holland, for example, seems to have long ago reached the practical minimum of profits: already in the last century her wealthy capitalists had a great part of their fortunes invested in the loans and joint-stock speculations of other countries: and this low rate of profit is ascribed to the heavy taxation, which had been in some measure forced on her by the circumstances of her position and history. The taxes indeed, besides their great amount, were many of them on necessaries, a kind of tax peculiarly injurious to industry and accumulation. But when the aggregate amount of taxation is very great, it is inevitable that recourse must be had for part of it to taxes of an objectionable character. And any taxes on consumption, when heavy, even if not operating on profits, have something of the same effect, by driving persons of moderate means to live abroad, often taking their capital with them. Although I by no means join with those political economists who think no state of national existence desirable in which there is not a rapid increase of wealth, I cannot overlook the many disadvantages to an independent nation from being brought prematurely to a stationary state, while the neighbouring countries continue advancing.

§3. The subject of protection to person and property, considered as afforded by government, ramifies widely, into a number of indirect channels. It embraces, for example, the whole subject of the perfection or inefficiency of the means provided for the ascertainment of rights and the redress of injuries. Person and property cannot be considered secure where the administration of justice is imperfect, either from defect of integrity or capacity in the tribunals, or because the delays, vexation, and expense accompanying their operation impose a heavy tax on those who appeal to them, and make it preferable to submit to any endurable amount of the evils which they are designed to remedy. In England there is no fault to be found with the administration of justice, in point of pecuniary integrity; a result which the progress of social improvement may also be supposed to have brought about in several other nations of Europe. But legal and judicial imperfections of other kinds are abundant; and, in England especially, are a large abatement from the value of the services which the government renders back to the people in return for our enormous taxation. In the first place, the incognoscibility (as Bentham termed it) of the law, and its extreme uncertainty, even to those who best know it, render a resort to the tribunals often necessary for obtaining justice, when, there being no dispute as to facts, no litigation ought to be required. In the next place, the procedure of the tribunals is so replete with delay, vexation, and expense, that the price at which justice is at last obtained is an evil outweighing a very considerable amount of injustice; and the wrong side, even that which the law considers such, has many chances of gaining its point, through the abandonment of litigation by the other party for want of funds, or through a compromise in which a sacrifice is made of just rights to terminate the suit, or through some technical quirk, whereby a decision is obtained on some other ground than the merits. This last detestable incident often happens without blame to the judge, under a system of law, of which a great part rests on no rational principles adapted to the present state of society, but was originally founded partly on a kind of whims and conceits, and partly on the principles and incidents of feudal tenure, (which now survive only as legal fictions;) and has only been very imperfectly adapted, as cases arose, to the changes which had taken place in society. Of all parts of the English legal system, the Court of Chancery, which has the best substantive law, has been incomparably the worst as to delay, vexation, and expense; and this is the only tribunal for most of the classes of cases which are in their nature the most complicated, such as cases of partnership, and the great range and variety of cases which come under the denomination of trust. The recent reforms in this Court have abated the mischief, but are still far from having removed it.

Fortunately for the prosperity of England, the greater part of the mercantile law is comparatively modern, and was made by the tribunals, by the simple process of recognizing and giving force of law to the usages which, from motives of convenience, had grown up among merchants themselves: so that this part of the law, at least, was substantially made by those who were most interested in its goodness: while the defects of the tribunals have been the less practically pernicious in reference to commercial transactions, because the importance of credit, which depends on character, renders the restraints of opinion (though, as daily experience proves, an insufficient) yet a very powerful, protection against those forms of mercantile dishonesty which are generally recognized as such.

The imperfections of the law, both in its substance and in its procedure, fall heaviest upon the interests connected with what is technically called *real* property; in the general language of European jurisprudence, immoveable property. With respect to all this portion of the wealth of the community, the law fails egregiously in the protection which it undertakes to provide. It fails, first, by the uncertainty, and the maze of technicalities, which make it impossible for any one, at however great an expense, to possess a title to land which he can positively know to be unassailable. It fails, secondly, in omitting to provide due evidence of transactions, by a proper registration of legal documents. It fails, thirdly, by creating a necessity for operose and expensive instruments and formalities (independently of fiscal burthens) on occasion of the purchase and sale, or even the lease or mortgage, of immoveable property. And, fourthly, it fails by the intolerable expense and delay of law proceedings, in almost all cases in which real property is concerned. There is no doubt that the greatest sufferers by the defects of the higher courts of civil law are the landowners. Legal expenses, either those of actual litigation, or of the preparation of legal instruments, form, I apprehend, no inconsiderable item in the annual expenditure of most persons of large landed property, and the saleable value of their land is greatly impaired, by the difficulty of giving to the buyer complete confidence in the title; independently of the legal expenses which accompany the transfer. Yet the landowners, though they have been masters of the legislation of England, to say the least since 1688, have never made a single move in the direction of law reform, and have been strenuous opponents of some of the improvements of which they would more particularly reap the benefit; especially that great one of a registration of contracts affecting land, which when proposed by a Commission of eminent real property lawyers, and introduced into the House of Commons by Lord Campbell, was so offensive to the general body of landlords, and was rejected by so large a majority, as to have long discouraged any repetition of the attempt.[2] This irrational hostility to improvement, in a case in which their own interest would be the most benefited by it, must be ascribed to an intense timidity on the subject of their titles, generated by the defects of the very law which they refuse to alter; and to a conscious ignorance, and incapacity of judgment, on all legal subjects, which makes them helplessly defer to the opinion of their professional advisers, heedless of the fact that every imperfection of the law, in proportion as it is burthensome to them, brings gain to the lawyer.

In so far as the defects of legal arrangements are a mere

2. Lord Westbury's recent Act is a material mitigation of this grievous defect in English law, and will probably lead to further improvements.

burthen on the landowner, they do not much affect the sources of production; but the uncertainty of the title under which land is held, must often act as a great discouragement to the expenditure of capital in its improvement; and the expense of making transfers, operates to prevent land from coming into the hands of those who would use it to most advantage; often amounting, in the case of small purchases, to more than the price of the land, and tantamount, therefore, to a prohibition of the purchase and sale of land in small portions, unless in exceptional circumstances. Such purchases, however, are almost everywhere extremely desirable, there being hardly any country in which landed property is not either too much or too little subdivided, requiring either that great estates should be broken down, or that small ones should be bought up and consolidated. To make land as easily transferable as stock, would be one of the greatest economical improvements which could be bestowed on a country; and has been shown, again and again, to have no insuperable difficulty attending it.

Besides the excellences or defects that belong to the law and judicature of a country as a system of arrangements for attaining direct practical ends, much also depends, even in an economical point of view, upon the moral influences of the law. Enough has been said in a former place, on the degree in which both the industrial and all other combined operations of mankind depend for efficiency on their being able to rely on one another for probity and fidelity to engagements; from which we see how greatly even the economical prosperity of a country is liable to be affected, by anything in its institutions by which either integrity and trustworthiness, or the contrary qualities, are encouraged. The law everywhere ostensibly favours at least pecuniary honesty and the faith of contracts; but if it affords facilities for evading those obligations, by trick and chicanery, or by the unscrupulous use of riches in instituting unjust or resisting just litigation; if there are ways and means by which persons may attain the ends of roguery, under the apparent sanction of the law; to that extent the law is demoralizing, even in regard to pecuniary integrity. And such cases are, unfortunately, frequent under the English system. If, again, the law, by a misplaced indulgence, protects idleness or prodigality against their natural consequences, or dismisses crime with inadequate penalties, the effect, both on the prudential and on the social virtues, is unfavourable. When the law, by its own dispensations and injunctions, establishes injustice between individual and individual; as all laws do which recognize any form of slavery; as the laws of all countries do, though not all in the same degree, in respect to the family relations; and as the laws of many countries do, though in still more unequal degrees, as between rich and poor; the effect on the moral sentiments of the people is still more disastrous. But these subjects introduce considerations so much larger and deeper than those of political economy, that I only advert to them in order not to pass wholly unnoticed, things superior in importance to those of which I treat.

CHAPTER IX

The Same Subject Continued

§1. HAVING spoken thus far of the effects produced by the excellences or defects of the general system of the law, I shall now touch upon those resulting from the special character of parts of it. As a selection must be made, I shall confine myself to a few leading topics. The portions of the civil law of a country which are of most importance economically (next to those which determine the *status* of the labourer, as slave, serf, or free), are those relating to the two subjects of Inheritance and Contract. Of the laws relating to contract, none are more important economically, than the laws of partnership, and those of insolvency. It happens that on all these three points, there is just ground for condemning some of the provisions of the English law.

With regard to Inheritance, I have, in an early chapter,[1] considered the general principles of the subject, and suggested what appear to me to be, putting all prejudices apart, the best dispositions which the law could adopt. Freedom of bequest as the general rule, but limited by two things: first, that if there are descendants, who, being unable to provide for themselves, would become burthensome to the state, the equivalent of whatever the state would accord to them should be reserved from the property for their benefit: and secondly, that no one person should be permitted to acquire, by inheritance, more than the amount of a moderate independence. In case of intestacy, the whole property to escheat to the state: which should be bound to make a just and reasonable provision for descendants, that is, such a provision as the parent or ancestor ought to have made, their circumstances, capacities, and mode of bringing up being considered.

The laws of inheritance, however, have probably several phases of improvement to go through, before ideas so far removed from present modes of thinking will be taken into serious considera-

1. [See below, pp. 368–88.]

tion: and as, among the recognized modes of determining the succession to property, some must be better and others worse, it is necessary to consider which of them deserves the preference. As an intermediate course, therefore, I would recommend the extension to all property, of the present English law of inheritance affecting personal property (freedom of bequest, and in case of intestacy, equal division): except that no rights should be acknowledged in collaterals, and that the property of those who have neither descendants nor ascendants, and make no will, should escheat to the state.

The laws of existing nations deviate from these maxims in two opposite ways. In England, and in most of the countries where the influence of feudality is still felt in the laws, one of the objects aimed at in respect to land and other immoveable property, is to keep it together in large masses: accordingly, in cases of intestacy, it passes, generally speaking (for the local custom of a few places is different), exclusively to the eldest son. And though the rule of primogeniture is not binding on testators, who in England have nominally the power of bequeathing their property as they please, any prorietor may so exercise this power as to deprive his immediate successor of it, by entailing the property on one particular line of his descendants: which, besides preventing it from passing by inheritance in any other than the prescribed manner, is attended with the incidental consequence of precluding it from being sold; since each successive possessor, having only a life interest in the property, cannot alienate it for a longer period than his own life. In some other countries, such as France, the law, on the contrary, compels division of inheritances; not only, in case of intestacy, sharing the property, both real and personal, equally among all the children, or (if there are no children) among all relatives in the same degree of propinquity; but also not recognizing any power of bequest, or recognizing it over only a limited portion of the property, the remainder being subjected to compulsory equal division.

Neither of these systems, I apprehend, was introduced, or is perhaps maintained, in the countries where it exists, from any general considerations of justice, or any foresight of economical consequences, but chiefly from political motives; in the one case to keep up large hereditary fortunes, and a landed aristocracy; in the other, to break these down, and prevent their resurrection. The first object, as an aim of national policy, I conceive to be eminently undesirable: with regard to the second, I have pointed out what seems to me a better mode of attaining it. The merit, or demerit, however, of either purpose, belongs to the general science of politics, not to the limited department of that science which is here treated of. Each of the two systems is a real and efficient instrument for the purpose intended by it; but each, as it appears to me, achieves that purpose at the cost of much mischief.

§2. There are two arguments of an economical character, which are urged in favour of primogeniture. One is, the stimulus applied to the industry and ambition of younger children, by leaving them to be the architects of their own fortunes. This argument was put by Dr Johnson in a manner more forcible than complimentary to an hereditary aristocracy, when he said, by way of recommendation of primogeniture, that it 'makes but one fool in a family'. It is curious that a defender of aristocratic institutions should be the person to assert that to inherit such a fortune as takes away any necessity for exertion, is generally fatal to activity and strength of mind: in the present state of education, however, the proposition, with some allowance for exaggeration, may be admitted to be true. But whatever force there is in the argument, counts in favour of limiting the eldest, as well as all the other children, to a mere provision, and dispensing with even the 'one fool' whom Dr Johnson was willing to tolerate. If unearned riches are so pernicious to the character, one does not see why, in order to withhold the poison from the junior members of a family, there should be no way but to unite all their separate potions, and administer them in the largest possible dose to one selected victim. It cannot be necessary to inflict this great evil on the eldest son, for want of knowing what else to do with a large fortune.

Some writers, however, look upon the effect of primogeniture in stimulating industry, as depending, not so much on the poverty of the younger children, as on the contrast between that poverty and the riches of the elder; thinking it indispensable to the activity and energy of the hive, that there should be a huge drone here and there, to impress the working bees with a due sense of the advantages of honey. 'Their inferiority in point of wealth', says Mr M'Culloch, speaking of the younger children, 'and their desire to escape from this lower station, and to attain to the same level with their elder brothers, inspires them with an energy and vigour they could not otherwise feel. But the advantage of preserving large estates from being frittered down by a scheme of equal division, is not limited to its influence over the younger children of their owners. It raises universally the standard of competence, and gives new force to the springs which set industry in motion. The manner of living among the great landlords is that in which every one is ambitious of being able to indulge; and their habits of expense, though sometimes injurious to themselves, act as powerful incentives to the ingenuity and enterprise of the other classes, who never think their fortunes sufficiently ample, unless they will enable them to emulate the splendour of the richest landlords; so that the custom of primogeniture seems to render all classes more industrious, and to augment at the same time, the mass of wealth and the scale of enjoyment.[2]

The portion of truth, I can hardly say contained in these observations, but recalled by them, I apprehend to be, that a state of complete equality of fortunes would not be favourable to active exertion for the increase of wealth. Speaking of the mass, it is as true of wealth as of most other distinctions – of talent, knowledge, virtue – that those who already have, or think they have, as much of it as their neighbours, will seldom exert themselves to acquire more. But it is not therefore necessary that society should provide a set of persons with large fortunes, to fulfil the social duty of standing to be looked at, with envy and admiration, by the aspiring poor. The fortunes which people have

2. *Principles of Political Economy*, ed. 1843, p. 264. There is much more to the same effect in the more recent treatise by the same author, 'On the Succession to Property vacant by Death'.

acquired for themselves, answer the purpose quite as well, indeed much better; since a person is more powerfully stimulated by the example of somebody who has earned a fortune, than by the mere sight of somebody who possesses one; and the former is necessarily an example of prudence and frugality as well as industry, while the latter much oftener sets an example of profuse expense, which spreads, with pernicious effect, to the very class on whom the sight of riches is supposed to have so beneficial an influence, namely, those whose weakness of mind, and taste for ostentation, makes 'the splendour of the richest landlords' attract them with the most potent spell. In America there are few or no hereditary fortunes; yet industrial energy, and the ardour of accumulation, are not supposed to be particularly backward in that part of the world. When a country has once fairly entered into the industrial career, which is the principal occupation of the modern, as war was that of the ancient and medieval world, the desire of acquisition by industry needs no factitious stimulus: the advantages naturally inherent in riches, and the character they assume of a test by which talent and success in life are habitually measured, are an ample security for their being pursued with sufficient intensity and zeal. As to the deeper consideration, that the diffusion of wealth, and not its concentration, is desirable, and that the more wholesome state of society is not that in which immense fortunes are possessed by a few and coveted by all, but that in which the greatest possible numbers possess and are contented with a moderate competency, which all may hope to acquire; I refer to it in this place, only to show, how widely separated, on social questions, is the entire mode of thought of the defenders of promigeniture, from that which is partially promulgated in the present treatise.

The other economical argument in favour of primogeniture, has special reference to landed property. It is contended that the habit of dividing inheritances equally, or with an approach to equality, among children, promotes the subdivision of land into portions too small to admit of being cultivated in an advantageous manner. This argument, eternally reproduced, has again and again been refuted by English and Continental writers. It proceeds on a supposition entirely at variance with that on which all the theorems of political economy are grounded. It assumes that mankind in general will habitually act in a manner opposed to their immediate and obvious pecuniary interest. For the division of the inheritance does not necessarily imply division of the land; which may be held in common, as is not unfrequently the case in France and Belgium; or may become the property of one of the coheirs, being charged with the shares of the others by way of mortgage; or they may sell it outright, and divide the proceeds. When the division of the land would diminish its productive power, it is the direct interest of the heirs to adopt some one of these arrangements. Supposing, however, what the argument assumes, that either from legal difficulties or from their own stupidity and barbarism, they would not, if left to themselves, obey the dictates of this obvious interest, but would insist upon cutting up the land bodily into equal parcels, with the effect of impoverishing themselves; this would be an objection to a law such as exists in France, of compulsory division, but can be no reason why testators should be discouraged from exercising the right of bequest in general conformity to the rule of equality, since it would always be in their power to provide that the division of the inheritance should take place without dividing the land itself. That the attempts of the advocates of primogeniture to make out a case by facts against the custom of equal division, are equally abortive, has been shown in a former place. In all countries, or parts of countries, in which the division of inheritances is accompanied by small holdings, it is because small holdings are the general system of the country, even on the estates of the great proprietors.

Unless a strong case of social utility can be made out for primogeniture, it stands sufficiently condemned by the general principles of justice; being a broad distinction in the treatment of one person and of another, grounded solely on an accident. There is no need, therefore, to make out any case of economical evil *against* primogentiure. Such a case, however, and a very strong one, may be made. It is a natural effect of primogeniture to make the landlords a needy class. The object of the institution, or custom, is to keep the land together in large masses, and this it commonly accomplishes; but the legal proprietor of a large domain is not necessarily *bona fide* owner of the whole income which it yields. It is usually charged, in each generation, with provisions for the other children. It is often charged still more heavily by the imprudent expenditure of the proprietor. Great landowners are generally improvident in their expenses; they live up to their incomes when at the highest, and if any change of circumstances diminishes their resources, some time elapses before they make up their minds to retrench. Spendthrifts in other classes are ruined, and disappear from society; but the spendthrift landlord usually holds fast to his land, even when he has become a mere receiver of its rents for the benefit of creditors. The same desire to keep up the 'splendour' of the family, which gives rise to the custom of primogeniture, indisposes the owner to sell a part in order to set free the remainder; their apparent are therefore habitually greater than their real means, and they are under a perpetual temptation to proportion their expenditure to the former rather than to the latter. From such causes as these, in almost all countries of great landowners, the majority of landed estates are deeply mortgaged; and instead of having capital to spare for improvements, it requires all the increased value of land, caused by the rapid increase of the wealth and population of the country, to preserve the class from being impoverished.

§3. To avert this impoverishment, recourse was had to the contrivance of entails, whereby the order of succession was irrevocably fixed, and each holder, having only a life interest, was unable to burthen his successor. The land thus passing, free from debt, into the possession of the heir, the family could not be ruined by the improvidence of its existing representative. The economical evils arising from this disposition of property were partly of the same kind, partly different, but on the whole greater, than those arising from primogeniture alone. The possessor could not now ruin his successors, but he could still ruin himself: he was not at all more likely than in the former case to have the means necessary for improving the property: while, even if he had, he was still less likely to employ them for that purpose, when the benefit was to accrue to a person whom the entail made independent of him, while he had probably younger children to provide for, in whose favour he could not now charge the estate. While thus disabled from being himself an improver, neither could he sell the estate to somebody who would; since entail precludes alienation. In general he has even been unable to grant leases beyond the term of his own life; 'for', says Blackstone, 'if such leases had been valid, then, under cover of long leases, the issue might have been virtually disinherited'; and it has been necessary in Great Britain to relax, by statute, the rigour of entails, in order to allow either of long leases, or of the execution of improvements at the expense of the estate. It may be added that the heir of entail, being assured of succeeding to the family property, however undeserving of it, and being aware of this from his earliest years, has much more than the ordinary chances of growing up idle, dissipated, and profligate.

In England, the power of entail is more limited by law, than in Scotland and in most other countries where it exists. A landowner can settle his property upon any number of persons successively who are living at the time, and upon one unborn person, on whose attaining the age of twenty-one, the entail expires, and the land becomes his absolute property. An estate may in this manner be transmitted through a son, or a son and grandson, living when the deed is executed, to an unborn child of that grandson. It has been maintained that this power of entail is not sufficiently extensive to do any mischief: in truth, however, it is much larger than it seems. Entails very rarely expire; the first heir of entail, when of age, joins with the existing possessor in resettling the estate, so as to prolong the entail for a further term. Large properties, therefore, are rarely free for any considerable period, from the restraints of a strict settlement; though the mischief is in one respect mitigated, since in the renewal of the settlement for one more generation, the estate is usually charged with a provision for younger children.

In an economical point of view, the best system of landed

property is that in which land is most completely an object of commerce; passing readily from hand to hand when a buyer can be found to whom it is worth while to offer a greater sum for the land, than the value of the income drawn from it by its existing possessor. This of course is not meant of ornamental property, which is a source of expense, not profit; but only of land employed for industrial uses, and held for the sake of the income which it affords. Whatever facilitates the sale of land, tends to make it a more productive instrument of the community at large; whatever prevents or restricts its sale, subtracts from its usefulness. Now, not only has entail this effect, but primogeniture also. The desire to keep land together in large masses, from other motives than that of promoting its productiveness, often prevents changes and alienations which would increase its efficiency as an instrument.

§4. On the other hand, a law which, like the French, restricts the power of bequest to a narrow compass, and compels the equal division of the whole or the greater part of the property among the children, seems to me, though on different grounds, also very seriously objectionable. The only reason for recognizing in the children any claim at all to more than a provision, sufficient to launch them in life, and enable them to find a livelihood, is grounded on the expressed or presumed wish of the parent; whose claim to dispose of what is actually his own, cannot be set aside by any pretensions of others to receive what is not theirs. To control the rightful owner's liberty of gift, by creating in the children a legal right superior to it, is to postpone a real claim to an imaginary one. To this great and paramount objection to the law, numerous secondary ones may be added. Desirable as it is that the parent should treat the children with impartiality, and not make an eldest son or a favourite, impartial division is not alway synonymous with equal division. Some of the children may, without fault of their own, be less capable than others of providing for themselves: some may, by other means than their own exertions, be already provided for: and impartiality may therefore require that the rule observed should not be one of equality, but of compensation. Even when equality is the object, there are sometimes better means of attaining it, than the inflexible rules by which law must necessarily proceed. If one of the coheirs, being of a quarrelsome or litigious disposition, stands upon his utmost rights, the law cannot make equitable adjustments; it cannot apportion the property as seems best for the collective interest of all concerned; if there are several parcels of land, and the heirs cannot agree about their value, the law cannot give a parcel to each, but every separate parcel must be either put up to sale or divided: if there is a residence, or a park or pleasure-ground, which would be destroyed, as such, by subdivision, it must be sold, perhaps at a great sacrifice both of money and of feeling. But what the law could not do, the parent could. By means of the liberty of bequest, all these points might be determined according to reason and the general interest of the persons concerned; and the spirit of the principle of equal division might be the better observed, because the testator was emancipated from its letter. Finally, it would not then be necessary, as under the compulsory system it is, that the law should interfere authoritatively in the concerns of individuals, not only on the occurrence of a death, but throughout life, in order to guard against the attempts of parents to frustrate the legal claims of their heirs, under colour of gifts and other alienations *inter vivos*.

In conclusion; all owners of property should, I conceive, have power to dispose by will of every part of it, but not to determine the person who should succeed to it after the death of all who were living when the will was made. Under what restrictions it should be allowable to bequeath property to one person for life, with remainder to another person already in existence, is a question belonging to general legislation, not to political economy. Such settlements would be no greater hindrance to alienation than any case of joint ownership, since the consent of persons actually in existence is all that would be necessary for any new arrangement respecting the property.

§5. From the subject of Inheritance I now pass to that of Contracts, and among these, to the important subject of the Laws of Partnership. How much of good or evil depends upon these laws, and how important it is that they should be the best possible, is evident to all who recognize in the extension of the co-operative principle in the larger sense of the term, the great economical necessity of modern industry. The progress of the productive arts requiring that many sorts of industrial occupation should be carried on by larger and larger capitals, the productive power of industry must suffer by whatever impedes the formation of large capitals through the aggregation of smaller ones. Capitals of the requisite magnitude belonging to single owners, do not, in most countries, exist in the needful abundance, and would be still less numerous if the laws favoured the diffusion instead of the concentration of property: while it is most undesirable that all those improved processes, and those means of efficiency and economy in production, which depend on the possession of large funds, should be monopolies in the hands of a few rich individuals, through the difficulties experienced by persons of moderate or small means in associating their capital. Finally, I must repeat my conviction, that the industrial economy which divides society absolutely into two portions, the payers of wages and the receivers of them, the first counted by thousands and the last by millions, is neither fit for, nor capable of, indefinite duration: and the possibility of changing this system for one of combination without dependence, and unity of interest instead of organized hostility, depends altogether upon the future developments of the Partnership principle.

Yet there is scarcely any country whose laws do not throw great, and in most cases, intentional obstacles in the way of the formation of any numerous partnership. In England it is already a serious discouragement, that differences among partners are, practically speaking, only capable of adjudication by the Court of Chancery: which is often worse than placing such questions out of the pale of all law; since any one of the disputant parties, who is either dishonest or litigious, can involve the others at his pleasure in the expense, trouble, and anxiety, which are the unavoidable accompaniments of a Chancery suit, without their having the power of freeing themselves from the infliction even by breaking up the association.[3] Besides this, it required, until lately, a separate Act of the legislature before any joint-stock association could legally constitute itself, and be empowered to act as one body. By a statute passed a few years ago, this necessity is done away; but the statute in question is described by competent authorities as a 'mass of confusion,' of which they say that there 'never was such an infliction' on persons entering into partnership.[4] When a number of persons, whether few or many, freely desire to unite their funds for a common undertaking, not asking any peculiar privilege, nor the power to dispossess any one of property, the law can have no good reason for throwing difficulties in the way of the realization of the project. On compliance with a few simple conditions of publicity, any body of persons ought to have the power of constituting themselves into a joint-stock company, or *société en nom collectif*, without asking leave either of any public officer or of parliament. As an association of many partners must practically be under the management of a few, every facility ought to be

3. Mr Cecil Fane, the Commissioner of the Bankruptcy Court, in his evidence before the Committee on the Law of Partnership, says: 'I remember a short time ago reading a written statement by two eminent solicitors, who said that they had known many partnership accounts go into Chancery, but that they never knew one come out. ... Very few of the persons who would be disposed to engage in partnerships of this kind' (co-operative associations of working men) 'have any idea of the truth, namely, that the decision of questions arising amongst partners is really impracticable.

'Do they not know that one partner may rob the other without any possibility of his obtaining redress? – The fact is so; but whether they know it or not, I cannot undertake to say.'

This flagrant injustice is, in Mr Fane's opinion, wholly attributable to the defects of the tribunal. 'My opinion is, that if there is one thing more easy than another, it is the settlement of partnership questions, and for the simple reason, that everything which is done in a partnership is entered in the books; the evidence therefore is at hand; if therefore a rational mode of proceeding were once adopted, the difficulty would altogether vanish.' – Minutes of Evidence annexed to the Report of the Select Committee on the Law of Partnership (1851), pp. 85–7.

4. Report, ut supra, p. 167.

afforded to the body for exercising the necessary control and check over those few, whether they be themselves members of the association, or merely its hired servants: and in this point the English system is still at a lamentable distance from the standard of perfection.

§6. Whatever facilities, however, English law might give to associations formed on the principles of ordinary partnership, there is one sort of joint-stock association which until the year 1855 it absolutely disallowed, and which could only be called into existence by a special act either of the legislature or of the Crown. I mean, associations with limited liability.

Associations with limited liability are of two kinds: in one, the liability of all the partners is limited, in the other that of some of them only. The first is the *société anonyme* of the French law, which in England had until lately no other name than that of 'chartered company': meaning thereby a joint-stock company whose shareholders, by a charter from the Crown or a special enactment of the legislature, stood exempted from any liability for the debts of the concern, beyond the amount of their subscriptions. The other species of limited partnership is that known to the French law under the name of *commandite*; of this, which in England is still unrecognized and illegal, I shall speak presently.

If a number of persons choose to associate for carrying on any operation of commerce or industry, agreeing among themselves and announcing to those with whom they deal that the members of the association do not undertake to be responsible beyond the amount of the subscribed capital; is there any reason that the law should raise objections to this proceeding, and should impose on them the unlimited responsibility which they disclaim? For whose sake? Not for that of the partners themselves; for it is they whom the limitation of responsibility benefits and protects. It must therefore be for the sake of third parties; namely, those who may have transactions with the association, and to whom it may run in debt beyond what the subscribed capital suffices to pay. But nobody is obliged to deal with the association: still less is any one obliged to give it unlimited credit. The class of persons with whom such associations have dealings are in general perfectly capable of taking care of themselves, and there seems no reason that the law should be more careful of their interests than they will themselves be; provided no false representation is held out, and they are aware from the first what they have to trust to. The law is warranted in requiring from all joint-stock associations with limited responsibility, not only that the amount of capital on which they profess to carry on business should either be actually paid up or security given for it (if, indeed, with complete publicity, such a requirement would be necessary), but also that such accounts should be kept, accessible to individuals, and if needful, published to the world, as shall render it possible to ascertain at any time the existing state of the company's affairs, and to learn whether the capital which is the sole security for the engagements into which they enter, still subsists unimpaired: the fidelity of such accounts being guarded by sufficient penalties. When the law has thus afforded to individuals all practicable means of knowing the circumstances which ought to enter into their prudential calculations in dealing with the company, there seems no more need for interfering with individual judgment in this sort of transactions, than in any other part of the private business of life.

The reason usually urged for such interference is, that the managers of an association with limited responsibility, not risking their whole fortunes in the event of loss, while in case of gain they might profit largely, are not sufficiently interested in exercising due circumspection, and are under the temptation of exposing the funds of the association to improper hazards. It is, however, well ascertained that associations with unlimited responsibility, if they have rich shareholders, can obtain, even when known to be reckless in their transactions, improper credit to an extent far exceeding what would be given to companies equally ill-conducted whose creditors had only the subscribed capital to rely on.[5] To whichever side the balance of evil inclines, it is a consideration of more importance to the shareholders themselves than to third parties; since, with proper securities

5. See the Report already referred to, pp. 145-158.

for publicity, the capital of an association with limited liability could not be engaged in hazards beyond those ordinarily incident to the business it carries on, without the facts being known, and becoming the subject of comments by which the credit of the body would be likely to be affected in quite as great a degree as the circumstances would justify. If, under securities for publicity, it were found in practice that companies, formed on the principle of unlimited responsiiblity, were more skilfully and more cautiously managed, companies with limited liability would be unable to maintain an equal competition with them; and would therefore rarely be formed, unless when such limitation was the only condition on which the necessary amount of capital could be raised: and in that case it would be very unreasonable to say that their formation ought to be prevented.

It may further be remarked, that although, with equality of capital, a company of limited liability offers a somewhat less security to those who deal with it, than one in which every shareholder is responsible with his whole fortune, yet even the weaker of these two securities is in some respects stronger than that which an individual capitalist can afford. In the case of an individual, there is such security as can be founded on his unlimited liability, but not that derived from publicity of transactions, or from a known and large amount of paid-up capital. This topic is well treated in an able paper by M. Coquelin, published in the *Revue des Deux Mondes* for July 1843.[6]

'While third parties who trade with individuals,' says this writer, 'scarcely ever know, except by approximation, and even that most vague and uncertain, what is the amount of capital responsible for the performance of contracts made with them, those who trade with a *société anonyme* can obtain full information if they seek it, and perform their operations with a feeling of confidence that cannot exist in the other case. Again, nothing is easier than for an individual trader to conceal the extent of his engagements, as no one can know it certainly but himself. Even his confidential clerk may be ignorant of it, as the loans he finds himself compelled to make may not all be of a character to

6. The quotation is from a translation published by Mr H. C. Carey, in an American periodical, Hunt's Merchant's Magazine, for May and June 1845.

require that they be entered in his day-book. It is a secret confined to himself; one which transpires rarely, and always slowly; one which is unveiled only when the catastrophe has occurred. On the contrary, the *société anonyme* neither can nor ought to borrow, without the fact becoming known to all the world – directors, clerks, shareholders, and the public. Its operations partake in some respects, of the nature of those of governments. The light of day penetrates in every direction, and there can be no secrets from those who seek for information. Thus all is fixed, recorded, known, of the capital and debts in the case of the *société anonyme*, while all is uncertain and unknown in the case of the individual trader. Which of the two, we would ask the reader, presents the most favourable aspect, or the surest guarantee, to the view of those who trade with them?

'Again, availing himself of the obscurity in which his affairs are shrouded, and which he desires to increase, the private trader is enabled, so long as his business appears prosperous, to produce impressions in regard to his means far exceeding the reality, and thus to establish a credit not justified by those means. When losses occur, and he sees himself threatened with bankruptcy, the world is still ignorant of his condition, and he finds himself enabled to contract debts far beyond the possibility of payment. The fatal day arrives, and the creditors find a debt much greater than had been anticipated, while the means of payment are as much less. Even this is not all. The same obscurity which has served him so well thus far, when desiring to magnify his capital and increase his credit, now affords him the opportunity of placing a part of that capital beyond the reach of his creditors. It becomes diminished, if not annihilated. It hides itself, and not even legal remedies, nor the activity of creditors, can bring it forth from the dark corners in which it is placed. ... Our readers can readily determine for themselves if practices of this kind are equally easy in the case of the *société anonyme*. We do not doubt that such things are possible, but we think that they will agree with us that from its nature, its organization, and the necessary publicity that attends all its actions, the liability to such occurrences is very greatly diminished.'

The laws of most countries, England included, have erred in

a twofold manner with regard to joint-stock companies. While they have been most unreasonably jealous of allowing such associations to exist, especially with limited responsibility, they have generally neglected the enforcement of publicity; the best security to the public against any danger which might arise from this description of partnerships; and a security quite as much required in the case of those associations of the kind in question, which, by an exception from their general practice, they suffered to exist. Even in the instance of the Bank of England, which holds a monopoly from the legislature, and has had partial control over a matter of so much public interest as the state of the circulating medium, it is only within these few years that any publicity has been enforced; and the publicity was at first of an extremely incomplete character, though now, for most practical purposes, probably at length sufficient.

§7. The other kind of limited partnership which demands our attention, is that in which the managing partner or partners are responsible with their whole fortunes for the engagements of the concern, but have others associated with them who contribute only definite sums, and are not liable for anything beyond, though they participate in the profits according to any rule which may be agreed on. This is called partnership *en commandite:* and the partners with limited liability (to whom, by the French law, all interference in the management of the concern is interdicted) are known by the name *commanditaires.* Such partnerships are not allowed by English law: in all private partnerships, whoever shares in the profits is liable for the debts, to as plenary an extent as the managing partner.

For such prohibition no satisfactory defence has ever, so far as I am aware, been made. Even the insufficient reason given against limiting the responsibility of shareholders in a joint-stock company does not apply here; there being no diminution of the motives to circumspect management, since all who take any part in the direction of the concern are liable with their whole fortunes. To third parties, again, the security is improved by the existence of a commandite; since the amount subscribed by commanditaires is all of it available to creditors, the commanditaires losing their whole investment before any creditor can lose anything; while, if instead of becoming partners to that amount, they had lent the sum at an interest equal to the profit they derived from it, they would have shared with the other creditors in the residue of the estate, diminishing *pro rata* the dividend obtained by all. While the practice of commandite thus conduces to the interest of creditors, it is often highly desirable for the contracting parties themselves. The managers are enabled to obtain the aid of a much greater amount of capital than they could borrow on their own security; and persons are induced to aid useful undertakings, by embarking limited portions of capital in them, when they would not, and often could not prudently, have risked their whole fortunes on the chances of the enterprise.

It may perhaps be thought that where due facilities are afforded to joint-stock companies, commandite partnerships are not required. But there are classes of cases to which the commandite principle must always be better adapted than the joint-stock principle. 'Suppose,' says M. Coquelin, 'an inventor seeking for a capital to carry his invention into practice. To obtain the aid of capitalists, he must offer them a share of the anticipated benefit; they must associate themselves with him in the chances of its success. In such a case, which of the forms would he select? Not a common partnership, certainly'; for various reasons, and especially the extreme difficulty of finding a partner with capital, willing to risk his whole fortune on the success of the invention.[7]

7. 'There has been a great deal of commiseration professed,' says Mr Duncan, solicitor, 'towards the poor inventor; he has been oppressed by the high cost of patents; but his chief oppression has been the partnership law, which prevents his getting any one to help him to develop his invention. He is a poor man, and therefore cannot give security to a creditor; no one will lend him money; the rate of interest offered, however high it may be, is not an attraction. But if by the alteration of the law he could allow capitalists to take an interest with him and share the profits, while the risk should be confined to the capital they embarked, there is very little doubt at all that he would frequently get assistance from capitalists; whereas at the present moment, with the law as it stands, he is completely destroyed, and his invention is useless to him; he struggles month after month; he applies

'Neither would he select the *société anonyme*,' or any other form
of joint-stock company, 'in which he might be superseded as
manager. He would stand, in such an association, on no better
footing than any other shareholder, and he might be lost in the
crowd; whereas, the association existing, as it were, by and for
him, the management would appear to belong to him as a matter
of right. Cases occur in which a merchant or a manufacturer,
without being precisely an inventor, has undeniable claims to the
management of an undertaking, from the possession of qualities
peculiarly calculated to promote its success. So great, indeed,'
continues M. Coquelin, 'is the necessity, in many cases, for the
limited partnership, that it is difficult to conceive how we could
dispense with or replace it': and in reference to his own country
he is probably in the right.

Where there is so great a readiness as in England, on the part
of the public, to form joint-stock associations, even without the
encouragement of a limitation of responsibility; commandite
partnership, though its prohibition is in principle quite indefensible, cannot be deemed to be, in a merely economical point of
view, of the imperative necessity which M. Coquelin ascribes to
it. Yet the inconveniences are not small, which arise indirectly
from provisions of law by which every one who shares in the
profits of a concern is subject to the full liabilities of an unlimited
partnership. It is impossible to say how many or what useful
modes of combination are rendered impracticable by such a state
of the law. It is sufficient for its condemnation that, unless in
some way relaxed, it is inconsistent with the payment of wages

---

again and again to the capitalist without avail. I know it practically in two
or three cases of patented inventions; especially one where parties with
capital were desirous of entering into an undertaking of great moment in
Liverpool, but five or six different gentlemen were deterred from doing so,
all feeling the strongest objection to what each one called the cursed partnership law.' Report, p. 155.

Mr Fane says, 'In the course of my professional life, as a Commissioner
of the Court of Bankruptcy, I have learned that the most unfortunate man
in the world is an inventor. The difficulty which an inventor finds in getting at capital involves him in all sorts of embarrassments, and he ultimately
is for the most part a ruined man, and somebody else gets possession of his
invention.' Ib. p. 82.

in part by a percentage on profits; in other words, the association of the operatives as virtual partners with the capitalist.

It is, above all, with reference to the improvement and elevation of the working classes that complete freedom in the conditions of partnership is indispensable. Combinations such as the associations of workpeople, described in a former chapter, are the most powerful means of effecting the social emancipation of the labourers through their own moral qualities. Nor is the liberty of association important solely for its examples of success, but fully as much so for the sake of attempts which would not succeed; but by their failure would give instruction more impressive than can be afforded by anything short of actual experience. Every theory of social improvement, the worth of which is capable of being brought to an experimental test, should be permitted, and even encouraged, to submit itself to that test. From such experiments the active portion of the working classes would derive lessons, which they would be slow to learn from the teaching of persons supposed to have interests and prejudices adverse to their good; would obtain the means of correcting, at no cost to society, whatever is now erroneous in their notions of the means of establishing their independence; and of discovering the conditions, moral, intellectual, and industrial, which are indispensably necessary for effecting without injustice, or for effecting at all, the social regeneration they aspire to.[9]

The French law of partnership is superior to the English in permitting commandite; and superior, in having no such unmanageable instrument as the Court of Chancery, all cases

8. It has been found possible to effect this through the Limited Liability Act, by erecting the capitalist and his workpeople into a Limited Company; as proposed by Messrs Briggs. [See above pp. 132–3.]

9. By an Act of the year 1852, called the Industrial and Provident Societies Act, for which the nation is indebted to the public-spirited exertions of Mr Slaney, industrial associations of working people are admitted to the statutory privileges of Friendly Societies. This not only exempts them from the formalities applicable to joint-stock companies, but provides for the settlement of disputes among the partners without recourse to the Court of Chancery. There are still some defects in the provisions of this Act, which hamper the proceedings of the Societies in several respects; as is pointed out in the Almanack of the Rochdale Equitable Pioneers for 1861.

arising from commercial transactions being adjudicated in a comparatively cheap and expeditious manner by a tribunal of merchants. In other respects the French system was, and I believe, still is, far worse than the English. A joint-stock company with limited responsibility cannot be formed without the express authorization of the department of government called the *Conseil d'Etat*, a body of administrators, generally entire strangers to industrial transactions, who have no interest in promoting enterprises, and are apt to think that the purpose of their institution is to restrain them; whose consent cannot in any case be obtained without an amount of time and labour which is a very serious hindrance to the commencement of an enterprise, while the extreme uncertainty of obtaining that consent at all is a great discouragement to capitalists who would be willing to subscribe. In regard to joint-stock companies without limitation of responsibility, which in England exist in such numbers and are formed with such facility, these associations cannot, in France, exist at all; for, in cases of unlimited partnership, the French law does not permit the division of the capital into transferable shares.

The best existing laws of partnership appear to be those of the New England States. According to Mr Carey,[10] 'nowhere is association so little trammelled by regulations as in New England; the consequence of which is, that it is carried to a greater extent there, and particularly in Massachusetts and Rhode Island, than in any other part of the world. In these states, the soil is covered with *compagnies anonymes*—chartered companies —for almost every conceivable purpose. Every town is a corporation for the management of its roads, bridges, and schools: which are, therefore, under the direct control of those who pay for them, and are consequently well managed. Academies and churches, lyceums and libraries, saving-fund societies, and trust companies, exist in numbers proportioned to the wants of the people, and all are corporations. Every district has its local bank, of a size to suit its wants, the stock of which is owned by the small capitalists of the neighbourhood, and managed by themselves; the consequence of which is, that in no part of the world

10. In a note appended to his translation of M. Coquelin's paper.

is the system of banking so perfect—so little liable to vibration in the amount of loans—the necessary effect of which is, that in none is the value of property so little affected by changes in the amount or value of the currency resulting from the movements of *their* own banking institutions. In the two states to which we have particularly referred, they are almost two hundred in number. Massachusetts, alone, offers to our view fifty-three insurance offices, of various forms, scattered through the state, and all incorporated. Factories are incorporated, and are owned in shares; and every one that has any part in the management of their concerns, from the purchase of the raw material to the sale of the manufactured article, is a part owner; while every one employed in them has a prospect of becoming one, by the use of prudence, exertion, and economy. Charitable associations exist in large numbers, and all are incorporated. Fishing vessels are owned in shares by those who navigate them; and the sailors of a whaling ship depend in a great degree, if not altogether, upon the success of the voyage for their compensation. Every master of a vessel trading in the Southern Ocean is a part owner, and the interest he possesses is a strong inducement to exertion and economy, by aid of which the people of New England are rapidly driving out the competition of other nations for the trade of that part of the world. Wherever settled, they exhibit the same tendency to combination of action. In New York they are the chief owners of the lines of packet ships, which are divided into shares, owned by the shipbuilders, the merchants, the master, and the mates; which last generally acquire the means of becoming themselves masters, and to this is due their great success. The system is the most perfectly democratic of any in the world. It affords to every labourer, every sailor, every operative, male or female, the prospect of advancement; and its results are precisely such as we should have reason to expect. In no part of the world are talent, industry, and prudence, so certain to be largely rewarded.'

The cases of insolvency and fraud on the part of chartered companies in America, which have caused so much loss and so much scandal in Europe, did not occur in the part of the Union to which this extract refers, but in other States, in which the right of association is much more fettered by legal restrictions, and in which, accordingly, joint-stock associations are not comparable in number or variety to those of New England. Mr Carey adds, 'A careful examination of the systems of the several states, can scarcely, we think, fail to convince the reader of the advantage resulting from permitting men to determine among themselves the terms upon which they will associate, and allowing the associations that may be formed to contract with the public as to the terms upon which they will trade together, whether of the limited or unlimited liability of the partners.' This principle has been adopted as the foundation of all recent English legislation on the subject.

§8. I proceed to the subject of Insolvency Laws.

Good laws on this subject are important, first and principally, on the score of public morals; which are on no point more under the influence of the law, for good and evil, than in a matter belonging so pre-eminently to the province of law as the preservation of pecuniary integrity. But the subject is also, in a merely economical point of view, of great importance. First, because the economical well-being of a people, and of mankind, depends in an especial manner upon their being able to trust each other's engagements. Secondly, because one of the risks, or expenses, of industrial operations is the risk or expense of what are commonly called bad debts, and every saving which can be effected in this liability is a diminution of cost of production; by dispensing with an item of outlay which in no way conduces to the desired end, and which must be paid for either by the consumer of the commodity, or from the general profits of capital, according as the burthen is peculiar or general.

The laws and practice of nations on this subject have almost always been in extremes. The ancient laws of most countries were all severity to the debtor. They invested the creditor with a power of coercion, more or less tyrannical, which he might use against his insolvent debtor, either to extort the surrender of hidden property, or to obtain satisfaction of a vindictive character, which might console him for the non-payment of the debt.

This arbitrary power has extended, in some countries, to making the insolvent debtor serve the creditor as his slave: in which plan there were at least some grains of common sense, since it might possibly be regarded as a scheme for making him work out the debt by his labour. In England the coercion assumed the milder form of ordinary imprisonment. The one and the other were the barbarous expedients of a rude age, repugnant to justice, as well as to humanity. Unfortunately the reform of them, like that of the criminal law generally, has been taken in hand as an affair of humanity only, not of justice: and the modish humanity of the present time, which is essentially a thing of one idea, has in this as in other cases, gone into a violent reaction against the ancient severity, and might almost be supposed to see in the fact of having lost or squandered other people's property, a peculiar title to indulgence. Everything in the law which attached disagreeable consequences to that fact, was gradually relaxed, or entirely got rid of: until the demoralizing effects of this laxity became so evident as to determine, by more recent legislation, a salutary though very insufficient movement in the reverse direction.

The indulgence of the laws to those who have made themselves unable to pay their just debts, is usually defended, on the plea that the sole object of the law should be, in case of insolvency, not to coerce the person of the debtor, but to get at his property, and distribute it fairly among the creditors. Assuming that this is and ought to be the sole object, the mitigation of the law was in the first instance carried so far as to sacrifice that object. Imprisonment at the discretion of a creditor was really a powerful engine for extracting from the debtor any property which he had concealed or otherwise made away with; and it remains to be shown by experience whether, in depriving creditors of this instrument, the law, even as last amended, has furnished them with a sufficient equivalent. But the doctrine, that the law has done all that ought to be expected from it, when it has put the creditors in possession of the property of an insolvent, is in itself a totally inadmissible piece of spurious humanity. It is the business of law to prevent wrong-doing, and not simply to patch up the consequences of it when it has been committed. The law is bound to

take care that insolvency shall not be a good pecuniary speculation; that men shall not have the privilege of hazarding other
people's property without their knowledge or consent, taking
the profits of the enterprise if it is successful, and if it fails throwing the loss upon the rightful owners; and that they shall not
find it answer to make themselves unable to pay their just debts,
by spending the money of their creditors in personal indulgence.
It is admitted that what is technically called fraudulent bankruptcy, the false pretence of inability to pay, is, when detected,
properly subject to punishment. But does it follow that insolvency
is not the consequence of misconduct because the inability to pay
may be real? If a man has been a spendthrift, or a gambler, with
property on which his creditors had a prior claim, shall he pass
scot-free because the mischief is consummated and the money
gone? Is there any very material difference in point of morality
between this conduct, and those other kinds of dishonesty which
go by the names of fraud and embezzlement?

Such cases are not a minority, but a large majority among
insolvencies. The statistics of bankruptcy prove the fact. 'By far
the greater part of all insolvencies arise from notorious misconduct; the proceedings of the Insolvent Debtors Court and of the
Bankruptcy Court will prove it. Excessive and unjustifiable
overtrading, or most absurd speculation in commodities, merely
because the poor speculator "thought they would get up", but
why he thought so he cannot tell; speculation in hops, in tea, in
silk, in corn – things with which he is altogether unacquainted;
wild and absurd investments in foreign funds, or in joint stocks;
these are among the most innocent causes of bankruptcy.'[11] The
experienced and intelligent writer from whom I quote, corrobor-
ates his assertion by the testimony of several of the official.
assignees of the Bankruptcy Court. One of them says, 'As far as
I can collect from the books and documents furnished by the
bankrupts, it seems to me that' in the whole number of cases
which occurred during a given time in the court to which he was
attached, 'fourteen have been ruined by speculations in things
with which they were unacquainted; three by neglecting book-

11. From a volume published in 1845, entitled *Credit the Life of Commerce*, by Mr J. H. Elliott.

keeping; ten by trading beyond their capital and means, and the consequent loss and expense of accommodation bills; forty-nine by expending more than they could reasonably hope their profits would be, though their business yielded a fair return; none by any general distress, or the falling off of any particular branch of trade.' Another of these officers says that, during a period of eighteen months, 'fifty-two cases of bankruptcy have come under my care. It is my opinion that thirty-two of these have arisen from an imprudent expenditure, and five partly from that cause, and partly from a pressure on the business in which the bankrupts were employed. Fifteen I attribute to improvident speculations, combined in many instances with an extravagant mode of life.'

To these citations the author adds the following statements from his personal means of knowledge. 'Many insolvencies are produced by tradesmen's indolence: they keep no books, or at least imperfect ones, which they never balance; they never take stock; they employ servants, if their trade be extensive, whom they are too indolent even to supervise, and then become insolvent. It is not too much to say, that one-half of all the persons engaged in trade, even in London, never take stock at all: they go on year after year without knowing how their affairs stand, and at last, like the child at school, they find to their surprise, but one halfpenny left in their pocket. I will venture to say that not one-fourth of all the persons in the provinces, either manufacturers, tradesmen, or farmers, ever take stock; nor in fact does one-half of them ever keep account-books, deserving any other name than memorandum books. I know sufficient of the concerns of five hundred small tradesmen in the provinces, to be enabled to say, that not one-fifth of them ever take stock, or keep even the most ordinary accounts. I am prepared to say of such tradesmen, from carefully prepared tables, giving every advantage where there has been any doubt as to the causes of their insolvency, that where nine happen from extravagance or dishonesty, one' at most 'may be referred to misfortune alone.'[12]

Is it rational to expect among the trading classes any high sense

12. pp. 50-1.

of justice, honour, or integrity, if the law enables men who act in this manner to shuffle off the consequences of their misconduct upon those who have been so unfortunate as to trust them; and practically proclaims that it looks upon insolvency thus produced, as a 'misfortune', not an offence?

It is, of course, not denied, that insolvencies do arise from causes beyond the control of the debtor, and that, in many more cases, his culpability is not of a high order; and the law ought to make a distinction in favour of such cases, but not without a searching investigation; nor should the case ever be let go without having ascertained, in the most complete manner practicable, not the fact of insolvency, but the cause of it. To have been trusted with money or money's worth, and to have lost or spent it, is *prima facie* evidence of something wrong: and it is not for the creditor to prove, which he cannot do in one case out of ten, that there has been criminality, but for the debtor to rebut the presumption, by laying open the whole state of affairs, and showing either that there has been no misconduct, or that the misconduct has been of an excusable kind. If he fail in this, he ought never to be dismissed without a punishment proportioned to the degree of blame which seems justly imputable to him; which punishment, however, might be shortened or mitigated in proportion as he appeared likely to exert himself in repairing the injury done.

It is a common argument with those who approve a relaxed system of insolvency laws, that credit, except in the great operations of commerce, is an evil; and that to deprive creditors of legal redress is a judicious means of preventing credit from being given. That which is given by retail dealers to unproductive consumers is, no doubt, to the excess to which it is carried, a considerably evil. This, however, is only true of large, and especially of long, credits; for there is credit whenever goods are not paid for before they quit the shop, or, at least, the custody of the seller; and there would be much inconvenience in putting an end to this sort of credit. But a large proportion of the debts on which insolvency laws take effect, are those due by small tradesmen to the dealers who supply them: and on no class of debts does the demoralization occasioned by a bad state of the law, operate more perniciously. These are commercial credits, which no one wishes to see curtailed; their existence is of great importance to the general industry of the country, and to numbers of honest, well-conducted persons of small means, to whom it would be a great injury that they should be prevented from obtaining the accommodation they need, and would not abuse, through the omission of the law to provide just remedies against dishonest or reckless borrowers.

But though it were granted that retail transactions, on any footing but that of ready money payment, are an evil, and their entire suppression a fit subject for legislation to aim at; a worse mode of compassing that object could scarcely be invented, than to permit those who have been trusted by others to cheat and rob them with impunity. The law does not generally select the vices of mankind as the appropriate instrument for inflicting chastisement on the comparatively innocent. When it seeks to discourage any course of action, it does so by applying inducements of its own, not by outlawing those who act in the manner it deems objectionable, and letting loose the predatory instincts of the worthless part of mankind to feed upon them. If a man has committed murder the law condemns him to death; but it does not promise impunity to anybody who may kill him for the sake of taking his purse. The offence of believing another's word, even rashly, is not so heinous that for the sake of discouraging it the spectacle should be brought home to every door, of triumphant rascality, with the law on its side, mocking the victims it has made. This pestilent example has been very widely exhibited since the relaxation of the insolvency laws. It is idle to expect that, even by absolutely depriving creditors of all legal redress, the kind of credit which is considered objectionable would really be very much checked. Rogues and swindlers are still an exception among mankind, and people will go on trusting each other's promises. Large dealers, in abundant business, would refuse credit, as many of them already do: but in the eager competition of a great town, or the dependent position of a village shopkeeper, what can be expected from the tradesman to whom a single customer is of importance, the beginner, perhaps, who is striving to get into business? He will take the risk, even if it were still greater; he is ruined if he cannot sell his goods, and he can be ruined if he is defrauded. Nor does it avail to say, that he ought to make proper inquiries, and ascertain the character of those to whom he supplies good on trust. In some of the most flagrant cases of profligate debtors which have come before the Bankruptcy Court, the swindler had been able to give, and had given, excellent references.

CHAPTER X

Of Interferences of Government Grounded on Erroneous Theories

§1. FROM the necessary functions of government, and the effects produced on the economical interests of society by their good or ill discharge, we proceed to the functions which belong to what I have termed, for want of a better designation, the optional class; those which are sometimes assumed by governments and sometimes not, and which it is not unanimously admitted that they ought to exercise.

Before entering on the general principles of the question, it will be advisable to clear from our path all those cases, in which government interference works ill because grounded on false views of the subject interfered with. Such cases have no connexion with any theory respecting the proper limits of interference. There are some things with which governments ought not to meddle, and other things with which they ought; but whether right or wrong in itself, the interference must work for ill, if government, not understanding the subject which it meddles with, meddles to bring about a result which would be mischievous. We will therefore begin by passing in review various false theories, which have from time to time formed the ground of acts of government more or less economically injurious.

Former writers on political economy have found it needful to devote much trouble and space to this department of their subject. It has now happily become possible, at least in our own country, greatly to abridge this purely negative part of our discussions. The false theories of political economy which have done so much mischief in times past, are entirely discredited among all who have not lagged behind the general progress of opinion; and few of the enactments which were once grounded on those theories still help to deform the statute-book. As the principles on which their condemnation rests have been fully set forth in other parts of this Treatise, we may here content ourselves with a few brief indications.

Of these false theories, the most notable is the doctrine of Protection to Native Industry; a phrase meaning the prohibition, or the discouragement by heavy duties, of such foreign commodities as are capable of being produced at home. If the theory involved in this system had been correct, the practical conclusions grounded on it would not have been unreasonable. The theory was, that to buy things produced at home was a national benefit, and the introduction of foreign commodities generally a national loss. It being at the same time evident that the interest of the consumer is to buy foreign commodities in preference to domestic whenever they are either cheaper or better, the interest of the consumer appeared in this respect to be contrary to the public interest; he was certain, if left to his own inclinations, to do what according to the theory was injurious to the public.

It was shown, however, in our analysis of the effects of international trade, as it had been often shown by former writers, that the importation of foreign commodities, in the common course of traffic, never takes place, except when it is, economically speaking, a national good, by causing the same amount of commodities to be obtained at a smaller cost of labour and capital to the country. To prohibit, therefore, this importation, or impose duties which prevent it, is to render the labour and capital of the country less efficient in production than they would otherwise be; and compel a waste, of the difference between the labour and capital necessary for the home production of the commodity, and that which is required for producing the things with which it can be purchased from abroad. The amount of national loss thus occasioned is measured by the excess of the price at which the commodity is produced, over that at which it could be imported. In the case of manufactured goods, the whole difference between the two prices is absorbed in indemnifying the producers for waste of labour, or of the capital which supports that labour. Those who are supposed to be benefited, namely, the makers of the protected articles, (unless they form an exclusive company, and have a monopoly against their own countrymen as well as against foreigners,) do not obtain higher profits than other people. All is sheer loss, to the country as well as to the consumer. When the protected article

278

is a product of agriculture – the waste of labour not being incurred on the whole produce, but only on what may be called the last instalment of it – the extra price is only in part an indemnity for waste, the remainder being a tax paid to the landlords.

The restrictive and prohibitory policy was originally grounded on what is called the Mercantile System, which representing the advantage of foreign trade to consist solely in bringing money into the country, gave artificial encouragement to exportation of goods, and discountenanced their importation. The only exceptions to the system were those required by the system itself. The materials and instruments of production were the subjects of a contrary policy, directed however to the same end; they were freely imported, and not permitted to be exported, in order that manufacturers, being more cheaply supplied with the requisites of manufacture, might be able to sell cheaper, and therefore to export more largely. For a similar reason, importation was allowed and even favoured, when confined to the productions of countries, which were supposed to take from the country still more than it took from them, thus enriching it by a favourable balance of trade. As part of the same system, colonies were founded, for the supposed advantage of compelling them to buy our commodities, or at all events not to buy those of any other country: in return for which restriction, we were generally willing to come under an equivalent obligation with respect to the staple productions of the colonists. The consequences of the theory were pushed so far, that it was not unusual even to give bounties on exportation, and induce foreigners to buy from us rather than from other countries, by a cheapness which we artificially produced, by paying part of the price for them out of our own taxes. This is a stretch beyond the point yet reached by any private tradesman in his competition for business. No shopkeeper, I should think, ever made a practice of bribing customers by selling goods to them at a permanent loss, making it up to himself from other funds in his possession.

The principle of the Mercantile Theory is now given up even by writers and governments who still cling to the restrictive system. Whatever hold that system has over men's minds, independently of the private interests exposed to real or apprehended loss by its abandonment, is derived from fallacies other than the old notion of the benefits of heaping up money in the country. The most effective of these is the specious plea of employing our own countrymen and our national industry, instead of feeding and supporting the industry of foreigners. The answer to this, from the principles laid down in former chapters, is evident. Without reverting to the fundamental theorem discussed in an early part of the present treatise, respecting the nature and sources of employment for labour, it is sufficient to say, what has usually been said by the advocates of free trade, that the alternative is not between employing our own people and foreigners, but between employing one class and another of our own people. The imported commodity is always paid for, directly or indirectly, with the produce of our own industry: that industry being at the same time rendered more productive, since, with the same labour and outlay, we are enabled to possess ourselves of a greater quantity of the article. Those who have not well considered the subject are apt to suppose that our exporting an equivalent in our own produce, for the foreign articles we consume, depends on contingencies – on the consent of foreign countries to make some corresponding relaxation of their own restrictions, or on the question whether those from whom we buy are induced by that circumstance to buy more from us; and that, if these things, or things equivalent to them, do not happen, the payment must be made in money. Now, in the first place, there is nothing more objectionable in a money payment than in payment by any other medium, if the state of the market makes it the most advantageous remittance; and the money itself was first acquired, and would again be replenished, by the export of an equivalent value of our own products. But, in the next place, a very short interval of paying in money would so lower prices as either to stop a part of the importation, or raise up a foreign demand for our produce, sufficient to pay for the imports. I grant that this disturbance of the equation of international demand would be in some degree to our disadvantage, in the purchase of other imported articles; and that a country which prohibits some foreign commodities, does, *caeteris paribus*, obtain those which it does not prohibit, at a less price than it would otherwise have to pay. To express the same thing in other words; a country which destroys or prevents altogether certain branches of foreign trade, thereby annihilating a general gain to the world, which would be shared in some proportion between itself and other countries – does, in some circumstances, draw to itself, at the expense of foreigners, a larger share than would else belong to it of the gain arising from that portion of its foreign trade which it suffers to subsist. But even this it can only be enabled to do, if foreigners do not maintain equivalent prohibitions or restrictions against its commodities. In any case, the justice or expediency of destroying one of two gains, in order to engross a rather larger share of the other, does not require much discussion: the gain, too, which is destroyed, being, in proportion to the magnitude of the transactions, the larger of the two, since it is the one which capital, left to itself, is supposed to seek by preference.

Defeated as a general theory, the Protectionist doctrine finds support in some particular cases, from considerations which, when really in point, involve greater interests than mere saving of labour; the interests of national subsistence and of national defence. The discussions on the Corn Laws have familiarized everybody with the plea, that we ought to be independent of foreigners for the food of the people; and the Navigation Laws were grounded, in theory and profession, on the necessity of keeping up a 'nursery of seamen' for the navy. On this last subject I at once admit, that the object is worth the sacrifice; and that a country exposed to invasion by sea, if it cannot otherwise have sufficient ships and sailors of its own to secure the means of manning on an emergency an adequate fleet, is quite right in obtaining those means, even at an economical sacrifice in point of cheapness of transport. When the English Navigation Laws were enacted, the Dutch, from their maritime skill and their low rate of profit at home, were able to carry for other nations, England included, at cheaper rates than those nations could carry for themselves: which placed all other countries at a great comparative disadvantage in obtaining experienced seamen for their ships of war. The Navigation Laws, by which this deficiency was remedied, and at the same time a blow struck against the maritime power of a nation with which England was then frequently engaged in hostilities, were probably, though economically disadvantageous, politically expedient. But English ships and sailors can now navigate as cheaply as those of any other country; maintaining at least an equal competition with the other maritime nations even in their own trade. The ends which may once have justified Navigation Laws, require them no longer, and afforded no reason for maintaining this invidious exception to the general rule of free trade.

With regard to subsistence, the plea of the Protectionists has been so often and so triumphantly met, that it requires little notice here. That country is the most steadily as well as the most abundantly supplied with food, which draws its supplies from the largest surface. It is ridiculous to found a general system of policy on so improbable a danger as that of being at war with all the nations of the world at once; or to suppose that, even if inferior at sea, a whole country could be blockaded like a town, or that the growers of food in other countries would not be as anxious not to lose an advantageous market, as we should be not to be deprived of their corn. On the subject, however, of subsistence, there is one point which deserves more especial consideration. In cases of actual or apprehended scarcity, many countries of Europe are accustomed to stop the exportation of food. Is this, or not, sound policy? There can be no doubt that in the present state of international morality, a people cannot, any more than an individual, be blamed for not starving itself to feed others. But if the greatest amount of good to mankind on the whole, were the end aimed at in the maxims of international conduct, such collective churlishness would certainly be condemned by them. Suppose that in ordinary circumstances the trade in food were perfectly free, so that the price in one country could not habitually exceed that in any other by more than the cost of carriage, together with a moderate profit to the importer. A general scarcity ensues, affecting all countries, but in unequal degrees. If the price rose in one country more than in others, it would be a proof that in that country the scarcity was severest, and that by permitting food to go freely thither from any other country, it would be spared from a less urgent necessity to relieve a greater. When the interests, therefore, of all countries are considered, free exportation is desirable. To the exporting country considered separately, it may, at least on the particular occasion, be an inconvenience: but taking into account that the country which is now the giver, will in some future season be the receiver, and the one that is benefited by the freedom, I cannot but think that even to the apprehension of food rioters it might be made apparent, that in such cases they should do to others what they would wish done to themselves.

In countries in which the Protection theory is declining, but not yet given up, such as the United States, a doctrine has come into notice which is a sort of compromise between free trade and restriction, namely, that protection for protection's sake is improper, but that there is nothing objectionable in having as much protection as may incidentally result from a tariff framed solely for revenue. Even in England, regret is sometimes expressed that a 'moderate fixed duty' was not preserved on corn, on account of the revenue it would yield. Independently, however, of the general impolicy of taxes on the necessaries of life, this doctrine overlooks the fact, that revenue is received only on the quantity imported, but that the tax is paid on the entire quantity consumed. To make the public pay much that the treasury may receive a little, is not an eligible mode of obtaining a revenue. In the case of manufactured articles the doctrine involves a palpable inconsistency. The object of the duty as a means of revenue, is inconsistent with its affording, even incidentally, any protection. It can only operate as protection in so far as it prevents importation; and to whatever degree it prevents importation, it affords no revenue.

The only case in which, on mere principles of political economy, protecting duties can be defensible, is when they are imposed temporarily (especially in a young and rising nation) in hopes of naturalizing a foreign industry, in itself perfectly suitable to the circumstances of the country. The superiority of one country over another in a branch of production, often arises only from having begun it sooner. There may be no inherent advantage on one part, or disadvantage on the other, but only a present superiority of acquired skill and experience. A country which has this skill and experience yet to acquire, may in other respects be better adapted to the production than those which were earlier in the field: and besides, it is a just remark of Mr Rae, that nothing has a greater tendency to promote improvements in any branch of production, than its trial under a new set of conditions. But it cannot be expected that individuals should, at their own risk, or rather to their certain loss, introduce a new manufacture, and bear the burthen of carrying it on until the producers have been educated up to the level of those with whom the processes are traditional. A protecting duty, continued for a reasonable time, might sometimes be the least inconvenient mode in which the nation can tax itself for the support of such an experiment. But it is essential that the protection should be confined to cases in which there is good ground of assurance that the industry which it fosters will after a time be able to dispense with it; nor should the domestic producers ever be allowed to expect that it will be continued to them beyond the time necessary for a fair trial of what they are capable of accomplishing.

The only writer, of any reputation as a political economist, who now adheres to the Protectionist doctrine, Mr H. C. Carey, rests its defence, in an economic point of view, principally on two reasons. One is, the great saving in cost of carriage, consequent on producing commodities at or very near to the place where they are to be consumed. The whole of the cost of carriage, both on the commodities imported and on those exported in exchange for them, he regards as a direct burthen on the producers, and not, as is obviously the truth, on the consumers. On whomsoever it falls, it is, without doubt, a burthen on the industry of the world. But it is obvious (and that Mr Carey does not see it, is one of the many surprising things in his book) that the burthen is only borne for a more than equivalent advantage. If the commodity is bought in a foreign country with domestic produce in spite of the double cost of carriage, the fact proves that, heavy as that cost may be, the saving in cost of production outweighs it, and the collective labour of the country is on the whole better remunerated than if the article were produced at home. Cost of carriage is a natural protecting duty, which free trade has no power to abrogate: and unless America gained more by obtaining her manufactures through the medium of her corn and cotton than she loses in cost of carriage, the capital employed in producing corn and cotton in annually increased quantities for the foreign market, would turn to manufactures instead. The natural advantages attending a mode of industry in which there is less cost of carriage to pay, can at most be only a justification for a temporary and merely tentative protection. The expenses of production being always greatest at first, it may happen that the home production, though really the most advantageous, may not become so until after a certain duration of pecuniary loss, which it is not to be expected that private speculators should incur in order that their successors may be benefited by their ruin. I have therefore conceded that in a new country a temporary protecting duty may sometimes be economically defensible; on condition, however, that it be strictly limited in point of time, and provision be made that during the latter part of its existence it be on a gradually decreasing scale. Such temporary protection is of the same nature as a patent, and should be governed by similar conditions.

The remaining argument of Mr Carey in support of the economic benefits of Protectionism, applies only to countries whose exports consist of agricultural produce. He argues, that by a trade of this description they actually send away their soil: the distant consumers not giving back to the land of the country, as home consumers would do, the fertilizing elements which they abstract from it. This argument deserves attention on account of the physical truth on which it is founded; a truth which has only lately come to be understood, but which is henceforth destined to be a permanent element in the thoughts of statesmen, as it must always have been in the destinies of nations. To the question of Protectionism, however, it is irrelevant. That the immense growth of raw produce in America to be consumed in Europe, is progresssively exhausting the soil of the Eastern, and even of the older Western States, and that both are already far less productive than formerly, is credible in itself, even if no one bore witness to it. But what I have already said respecting cost of carriage, is true also of the cost of manuring. Free trade does not compel America to export corn: she would cease to do so if it ceased to be to her advantage. As, then, she would not persist in exporting raw produce and importing manufactures, any longer than the labour she saved by doing so exceeded what the carriage cost her, so when it became necessary for her to replace in the soil the elements of fertility which she had sent away, if the saving in cost of production were more than equivalent to the cost of carriage and of manure together, manure would be imported; and if not, the export of corn would cease. It is evident that one of these two things would already have taken place, if there had not been near at hand a constant succession of new soils, not yet exhausted of their fertility, the cultivation of which enables her, whether judiciously or not, to postpone the question of manure. As soon as it no longer answers better to break up new soils than to manure the old, America will either become a regular importer of manure, or will, without protecting duties, grow corn for herself only, and manufacturing for herself, will make her manure, as Mr Carey desires, at home.[1]

For these obvious reasons, I hold Mr Carey's economic arguments for Protectionism to be totally invalid. The economic, however, is far from being the strongest point of his case. American Protectionists often reason extremely ill; but it is an injustice to them to suppose that their Protectionist creed rests

1. To this Mr Carey would reply (indeed he has already so replied in advance) that of all commodities manure is the least susceptible of being conveyed to a distance. This is true of sewage, and of stable manure, but not true of the ingredients to which those manures owe their efficiency. These, on the contrary, are chiefly substances containing great fertilizing power in small bulk; substances of which the human body requires but a small quantity, and hence peculiarly susceptible of being imported; the mineral alkalies and the phosphates. The question indeed mainly concerns the phosphates, for of the alkalies, soda is procurable everywhere; while potass, being one of the constituents of granite and the other feldspathic rocks, exists in many subsoils, by whose progressive decomposition it is renewed, a large quantity also being brought down in the deposits of rivers. As for the phosphates, they, in the very convenient form of pulverized bones, are a regular article of commerce, largely imported into England; as they are sure to be into any country where the conditions of industry make it worth while to pay the price.

upon nothing superior to an economic blunder. Many of them have been led to it, much more by consideration for the higher interests of humanity, than by purely economic reasons. They, and Mr Carey at their head, deem it a necessary condition of human improvement that towns should abound; that men should combine their labour, by means of interchange – with near neighbours, with people of pursuits, capacities, and mental cultivation different from their own, sufficiently close at hand for mutual sharpening of wits and enlarging of ideas – rather than with people on the opposite side of the globe. They believe that a nation all engaged in the same, or nearly the same, pursuit – a nation all agricultural – cannot attain a high state of civilization and culture. And for this there is a great foundation of reason. If the difficulty can be overcome, the United States, with their free institutions, the universal schooling and their omnipresent press, are the people to do it; but whether this is possible or not is still a problem. So far, however, as it is an object to check the excessive dispersion of the population, Mr Wakefield has pointed out a better way; to modify the existing method of disposing of the unoccupied lands, by raising the price, instead of lowering it, or giving away the land gratuitously, as is largely done since the passing of the Homestead Act. To cut the knot in Mr Carey's fashion, by Protectionism, it would be necessary that Ohio and Michigan should be protected against Massachusetts as well as against England: for the manufactories of New England, no more than those of the old country, accomplish his desideratum of bringing a manufacturing population to the doors of the Western farmer. Boston and New York do not supply the want of local towns to the Western prairies, any better than Manchester; and it is as difficult to get back the manure from the one place as from the other.

There is only one part of the Protectionist scheme which requires any further notice: its policy towards colonies, and foreign dependencies; that of compelling them to trade exclusively with the dominant country. A country which thus secures to itself an extra foreign demand for its commodities, undoubtedly gives itself some advantage in the distribution of the general gains of the commercial world. Since, however, it causes the industry and capital of the colony to be diverted from channels, which are proved to be the most productive, inasmuch as they are those into which industry and capital spontaneously tend to flow; there is a loss, on the whole, to the productive powers of the world, and the mother country does not gain so much as she makes the colony lose. If, therefore, the mother country refuses to acknowledge any reciprocity of obligation, she imposes a tribute on the colony in an indirect mode, greatly more oppressive and injurious that the direct. But if, with a more equitable spirit, she submits herself to corresponding restrictions for the benefit of the colony, the result of the whole transaction is the ridiculous one, that each party loses much, in order that the other may gain a little.

§2. Next to the system of Protection, among mischievous interferences with the spontaneous course of industrial transactions, may be noticed certain interferences with contracts. One instance is that of the Usury Laws. These originated in a religious prejudice against receiving interest on money, derived from that fruitful source of mischief in modern Europe, the attempted adaptation to Christianity of doctrines and precepts drawn from the Jewish law. In Mahomedan nations the receiving of interest is formally interdicted, and rigidly abstained from: and Sismondi has noticed, as one among the causes of the industrial inferiority of the Catholic, compared with the Protestant parts of Europe, that the Catholic Church in the middle ages gave its sanction to the same prejudice; which subsists, impaired but not destroyed, wherever that religion is acknowledged. Where law or conscientious scruples prevent lending at interest, the capital which belongs to persons not in business is lost to productive purposes, or can be applied to them only in peculiar circumstances of personal connexion, or by a subterfuge. Industry is thus limited to the capital of the undertakers, and to what they can borrow from persons not bound by the same laws or religion as themselves. In Mussulman countries the bankers and money dealers are either Hindoos, Armenians, or Jews.

In more improved countries, legislation no longer discountenances the receipt of an equivalent for money lent; but it has everywhere interfered with the free agency of the lender and borrower, by fixing a legal limit to the rate of interest, and making the receipt of more than the appointed maximum a penal offence. This restriction, though approved by Adam Smith, has been condemned by all enlightened persons since the triumphant onslaught made upon it by Bentham in his 'Letters on Usury', which may still be referred to as the best extant writing on the subject.

Legislators may enact and maintain Usury Laws from one of two motives: ideas of public policy, or concern for the interest of the parties in the contract; in this case, of one party only, the borrower. As a matter of policy, the notion may possibly be, that it is for the general good that interest should be low. It is however a misapprehension of the causes which influence commercial transactions, to suppose that the rate of interest is really made lower by law, than it would be made by the spontaneous play of supply and demand. If the competition of borrowers, left unrestrained, would raise the rate of interest to six per cent, this proves that at five there would be a greater demand for loans, than there is capital in the market to supply. If the law in these circumstances permits no interest beyond five per cent, there will be some lenders, who not choosing to disobey the law, and not being in a condition to employ their capital otherwise, will content themselves with the legal rate: but others, finding that in a season of pressing demand, more may be made of their capital by other means than they are permitted to make by lending it, will not lend it at all; and the loanable capital, already too small for the demand, will be still further diminished. Of the disappointed candidates there will be many at such periods, who must have their necessities supplied at any price, and these will readily find a third section of lenders, who will not be averse to join in a violation of the law, either by circuitous transactions partaking of the nature of fraud, or by relying on the honour of the borrower. The extra expense of the roundabout mode of proceeding, and an equivalent for the risk of non-payment and of legal penalties, must be paid by the borrower, over and above the extra interest which would have been required of him by the general state of the market. The laws which were intended to lower the price paid by him for pecuniary accommodation, end thus in greatly increasing it. These laws have also a directly demoralizing tendency. Knowing the difficulty of detecting an illegal pecuniary transaction between two persons, in which no third person is involved, so long as it is the interest of both to keep the secret, legislators have adopted the expedient of tempting the borrower to become the informer, by making the annulment of the debt a part of the penalty for the offence; thus rewarding men for first obtaining the property of others by false promises, and then not only refusing payment, but invoking legal penalties on those who have helped them in their need. The moral sense of mankind very rightly infamizes those who resist an otherwise just claim on the ground of usury, and tolerates such a plea only when resorted to as the best legal defence available against an attempt really considered as partaking of fraud or extortion. But this very severity of public opinion renders the enforcement of the laws so difficult, and the infliction of the penalties so rare, that when it does occur it merely victimizes an individual, and has no effect on general practice.

In so far as the motive of the restriction may be supposed to be, not public policy, but regard for the interest of the borrower, it would be difficult to point out any case in which such tenderness on the legislator's part is more misplaced. A person of sane mind, and of the age at which persons are legally competent to conduct their own concerns, must be presumed to be a sufficient guardian of his pecuniary interests. If he may sell an estate, or grant a release, or assign away all his property, without control from the law, it seems very unnecessary that the only bargain which he cannot make without its intermeddling, should be a loan of money. The law seems to presume that the money-lender, dealing with necessitous persons, can take advantage of their necessities, and exact conditions limited only by his own pleasure. It might be so if there were only one money-lender within reach. But when there is the whole monied capital of a wealthy community to resort to, no borrower is placed under any disadvantage in the market merely by the urgency of his need. If he cannot borrow at the interest paid by other people, it must be because he cannot give such good security: and competition will limit the extra demand to a fair equivalent for the risk of his proving insolvent. Though the law intends favour to the borrower, it is to him above all that injustice is, in this case, done by it. What can be more unjust than that a person who cannot give perfectly good security, should be prevented from borrowing of persons who are willing to lend money to him, by their not being permitted to receive the rate of interest which would be a just equivalent for their risk? Through the mistaken kindness of the law, he must either go without the money which is perhaps necessary to save him from much greater losses, or be driven to expedients of a far more ruinous description, which the law either has not found it possible, or has not happened, to interdict.

Adam Smith rather hastily expressed the opinion, that only two kinds of persons, 'prodigals and projectors', could require to borrow money at more than the market rate of interest. He should have included all persons who are in any pecuniary difficulties, however temporary their necessities may be. It may happen to any person in business, to be disappointed of the resources on which he had calculated for meeting some engagement, the non-fulfilment of which on a fixed day would be bankruptcy. In periods of commercial difficulty, this is the condition of many prosperous mercantile firms, who become competitors for the small amount of disposable capital which, in a time of general distrust, the owners are willing to part with. Under the English usury laws, now happily abolished, the limitations imposed by those laws were felt as a most serious aggravation of every commercial crisis. Merchants who could have obtained the aid they required at an interest of seven or eight per cent for short periods, were obliged to give 20 or 30 per cent, or to resort to forced sales of goods at a still greater loss. Experience having obtruded these evils on the notice of Parliament, the sort of compromise took place, of which English legislation affords so many instances, and which helps to make our laws and policy the mass of inconsistency that they are. The law was reformed as a person reforms a tight shoe, who cuts a hole in it where it pinches hardest, and continues to wear it. Retaining the erroneous principle as a general rule, Parliament allowed an exception in the case in which the practical mischief was most flagrant. It left the usury laws unrepealed, but exempted bills of exchange, of not more than three months date, from their operation. Some years afterwards the laws were repealed in regard to all other contracts, but left in force as to all those which relate to land. Not a particle of reason could be given for making this extra-ordinary distinction: but the 'agricultural mind' was of opinion that the interest on mortgages, though it hardly ever came up to the permitted point, would came up to a still higher point; and the usury laws were maintained that the landlords might as they thought, be enabled to borrow below the market rate, as the corn-laws were kept up that the same class might be able to sell corn above the market rate. The modesty of the pretension was quite worthy of the intelligence which could think that the end aimed at was in any way forwarded by the means used.

With regard to the 'prodigals and projectors' spoken of by Adam Smith; no law can prevent a prodigal from ruining him-self, unless it lays him or his property under actual restraint, according to the unjustifiable practice of the Roman Law and some of the Continental systems founded on it. The only effect of usury laws upon a prodigal, is to make his ruin rather more expeditious, by driving him to a disreputable class of money-dealers, and rendering the conditions more onerous by the extra risk created by the law. As for projectors, (a term, in its unfav-ourable sense, rather unfairly applied to every person who has a project); such laws may put a veto upon the prosecution of the most promising enterprise, when planned, as it generally is, by a person who does not possess capital adequate to its successful completion. Many of the greatest improvements were at first looked shyly on by capitalists, and had to wait long before they found one sufficiently adventurous to be the first in a new path: many years elapsed before Stephenson could convince even the enterprising mercantile public of Liverpool and Manchester, of the advantage of substituting railways for turnpike roads; and plans on which great labour and large sums have been expended with little visible result (the epoch in their progress when pre-dictions of failure are most rife) may be indefinitely suspended, or altogether dropped, and the outlay all lost, if, when the original funds are exhausted, the law will not allow more to be raised on the terms on which people are willing to expose it to the chances of an enterprise not yet secure of success.

§3. Loans are not the only kind of contract, of which governments have thought themselves qualified to regulate the conditions better than the persons interested. There is scarcely any commodity which they have not, at some place or time, endeavoured to make either dearer or cheaper than it would be if left to itself. The most plausible case for artificially cheapening a commodity, is that of food. The desirableness of the object is in this case undeniable. But since the average price of food, like that of other things, conforms to the cost of production, with the addition of the usual profit; if this price is not expected by the farmer, he will, unless compelled by law, produce no more than he requires for his own consumption: and the law, therefore, if absolutely determined to have food cheaper, must substitute, for the ordinary motives to cultivation, a system of penalties. If it shrinks from doing this, it has no resource but that of taxing the whole nation, to give a bounty or premium to the grower or importer of corn, thus giving everybody cheap bread at the expense of all: in reality a largess to those who do not pay taxes, at the expense of those who do; one of the forms of a practice essentially bad, that of converting the working classes into unworking classes by making them a present of subsistence.

It is not however so much the general or average price of food, as its occasional high price in times of emergency, which governments have studied to reduce. In some cases, as for example the famous 'maximum' of the revolutionary government of 1793, the compulsory regulation was an attempt by the ruling powers to counteract the necessary consequences of their own acts; to scatter an indefinite abundance of the circulating medium with one hand, and keep down prices with the other; a thing manifestly impossible under any régime except one of unmitigated terror. In case of actual scarcity, governments are often urged, as they were in the Irish emergency of 1847, to take measures of some sort for moderating the price of food. But the price of a thing cannot be raised by deficiency of supply, beyond what is sufficient to make a corresponding reduction of the consumption; and if a government prevents this reduction from being brought about by a rise of price, there remains no mode of effecting it unless by taking possession of all the food, and serving it out in rations, as in a besieged town. In a real scarcity, nothing can afford general relief, except a determination by the richer classes to diminish their own consumption. If they buy and consume their usual quantity of food, and content themselves with giving money, they do no good. The price is forced up until the poorest competitors have no longer the means of competing, and the privation of food is thrown exclusively upon the indigent, the other classes being only affected pecuniarily. When the supply is insufficient, somebody must consume less, and if every rich person is determined not to be that somebody, all they do by subsidizing their poor competitors is to force up the price so much the higher, with no effect but to enrich the corn-dealers, the very reverse of what is desired by those who recommend such measures. All that governments can do in these emergencies, is to counsel a general moderation in consumption, and to interdict such kinds of it as are not of primary importance. Direct measures at the cost of the state, to procure food from a distance, are expedient when from peculiar reasons the thing is not likely to be done by private speculation. In any other case they are a great error. Private speculators, will not, in such cases, venture to compete with the government; and though a government can do more than any one merchant, it cannot do nearly so much as all merchants.

§4. Governments, however, are oftener chargeable with having attempted, too successfully, to make things dear, than with having aimed by wrong means at making them cheap. The usual instrument for producing artificial dearness is monopoly. To confer a monopoly upon a producer or leader, or upon a set of producers or dealers not too numerous to combine, is to give them the power of levying any amount of taxation on the public, for their individual benefit, which will not make the public forego the use of the commodity. When the sharers in the monopoly are so numerous and so widely scattered that they are prevented from combining, the evil is considerably less: but even then the competition is not so active among a limited as among an unlimited number. Those who feel assured of a fair average proportion in the general business, are seldom eager to get a larger share by foregoing a portion of their profits. A limitation of competition, however partial, may have mischievous effects quite disproportioned to the apparent cause. The mere exclusion of foreigners, from a branch of industry open to the free competition of every native, has been known, even in England, to render that branch a conspicuous exception to the general industrial energy of the country. The silk manufacture of England remained far behind that of other countries of Europe, so long as the foreign fabrics were prohibited. In addition to the tax levied for the profit, real or imaginary, of the monopolists, the consumer thus pays an additional tax for their laziness and incapacity. When relieved from the immediate stimulus of competition, producers and dealers grow indifferent to the dictates of their ultimate pecuniary interest; preferring to the most hopeful prospects, the present ease of adhering to routine. A person who is already thriving, seldom puts himself out of his way to commence even a lucrative improvement, unless urged by the additional motive of fear lest some rival should supplant him by getting possession of it before him.

The condemnation of monopolies ought not to extend to patents, by which the originator of an improved process is allowed to enjoy, for a limited period, the exclusive privilege of using his own improvement. This is not making the commodity dear for his benefit, but merely postponing a part of the increased cheapness which the public owe to the inventor, in order to compensate and reward him for the service. That he ought to be both compensated and rewarded for it, will not be denied, and also that if all were at once allowed to avail themselves of his ingenuity, without having shared the labours or the expenses which he had to incur in bringing his idea into a practical shape, either such expenses and labours would be undergone by nobody except very opulent and very public-spirited persons, or the state must put a value on the service rendered by an inventor, and make him a pecuniary grant. This has been done in some instances, and may be done without inconvenience in cases of very conspicuous public benefit; but in general an exclusive privilege, of temporary duration, is preferable; because it leaves nothing to any one's discretion; because the reward conferred by it depends upon the invention's being found useful, and the greater the usefulness the greater the reward; and because it is paid by the very persons to whom the service is rendered, the consumers of the commodity. So decisive, indeed, are these considerations, that if the system of patents were abandoned for that of rewards by the state, the best shape which these could assume would be that of a small temporary tax, imposed for the inventor's benefit, on all persons making use of the invention. To this, however, or to any other system which would vest in the state the power of deciding whether an inventor should derive any pecuniary advantage from the public benefit which he confers, the objections are evidently stronger and more fundamental that the strongest which can possibly be urged against patents. It is generally admitted that the present Patent Laws need much improvement; but in this case, as well as in the closely analogous one of Copyright, it would be a gross immorality in the law to set everybody free to use a person's work without his consent, and without giving him an equivalent. I have seen with real alarm several recent attempts, in quarters carrying some authority, to impugn the principle of patents altogether; attempts which, if practically successful, would enthrone free stealing under the prostituted name of free trade, and make the men of brains, still more than at present, the needy retainers and dependents of the men of money-bags.

§5. I pass to another kind of government interference, in which the end and the means are alike odious, but which existed in England until not more than a generation ago, and in France up to the year 1864. I mean the laws against combinations of workmen to raise wages; laws enacted and maintained for the declared purpose of keeping wages low, as the famous Statute of Labourers was passed by a legislature of employers, to prevent the labouring class, when its numbers had been thinned by a pestilence, from taking advantage of the diminished competition to obtain higher wages. Such laws exhibit the infernal spirit of the slave master, when to retain the working classes in avowed slavery has ceased to be practicable.

If it were possible for the working classes, by combining among themselves, to raise or keep up the general rate of wages, it needs hardly be said that this would be a thing not to be punished, but to be welcomed and rejoiced at. Unfortunately the effect is quite beyond attainment by such means. The multitudes who compose the working class are too numerous and too widely scattered to combine at all, much more to combine effectually. If they could do so, they might doubtless succeed in diminishing the hours of labour, and obtaining the same wages for less work. They would also have a limited power of obtaining, by combination, an increase of general wages at the expense of profits. But the limits of this power are narrow; and were they to attempt to strain it beyond those limits, this could only be accomplished by keeping a part of their number permanently out of employment. As support from public charity would of course be refused to those who could get work and would not accept it, they would be thrown for support upon the trades union of which they were members; and the workpeople collectively would be no better off than before, having to support the same numbers out of the same aggregate wages. In this way, however, the class would have its attention forcibly drawn to the fact of a superfluity of numbers, and to the necessity, if they would have high wages, of proportioning the supply of labour to the demand.

Combinations to keep up wages are sometimes successful, in trades where the workpeople are few in number, and collected in a small number of local centres. It is questionable if combinations ever had the smallest effect on the permanent remuneration of spinners or weavers; but the journeymen type-founders, by a close combination, are able, it is said, to keep up a rate of wages much beyond that which is usual in employments of equal hardness and skill; and even the tailors, a much more numerous class, are understood to have had, to some extent, a similar success. A rise of wages, thus confined to particular employments, is not (like a rise of general wages) defrayed from profits, but raises the value and price of the particular article, and falls on the consumer; the capitalist who produces the commodity being only injured in so far as the high price tends to narrow the market; and not even then, unless it does so in a greater ratio than that of the rise of price: for though, at higher wages, he employs, with a given capital, fewer workpeople, and obtains less of the commodity, yet if he can sell the whole of this diminished quantity at the higher price, his profits are as great as before.

This partial rise of wages, if not gained at the expense of the remainder of the working class, ought not to be regarded as an evil. The consumer, indeed, must pay for it; but cheapness of goods is desirable only when the cause of it is that their production costs little labour, and not when occasioned by that labour's being ill remunerated. It may appear, indeed, at first sight, that the high wages of the type-founders (for example) are obtained at the general cost of the labouring class. This high remuneration either causes fewer persons to find employment in the trade, or if not, must lead to the investment of more capital in it, at the expense of other trades: in the first case, it throws an additional number of labourers on the general market; in the second, it withdraws from that market a portion of the demand: effects, both of which are injurious to the working classes. Such, indeed, would really be the result of a successful combination in a particular trade or trades, for some time after its formation; but when it is a permanent thing, the principles so often insisted upon in this treatise, show that it can have no such effect. The habitual earnings of the working classes at large can be affected by nothing but the habitual requirements of the labouring people: these indeed may be altered, but while they remain the same, wages never fall permanently below the standard of these requirements, and do not long remain above that standard. If there had been no combinations in particular trades, and the wages of those trades had never been kept above the common level, there is no reason to suppose that the common level would have been at all higher than it now is. There would merely have been a greater number of people altogether, and a smaller number of exceptions to the ordinary low rate of wages.

If, therefore, no improvement were to be hoped for in the general circumstances of the working classes, the success of a portion of them, however small, in keeping their wages by combination above the market rate, would be wholly a matter of satisfaction. But when the elevation of the character and condition of the entire body has at last become a thing not beyond the reach of rational effort, it is time that the better paid classes of skilled artisans should seek their own advantage in common with, and not by the exclusion of, their fellow-labourers. While they continue to fix their hopes on hedging themselves in against competition, and protecting their own wages by shutting out others from access to their employment, nothing better can be expected from them than that total absence of any large and generous aims, that almost open disregard of all other objects than high wages and little work for their own small body, which were so deplorably evident in the proceedings and manifestoes of the Amalgamated Society of Engineers during their quarrel with their employers. Success, even if attainable, in raising up a protected class of working people, would now be a hindrance, instead of a help, to the emancipation of the working classes at large.

But though combinations to keep up wages are seldom effectual, and when effectual, are, for the reasons which I have assigned, seldom desirable, the right of making the attempt is one which cannot be refused to any portion of the working population without great injustice, or without the probability of fatally misleading them respecting the circumstances which determine their condition. So long as combinations to raise wages were prohibited by law, the law appeared to the operatives to be the real cause of the low wages which there was no denying that it had done its best to produce. Experience of strikes has been the best teacher of the labouring classes on the subject of the relation between wages and the demand and supply of labour: and it is most important that this course of instruction should not be disturbed.

It is a great error to condemn, *per se* and absolutely, either trades unions or the collective action of strikes. Even assuming that a strike must inevitably fail whenever it attempts to raise wages above that market rate which is fixed by the demand and supply; demand and supply are not physical agencies, which thrust a given amount of wages into a labourer's hand without the participation of his own will and actions. The market rate is not fixed for him by some self-acting instrument, but is the result of bargaining between human beings – of what Adam Smith calls 'the higgling of the market'; and those who do not 'higgle' will long continue to pay, even over a counter, more than the market price for their purchases. Still more might poor labourers who have to do with rich employers, remain long without the amount of wages which the demand for their labour would justify, unless, in vernacular phrase, they stood out for it: and how can they stand out for terms without organized concert? What chance would any labourer have, who struck singly for an advance of wages? How could he even know whether the state of the market admitted of a rise, except by consultation with his fellows, naturally leading to concerted action? I do not hesitate to say that associations of labourers, of a nature similar to trades unions, far from being a hindrance to a free market for labour, are the necessary instrumentality of that free market; the indispensable means of enabling the sellers of labour to take due care of their own interests under a system of competition. There is an ulterior consideration of much importance, to which attention was for the first time drawn by Professor Fawcett, in an article in the *Westminster Review*. Experience has at length enabled the more intelligent trades to take a tolerably correct measure of the circumstances on which the success of a strike for an advance of wages depends. The workmen are now nearly as well informed as the master, of the state of the market for his commodities; they can calculate his gains and his expenses, they know when his trade is or is not prosperous, and only when it is, are they ever again likely to strike for higher wages; which wages their known readiness to strike makes their employers for the most part willing, in that case, to concede. The tendency, therefore, of this state of things is to make a rise of wages in any particular trade usually consequent upon a rise of profits, which, as Mr Fawcett observes, is a commencement of that regular participation of the labourers in the profits derived from their labour, every tendency to which, for the reasons stated in a previous chapter,[2] it is so important to encourage, since to it we have chiefly to look for any radical improvement in the social and economical relations between labour and capital. Strikes, therefore, and the trade societies which render strikes possible, are for these various reasons not a mischievous, but on the contrary, a valuable part of the existing machinery of society.

It is, however, an indispensable condition of tolerating combinations, that they should be voluntary. No severity, necessary to the purpose, is too great to be employed against attempts to compel workmen to join a union, or take part in a strike by threats or violence. Mere moral compulsion, by the expression of opinion, the law ought not to interfere with; it belongs to more enlightened opinion to restrain it, by rectifying the moral sentiments of the people. Other questions arise when the combination, being voluntary, proposes to itself objects really contrary to the public good. High wages and short hours are generally good objects, or, at all events, may be so: but in many trades unions, it is among the rules that there shall be no task work, or no difference of pay between the most expert workmen and the most unskilful, or that no member of the union shall earn more than a certain sum per week, in order that there may be more employment for the rest; and the abolition of piece work, under more or less of modification, held a conspicuous place among the demands of the Amalgamated Society. These are combinations to effect objects which are pernicious. Their success, even when only partial, is a public mischief; and were it complete, would be equal in magnitude to almost any of the evils arising from bad economical legislation. Hardly anything worse can be said of the worst laws on the subject of industry and its remuneration, consistent with the personal freedom of the labourer, than that they place the energetic and the idle, the skilful and the incompetent, on a level: and this, in so far as it is in itself

2. Supra, Bk. V, Ch. VII.

possible, it is the direct tendency of the regulations of these unions to do. It does not, however, follow as a consequence that the law would be warranted in making the formation of such associations illegal and punishable. Independently of all considerations of constitutional liberty, the best interests of the human race imperatively require that all economical experiments, voluntarily undertaken, should have the fullest licence, and that force and fraud should be the only means of attempting to benefit themselves, which are interdicted to the less fortunate classes of the community.[3]

§6. Among the modes of undue exercise of the power of government, on which I have commented in this chapter, I have included only such as rest on theories which have still more or less of footing in the most enlightened countries. I have not spoken of some which have done still greater mischief in times not long past, but which are now generally given up, at least in theory, though enough of them still remains in practice to make it impossible as yet to class them among exploded errors.

The notion, for example, that a government should choose opinions for the people, and should not suffer any doctrines in politics, morals, law, or religion, but such as it approves, to be printed or publicly professed, may be said to be altogether abandoned as a general thesis. It is now well understood that a régime of this sort is fatal to all prosperity, even of an economical kind: that the human mind when prevented either by fear of the law

3. Whoever desires to understand the question of Trade Combinations as seen from the point of view of the working people, should make himself acquainted with a pamphlet published in 1860, under the title 'Trades Unions and Strikes, their Philosophy and Intention; by T. J. Dunning, Secretary to the London Consolidated Society of Bookbinders'. There are many opinions in this able tract in which I only partially, and some in which I do not at all, coincide. But there are also many sound arguments, and an instructive exposure of the common fallacies of opponents. Readers of other classes will see with surprise, not only how great a portion of truth the Unions have on their side, but how much less flagrant and condemnable even their errors appear, when seen under the aspect in which it is only natural that the working classes should themselves regard them.

or by fear of opinion from exercising its faculties freely on the most important subjects, acquires a general torpidity and imbecility, by which, when they reach a certain point, it is disqualified from making any considerable advances even in the common affairs of life, and which, when greater still, make it gradually lose even its previous attainments. There cannot be a more decisive example than Spain and Portugal, for two centuries after the Reformation. The decline of those countries in national greatness, and even in material civilization, while almost all the other nations of Europe were uninterruptedly advancing, has been ascribed to various causes, but there is one which lies at the foundation of them all: the Holy Inquisition, and the system of mental slavery of which it is the symbol.

Yet although these truths are very widely recognized, and freedom both of opinion and of discussion is admitted as an axiom in all free countries, this apparent liberality and tolerance has acquired so little of the authority of a principle, that it is always ready to give way to the dread or horror inspired by some particular sort of opinions. Within the last fifteen or twenty years several individuals have suffered imprisonment, for the public profession, sometimes in a very temperate manner, of disbelief in religion; and it is probable that both the public and the government, at the first panic which arises on the subject of Chartism or Communism, will fly to similar means for checking the propagation of democratic or anti-property doctrines. In this country, however, the effective restraints on mental freedom proceed much less from the law or the government, than from the intolerant temper of the national mind; arising no longer from even as respectable a source as bigotry or fanaticism, but rather from the general habit, both in opinion and conduct, of making adherence to custom the rule of life, and enforcing it, by social penalties, against all persons who, without a party to back them, assert their individual independence.

CHAPTER XI

Of the Grounds and Limits
of the Laisser-faire or
Non-interference Principle

§1. WE have now reached the last part of our undertaking; the discussion, so far as suited to this treatise (that is, so far as it is a question of principle, not detail) of the limits of the province of government: the question, to what objects governmental intervention in the affairs of society may or should extend, over and above those which necessarily appertain to it. No subject has been more keenly contested in the present age: the contest, however, has chiefly taken place round certain select points, with only flying excursions into the rest of the field. Those indeed who have discussed any particular question of government interference, such as state education (spiritual or secular), regulation of hours of labour, a public provision for the poor, &c., have often dealt largely in general arguments, far outstretching the special application made of them, and have shown a sufficiently strong bias either in favour of letting things alone, or in favour of meddling; but have seldom declared, or apparently decided in their own minds, how far they would carry either principle. The supporters of interference have been content with asserting a general right and duty on the part of government to intervene, wherever its intervention would be useful: and when those who have been called the *laisser-faire* school have attempted any definite limitation of the province of government, they have usually restricted it to the protection of person and property against force and fraud; a definition to which neither they nor any one else can deliberately adhere, since it excludes, as has been shown in a preceding chapter,[1] some of the most indispensable and unanimously recognized of the duties of government.

Without professing entirely to supply this deficiency of a general theory, on a question which does not, as I conceive,

1. Supra, Bk. V, Ch. I.

admit of any universal solution, I shall attempt to afford some little aid towards the resolution of this class of questions as they arise, by examining, in the most general point of view in which the subject can be considered, what are the advantages, and what the evils or inconveniences, of government interference.

We must set out by distinguishing between two kinds of intervention by the government, which, though they may relate to the same subject, differ widely in their nature and effects, and require, for their justification, motives of a very different degree of urgency. The intervention may extend to controlling the free agency of individuals. Government may interdict all persons from doing certain things; or from doing them without its authorization; or may prescribe to them certain things to be done, or a certain manner of doing things which it is left optional with them to do or to abstain from. This is the *authoritative* interference of government. There is another kind of intervention which is not authoritative: when a government, instead of issuing a command and enforcing it by penalties, adopts the course so seldom resorted to by governments, and of which such important use might be made, that of giving advice and promulgating information; or when, leaving individuals free to use their own means of pursuing any object of general interest, the government, not meddling with them, but not trusting the object solely to their care, establishes, side by side with their arrangements, an agency of its own for a like purpose. Thus, it is one thing to maintain a Church Establishment, and another to refuse toleration to other religions, or to persons professing no religion. It is one thing to provide schools or colleges, and another to require that no person shall act as an instructor of youth without a government licence. There might be a national bank, or a government manufactory, without any monopoly against private banks and manufactories. There might be a post-office, without penalties against the conveyance of letters by any other means. There may be a corps of government engineers for civil purposes, while the profession of a civil engineer is free to be adopted by every one. There may be public hospitals, without any restriction upon private medical or surgical practice.

§2. It is evident, even at first sight, that the authoritative form of government intervention has a much more limited sphere of legitimate action than the other. It requires a much stronger necessity to justify it in any case; while there are large departments of human life from which it must be unreservedly and imperiously excluded. Whatever theory we adopt respecting the foundation of the social union, and under whatever political institutions we live, there is a circle around every individual human being, which no government, be it that of one, of a few, or of the many, ought to be permitted to overstep: there is a part of the life of every person who has come to years of discretion, within which the individuality of that person ought to reign uncontrolled either by any other individual or by the public collectively. That there is, or ought to be, some space in human existence thus entrenched around, and sacred from authoritative intrusion, no one who professes the smallest regard to human freedom or dignity will call in question: the point to be determined is, where the limit should be placed; how large a province of human life this reserved territory should include. I apprehend that it ought to include all that part which concerns only the life, whether inward or outward, of the individual, and does not affect the interests of others, or affects them only through the moral influence of example. With respect to the domain of the inward consciousness, the thoughts and feelings, and as much of external conduct as is personal only, involving no consequences, none at least of a painful or injurious kind, to other people: I hold that it is allowable in all, and in the more thoughtful and cultivated often a duty, to assert and promulgate, with all the force they are capable of, their opinion of what is good or bad, admirable or contemptible, but not to compel others to conform to that opinion; whether the force used is that of extra-legal coercion, or exerts itself by means of the law.

Even in those portions of conduct which do affect the interest of others, the onus of making out a case always lies on the defenders of legal prohibitions. It is not a merely constructive or presumptive injury to others, which will justify the interference of law with individual freedom. To be prevented from doing what one is inclined to, from acting according to one's own judgment of what is desirable, is not only always irksome, but always tends, *pro tanto*, to starve the development of some portion of the bodily or mental faculties, either sensitive or active; and unless the conscience of the individual goes freely with the legal restraint, it partakes, either in a great or in a small degree, of the degradation of slavery. Scarcely any degree of utility, short of absolute necessity, will justify a prohibitory regulation, unless it can also be made to recommend itself to the general conscience; unless persons of ordinary good intentions either believe already, or can be induced to believe, that the thing prohibited is a thing which they ought not to wish to do.

It is otherwise with governmental interferences which do not restrain individual free agency. When a government provides means of fulfilling a certain end, leaving individuals free to avail themselves of different means if in their opinion preferable, there is no infringement of liberty, no irksome or degrading restraint. One of the principal objections to government interference is then absent. There is, however, in almost all forms of government agency, one thing which is compulsory; the provision of the pecuniary means. These are derived from taxation; or, if existing in the form of an endowment derived from public property, they are still the cause of as much compulsory taxation as the sale or the annual proceeds of the property would enable to be dispensed with.[2] And the objection necessarily attaching to compulsory contributions, is almost always greatly aggravated by the expensive precautions and onerous restrictions, which are indispensable to prevent evasion of a compulsory tax.

2. The only cases in which government agency involves nothing of a compulsory nature, are the rare cases in which, without any artificial monopoly, it pays its own expenses. A bridge built with public money, on which tolls are collected sufficient to pay not only all current expenses, but the interest of the original outlay, is one case in point. The government railways in Belgium and Germany are another example. The Post Office, if its monopoly were abolished, and it still paid its expenses, would be another.

§3. A second general objection to government agency, is that every increase of the functions devolving on the government is an increase of its power, both in the form of authority, and still more, in the indirect form of influence. The importance of this consideration, in respect of political freedom, has in general been quite sufficiently recognized, at least in England, but many, in latter times, have been prone to think that limitation of the powers of the government is only essential when the government itself is badly constituted; when it does not represent the people, but is the organ of a class, or coalition of classes: and that a government of sufficiently popular constitution might be trusted with any amount of power over the nation, since its power would be only that of the nation over itself. This might be true, if the nation, in such cases, did not practically mean a mere majority of the nation, and if minorities were only capable of oppressing, but not of being oppressed. Experience, however, proves that the depositaries of power who are mere delegates of the people, that is of a majority, are quite as ready (when they think they can count on popular support) as any organs of oligarchy, to assume arbitrary power, and encroach unduly on the liberty of private life. The public collectively is abundantly ready to impose, not only its generally narrow views of its interests, but its abstract opinions, and even its tastes, as laws binding upon individuals. And the present civilization tends so strongly to make the power of persons acting in masses the only substantial power in society, that there never was more necessity for surrounding individual independence of thought, speech, and conduct, with the most powerful defences, in order to maintain that originality of mind and individuality of character, which are the only source of any real progress, and of most of the qualities which make the human race much superior to any herd of animals. Hence it is no less important in a democratic than in any other government, that all tendency on the part of public authorities to stretch their interference, and assume a power of any sort which can easily be dispensed with, should be regarded with unremitting jealousy. Perhaps this is even more important in a democracy than in any other form of political society; because where public opinion is sovereign, an individual who is oppressed by the sovereign does not, as in most other states of things, find a rival power to which he can appeal for relief, or, at all events, for sympathy.

§4. A third general objection to government agency, rests on the principle of the division of labour. Every additional function undertaken by the government, is a fresh occupation imposed upon a body already overcharged with duties. A natural consequence is that most things are ill done; much not done at all, because the government is not able to do it without delays which are fatal to its purpose; that the more troublesome and less showy, of the functions undertaken, are postponed or neglected, and an excuse is always ready for the neglect; while the heads of the administration have their minds so fully taken up with official details, in however perfunctory a manner superintended, that they have no time or thought to spare for the great interests of the state, and the preparation of enlarged measures of social improvement.

But these inconveniences, though real and serious, result much more from the bad organization of governments, than from the extent and variety of the duties undertaken by them. Government is not a name for some one functionary, or definite number of functionaries : there may be almost any amount of division of labour within the administrative body itself. The evil in question is felt in great magnitude under some of the governments of the Continent, where six or eight men, living at the capital and known by the name of ministers, demand that the whole public business of the country shall pass, or be supposed to pass, under their individual eye. But the inconvenience would be reduced to a very manageable compass, in a country in which there was a proper distribution of functions between the central and local officers of government, and in which the central body was divided into a sufficient number of departments. When Parliament thought it expedient to confer on the government an inspecting and partially controlling authority over railways, it did not add railways to the department of the Home Minister, but created a Railway Board. When it determined to have a

central superintending authority for pauper administration, it
established the Poor Law Commission. There are few countries
in which a greater number of functions are discharged by public
officers, than in some states of the American Union, particularly the New England States; but the division of labour in
public business is extreme; most of these officers being not
even amenable to any common superior, but performing their
duties freely, under the double check of election by their
townsmen, and civil as well as criminal responsibility to the
tribunals.

It is, no doubt, indispensable to good government that the
chiefs of the administration, whether permanent or temporary,
should extend a commanding, though general, view over the
ensemble of all the interests confided, in any degree, to the responsibility of the central power. But with a skilful internal
organization of the administrative machine, leaving to subordinates, and as far as possible, to local subordinates, not only the
execution, but to a greater degree the control, of details; holding
them accountable for the results of their acts rather than for the
acts themselves, except where these come within the cognizance
of the tribunals; taking the most effectual securities for honest
and capable appointments; opening a broad path to promotion
from the inferior degrees of the administrative scale to the
superior; leaving, at each step, to the functionary, a wider range
in the origination of measures, so that, in the highest grade of
all, deliberation might be concentrated on the great collective
interests of the country in each department; if all this were done,
the government would not probably be overburthened by any
business, in other respects fit to be undertaken by it; though
the overburthening would remain as a serious addition to the
inconveniences incurred by its undertaking any which was
unfit.

§5. But though a better organization of governments would
greatly diminish the force of the objection to the mere multiplication of their duties, it would still remain true that in all the more
advanced communities, the great majority of things are worse

done by the intervention of government, than the individuals most interested in the matter would do them, or cause them to be done, if left to themselves. The grounds of this truth are expressed with tolerable exactness in the popular dictum, that people understand their own business and their own interests better, and care for them more, than the government does, or can be expected to do. This maxim holds true throughout the greatest part of the business of life, and wherever it is true we ought to condemn every kind of government intervention that conflicts with it. The inferiority of government agency, for example, in any of the common operations of industry or commerce, is proved by the fact, that it is hardly ever able to maintain itself in equal competition with individual agency, where the individuals possess the requisite degree of industrial enterprise, and can command the necessary assemblage of means. All the facilities which a government enjoys of access to information; all the means which it possesses of remunerating, and therefore of commanding, the best available talent in the market – are not an equivalent for the one great disadvantage of an inferior interest in the result.

It must be remembered, besides, that even if a government were superior in intelligence and knowledge to any single individual in the nation, it must be inferior to all the individuals of the nation taken together. It can neither possess in itself, nor enlist in its service, more than a portion of the acquirements and capacities which the country contains, applicable to any given purpose. There must be many persons equally qualified for the work with those whom the government employs, even if it selects its instruments with no reference to any consideration but their fitness. Now these are the very persons into whose hands, in the cases of most common occurrence, a system of individual agency naturally tends to throw the work, because they are capable of doing it better or on cheaper terms than any other persons. So far as this is the case, it is evident that government, by excluding or even by superseding individual agency, either substitutes a less qualified instrumentality for one better qualified, or at any rate substitutes its own mode of accomplishing the work, for all the variety of modes which would be tried by a number of equally qualified persons aiming at the same end; a competition by many degrees more propitious to the progress of improvement, than any uniformity of system.

§6. I have reserved for the last place one of the strongest of the reasons against the extension of government agency. Even if the government could comprehend within itself, in each department, all the most eminent intellectual capacity and active talent of the nation, it would not be the less desirable that the conduct of a large portion of the affairs of the society should be left in the hands of the persons immediately interested in them. The business of life is an essential part of the practical education of a people; without which, book and school instruction, though most necessary and salutary, does not suffice to qualify them for conduct, and for the adaptation of means to ends. Instruction is only one of the desiderata of mental improvement; another, almost as indispensable, is a vigorous exercise of the active energies; labour, contrivance, judgment, self-control : and the natural stimulus to these is the difficulties of life. This doctrine is not to be confounded with the complacent optimism, which represents the evils of life as desirable things, because they call forth qualities adapted to combat with evils. It is only because the difficulties exist, that the qualities which combat with them are of any value. As practical beings it is our business to free human life from as many as possible of its difficulties, and not to keep up a stock of them as hunters preserve game, for the exercise of pursuing it. But since the need of active talent and practical judgment in the affairs of life can only be diminished, and not, even on the most favourable supposition, done away with, it is important that those endowments should be cultivated not merely in a select few, but in all, and that the cultivation should be more varied and complete than most persons are able to find in the narrow sphere of their merely individual interests. A people among whom there is no habit of spontaneous action for a collective interest—who look habitually to their government to command or prompt them in all matters of joint concern—who expect to have everything done for them, except what can be made an affair of mere habit and routine — have their faculties only half developed; their education is defective in one of its most important branches.

Not only is the cultivation of the active faculties by exercise, diffused through the whole community, in itself one of the most valuable of national possessions: it is rendered, not less, but more, necesary, when a high degree of that indispensable culture is systematically kept up in the chiefs and functionaries of the state. There cannot be a combination of circumstances more dangerous to human welfare, than that in which intelligence and talent are maintained at a high standard within a governing corporation, but starved and discouraged outside the pale. Such a system, more completely than any other, embodies the idea of despotism, by arming with intellectual superiority as an additional weapon, those who have already the legal power. It approaches as nearly as the organic difference between human beings and other animals admits, to the government of sheep by their shepherd, without anything like so strong an interest as the shepherd has in the thriving condition of the flock. The only security against political slavery, is the check maintained over governors, by the diffusion of intelligence, activity, and public spirit among the governed. Experience proves the extreme difficulty of permanently keeping up a sufficiently high standard of those qualities; a difficulty which increases, as the advance of civilization and security removes one after another of the hardships, embarrassments, and dangers against which individuals had formerly no resource but in their own strength, skill, and courage. It is therefore of supreme importance that all classes of the community, down to the lowest, should have much to do for themselves; that as great a demand should be made upon their intelligence and virtue as it is in any respect equal to; that the government should not only leave as far as possible to their own faculties the conduct of whatever concerns themselves alone, but should suffer them, or rather encourage them, to manage as many as possible of their joint concerns by voluntary co-operation; since this discussion and management of collective interests is the great school of that public spirit, and the great source of that intelligence of public affairs, which are always regarded as the distinctive character of the public of free countries.

A democratic constitution, not supported by democratic institutions in detail, but confined to the central government, not only is not political freedom, but often creates a spirit precisely the reverse, carrying down to the lowest grade in society the desire and ambition of political domination. In some countries the desire of the people is for not being tyrannized over, but in others it is merely for an equal chance to everybody of tyrannizing. Unhappily this last state of the desires is fully as natural to mankind as the former, and in many of the conditions even of civilized humanity, is far more largely exemplified. In proportion as the people are accustomed to manage their affairs by their own active intervention, instead of leaving them to the government, their desires will turn to repelling tyranny, rather than to tyrannizing: while in proportion as all real initiative and direction resides in the government, and individuals habitually feel and act as under its perpetual tutelage, popular institutions develop in them not the desire of freedom, but an unmeasured appetite for place and power: diverting the intelligence and activity of the country from its principal business, to a wretched competition for the selfish prizes and the petty vanities of office.

§7. The preceding are the principal reasons, of a general character, in favour of restricting to the narrowest compass the intervention of a public authority in the business of the community: and few will dispute the more than sufficiency of these reasons, to throw, in every instance, the burthen of making out a strong case, not on those who resist, but on those who recommend, government interference. *Laisser-faire*, in short, should be the general practice: every departure from it, unless required by some great good, is a certain evil.

The degree in which the maxim, even in the cases to which it is most manifestly applicable, has heretofore been infringed by governments, future ages will probably have difficulty in crediting. Some idea may be formed of it from the description of M.

Dunoyer[3] of the restraints imposed on the operations of manufacture under the old government of France, by the meddling and regulating spirit of legislation.

'La société exerçait sur la fabrication la juridiction la plus illimitée et la plus arbitraire : elle disposait sans scrupule des facultés des fabricants; elle décidait qui pourrait travailler, quelle chose on pourrait faire, quels matériaux on devrait employer, quels procédés il faudrait suivre, quelles formes on donnerait aux produits, etc. Il ne suffisait pas de faire bien, de faire mieux, il fallait faire suivant les règles. Qui ne connaît ce règlement de 1670, qui préscrivait de saisir et de clouer au poteau, avec le nom des auteurs, les marchandises non conformes aux règles tracées, et qui, à la seconde récidive, voulait que les fabricants y fussent attachés eux mêmes? Il ne s'agissait pas de consulter le goût des consommateurs, mais de se conformer aux volontés de la loi. Des légions d'inspecteurs, de commissaires, de contrôleurs, de jurés, de gardes, étainet chargés de les faire exécuter; on brisait les métiers, on brûlait les produits qui n'y étaient pas conformes : les améliorations étaient punies; on mettait les inventeurs à l'amende. On soumettait à des règles différentes la fabrication des objets destinés à la consommation intérieure et celle des produits destinés au commerce étranger. Un artisan n'était pas le maître de choisir le lieu de son établissement, ni de travailler en toute saison, ni de travailler pour tout le monde. Il existe un décret du 30 Mars 1700, qui borne à dix-huit villes le nombre des lieux où l'on pourra faire des bas au métier; un arrêt du 18 Juin 1723 enjoint aux fabricants de Rouen de suspendre leurs travaux du 1er Juillet au 15 Septembre, affin de faciliter ceux de la récolte; Louis XIV., quand il voulut entreprendre la colonnade du Louvre, défendit aux particuliers d'employer des ouvriers sans sa permission, sous peine de 10,000 livres d'amende, et aux ouvriers de travailler pour les particuliers, sous peine, pour la première fois, de la prison, et pour la seconde, des galères.'

That these and similar regulations were not a dead letter, and that the officious and vexatious meddling was prolonged down to the French Revolution, we have the testimony of Roland, the

3. *De la Liberté du Travail*, Vol. II, pp. 353-4.

Girondist minister.[4] 'I have seen', says he, 'eighty, ninety, a hundred pieces of cotton or woollen stuff cut up, and completely destroyed. I have witnessed similar scenes every week for a number of years. I have seen manufactured goods confiscated; heavy fines laid on the manufacturers; some pieces of fabric were burnt in public places, and at the hours of market: others were fixed to the pillory, with the name of the manufacturer inscribed upon them, and he himself was threatened with the pillory, in case of a second offence. All this was done under my eyes, at Rouen, in conformity with existing regulations, or ministerial orders. What crime deserved so cruel a punishment? Some defects in the materials employed, or in the texture of the fabric, or even in some of the threads of the warp.

'I have frequently seen manufacturers visited by a band of satellites who put all in confusion in their establishments, spread terror in their families, cut the stuffs from the frames, tore off the warp from the looms, and carried them away as proofs of infringement; the manufacturers were summoned, tried, and condemned: their goods confiscated; copies of their judgment of confiscation posted up in every public place; fortune, reputation, credit, all was lost and destroyed. And for what offence? Because they had made of worsted, a kind of cloth called shag, such as the English used to manufacture, and even sell in France, while the French regulations stated that that kind of cloth should be made with mohair. I have seen other manufacturers treated in the same way, because they had made camlets of a particular width, used in England and Germany, for which there was a great demand from Spain, Portugal, and other countries, and from several parts of France, while the French regulations prescribed other widths for camlets.'

The time is gone by, when such applications as these of the principle of 'paternal government' would be attempted, in even the least enlightened country of the European commonwealth of nations. In such cases as those cited, all the general objections to government interference are valid, and several of them in nearly their highest degree. But we must now turn to the second part

4. I quote at second hand, from Mr Carey's *Essay on the Rate of Wages*, pp. 195–6.

of our task, and direct our attention to cases, in which some of those general objections are altogether absent, while those which can never be got rid of entirely, are overruled by counter-considerations of still greater importance.

We have observed that, as a general rule, the business of life is better performed when those who have an immediate interest in it are left to take their own course, uncontrolled either by the mandate of the law or by the meddling of any public functionary. The persons, or some of the persons, who do the work, are likely to be better judges than the government, of the means of attaining the particular end at which they aim. Were we to suppose, what is not very probable, that the government has possessed itself of the best knowledge which had been acquired up to a given time by the persons most skilled in the occupation; even then, the individual agents have so much stronger and more direct an interest in the result, that the means are far more likely to be improved and perfected if left to their uncontrolled choice. But if the workman is generally the best selector of means, can it be affirmed with the same universality, that the consumer, or person served, is the most competent judge of the end? Is the buyer always qualified to judge of the commodity? If not, the presumption in favour of the competition of the market does not apply to the case; and if the commodity be one, in the quality of which society has much at stake, the balance of advantages may be in favour of some mode and degree of intervention, by the authorized representatives of the collective interest of the state.

§8. Now, the proposition that the consumer is a competent judge of the commodity, can be admitted only with numerous abatements and exceptions. He is generally the best judge (though even this is not true universally) of the material objects produced for his use. These are destined to supply some physical want, or gratify some taste or inclination, respecting which wants or inclinations there is no appeal from the person who feels them; or they are the means and appliances of some occupation, for the use of the persons engaged in it, who may be presumed to be judges of the things required in their own habitual employment.

But there are other things, of the worth of which the demand of the market is by no means a test; things of which the utility does not consist in ministering to inclinations, nor in serving the daily uses of life, and the want of which is least felt where the need is greatest. This is peculiarly true of those things which are chiefly useful as tending to raise the character of human beings. The uncultivated cannot be competent judges of cultivation. Those who most need to be made wiser and better, usually desire it least, and if they desired it, would be incapable of finding the way to it by their own lights. It will continually happen, on the voluntary system, that the end not being desired, the means will not be provided at all, or that, the persons requiring improvement having an imperfect or altogether erroneous conception of what they want, the supply called forth by the demand of the market will be anything but what is really required. Now any well-intentioned and tolerably civilized government may think, without presumption, that it does or ought to possess a degree of cultivation above the average of the community which it rules, and that it should therefore be capable of offering better education and better instruction to the people, than the greater number of them would spontaneously demand. Education, therefore, is one of those things which it is admissible in principle that a government should provide for the people. The case is one to which the reasons of the non-interference principle do not necessarily or universally extend.[5]

5. In opposition to these opinions, a writer, with whom on many points I agree, but whose hostility to government intervention seems to me too indiscriminate and unqualified, M. Dunoyer, observes, that instruction, however good in itself, can only be useful to the public in so far as they are willing to receive it, and that the best proof that the instruction is suitable to their wants is its success as a pecuniary enterprise. This argument seems no more conclusive respecting instruction for the mind, than it would be respecting medicine for the body. No medicine will do the patient any good if he cannot be induced to take it; but we are not bound to admit as a corollary from this, that the patient will select the right medicine without assistance. Is it not probable that a recommendation, from any quarter which he respects, may induce him to accept a better medicine than he would spontaneously have chosen? This is, in respect to education, the very point in debate. Without doubt, instruction which is so far in advance of the people that they cannot be induced to avail themselves of it, is to them

With regard to elementary education, the exception to ordinary rules may, I conceive, justifiably be carried still further. There are certain primary elements and means of knowledge, which it is in the highest degree desirable that all human beings born into the community should acquire during childhood. If their parents, or those on whom they depend, have the power of obtaining for them this instruction, and fail to do it, they commit a double breach of duty, towards the children themselves, and towards the members of the community generally, who are all liable to suffer seriously from the consequences of ignorance and want of education in their fellow-citizens. It is therefore an allowable exercise of the powers of government, to impose on parents the legal obligation of giving elementary instruction to children. This, however, cannot fairly be done, without taking measures to insure that such instruction shall be always accessible to them, either gratuitously or at a trifling expense.

It may indeed be objected that the education of children is one of those expenses which parents, even of the labouring class, ought to defray; that it is desirable that they should feel it incumbent on them to provide by their own means for the fulfilment of their duties, and that by giving education at the cost of others, just as much by giving subsistence, the standard of necessary wages is proportionally lowered, and the springs of

---

of no more worth than if it did not exist. But between what they spontaneously choose, and what they will refuse to accept when offered, there is a breadth of interval proportioned to their deference for the recommender. Besides, a thing of which the public are bad judges, may require to be shown to them and pressed on their attention for a long time, and to prove its advantages by long experience, before they learn to appreciate it, yet they may learn at last; which they might never have done, if the thing had not been thus obtruded upon them in act, but only recommended in theory. Now, a pecuniary speculation cannot wait years, or perhaps generations for success; it must succeed rapidly, or not at all. Another consideration which M. Dunoyer seems to have overlooked, is, that institutions and modes of tuition which never could be made sufficiently popular to repay, with a profit, the expenses incurred on them, may be invaluable to the many by giving the highest quality of education to the few, and keeping up the perpetual succession of superior minds, by whom knowledge is advanced, and the community urged forward in civilization.

exertion and self-restraint is so much relaxed. This argument could, at best, be only valid if the question were that of substituting a public provision for what individuals would otherwise do for themselves; if all parents in the labouring class recognized and practised the duty of giving instruction to their children at their own expense. But inasmuch as parents do not practise this duty, and do not include education among those necessary expenses which their wages must provide for, therefore the general rate of wages is not high enough to bear those expenses, and they must be borne from some other source. And this is not one of the cases in which the tender of help perpetuates the state of things which renders help necessary. Instruction, when it is really such, does not enervate, but strengthens as well as enlarges the active faculties: in whatever manner acquired, its effect on the mind is favourable to the spirit of independence: and when, unless had gratuitously, it would not be had at all, help in this form has the opposite tendency to that which in so many other cases makes it objectionable; it is help towards doing without help.

In England, and most European countries, elementary instruction cannot be paid for, at its full cost, from the common wages of unskilled labour, and would not if it could. The alternative, therefore, is not between government and private speculation, but between a government provision and voluntary charity: between interference by government, and interference by associations of individuals, subscribing their own money for the purpose, like the two great School Societies. It is, of course, not desirable that anything should be done by funds derived from compulsory taxation, which is already sufficiently well done by individual liberality. How far this is the case with school instruction, is, in each particular instance, a question of fact. The education provided in this country on the voluntary principle has of late been so much discussed, that it is needless in this place to criticize it minutely, and I shall merely express my conviction, that even in quantity it is, and is likely to remain, altogether insufficient, while in quality, though with some slight tendency to improvement, it is never good except by some rare accident, and generally so bad as to be little more than nominal. I hold it therefore the duty of the government to supply the defect, by giving pecuniary support to elementary schools, such as to render them accessible to all the children of the poor, either freely, or for a payment too inconsiderable to be sensibly felt.

One thing must be strenuously insisted on; that the government must claim no monopoly for its education, either in the lower or in the higher branches; must exert neither authority nor influence to induce the people to resort to its teachers in preference to others, and must confer no peculiar advantages on those who have been instructed by them. Though the government teachers will probably be superior to the average of private instructors, they will not embody all the knowledge and sagacity to be found in all instructors taken together, and it is desirable to leave open as many roads as possible to the desired end. It is not endurable that a government should, either *de jure* or *de facto*, have a complete control over the education of the people. To possess such a control, and actually exert it, is to be despotic. A government which can mould the opinions and sentiments of the people from their youth upwards, can do with them whatever it pleases. Though a government, therefore, may, and in many cases ought to, establish schools and colleges, it must neither compel nor bribe any person to come to them; nor ought the power of individuals to set up rival establishments, to depend in any degree upon its authorization. It would be justified in requiring from all the people that they shall possess instruction in certain things, but not in prescribing to them how or from whom they shall obtain it.

§9. In the matter of education, the intervention of government is justifiable, because the case is not one in which the interest and judgment of the consumer are a sufficient security for the goodness of the commodity. Let us now consider another class of cases, where there is no person in the situation of a consumer, and where the interest and judgment to be relied on are those of the agent himself; as in the conduct of any business in which he is exclusively interested, or in entering into any contract or engagement by which he himself is to be bound.

The ground of the practical principle of non-interference must here be, that most persons take a juster and more intelligent view of their own interest, and of the means of promoting it, than can either be prescribed to them by a general enactment of the legislature, or pointed out in the particular case by a public functionary. The maxim is unquestionably sound as a general rule; but there is no difficulty in perceiving some very large and conspicuous exceptions to it. These may be classed under several heads.

First:— The individual who is presumed to be the best judge of his own interests may be incapable of judging or acting for himself; may be a lunatic, an idiot, an infant: or though not wholly incapable, may be of immature years and judgment. In this case the foundation of the *laisser-faire* principle breaks down entirely. The person most interested is not the best judge of the matter, nor a competent judge at all. Insane persons are everywhere regarded as proper objects of the care of the state.[6] In the case of children and young persons, it is common to say, that though they cannot judge for themselves, they have their parents or other relatives to judge for them. But this removes the question

6. The practice of the English law with respect to insane persons, especially on the all-important point of the ascertainment of insanity, most urgently demands reform. At present no persons, whose property is worth coveting, and whose nearest relations are unscrupulous, or on bad terms with them, are secure against a commission of lunacy. At the instance of the persons who would profit by their being declared insane, a jury may be impanelled and an investigation held at the expense of the property, in which all their personal peculiarities, with all the additions made by the lying gossip of low servants, are poured into the credulous ears of twelve petty shopkeepers, ignorant of all ways of life except those of their own class, and regarding every trait of individuality in character or taste as eccentricity, and all eccentricity as either insanity or wickedness. If this sapient tribunal gives the desired verdict, the property is handed over to perhaps the last persons whom the rightful owner would have desired or suffered to possess it. Some recent instances of this kind of investigation have been a scandal to the administration of justice. Whatever other changes in this branch of law may be made, two at least are imperative: first, that, as in other legal proceedings, the expenses should not be borne by the person on trial, but by the promoters of the inquiry, subject to recovery of costs in case of success: and secondly, that the property of a person declared insane, should in no case be made over to heirs while the proprietor is alive, but should be managed by a public officer until his death or recovery.

into a different category; making it no longer a question whether the government should interfere with individuals in the direction of their own conduct and interests, but whether it should leave absolutely in their power the conduct and interests of somebody else. Parental power is as susceptible of abuse as any other power, and is, as a matter of fact, constantly abused. If laws do not succeed in preventing parents from brutally ill-treating, and even from murdering their children, far less ought it to be presumed that the interests of children will never be sacrificed, in more commonplace and less revolting ways, to the selfishness or the ignorance of their parents. Whatever it can be clearly seen that parents ought to do or forbear for the interest of children, the law is warranted, if it is able, in compelling to be done or forborne, and is generally bound to do so. To take an example from the peculiar province of political economy; it is right that children, and young persons not yet arrived at maturity, should be protected so far as the eye and hand of the state can reach, from being over-worked. Labouring for too many hours in the day, or on work beyond their strength, should not be permitted to them, for if permitted it may always be compelled. Freedom of contract, in the case of children, is but another word for freedom of coercion. Education also, the best which circumstances admit of their receiving, is not a thing which parents or relatives, from indifference, jealousy, or avarice, should have it in their power to withhold.

The reasons for legal intervention in favour of children, apply not less strongly to the case of those unfortunate slaves and victims of the most brutal part of mankind, the lower animals. It is by the grossest misunderstanding of the principles of liberty, that the infliction of exemplary punishment on ruffianism practised towards these defenceless creatures, has been treated as a meddling by government with things beyond its province; an interference with domestic life. The domestic life of domestic tyrants is one of the things which it is the most imperative on the law to interfere with; and it is to be regretted that metaphysical scruples respecting the nature and source of the authority of government, should induce many warm supporters of laws against cruelty to animals, to seek for a justification of such laws in the incidental consequences of the indulgence of ferocious habits to the interests of human beings, rather than in the intrinsic merits of the case itself. What it would be the duty of a human being, possessed of the requisite physical strength, to prevent by force if attempted in his presence, it cannot be less incumbent on society generally to repress. The existing laws of England on the subject are chiefly defective in the trifling, often almost nominal, maximum, to which the penalty even in the worst cases is limited.

Among those members of the community whose freedom of contract ought to be controlled by the legislature for their own protection, on account (it is said) of their dependent position, it is frequently proposed to include women : and in the existing Factory Acts, their labour, in common with that of young persons, has been placed under peculiar restrictions. But the classing together, for this and other purposes, of women and children, appears to me both indefensible in principle and mischievous in practice. Children below a certain age *cannot* judge or act for themselves; up to a considerably greater age they are inevitably more or less disqualified for doing so; but women are as capable as men of appreciating and managing their own concerns, and the only hindrance to their doing so arises from the injustice of their present social position. When the law makes everything which the wife acquires, the property of the husband, while by compelling her to live with him it forces her to submit to almost any amount of moral and even physical tyranny which he may choose to inflict, there is some ground for regarding every act done by her as done under coercion : but it is the great error of reformers and philanthropists in our time, to nibble at the consequences of unjust power, instead of redressing the injustice itself. If women had as absolute a control as men have, over their own persons and their own patrimony or acquisitions, there would be no plea for limiting their hours of labouring for themselves, in order that they might have time to labour for the husband, in what is called, by the advocates of restriction, *his* home. Women employed in factories are the only women in the labouring rank of life whose position is not that of slaves and drudges; precisely because they cannot easily be compelled to work and earn wages in factories against their will. For improving the condition of women, it should, in the contrary, be an object to give them the readiest access to independent industrial employment, instead of closing, either entirely or partially, that which is already open to them.

§10. A second exception to the doctrine that individuals are the best judges of their own interest, is when an individual attempts to decide irrevocably now, what will be best for his interest at some future and distant time. The presumption in favour of individual judgment is only legitimate, where the judgment is grounded on actual, and especially on present, personal experience; not where it is formed antecedently to experience, and not suffered to be reversed even after experience has condemned it. When persons have bound themselves by a contract, not simply to do some one thing, but to continue doing something for ever or for a prolonged period, without any power of revoking the engagement, the presumption which their perseverance in that course of conduct would otherwise raise in favour of its being advantageous to them, does not exist; and any such presumption which can be grounded on their having voluntarily entered into the contract, perhaps at an early age, and without any real knowledge of what they undertook, is commonly next to null. The practical maxim of leaving contracts free, is not applicable without great limitations in case of engagement in perpetuity; and the law should be extremely jealous of such engagements; should refuse its sanction to them, when the obligations they impose are such as the contracting party cannot be a competent judge of; if it ever does sanction them, it should take every possible security for their being contracted with foresight and deliberation; and in compensation for not permitting the parties themselves to revoke their engagement, should grant them a release from it, on a sufficient case being made out before an impartial authority. These considerations are eminently applicable to marriage, the most important of all cases of engagement for life.

§11. The third exception which I shall notice, to the doctrine that government cannot manage the affairs of individuals as well as the individuals themselves, has reference to the great class of cases in which the individuals can only manage the concern by delegated agency, and in which the so-called private management is, in point of fact, hardly better entitled to be called management by the persons interested, than administration by a public officer. Whatever, if left to spontaneous agency, can only be done by joint-stock associations, will often be as well, and sometimes better done, as far as the actual work is concerned, by the state. Government management is, indeed, proverbially jobbing, careless, and ineffective, but so likewise has generally been joint-stock management. The directors of a joint-stock company, it is true, are always shareholders; but also the members of a government are invariably taxpayers; and in the case of directors, no more than in that of governments, is their proportional share of the benefits of good management, equal to the interest they may possibly have in mismanagement, even without reckoning the interest of their case. It may be objected, that the shareholders, in their collective character, exercise a certain control over the directors, and have almost always full power to remove them from office. Practically, however, the difficulty of exercising this power is found to be so great, that it is hardly ever exercised except in cases of such flagrantly unskilful, or, at least, unsuccessful management, as would generally produce the ejection from office of managers appointed by the government. Against the very ineffectual security afforded by meetings of shareholders, and by their individual inspection and inquiries, may be placed the greater publicity and more active discussion and comment, to be expected in free countries with regard to affairs in which the general government takes part. The defects, therefore, of government management, do not seem to be necessarily much greater, if necessarily greater at all, than those of management by joint-stock.

The true reasons in favour of leaving to voluntary associations all such things as they are competent to perform, would exist in equal strength if it were certain that the work itself would be as well or better done by public officers. These reasons have been already pointed out: the mischief of overloading the chief functionaries of government with demands on their attention, and diverting them from duties which they alone can discharge, to objects which can be sufficiently well attained without them; the danger of unnecessarily swelling the direct power and indirect influence of government, and multiplying occasions of collision between its agents and private citizens; and the inexpediency of concentrating in a dominant bureaucracy, all the skill and experience in the management of large interests, and all the power of organized action, existing in the community; a practice which keeps the citizens in a relation to the government like that of children to their guardians, and is a main cause of the inferior capacity for political life which has hitherto characterized the over-governed countries of the Continent, whether with or without the forms of representative government.[7]

But although, for these reasons, most things which are likely to be even tolerably done by voluntary associations, should, generally speaking, be left to them; it does not follow that the manner in which those associations perform their work should be entirely uncontrolled by the government. There are many cases in which the agency, of whatever nature, by which a service is performed, is certain, from the nature of the case, to be virtually single; in which a practical monopoly, with all the power it confers of taxing the community, cannot be prevented from existing. I have already more than once adverted to the case of the gas and water companies, among which, though perfect

7. A parallel case may be found in the distaste for politics, and absence of public spirit, by which women, as a class, are characterized in the present state of society, and which is often felt and complained of by political reformers, without, in general, making them willing to recognise, or desirous to remove, its cause. It obviously arises from their being taught, both by institutions and by the whole of their education, to regard themselves as entirely apart from politics. Wherever they have been politicians, they have shown as great interest in the subject, and as great aptitude for it, according to the spirit of their time, as the men with whom they were contemporaries: in that period of history (for example) in which Isabella of Castile and Elizabeth of England were, not rare exceptions, but merely brilliant examples of a spirit and capacity very largely diffused among women of high station and cultivation in Europe.

freedom is allowed to competition, none really takes place, and practically they are found to be even more irresponsible, and unapproachable by individual complaints, than the government. There are the expenses without the advantages of plurality of agency; and the charge made for services which cannot be dispensed with, is, in substance, quite as much compulsory taxation as if imposed by law; there are few householders who make any distinction between their 'water rate' and other local taxes. In the case of these particular services, the reasons preponderate in favour of their being performed, like the paving and cleansing of the streets, not certainly by the general government of the state, but by the municipal authorities of the town, and the expense defrayed, as even now it in fact is, by a local rate. But in the many analogous cases which it is best to resign to voluntary agency, the community needs some other security for the fit performance of the service than the interest of the managers; and it is the part of the government, either to subject the business to reasonable conditions for the general advantage, or to retain such power over it, that the profits of the monopoly may at least be obtained for the public. This applies in the case of a road, a canal, or a railway. These are always, in a great degree, practical monopolies; and a government which concedes such monopoly unreservedly to a private company, does much the same thing as if it allowed an individual or an association to levy any tax they chose, for their own benefit, on all the malt produced in the country, or on all the cotton imported into it. To make the concession for a limited time is generally justifiable, on the principle which justifies patents for invention: but the state should either reserve to itself a reversionary property in such public works, or should retain, and freely exercise, the right of fixing a maximum of fares and charges, and, from time to time, varying that maximum. It is perhaps necessary to remark, that the state may be the proprietor of canals or railways without itself working them; and that they will almost always be better worked by means of a company, renting the railway or canal for a limited period from the state.

§12. To a fourth case of exception I must request particular attention, it being one to which as it appears to me, the attention of political economists has not yet been sufficiently drawn. There are matters in which the interference of law is required, not to overrule the judgment of individuals respecting their own interest, but to give effect to that judgment: they being unable to give effect to it except by concert, which concert again cannot be effectual unless it receives validity and sanction from the law. For illustration, and without prejudging the particular point, I may advert to the question of diminishing the hours of labour. Let us suppose, what is at least supposable, whether it be the fact or not – that a general reduction of the hours of factory labour, say from ten to nine, would be for the advantage of the work-people: that they would receive as high wages, or nearly as high, for nine hours' labour as they receive for ten. If this would be the result, and if the operatives generally are convinced that it would, the limitation, some may say, will be adopted spontaneously. I answer, that it will not be adopted unless the body of operatives bind themselves to one another to abide by it. A workman who refused to work more than nine hours while there were others who worked ten, would either not be employed at all, or if employed, must submit to lose one-tenth of his wages. However convinced, therefore, he may be that it is the interest of the class to work short time, it is contrary to his own interest to set the example, unless he is well assured that all or most others will follow it. But suppose a general agreement of the whole class: might not this be effectual without the sanction of law? Not unless enforced by opinion with a rigour practically equal to that of law. For however beneficial the observance of the regulation might be to the class collectively, the immediate interest of every individual would lie in violating it: and the more numerous those were who adhered to the rule, the more would individuals gain by departing from it. If nearly all restricted themselves to nine hours, those who chose to work for ten would gain all the advantages of the restriction, together with the profit from infringing it; they would get ten hours'

wages for nine hours' work, and an hour's wages besides. I grant
that if a large majority adhered to the nine hours, there would
be no harm done; the benefit would be, in the main, secured to
the class, while those individuals who preferred to work harder
and earn more, would have an opportunity of doing so. This
certainly would be the state of things to be wished for; and
assuming that a reduction of hours without any diminution of
wages could take place without expelling the commodity from
some of its markets – which is in every particular instance a
question of fact, not of principle – the manner in which it
would be most desirable that this effect should be brought about,
would be by a quiet change in the general custom of the trade;
short hours becoming, by spontaneous choice, the general practice, but those who chose to deviate from it having the fullest
liberty to do so. Probably, however, so many would prefer the
ten hours' work on the improved terms, that the limitation could
not be maintained as a general practice : what some did from
choice, others would soon be obliged to do from necessity, and
those who had chosen long hours for the sake of increased wages,
would be forced in the end to work long hours for no greater
wages than before. Assuming then that it really would be the
interest of each to work only nine hours if he could be assured
that all others would do the same, there might be no means of
attaining this object but by converting their supposed mutual
agreement into an engagement under penalty, by consenting to
have it enforced by law. I am not expressing any opinion in
favour of such an enactment, which has never in this country
been demanded, and which I certainly should not, in present
circumstances, recommend : but it serves to exemplify the
manner in which classes of persons may need the assistance of
law, to give effect to their deliberate collective opinion of their
own interest, by affording to every individual a guarantee that
his competitors will pursue the same course, without which he
cannot safely adopt it himself.

Another exemplification of the same principle is afforded by
what is known as the Wakefield system of colonization. This
system is grounded on the important principle, that the degree of
productiveness of land and labour depends on their being in a

due proportion to one another; that if a few persons in a newly-settled country attempt to occupy and appropriate a large district, or if each labourer becomes too soon an occupier and cultivator of land, there is a loss of productive power, and a great retardation of the progress of the colony in wealth and civilization: that nevertheless the instinct (as it may almost be called) of appropriation, and the feelings associated in old countries with landed proprietorship, induce almost every emigrant to take possession of as much land as he has the means of acquiring, and every labourer to become at once a proprietor, cultivating his own land with no other aid than that of his family. If this propensity to the immediate possession of land could be in some degree restrained, and each labourer induced to work a certain number of years on hire before he became a landed proprietor, a perpetual stock of hired labourers could be maintained, available for roads, canals, works of irrigation, &c., and for the establishment and carrying on of the different branches of town industry; whereby the labourer, when he did at last become a landed proprietor, would find his land much more valuable, through access to markets, and facility of obtaining hired labour. Mr Wakefield therefore proposed to check the premature occupation of land, and dispersion of the people, by putting upon all unappropriated lands a rather high price, the proceeds of which were to be expended in conveying emigrant labourers from the mother country.

This salutary provision, however, has been objected to, in the name and on the authority of what was represented as the great principle of political economy, that individuals are the best judges of their own interest. It was said, that when things are left to themselves, land is appropriated and occupied by the spontaneous choice of individuals, in the quantities and at the times most advantageous to each person, and therefore to the community generally; and that to interpose artificial obstacles to their obtaining land, is to prevent them from adopting the course which in their own judgment is most beneficial to them, from a self-conceited notion of the legislator, that he knows what is most for their interest, better than they do themselves. Now this is a complete misunderstanding, either of the system itself, or of the principle with which it is alleged to conflict. The oversight is similar to that which we have just seen exemplified on the subject of hours of labour. However beneficial it might be to the colony in the aggregate, and to each individual composing it, that no one should occupy more land than he can properly cultivate, nor become a proprietor until there are other labourers ready to take his place in working for hire; it can never be the interest of an individual to exercise this forbearance, unless he is assured that others will do so too. Surrounded by settlers who have each their thousand acres, how is he benefited by restricting himself to fifty? or what does a labourer gain by deferring the acquisition altogether for a few years, if all other labourers rush to convert their first earnings into estates in the wilderness, several miles apart from one another? If they, by seizing on land, prevent the formation of a class of labourers for wages, he will not, by postponing the time of his becoming a proprietor, be enabled to employ the land with any greater advantage when he does obtain it; to what end therefore should he place himself in what will appear to him and others a position of inferiority, by remaining a hired labourer, when all around him are proprietors? It is the interest of each to do what is good for all, but only if others will do likewise.

The principle that each is the best judge of his own interest, understood as these objectors understand it, would prove that governments ought not to fulfil any of their acknowledged duties – ought not, in fact, to exist at all. It is greatly the interest of the community, collectively and individually, not to rob or defraud one another: but there is not the less necessity for laws to punish robbery and fraud; because, though it is the interest of each that nobody should rob or cheat, it is not any one's interest to refrain from robbing and cheating others when all others are permitted to rob and cheat him. Penal laws exist at all, chiefly for this reason – because even an unanimous opinion that a certain line of conduct is for the general interest, does not always make it people's individual interest to adhere to that line of conduct.

§13. Fifthly; the argument against government interference grounded on the maxim that individuals are the best judges of their own interest, cannot apply to the very large class of cases, in which those acts of individuals with which the government claims to interfere, are not done by those individuals for their own interest, but for the interest of other people. This includes, among other things, the important and much agitated subject of public charity. Though individuals should, in general, be left to do for themselves whatever it can reasonably be expected that they should be capable of doing, yet when they are at any rate not to be left to themselves, but to be helped by other people, the question arises whether it is better that they should receive this help exclusively from individuals, and therefore uncertainly and casually, or by systematic arrangements, in which society acts through its organ, the state.

This brings us to the subject of Poor Laws; a subject which would be of very minor importance if the habits of all classes of the people were temperate and prudent, and the diffusion of property satisfactory; but of the greatest moment in a state of things so much the reverse of this, in both points, as that which the British islands present.

Apart from any metaphysical considerations respecting the foundation of morals or of the social union, it will be admitted to be right that human beings should help one another; and the more so, in proportion to the urgency of the need: and none needs help so urgently as one who is starving. The claim to help, therefore, created by destitution, is one of the strongest which can exist; and there is *prima facie* the amplest reason for making the relief of so extreme an exigency as certain to those who require it, as by any arrangements of society it can be made.

On the other hand, in all cases of helping, there are two sets of consequences to be considered; the consequences of the assistance, and the consequences of relying on the assistance. The former are generally beneficial, but the latter, for the most part, injurious; so much so, in many cases, as greatly to outweigh the value of the benefit. And this is never more likely to happen than in the very cases where the need of help is the most intense. There are few things for which it is more mischievous that people should rely on the habitual aid of others, than for the means of subsistence, and unhappily there is no lesson which they more easily learn. The problem to be solved is therefore one of peculiar nicety as well as importance; how to give the greatest amount of needful help, with the smallest encouragement to undue reliance on it.

Energy and self-dependence are, however, liable to be impaired by the absence of help, as well as by its excess. It is even more fatal to exertion to have no hope of succeeding by it, than to be assured of succeeding without it. When the condition of any one is so disastrous that his energies are paralysed by discouragement, assistance is a tonic, not a sedative: it braces instead of deadening the active faculties: always provided that the assistance is not such as to dispense with self-help, by substituting itself for the person's own labour, skill, and prudence, but is limited to affording him a better hope of attaining success by those legitimate means. This accordingly is a test to which all plans of philanthropy and benevolence should be brought, whether intended for the benefit of individuals or of classes, and whether conducted on the voluntary or on the government principle.

In so far as the subject admits of any general doctrine or maxim, it would appear to be this – that if assistance is given in such a manner that the condition of the person helped is as desirable as that of the person who succeeds in doing the same thing without help, the assistance, if capable of being previously calculated on, is mischievous: but if, while available to everybody, it leaves to every one a strong motive to do without it if he can, it is then for the most part beneficial. This principle, applied to a system of public charity, is that of the Poor Law of 1834. If the condition of a person receiving relief is made as eligible as that of the labourer who supports himself by his own exertions, the system strikes at the root of all individual industry and self-government; and, if fully acted up to, would require as its supplement an organized system of compulsion, for governing and setting to work like cattle, those who had been removed from the influence of the motives that act on human beings. But if, consistently with guaranteeing all persons against absolute want, the condition of those who are supported by legal charity can be kept considerably less desirable than the condition of those who find support for themselves, none but beneficial consequences can arise from a law which renders it impossible for any person, except by his own choice, to die from insufficiency of food. That in England at least this supposition can be realized, is proved by the experience of a long period preceding the close of the last century, as well as by that of many highly pauperized districts in more recent times, which have been dispauperized by adopting strict rules of poor-law administration, to the great and permanent benefit of the whole labouring class. There is probably no country in which, by varying the means suitably to the character of the people, a legal provision for the destitute might not be made compatible with the observance of the conditions necessary to its being innocuous.

Subject to these conditions, I conceive it to be highly desirable, that the certainty of subsistence should be held out by law to the destitute able-bodied, rather than that their relief should depend on voluntary charity. In the first place, charity almost always does too much or too little: it lavishes its bounty in one place, and leaves people to starve in another. Secondly, since the state must necessarily provide subsistence for the criminal poor while undergoing punishment, not to do the same for the poor who have not offended is to give a premium on crime. And lastly, if the poor are left to individual charity, a vast amount of mendacity is inevitable. What the state may and should abandon to private charity, is the task of distinguishing between one case of real necessity and another. Private charity can give more to the more deserving. The state must act by general rules. It cannot undertake to discriminate between the deserving and the undeserving indigent. It owes no more than subsistence to the first, and can give no less to the last. What is said about the injustice of a law which has no better treatment for the merely unfortunate poor than for the ill-conducted, is founded on a misconception of the province of law and public authority. The dispensers of public relief have no business to be inquisitors. Guardians and overseers are not fit to be trusted to give or withhold other people's money according to their verdict on the morality of the person soliciting it; and it would show much ignorance of the ways of mankind to suppose that such persons, even in the almost impossible case of their being qualified, will take the trouble of ascertaining and sifting the past conduct of a person in distress, so as to form a rational judgment on it. Private charity can make these distinctions; and in bestowing its own money, is entitled to do so according to its own judgment. It should understand that this is its peculiar and appropriate province, and that it is commendable or the contrary, as it exercises the function with more or less discernment. But the administrators of a public fund ought not to be required to do more for anybody, than that minimum which is due even to the worst. If they are, the indulgence very speedily becomes the rule, and refusal the more or less capricious or tyrannical exception.

§14. Another class of cases which fall within the same general principle as the case of public charity, are those in which the acts done by individuals, though intended solely for their own benefit, involve consequences extending indefinitely beyond them, to interests of the nation or of posterity, for which society in its collective capacity is alone able, and alone bound, to provide. One of these cases is that of Colonization. If it is desirable, as no one will deny it to be, that the planting of colonies should be conducted, not with an exclusive view to the private interests of the first founders, but with a deliberate regard to the permanent welfare of the nations afterwards to arise from these small beginnings; such regard can only be secured by placing the enterprise, from its commencement, under regulations constructed with the foresight and enlarged views of philosophical legislators; and the government alone has power either to frame such regulations, or to enforce their observance.

The question of government intervention in the work of Colonization involves the future and permanent interests of civilization itself, and far outstretches the comparatively narrow limits of purely economical considerations. But even with a view to those considerations alone, the removal of population from the overcrowded to the unoccupied parts of the earth's surface is one of those works of eminent social usefulness, which most require, and which at the same time best repay, the intervention of government.

To appreciate the benefits of colonization, it should be considered in its relation, not to a single country, but to the collective economical interests of the human race. The question is in general treated too exclusively as one of distribution; of relieving one labour market and supplying another. It is this, but it is also a question of production, and of the most efficient employment of the productive resources of the world. Much has been said of the good economy of importing commodities from the place where they can be bought cheapest; while the good economy of producing them where they can be produced cheapest, is comparatively little thought of. If to carry consumable goods from the places where they are superabundant to those where they are scarce, is a good pecuniary speculation, is it not an equally good speculation to do the same thing with regard to labour and instruments? The exportation of labourers and capital from old to new countries, from a place where their productive power is less, to a place where it is greater, increases by so much the aggregate produce of the labour and capital of the world. It adds to the joint wealth of the old and the new country, what amounts in a short period to many times the mere cost of effecting the transport. There needs be no hesitation in affirming that Colonization, in the present state of the world, is the best affair of business, in which the capital of an old and wealthy country can engage.

It is equally obvious, however, that Colonization on a great scale can be undertaken, as an affair of business, only by the government, or by some combination of individuals in complete understanding with the government; except under such very peculiar circumstances as those which succeeded the Irish famine. Emigration on the voluntary principle rarely has any material influence in lightening the pressure of population in the old country, though as far as it goes it is doubtless a benefit to the colony. Those labouring persons who voluntarily emigrate are seldom the very poor; they are small farmers with some little capital, or labourers who have saved something, and who, in removing only their own labour from the crowded labour-market, withdraw from the capital of the country a fund which maintained and employed more labourers than themselves. Besides, this portion of the community is so limited in number, that it might be removed entirely, without making any sensible impression upon the numbers of the population, or even upon the annual increase. Any considerable emigration of labour is only practicable, when its cost is defrayed, or at least advanced, by others than the emigrants themselves. Who then is to advance it? Naturally, it may be said, the capitalists of the colony, who require the labour, and who intend to employ it. But to this there is the obstacle, that a capitalist, after going to the expense of carrying out labourers, has no security that he shall be the person to derive any benefit from them. If all the capitalists of the colony were to combine, and bear the expense by subscription, they would still have no security that the labourers, when there, would continue to work for them. After working for a short time and earning a few pounds, they always, unless prevented by the government, squat on unoccupied land, and work only for themselves. The experiment has been repeatedly tried whether it was possible to enforce contracts for labour, or the repayment of the passage money of emigrants to those who advanced it, and the trouble and expense have always exceeded the advantage. The only other resource is the voluntary contributions of parishes or individuals, to rid themselves of surplus labourers who are already, or who are likely to become, locally chargeable on the poor-rate. Were this speculation to become general, it might produce a sufficient amount of emigration to clear off the existing unemployed population, but not to raise the wages of the employed: and the same thing would require to be done over again in less than another generation.

One of the principal reasons why Colonization should be a national undertaking, is that in this manner alone, save in highly exceptional cases, can emigration be self-supporting. The exportation of capital and labour to a new country being, as before observed, one of the best of all affairs of business, it is absurd that it should not, like other affairs of business, repay its own expenses. Of the great addition which it makes to the produce of the world, there can be no reason why a sufficient portion should not be intercepted, and employed in reimbursing the outlay incurred in effecting it. For reasons already given, no individual, or body of individuals, can reimburse themselves for the expense; the government, however, can. It can take from the annual increase of wealth, caused by the emigration, the fraction which suffices to repay with interest what the emigration has cost. The expenses of emigration to a colony ought to be borne by the colony; and this, in general, is only possible when they are borne by the colonial government.

Of the modes in which a fund for the support of colonization can be raised in the colony, none is comparable in advantage to that which was first suggested, and so ably and perseveringly advocated, by Mr Wakefield : the plan of putting a price on all unoccupied land, and devoting the proceeds to emigration. The unfounded and pedantic objections to this plan have been answered in a former part of this chapter : we have now to speak of its advantages. First, it avoids the difficulties and discontents incident to raising a large annual amount by taxation; a thing which is almost useless to attempt with a scattered population of settlers in the wilderness, who, as experience proves, can seldom be compelled to pay direct taxes, except at a cost exceeding their amount; while in an infant community indirect taxation soon reaches its limit. The sale of lands is thus by far the easiest mode of raising the requisite funds. But it has other and still greater recommendations. It is a beneficial check upon the tendency of a population of colonists to adopt the tastes and inclinations of savage life, and to disperse so widely as to lose all the advantages of commerce, of markets, of separation of employments, and combination of labour. By making it necessary for those who emigrate at the expense of the fund, to earn a considerable sum before they can become landed proprietors, it keeps up a perpetual succession of labourers for hire, who in every country are a most important auxiliary even to peasant proprietors : and by diminishing the eagerness of agricultural speculators to add to their domain, it keeps the settlers within reach of each other for purposes of co-operation, arranges a numerous body of them within easy distance of each centre of foreign commerce and non-agricultural industry, and insures the formation and rapid growth of towns and town products. This concentration, compared with the dispersion which uniformly occurs when unoccupied land can be had for nothing, greatly accelerates the attainment of prosperity, and enlarges the fund which may be drawn upon for further emigration. Before the adoption of the Wakefield system, the early years of all new colonies were full of hardship and difficulty: the last colony founded on the old principle, the Swan River settlement, being one of the most characteristic instances. In all subsequent colonization, the Wakefield principle has been acted upon, though imperfectly, a part only of the proceeds of the sale of land being devoted to emigration: yet wherever it has been introduced at all, as in South Australia, Victoria, and New Zealand, the restraint put upon the dispersion of the settlers, and the influx of capital caused by the assurance of being able to obtain hired labour, has, in spite of many difficulties and much mismanagement, produced a suddenness and rapidity of prosperity more like fable than reality.[8]

The self-supporting system of Colonization, once established, would increase in efficiency every year; its effect would tend to increase in geometrical progression: for since every able-bodied emigrant, until the country is fully peopled, adds in a very short time to its wealth, over and above his own consumption, as much as would defray the expense of bringing out another emigrant, it follows that the greater the number already sent, the greater number might continue to be sent, each emigrant laying the foundation of a succession of other emigrants at short intervals without fresh expense, until the colony is filled up. It would

8. The objections which have been made, with so much virulence, in some of these colonies, to the Wakefield system, apply, in so far as they have any validity, not to the principle, but to some provisions which are no part of the system, and have been most unnecessarily and improperly engrafted on it; such as the offering only a limited quantity of land for sale, and that by auction, and in lots of not less than 640 acres, instead of selling all land which is asked for, and allowing to the buyer unlimited freedom of choice, both as to quantity and situation, at a fixed price.

therefore be worth while, to the mother country, to accelerate the early stages of this progression, by loans to the colonies for the purpose of emigration, repayable from the fund formed by the sales of land. In thus advancing the means of accomplishing a large immediate emigration, it would be investing that amount of capital in the mode, of all others, most beneficial to the colony; and the labour and savings of these emigrants would hasten the period at which a large sum would be available from sales of land. It would be necessary, in order not to overstock the labour market, to act in concert with the persons disposed to remove their own capital to the colony. The knowledge that a large amount of hired labour would be available, in so productive a field of employment, would insure a large emigration of capital from a country, like England, of low profits and rapid accumulation: and it would only be necessary not to send out a greater number of labourers at one time, than this capital could absorb and employ at high wages.

Inasmuch as, on this system, any given amount of expenditure, once incurred, would provide not merely a single emigration, but a perpetually flowing stream of emigrants, which would increase in breadth and depth as it flowed on; this mode of relieving overpopulation has a recommendation, not possessed by any other plan ever proposed for making head against the consequences of increase without restraining the increase itself: there is an element of indefiniteness in it; no one can perfectly foresee how far its influence, as a vent for surplus population, might possibly reach. There is hence the strongest obligation on the government of a country like our own, with a crowded population, and unoccupied continents under its command, to build, as it were, and keep open, in concert with the colonial governments, a bridge from the mother country to those continents, by establishing the self-supporting system of colonization on such a scale, that as great an amount of emigration as the colonies can at the time accommodate, may at all times be able to take place without cost to the emigrants themselves.

The importance of these considerations, as regards the British islands, has been of late considerably diminished by the unparalleled amount of spontaneous emigration from Ireland; an emigration not solely of small farmers, but of the poorest class of agricultural labourers, and which is at once voluntary and self-supporting, the succession of emigrants being kept up by funds contributed from the earnings of their relatives and connexions who had gone before. To this has been added a large amount of voluntary emigration to the seats of the gold discoveries, which has partly supplied the wants of our most distant colonies, where, both for local and national interests, it was most of all required. But the stream of both these emigrations has already considerably slackened, and though that from Ireland has since partially revived, it is not certain that the aid of government in a systematic form, and on the self-supporting principle, will not again become necessary to keep the communication open between the hands needing work in England, and the work which needs hands elsewhere.

§15. The same principle which points out colonization, and the relief of the indigent, as cases to which the principal objection to government interference does not apply, extends also to a variety of cases, in which important public services are to be performed, while yet there is no individual specially interested in performing them, nor would any adequate remuneration naturally or spontaneously attend their performance. Take for instance a voyage of geographical or scientific exploration. The information sought may be of great public value, yet no individual would derive any benefit from it which would repay the expense of fitting out the expedition; and there is no mode of intercepting the benefit on its way to those who profit by it, in order to levy a toll for the remuneration of its authors. Such voyages are, or might be, undertaken by private subscription; but this is a rare and precarious resource. Instances are more frequent in which the expense has been borne by public companies or philanthropic associations; but in general such enterprises have been conducted at the expense of government, which is thus enabled to entrust them to the persons in its judgment best qualified for the task. Again, it is a proper office of government to build and maintain lighthouses, establish buoys, &c. for the security of navigation: for since it is impossible that the ships at sea which are benefited by a lighthouse, should be made to pay a toll on the occasion of its use, no one would build lighthouses from motives of personal interest, unless indemnified and rewarded from a compulsory levy made by the state. There are many scientific researches, of great value to a nation and to mankind, requiring assiduous devotion of time and labour, and not unfrequently great expense, by persons who can obtain a high price for their services in other ways. If the government had no power to grant indemnity for expense, and remuneration for time and labour thus employed, such researches could only be undertaken by the very few persons who, with an independent fortune, unite technical knowledge, laborious habits, and either great public spirit, or an ardent desire of scientific celebrity.

Connected with this subject is the question of providing, by means of endowments or salaries, for the maintenance of what has been called a learned class. The cultivation of speculative knowledge, though one of the most useful of all employments, is a service rendered to a community collectively, not individually, and one consequently for which it is, *prima facie*, reasonable that the community collectively should pay; since it gives no claim on any individual for a pecuniary remuneration; and unless a provision is made for such services from some public fund, there is not only no encouragement to them, but there is as much discouragement as is implied in the impossibility of gaining a living by such pursuits, and the necessity consequently imposed on most of those who would be capable of them, to employ the greatest part of their time in gaining a subsistence. The evil, however, is greater in appearance than in reality. The greatest things, it has been said, have generally been done by those who had the least time at their disposal; and the occupation of some hours every day in a routine employment, has often been found compatible with the most brilliant achievements in literature and philosophy. Yet there are investigations and experiments which require not only a long but a continuous devotion of time and attention: there are also occupations which so engross and fatigue the mental faculties, as to be inconsistent with any vigorous employment of them upon other subjects, even in intervals of leisure. It is highly desirable, therefore, that there should be a mode of insuring to the public the services of scientific discoverers, and perhaps of some other classes of savants, by affording them the means of support consistently with devoting a sufficient portion of time to their peculiar pursuits. The fellowships of the Universities are an institution excellently adapted for such a purpose; but are hardly ever applied to it, being bestowed, at the best, as a reward for past proficiency, in committing to memory what has been done by others, and not as the salary of future labours in the advancement of knowledge. In some countries, Academies of science, antiquities, history, &c., have been formed, with emoluments annexed. The most effectual plan, and at the same time least liable to abuse, seems to be that of conferring Professorships, with duties of instruction attached to them. The occupation of teaching a branch of knowledge, at least in its higher departments, is a help rather than an impediment to the systematic cultivation of the subject itself. The duties of a professorship almost always leave much time for original researches; and the greatest advances which have been made in the various sciences, both moral and physical, have originated with those who were public teachers of them; from Plato and Aristotle to the great names of the Scotch, French, and German Universities. I do not mention the English, because until very lately their professorships have been, as is well known, little more than nominal. In the case, too, of a lecturer in a great institution of education, the public at large has the means of judging, if not the quality of the teaching, at least the talents and industry of the teacher; and it is more difficult to misemploy the power of appointment to such an office, than to job in pensions and salaries to persons not so directly before the public eye.

It may be said generally, that anything which it is desirable should be done for the general interests of mankind or of future generations, or for the present interests of those members of the community who require external aid but which is not of a nature to remunerate individuals or associations for undertaking it, is in itself a suitable thing to be undertaken by government: though, before making the work their own, governments ought always to consider if there be any rational probability of its being done on what is called the voluntary principle, and if so, whether it is likely to be done in a better or more effectual manner by government agency, than by the zeal and liberality of individuals.

§16. The preceding heads comprise, to the best of my judgment, the whole of the exceptions to the practical maxim, that the business of society can be best performed by private and voluntary agency. It is, however, necessary to add, that the intervention of government cannot always practically stop short at the limit which defines the cases intrinsically suitable for it. In the particular circumstances of a given age or nation, there is scarcely anything really important to the general interest, which it may not be desirable, or even necessary, that the government should take upon itself, not because private individuals cannot effectually perform it, but because they will not. At some times and places, there will be no roads, docks, harbours, canals, works of irrigation, hospitals, schools, colleges, printing-presses, unless the government establishes them; the public being either too poor to command the necessary resources, or too little advanced in intelligence to appreciate the ends, or not sufficiently practised in joint action to be capable of the means. This is true, more or less, of all countries inured to despotism, and particularly of those in which there is a very wide distance in civilization between the people and the government: as in those which have been conquered and are retained in subjection by a more energetic and more cultivated people. In many parts of the world, the people can do nothing for themselves which requires large means and combined action: all such things are left undone, unless done by the state. In these cases, the mode in which the government can most surely demonstrate the sincerity with which it intends the greatest good of its subjects, is by doing the things which are made incumbent on it by the helplessness of the public, in such a manner as shall tend not to increase and perpetuate, but to correct, that helplessness. A good government will give all its aid in such a shape, as to encourage and nurture any rudiments it may find of a spirit of individual exertion. It will be assiduous in removing obstacles and discouragements to voluntary enterprise, and in giving whatever facilities and whatever direction and guidance may be necessary: its pecuniary means will be applied, when practicable, in aid of private efforts rather than in supersession of them, and it will call into play its machinery of rewards and honours to elicit such efforts. Government aid, when given merely in default of private enterprise, should be so given as to be as far as possible a course of education for the people in the art of accomplishing great objects by individual energy and voluntary co-operation.

I have not thought it necessary here to insist on that part of the functions of government which all admit to be indispensable, the function of prohibiting and punishing such conduct on the part of individuals in the exercise of their freedom, as is clearly injurious to other persons, whether the case be one of force, fraud, or negligence. Even in the best state which society has yet reached, it is lamentable to think how great a proportion of all the efforts and talents in the world are employed in merely neutralizing one another. It is the proper end of government to reduce this wretched waste to the smallest possible amount, by taking such measures as shall cause the energies now spent by mankind in injuring one another, or in protecting themselves against injury, to be turned to the legitimate employment of the human faculties, that of compelling the powers of nature to be more and more subservient to physical and moral good.

APPENDIX

BOOK II

DISTRIBUTION

CHAPTER I

Of Property

§1. The principles which have been set forth in the first part of this Treatise, are, in certain respects, strongly distinguished from those, on the consideration of which we are now about to enter. The laws and conditions of the production of wealth, partake of the character of physical truths. There is nothing optional, or arbitrary in them. Whatever mankind produce, must be produced in the modes, and under the conditions, imposed by the constitution of external things, and by the inherent properties of their own bodily and mental structure. Whether they like it or not, their productions will be limited by the amount of their previous accumulation, and, that being given, it will be proportional to their energy, their skill, the perfection of their machinery, and their judicious use of the advantages of combined labour. Whether they like it or not, a double quantity of labour will not raise, on the same land, a double quantity of food, unless some improvement takes place in the processes of cultivation. Whether they like it or not, the unproductive expenditure of individauls will *pro tanto* tend to impoverish the community, and only their productive expenditure will enrich it. The opinions, or the wishes, which may exist on these different matters, do not control the things themselves. We cannot, indeed, foresee to what extent the modes of production may be altered, or the productiveness of labour increased, by future extensions of our knowledge of the laws of nature, suggesting new processes of industry of which we have at present no conception. But howsoever we may succeed in making for ourselves more space within the limits set by the constitution of things, we know that there must be limits. We cannot alter the ultimate properties either of matter or mind, but can only employ those properties more or less successfully, to bring about the events in which we are interested.

It is not so with the Distribution of Wealth. That is a matter of human institution solely. The things once there, mankind, individually or collectively, can do with them as they like. They can place them at the disposal of whomsoever they please, and on whatever terms. Further, in the social state, in every state except total solitude, any disposal whatever of them can only take place by the consent of society, or rather of those who dispose of its active force. Even what a person has produced by his individual toil, unaided by any one, he cannot keep, unless by the permission of society. Not only can society take it from him, but individuals could and would take it from him, if society only remained passive; if it did not either interfere *en masse*, or employ and pay people for the purpose of preventing him from being disturbed in the possession. The distribution of wealth, therefore, depends on the laws and customs of society. The rules by which it is determined, are what the opinions and feelings of the ruling portion of the community make them, and are very different in different ages and countries; and might be still more different, if mankind so chose.

The opinions and feelings of mankind, doubtless, are not a matter of chance. They are consequences of the fundamental laws of human nature, combined with the existing state of knowledge and experience, and the existing condition and social institutions and intellectual and moral culture. But the laws of the generation of human opinions are not within our present subject. They are part of the general theory of human progress, a far larger and more difficult subject of inquiry than political economy. We have here to consider, not the causes, but the consequences of the rules according to which wealth may be distributed. Those, at least, are as little arbitrary, and have as much the character of physical laws, as the laws of production. Human beings can control their own acts, but not the consequences of their acts either to themselves or to others. Society can subject the distribution of wealth to whatever rules it thinks best; but what practical results will flow from the operation of those rules, must be discovered, like any other physical or mental truths, by observation and reasoning.

We proceed, then, to the consideration of the different modes of distributing the produce of land and labour, which have been adopted in practice, or may be conceived in theory. Among these, our attention is first claimed by that primary and fundamental institution, on which, unless in some exceptional and very limited cases, the economical arrangements of society have always rested, though in its secondary features it has varied, and is liable to vary. I mean, of course, the institution of individual property.

§2. Private property, as an institution, did not owe its origin to any of those considerations of utility, which plead for the maintenance of it when established. Enough is known of rude ages, both from history and from analogous states of society in our own time, to show, that tribunals (which always precede laws) were originally established, not to determine rights, but to repress violence and terminate quarrels. With this object chiefly in view, they naturally enough gave legal effect to first occupancy, by treating as the aggressor the person who first commenced violence, by turning, or attempting to turn, another out of possession. The preservation of the peace, which was the original object of civil government, was thus attained; while by confirming, to those who already possessed it, even what was not the fruit of personal exertion, a guarantee was incidentally given to them and others that they would be protected in what was so.

In considering the institution of property as a question in social philosophy, we must leave out of consideration its actual origin in any of the existing nations of Europe. We may suppose a community unhampered by any previous possession; a body of colonists, occupying for the first time an uninhabited country; bringing nothing with them but what belonged to them in common, and having a clear field for the adoption of the institutions and polity which they judged most expedient; required, therefore, to choose whether they would conduct the work of production on the principle of individual property, or on some system of common ownership and collective agency.

If private property were adopted, we must presume that it would be accompanied by none of the initial inequalities and injustices which obstruct the beneficial operation of the principle in old societies. Every full-grown man or woman, we must suppose, would be secured in the unfettered use and disposal of his or her bodily and mental faculties; and the instruments of production, the land and tools, would be divided fairly among them, so that all might start, in respect to outward appliances, on equal terms. It is possible also to conceive that in this original apportionment, compensation might be made for the injuries of nature, and the balance redressed by assigning to the less robust members of the community advantages in the distribution, sufficient to put them on a par with the rest. But the division, once made, would not again be interfered with; individuals would be left to their own exertions and to the ordinary chances, for making an advantageous use of what was assigned to them. If individual property, on the contrary, were excluded, the plan which must be adopted would be to hold the land and all instruments of production as the joint property of the community, and to carry on the operations of industry on the common account. The direction of the labour of the community would devolve upon a magistrate or magistrates, whom we may suppose elected by the suffrages of the community, and whom we must assume to be voluntarily obeyed by them. The division of the produce would in like manner be a public act. The principle might either be that of complete equality, or of apportionment to the necessities or deserts of individuals, in whatever manner might be conformable to the ideas of justice or policy prevailing in the community.

Examples of such associations, on a small scale, are the monastic orders, the Moravians, the followers of Rapp, and others: and from the hopes which they hold out of relief from the miseries and iniquities of a state of much inequality of wealth, schemes for a larger application of the same idea have reappeared and become popular at all periods of active speculation on the first principles of society. In an age like the present, when a general reconsideration of all first principles is felt to be inevitable, and when more than at any former period of history the suffering portions of the community have a voice in the discussion, it was impossible but that ideas of this nature should spread far and wide. The late revolutions in Europe have thrown up a great amount of speculation of this character, and an unusual share of attention has consequently been drawn to the various forms which these ideas have assumed: nor is this attention likely to diminish, but on the contrary, to increase more and more.

The assailants of the principle of individual property may be divided into two classes: those whose scheme implies absolute equality in the distribution of the physical means of life and enjoyment, and those who admit inequality, but grounded on some principle, or supposed principle, of justice or general expediency, and not, like so many of the existing social inequalities, dependent on accident alone. At the head of the first class, as the earliest of those belonging to the present generation, must be placed Mr Owen and his followers. M. Louis Blanc and M. Cabet have more recently become conspicuous as apostles of similar doctrines (though the former advocates equality of distribution only as a transition to a still higher standard of justice, that all should work according to their capacity, and receive according to their wants). The characteristic name for this economical system is Communism, a word of continental origin, only of late introduced into this country. The word Socialism, which originated among the English Communists, and was assumed by them as a name to designate their own doctrine, is now, on the Continent, employed in a larger sense; not necessarily implying Communism, or the entire abolition of private property, but applied to any system which requires that the land and the instruments of production should be the property, not of individuals, but of communities or associations, or of the government. Among such systems, the two of highest intellectual pretension are those which, from the names of their real or reputed authors, have been called St Simonism and Fourierism; the former, defunct as a system, but which during the few years of public promulgation, sowed the seeds of nearly all the Socialist tendencies which have since spread so widely in France: the second, still flourishing in the number, talent, and zeal of its adherents.

§3. Whatever may be the merits or defects of these various schemes, they cannot be truly said to be impracticable. No reasonable person can doubt that a village community, composed of a few thousand inhabitants cultivating in joint ownership the same extent of land which at present feeds that number of people, and producing by combined labour and the most improved processes the manufactured articles which they required, could raise an amount of productions sufficient to maintain them in comfort; and would find the means of obtaining, and if need be, exacting, the quantity of labour necessary for this purpose, from every member of the association who was capable of work.

The objection ordinarily made to a system of community of property and equal distribution of the produce, that each person would be incessantly occupied in evading his fair share of the work, points, undoubtedly, to a real difficulty. But those who urge this objection, forget to how great an extent the same difficulty exists under the system on which nine-tenths of the business of society is now conducted. The objection supposes, that honest and efficient labour is only to be had from those who are themselves individually to reap the benefit of their own exertions. But how small a part of all the labour performed in England, from the lowest paid to the highest, is done by persons working for their own benefit. From the Irish reaper or hodman to the chief justice or the minister of state, nearly all the work of society is remunerated by day wages or fixed salaries. A factory operative has less personal interest in his work than a member of a Communist association, since he is not, like him, working for a partnership of which he is himself a member. It will no doubt be said, that though the labourers themselves have not, in most cases, a personal interest in their work, they are watched and superintended, and their labour directed, and the mental part of the labour performed, by persons who have. Even this, however, is far from being universally the fact. In all public, and many of the largest and most successful private undertakings, not only the labours of detail, but the control and superintendence are entrusted to salaried officers. And though the 'master's eye', when the master is vigilant and intelligent, is of proverbial value, it must be remembered that in a Socialist farm or manufactory, each labourer would be under the eye not of one master, but of the whole community. In the extreme case of obstinate perseverance in not performing the due share of work, the community would have the same resources which society now has for compelling conformity to the necessary conditions of the association. Dismissal, the only remedy at present, is no remedy when any other labourer who may be engaged does no better than his predecessor : the power of dismissal only enables an employer to obtain from his workmen the customary amount of labour, but that customary labour may be of any degree of inefficiency. Even the labourer who loses his employment by idleness or negligence, has nothing worse to suffer, in the most unfavourable case, than the discipline of a workhouse, and if the desire to avoid this be a sufficient motive in the one system, it would be sufficient in the other. I am not undervaluing the strength of the incitement given to labour when the whole or a large share of the benefit of extra exertion belongs to the labourer. But under the present system of industry this incitement, in the great majority of cases, does not exist. If Communistic labour might be less vigorous than that of a peasant proprietor, or a workman labouring on his own account, it would probably be more energetic than that of a labourer for hire, who has no personal interest in the matter at all. The neglect by the uneducated classes of labourers for hire, of the duties which they engage to perform, is in the present state of society most flagrant. Now it is an admitted condition of the Communist scheme that all shall be educated : and this being supposed, the duties of the members of the association would doubtless be as diligently performed as those of the generality of salaried officers in the middle or higher classes; who are not supposed to be necessarily unfaithful to their trust, because so long as they are not dismissed, their pay is the same in however lax a manner their duty is fulfilled. Undoubtedly, as a general rule, remuneration by fixed salaries does not in any class of functionaries produce the maximum of zeal: and this is as much as can be reasonably alleged against Communistic labour.

That even this inferiority would necessarily exist, is by no means so certain as is assumed by those who are little used to carry their minds beyond the state of things with which they are familiar. Mankind are capable of a far greater amount of public spirit than the present age is accustomed to suppose possible. History bears witness to the success with which large bodies of human beings may be trained to feel the public interest their own. And no soil could be more favourable to the growth of such a feeling, than a Communist association, since all the ambition, and the bodily and mental activity, which are now exerted in the pursuit of separate and self-regarding interests, would require another sphere of employment, and would naturally find it in the pursuit of the general benefit of the community. The same cause, so often assigned in explanation of the devotion of the Catholic priest or monk to the interest of his order – that he has no interest apart from it – would, under Communism, attach the citizen to the community. And independently of the public motive, every member of the association would be amenable to the most universal, and one of the strongest of personal motives, that of public opinion. The force of this motive in deterring from any act or omission positively reproved by the community, no one is likely to deny; but the power also of emulation, in exciting to the most strenuous exertions for the sake of the approbation and admiration of others, is borne witness to by experience in every situation in which human beings publicly compete with one another, even if it be in things frivolous, or from which the public derive no benefit. A contest, who can do most for the common good, is not the kind of competition which Socialists repudiate. To what extent, therefore, the energy of labour would be diminished by Communism, or whether in the long run it would be diminished at all, must be considered for the present an undecided question.

Another of the objections to Communism is similar to that, so often urged against poor-laws: that if every member of the community were assured of subsistence for himself and any number of children, on the sole condition of willingness to work, prudential restraint on the multiplication of mankind would be at an end, and population would start forward at a rate which would reduce the community through successive stages of increasing discomfort to actual starvation. There would certainly be much ground for this apprehension if Communism provided no motives to restraint, equivalent to those which it would take away. But Communism is precisely the state of things in which opinion might be expected to declare itself with greatest intensity against this kind of selfish intemperance. Any augmentation of numbers which diminished the comfort or increased the toil of the mass, would then cause (which now it does not) immediate and unmistakeable inconvenience to every individual in the association; inconvenience which could not then be imputed to the avarice of employers, or the unjust privileges of the rich. In such altered circumstances opinion could not fail to reprobate, and if reprobation did not suffice, to repress by penalties of some description, this or any other culpable self-indulgence at the expense of the community. The Communistic scheme, instead of being peculiarly open to the objection drawn from danger of over-population, has the recommendation of tending in an especial degree to the prevention of that evil.

A more real difficulty is that of fairly apportioning the labour of the community among its members. There are many kinds of work, and by what standard are they to be measured one against another? Who is to judge how much cotton spinning, or distributing goods from the stores, or bricklaying, or chimney sweeping, is equivalent to so much ploughing? The difficulty of making the adjustment between different qualities of labour is so strongly felt by Communist writers that they have usually thought it necessary to provide that all should work by turns at every description of useful labour: an arrangement which by putting an end to the division of employments, would sacrifice so much of the advantage of co-operative production as greatly to diminish the productiveness of labour. Besides, even in the same kind of work, nominal equality of labour would be so great a real inequality, that the feeling of justice would revolt against its being enforced. All persons are not equally fit for all labour; and the same quantity of labour is an unequal burthen

357

on the weak and the strong, the hardy and the delicate, the quick and the slow, the dull and the intelligent.

But these difficulties, though real, are not necessarily insuperable. The apportionment of work to the strength and capacities of individuals, the mitigation of a general rule to provide for cases in which it would operate harshly, are not problems to which human intelligence, guided by a sense of justice, would be inadequate. And the worst and most unjust arrangement which could be made of these points, under a system aiming at equality, would be so far short of the inequality and injustice with which labour (not to speak of remuneration) is now apportioned, as to be scarcely worth counting in the comparison. We must remember too that Communism, as a system of society, exists only in idea; that its difficulties, at present, are much better understood than its resources; and that the intellect of mankind is only beginning to contrive the means of organizing it in detail, so as to overcome the one and derive the greatest advantage from the other.

If, therefore, the choice were to be made between Communism with all its chances, and the present state of society with all its sufferings and injustices; if the institution of private property necessarily carried with it as a consequence, that the produce of labour should be apportioned as we now see it, almost in an inverse ratio to the labour – the largest portions to those who have never worked at all, the next largest to those whose work is almost nominal, and so in a descending scale, the remuneration dwindling as the work grows harder and more disagreeable, until the most fatiguing and exhausting bodily labour cannot count with certainty on being able to earn even the necessaries of life; if this, or Communism, were the alternative, all the difficulties, great or small, of Communism would be but as dust in the balance. But to make the comparison applicable, we must compare Communism at its best, with the régime of individual property, not as it is, but as it might be made. The principle of private property has never yet had a fair trial in any country; and less so, perhaps, in this country than in some others. The social arrangements of modern Europe commenced from a distribution of property which was the result, not of just partition, or acquisition by industry, but of conquest and violence: and notwithstanding what industry has been doing for many centuries to modify the work of force, the system still retains many and large traces of its origin. The laws of property have never yet conformed to the principles on which the justification of private property rests. They have made property of things which never ought to be property, and absolute property where only a qualified property ought to exist. They have not held the balance fairly between human beings, but have heaped impediments upon some, to give advantage to others; they have purposely fostered inequalities, and prevented all from starting fair in the race. That all should indeed start on perfectly equal terms, is inconsistent with any law of private property: but if as much pains as has been taken to aggravate the inequality of chances arising from the natural working of the principle, had been taken to temper that inequality by every means not subversive of the principle itself; if the tendency of legislation had been to favour the diffusion, instead of the concentration of wealth – to encourage the subdivision of the large masses, instead of striving to keep them together; the principle of individual property would have been found to have no necessary connexion with the physical and social evils which almost all Socialist writers assume to be inseparable from it.

Private property, in every defence made of it, is supposed to mean, the guarantee to individuals, of the fruits of their own labour and abstinence. The guarantee to them of the fruits of the labour and abstinence of others, transmitted to them without any merit or exertion of their own, is not of the essence of the institution, but a mere incidental consequence, which when it reaches a certain height, does not promote, but conflicts with the ends which render private property legitimate. To judge of the final destination of the institution of property, we must suppose everything rectified, which causes the institution to work in a manner opposed to that equitable principle, of proportion between remuneration and exertion, on which in every vindication of it that will bear the light, it is assumed to be grounded. We must also suppose two conditions realized, without which neither Communism nor any other laws or institutions could make the condition of the mass of mankind other than degraded and miserable. One of these conditions is, universal education; the other, a due limitation of the numbers of the community. With these, there could be no poverty even under the present social institutions: and these being supposed, the question of Socialism is not, as generally stated by Socialists, a question of flying to the sole refuge against the evils which now bear down humanity; but a mere question of comparative advantages, which futurity must determine. We are too ignorant either of what individual agency in its best form, or Socialism in its best form, can accomplish, to be qualified to decide which of the two will be the ultimate form of human society.

If a conjecture may be hazarded, the decision will probably depend mainly on one consideration, viz. which of the two systems is consistent with the greatest amount of human liberty and spontaneity. After the means of subsistence are assured, the next in strength of the personal wants of human beings is liberty; and (unlike the physical wants, which as civilization advances become more moderate and more amenable to control) it increases instead of diminishing in intensity, as the intelligence and the moral faculties are more developed. The perfection both of social arrangements and of practical morality would be, to secure to all persons complete independence and freedom of action, subject to no restriction but that of not doing injury to others: and the education which taught or the social institutions which required them to exchange the control of their own actions for any amount of comfort or affluence, or to renounce liberty for the sake of equality, would deprive them of one of the most elevated characteristics of human nature. It remains to be discovered how far the preservation of this characteristic would be found compatible with the communistic organization of society. No doubt, this, like all the other objections to the Socialist schemes, is vastly exaggerated. The members of the association need not be required to live together more than they do now, nor need they be controlled in the disposal of their individual share of the produce, and of the probably large amount of leisure which, if they limited their production to things really worth producing, they would possess. Individuals need not be chained to an occupation, or to a particular locality. The restraints of Communism would be freedom in comparison with the present condition of the majority of the human race. The generality of labourers in this and most other countries, have as little choice of occupation or freedom of locomotion, are practically as dependent on fixed rules and on the will of others, as they could be on any system short of actual slavery; to say nothing of the entire domestic subjection of one half the species, to which it is the signal honour of Owenism and most other forms of Socialism that they assign equal rights, in all respects, with those of the hitherto dominant sex. But it is not by comparison with the present bad state of society that the claims of Communism can be estimated; nor is it sufficient that it should promise greater personal and mental freedom than is now enjoyed by those who have not enough of either to deserve the name. The question is whether there would be any asylum left for individuality of character; whether public opinion would not be a tyrannical yoke; whether the absolute dependence of each on all, and surveillance of each by all, would not grind all down into a tame uniformity of thoughts, feelings, and actions. This is already one of the glaring evils of the existing state of society, notwithstanding a much greater diversity of education and pursuits, and a much less absolute dependence of the individual on the mass, than would exist in the Communistic régime. No society in which eccentricity is a matter of reproach, can be in a wholesome state. It is yet to be ascertained whether the Communistic scheme would be consistent with that multiform development of human nature, those manifold unlikenesses, that diversity of tastes and talents, and variety of intellectual points of view, which not only form a great part of the interest of human life, but by bringing intellects into a stimulating collision, and by presenting to each innumerable notions that he would not have conceived of himself, are the mainspring of mental and moral progression.

§4. I have thus far confined my observations to the Communistic doctrine, which forms the extreme limit of Socialism; according to which not only the instruments of production, the land and capital, are the joint property of the community, but the produce is divided and the labour apportioned, as far as possible, equally. The objections, whether well or ill grounded, to which Socialism is liable, apply to this form of it in their greatest force. The other varieties of Socialism mainly differ from Communism, in not relying solely on what M. Louis Blanc calls the point of honour of industry, but retaining more or less of the incentives to labour derived from private pecuniary interest. Thus it is already a modification of the strict theory of Communism, when the principle is professed of proportioning remuneration to labour. The attempts which have been made in France to carry Socialism into practical effect, by associations of workmen manufacturing on their own account, mostly began by sharing the remuneration equally, without regard to the quantity of work done by the individual: but in almost every case this plan was after a short time abandoned, and recourse was had to working by the piece. The original principle appeals to a higher standard of justice, and is adapted to a much higher moral condition of human nature. The proportioning of remuneration to work done, is really just, only in so far as the more or less of the work is a matter of choice: when it depends on natural difference of strength or capacity, this principle of remuneration is in itself an injustice: it is giving to those who have; assigning most to those who are already most favoured by nature. Considered however, as a compromise with the selfish type of character formed by the present standard of morality, and fostered by the existing social institutions, it is highly expedient; and until education shall have been entirely regenerated, is far more likely to prove immediately successful, than an attempt at a higher ideal.

The two elaborate forms of non-communistic Socialism known as St Simonism and Fourierism, are totally free from the objections usually urged against Communism; and though they are open to others of their own, yet by the great intellectual power which in many respects distinguishes them, and by their large and philosophic treatment of some of the fundamental problems of society and morality, they may justly be counted among the most remarkable productions of the past and present age.

The St Simonian scheme does not contemplate an equal, but an unequal division of the produce; it does not propose that all should be occupied alike, but differently, according to their vocation or capacity; the function of each being assigned, like grades in a regiment, by the choice of the directing authority, and the remuneration being by salary, proportioned to the importance, in the eyes of that authority, of the function itself, and the merits of the person who fulfils it. For the constitution of the ruling body, different plans might be adopted, consistently with the essentials of the system. It might be appointed by popular suffrage. In the idea of the original authors, the rulers were supposed to be persons of genius and virtue, who obtained the voluntary adhesion of the rest by the force of mental superiority. That the scheme might in some peculiar states of society work with advantage, is not improbable. There is indeed a successful experiment, of a somewhat similar kind, on record, to which I have once alluded; that of the Jesuits in Paraguay. A race of savages, belonging to a portion of mankind more averse to consecutive exertion for a distant object than any other authentically known to us, was brought under the mental dominion of civilized and instructed men who were united among themselves by a system of community of goods. To the absolute authority of these men they reverentially submitted themselves, and were induced by them to learn the arts of civilized life, and to practise labours for the community, which no inducement that could have been offered would have prevailed on them to practise for themselves. This social system was of short duration, being prematurely destroyed by diplomatic arrangements and foreign force. That it could be brought into action at all was probably owing to the immense distance in point of knowledge and intellect which separated the few rulers from the whole body of the ruled, without any intermediate orders, either social or intellectual. In any other circumstances it would probably have been a complete failure. It supposes an absolute despotism in the heads of the association; which would probably not be much improved if the depositaries of the despotism (contrary to the views of the authors of the system) were varied from time to time according to the result of a popular canvass. But to suppose that one or a few human beings, howsoever selected, could, by whatever machinery of subordinate agency, be qualified to adapt each person's work to his capacity, and proportion each person's remuneration to his merits – to be, in fact, the dispensers of distributive justice to every member of a community; or that any use which they could make of this power would give general satisfaction, or would be submitted to without the aid of force – is a supposition almost too chimerical to be reasoned against. A fixed rule, like that of equality, might be acquiesced in, and so might chance, or an external necessity; but that a handful of human beings should weigh everybody in the balance, and give more to one and less to another at their sole pleasure and judgment, would not be borne, unless from persons believed to be more than men, and backed by supernatural terrors.

The most skilfully combined, and with the greatest foresight of objections, of all the forms of Socialism, is that commonly known as Fourierism. This system does not contemplate the abolition of private property, nor even of inheritance: on the contrary, it avowedly takes into consideration, as an element in the distribution of the produce, capital as well as labour. It proposes that the operations of industry should be carried on by associations of about two thousand members, combining their labour on a district of about a square league in extent, under the guidance of chiefs selected by themselves. In the distribution, a certain minimum is first assigned for the subsistence of every member of the community, whether capable or not of labour. The remainder of the produce is shared in certain proportions, to be determined beforehand, among the three elements, Labour, Capital, and Talent. The capital of the community may be owned in unequal shares by different members, who would in that case receive, as in any other joint-stock company, proportional dividends. The claim of each person on the share of the produce apportioned to talent is estimated by the grade or rank which the individual occupies in the several groups of labourers to which he or she belongs; these grades being in all cases conferred by the choice of his or her companions. The remuneration, when received, would not of necessity be expended or enjoyed in common; there would be separate *ménages* for all who preferred them, and no other community of living is contemplated, than that all the members of the association should reside in the same pile of buildings; for saving of labour and expense, not only in building, but in every branch of domestic economy; and in order that, the whole of the buying and selling operations of the community being performed by a single agent, the enormous portion of the produce of industry now carried off by the profits of mere distributors might be reduced to the smallest amount possible.

This system, unlike Communism, does not, in theory at least, withdraw any of the motives to exertion which exist in the present state of society. On the contrary, if the arrangement worked according to the intentions of its contrivers, it would even strengthen those motives; since each person would have much more certainty of reaping individually the fruits of increased skill or energy, bodily or mental, than under the present social arrangements can be felt by any but those who are in the most advantageous positions, or to whom the chapter of accidents is more than ordinarily favourable. The Fourierists, however, have still another resource. They believe that they have solved the great and fundamental problem of rendering labour attractive. That this is not impracticable, they contend by very strong arguments; in particular by one which they have in common with the Owenites, viz., that scarcely any labour, however severe, undergone by human beings for the sake of subsistence, exceeds in intensity that which other human beings, whose subsistence is already provided for, are found ready and even eager to undergo for pleasure. This certainly is a most significant fact, and one from which the student in social philosophy may draw important instruction. But the argument founded on it may easily be stretched too far. If occupations full of discomfort and fatigue are freely pursued by many persons as amusements, who does not see that they are amusements exactly because they are pursued freely, and may be discontinued at pleasure? The liberty of quitting a position often makes the whole difference between its being painful and pleasurable. Many a person remains in the same town, street, or house from January to December, without a wish or a thought tending towards removal, who, if confined to that same place by the mandate of authority, would find the imprisonment absolutely intolerable.

According to the Fourierists, scarcely any kind of useful labour is naturally and necessarily disagreeable, unless it is either regarded as dishonourable, or is immoderate in degree, or destitute of the stimulus of sympathy and emulation. Excessive toil needs not, they contend, be undergone by any one, in a society in which there would be no idle class, and no labour wasted, as so enormous an amount of labour is now wasted, in useless things; and where full advantage would be taken of the power of association, both in increasing the efficiency of production, and in economizing consumption. The other requisites for rendering labour attractive would, they think, be found in the execution of all labour by social groups, to any number of which the same individual might simultaneously belong, at his or her own choice; their grade in each being determined by the degree of service which they were found capable of rendering, as appreciated by the suffrages of their comrades. It is inferred from the diversity of tastes and talents, that every member of the community would be attached to several groups, employing themselves in various kinds of occupation, some bodily, others mental, and would be capable of occupying a high place in some one or more; so that a real equality, or something more nearly approaching to it than might at first be supposed, would practically result: not from the compression, but, on the contrary, from the largest possible development, of the various natural superiorities residing in each individual.

Even from so brief an outline, it must be evident that this system does no violence to any of the general laws by which human action, even in the present imperfect state of moral and intellectual cultivation, is influenced; and that it would be extremely rash to pronounce it incapable of success, or unfitted to realize a great part of the hopes founded on it by its partisans. With regard to this, as to all other varieties of Socialism, the thing to be desired, and to which they have a just claim, is opportunity of trial. They are all capable of being tried on a moderate scale, and at no risk, either personal or pecuniary, to any except those who try them. It is for experience to determine how far or how soon any one or more of the possible systems of community of property will be fitted to substitute itself for the 'organization of industry' based on private ownership of land and capital. In the meantime we may, without attempting to limit the ultimate capabilities of human nature, affirm, that the political economist, for a considerable time to come, will be chiefly concerned with the conditions of existence and progress belonging to a society founded on private property and individual competition; and that the object to be principally aimed at in the present stage of human improvement, is not the subversion of the system of individual property, but the improvement of it, and the full participation of every member of the community in its benefits.

CHAPTER II

The Same Subject Continued

§1. It is next to be considered, what is included in the idea of private property, and by what considerations the application of the principle should be bounded.

The institution of property, when limited to its essential elements, consists in the recognition, in each person, of a right to the exclusive disposal of what he or she have produced by their own exertions, or received either by gift or by fair agreement, without force or fraud, from those who produced it. The foundation of the whole is, the right of producers to what they themselves have produced. It may be objected, therefore, to the institution as it now exists, that it recognizes rights of property in individuals over things which they have not produced. For example (it may be said) the operatives in a manufactory create, by their labour and skill, the whole produce; yet, instead of its belonging to them, the law gives them only their stipulated hire, and transfers the produce to some one who has merely supplied the funds, without perhaps contributing anything to the work itself, even in the form of superintendence. The answer to this is, that the labour of manufacture is only one of the conditions which must combine for the production of the commodity. The labour cannot be carried on without materials and machinery, nor without a stock of necessaries provided in advance, to maintain the labourers during the production. All these things are the fruits of previous labour. If the labourers were possessed of them, they would not need to divide the produce with any one; but while they have them not, an equivalent must be given to those who have, both for the antecedent labour, and for the abstinence by which the produce of that labour, instead of being expended on indulgences, has been reserved for this use. The capital may not have been, and in most cases was not, created by the labour and abstinence of the present possessor; but it was created by the labour and abstinence of some former person, who may indeed have been wrongfully dispossessed of it, but who, in the present age of the world, much more probably transferred his claims to the present capitalist by gift or voluntary contract: and the abstinence at least must have been continued by each successive owner, down to the present. If it be said, as it may with truth, that those who have inherited the savings of others have an advantage which they may have in no way deserved, over the industrious whose predecessors have not left them anything; I not only admit, but strenuously contend, that this unearned advantage should be curtailed, as much as is consistent with justice to those who thought fit to dispose of their savings by giving them to their descendants. But while it is true that the labourers are at a disadvantage compared with those whose predecessors have saved, it is also true that the labourers are far better off than if those predecessors had not saved. They share in the advantage, though not to an equal extent with the inheritors. The terms of co-operation between present labour and the fruits of past labour and saving, are a subject for adjustment between the two parties. Each is necessary to the other. The capitalists can do nothing without labourers, nor the labourers without capital. If the labourers compete for employment, the capitalists on their part compete for labour, to the full extent of the circulating capital of the country. Competition is often spoken of as if it were necessarily a cause of misery and degradation to the labouring class; as if high wages were not precisely as much a product of competition as low wages. The remuneration of labour is as much the result of the law of competition in the United States, as it is in Ireland, and much more completely so than in England.

The right of property includes, then, the freedom of acquiring by contract. The right of each to what he has produced, implies a right to what has been produced by others, if obtained by their free consent; since the producers must either have given it from good will, or exchanged it for what they esteemed an equivalent, and to prevent them from doing so would be to infringe their right of property in the product of their own industry.

§2. Before proceeding to consider the things which the principle of individual property does not include, we must specify one more thing which it does include: and this is, that a title, after a certain period, should be given by prescription. According to the fundamental idea of property, indeed, nothing ought to be treated as such, which has been acquired by force or fraud, or appropriated in ignorance of a prior title vested in some other person; but it is necessary to the security of rightful possessors, that they should not be molested by charges of wrongful acquisition, when by the lapse of time witnesses must have perished or been lost sight of, and the real character of the transaction can no longer be cleared up. Possession which has not been legally questioned within a moderate number of years, ought to be, as by the laws of all nations it is, a complete title. Even when the acquisition was wrongful, the dispossession, after a generation has elapsed, of the probably *bona fide* possessors, by the revival of a claim which had been long dormant, would generally be a greater injustice, and almost always a greater private and public mischief, than leaving the original wrong without atonement. It may seem hard, that a claim, originally just, should be defeated by mere lapse of time; but there is a time after which, (even looking at the individual case, and without regard to the general effect on the security of possessors,) the balance of hardship turns the other way. With the injustices of men, as with the convulsions and disasters of nature, the longer they remain unrepaired, the greater become the obstacles to repairing them, arising from the aftergrowths which would have to be torn up or broken through. In no human transactions, not even in the simplest and clearest, does it follow that a thing is fit to be done now, because it was fit to be done sixty years ago. It is scarcely needful to remark, that these reasons for not disturbing acts of injustice of old date, cannot apply to unjust systems or institutions; since a bad law or usage is not one bad act, in the remote past, but a perpetual repetition of bad acts, as long as the law or usage lasts.

Such, then, being the essentials of private property, it is now to be considered, to what extent the forms in which the institution has existed in different states of society, or still exists, are necessary consequences of its principle, or are recommended by the reasons on which it is grounded.

§3. Nothing is implied in property but the right of each to his (or her) own faculties, to what he can produce by them, and to whatever he can get for them in a fair market: together with his right to give this to any other person if he chooses, and the right of that other to receive and enjoy it.

It follows, therefore, that although the right of bequest, or gift after death, forms part of the idea of private property, the right of inheritance, as distinguished from bequest, does not. That the property of persons who have made no disposition of it during their lifetime, should pass first to their children, and failing them, to the nearest relations, may be a proper arrangement or not, but is no consequence of the principle of private property. Although there belong to the decision of such questions many considerations besides those of political economy, it is not foreign to the plan of this work to suggest, for the judgment of thinkers, the view of them which most recommends itself to the writer's mind.

No presumption in favour of existing ideas on this subject is to be derived from their antiquity. In early ages, the property of a deceased person passed to his children and nearest relatives by so natural and obvious an arrangement, that no other was likely to be even thought of in competition with it. In the first place, they were usually present on the spot: they were in possession, and if they had no other title, had that, so important in an early state of society, of first occupancy. Secondly, they were already, in a manner, joint owners of his property during his life. If the property was in land, it had generally been conferred by the State on a family rather than on an individual: if it consisted of cattle or moveable goods, it had probably been acquired, and was certainly protected and defended, by the united efforts of all members of the family who were of an age to work or fight. Exclusive individual property, in the modern sense, scarcely entered into the ideas of the time; and when the first magistrate of the association died, he really left nothing vacant but his own share in the division, which devolved on the member of the family who succeeded to his authority. To have disposed of the property otherwise, would have been to break up a little commonwealth, united by ideas, interest, and habits, and to cast them adrift on the world. These considerations, though rather felt than reasoned about, had so great an influence on the minds of mankind, as to create the idea of an inherent right in the children to the possessions of their ancestor; a right which it was not competent to himself to defeat. Bequest, in a primitive state of society, was seldom recognized; a clear proof, were there no other, that property was conceived in a manner totally different from the conception of it in the present time.[1]

But the feudal family, the last historical form of patriarchal life, has long perished, and the unit of society is not now the family or clan, composed of all the reputed descendants of a common ancestor, but the individual; or at most a pair of individuals, with their unemancipated children. Property is now inherent in individuals, not in families: the children when grown up do not follow the occupations or fortunes of the parent: if they participate in the parent's pecuniary means it is at his or her pleasure, and not by a voice in the ownership and government of the whole, but generally by the exclusive enjoyment of a part: and in this country at least (except as far as entails or settlements are an obstacle) it is in the power of parents to disinherit even their children, and leave their fortune to strangers. More distant relatives are in general almost as completely detached from the family and its interests as if they were in no way connected with it. The only claim they are supposed to have on their richer relations, is to a preference, *cæteris paribus*, in good offices, and some aid in case of actual necessity.

So great a change in the constitution of society must make a considerable difference in the grounds on which the disposal of property by inheritance should rest. The reasons usually assigned by modern writers for giving the property of a person who dies intestate, to the children, or nearest relatives, are first, the sup-

1. See, for admirable illustrations of this and many kindred points, Mr Maine's profound work on Ancient Law and its relation to Modern Ideas.

position that in so disposing of it, the law is more likely than in any other mode to do what the proprietor would have done, if he had done anything; and secondly, the hardship, to those who lived with their parents and partook in their opulence, of being cast down from the enjoyments of wealth into poverty and privation.

There is some force in both these arguments. The law ought, no doubt, to do for the children or dependents of an intestate, whatever it was the duty of the parent or protector to have done, so far as this can be known by any one besides himself. Since, however, the law cannot decide on individual claims, but must proceed by general rules, it is next to be considered what these rules should be.

We may first remark, that in regard to collateral relatives, it is not, unless on grounds personal to the particular individual, the duty of any one to make a pecuniary provision for them. No one now expects it, unless there happens to be no direct heirs; nor would it be expected even then, if the expectation were not created by the provisions of the law in case of intestacy. I see, therefore, no reason why collateral inheritance should exist at all. Mr Bentham long ago proposed, and other high authorities have agreed in the opinion, that if there are no heirs either in the descending or in the ascending line, the property, in case of intestacy, should escheat to the State. With respect to the more remote degrees of collateral relationship, the point is not very likely to be disputed. Few will maintain that there is any good reason why the accumulations of some childless miser should on his death (as every now and then happens) go to enrich a distant relative who never saw him, who perhaps never knew himself to be related to him until there was something to be gained by it, and who had no moral claim upon him of any kind, more than the most entire stranger. But the reason of the case applies alike to all collaterals, even in the nearest degree. Collaterals have no real claims, but such as may be equally strong in the case of non-relatives; and in the one case as in the other, where valid claims exist, the proper mode of paying regard to them is by bequest.

The claims of children are of a different nature: they are real, and indefeasible. But even of these, I venture to think that the measure usually taken is an erroneous one: what is due to children is in some respects underrated, in others, as it appears to me, exaggerated. One of the most binding of all obligations, that of not bringing children into the world unless they can be maintained in comfort during childhood, and brought up with a likelihood of supporting themselves when of full age, is both disregarded in practice and made light of in theory in a manner disgraceful to human intelligence. On the other hand, when the parent possesses property, the claims of the children upon it seem to me to be the subject of an opposite error. Whatever fortune a parent may have inherited, or still more, may have acquired, I cannot admit that he owes to his children, merely because they are his children, to leave them rich, without the necessity of any exertion. I could not admit it, even if to be so left were always, and certainly, for the good of the children themselves. But this is in the highest degree uncertain. It depends on individual character. Without supposing extreme cases, it may be affirmed that in a majority of instances the good not only of society but of the individuals would be better consulted by bequeathing to them a moderate, than a large provision. This, which is a common-place of moralists ancient and modern, is felt to be true by many intelligent parents, and would be acted upon much more frequently, if they did not allow themselves to consider less what really is, than what will be thought by others to be, advantageous to the children.

The duties of parents to their children are those which are indissolubly attached to the fact of causing the existence of a human being. The parent owes to society to endeavour to make the child a good and valuable member of it, and owes to the children to provide, so far as depends on him, such education, and such appliances and means, as will enable them to start with a fair chance of achieving by their own exertions a successful life. To this every child has a claim; and I cannot admit, that as a child he has a claim to more. There is a case in which these obligations present themselves in their true light, without any extrinsic circumstances to disguise or confuse them: it is that of an illegitimate child. To such a child it is generally felt that there is due from the parent, the amount of provision for his welfare which will enable him to make his life on the whole a desirable one. I hold that to no child, merely as such, anything more is due, than what is admitted to be due to an illegitimate child: and that no child for whom thus much has been done, has, unless on the score of previously raised expectations, any grievance, if the remainder of the parent's fortune is devoted to public uses, or to the benefit of individuals on whom in the parent's opinion it is better bestowed.

In order to give the children that fair chance of a desirable existence, to which they are entitled, it is generally necessary that they should not be brought up from childhood in habits of luxury which they will not have the means of indulging in after life. This, again, is a duty often flagrantly violated by possessors of terminable incomes, who have little property to leave. When the children of rich parents have lived, as it is natural they should do, in habits corresponding to the scale of expenditure in which the parents indulge, it is generally the duty of the parents to make a greater provision for them, than would suffice for children otherwise brought up. I say generally, because even here there is another side to the question. It is a proposition quite capable of being maintained, that to a strong nature which has to make its way against narrow circumstances, to have known early some of the feelings and experiences of wealth, is an advantage both in the formation of character and in the happiness of life. But allowing that children have a just ground of complaint, who have been brought up to require luxuries which they are not afterwards likely to obtain, and that their claim, therefore, is good to a provision bearing some relation to the mode of their bringing up; this, too, is a claim which is particularly liable to be stretched further than its reasons warrant. The case is exactly that of the younger children of the nobility and landed gentry, the bulk of whose fortune passes to the eldest son. The other sons, who are usually numerous, are brought up in the same habits of luxury as the future heir, and they receive, as a younger brother's portion, generally what the reason of the case dictates, namely, enough to support, in the habits of life to which they are accustomed, themselves, but not a wife or children. It really is no grievance to any man, that for the means of marrying and of supporting a family, he has to depend on his own exertions.

A provision, then, such as is admitted to be reasonable in the case of illegitimate children, for younger children, wherever in short the justice of the case, and the real interests of the individuals and of society, are the only things considered, is, I conceive, all that parents owe to their children, and all, therefore, which the state owes to the children of those who die intestate. The surplus, if any, I hold that it may rightfully appropriate to the general purposes of the community. I would not, however, be supposed to recommend that parents should never do more for their children than what, merely as children, they have a moral right to. In some cases it is imperative, in many laudable, and in all allowable, to do much more. For this, however, the means are afforded by the liberty of bequest. It is due, not to the children but to the parents, that they should have the power of showing marks of affection, of requiting services and sacrifices, and of bestowing their wealth according to their own preferences, or their own judgment of fitness.

§4. Whether the power of bequest should itself be subject to limitation, is an ulterior question of great importance. Unlike inheritance *ab intestato*, bequest is one of the attributes of property: the ownership of a thing cannot be looked upon as complete without the power of bestowing it, at death or during life, at the owner's pleasure: and all the reasons, which recommend that private property should exist, recommend *pro tanto* this extension of it. But property is only a means to an end, not itself the end. Like all other proprietary rights, and even in a greater degree than most, the power of bequest may be so exercised as to conflict with the permanent interests of the human race. It does so, when, not content with bequeathing an estate to A, the testator prescribes that on A's death it shall pass to his eldest son, and to that son's son, and so on for ever. No doubt, persons have occasionally exerted themselves more strenuously to acquire a fortune from the hope of founding a family in perpetuity; but the mischiefs to society of such perpetuities outweigh the value of this incentive to exertion, and the incentives in the case of those who have the opportunity of making large fortunes are strong enough without it. A similar abuse of the power of bequest is committed when a person who does the meritorious act of leaving property for public uses, attempts to prescribe the details of its application in perpetuity; when in founding a place of education, (for instance) he dictates, for ever, what doctrines shall be taught. It being impossible that any one should know what doctrines will be fit to be taught after he has been dead for centuries, the law ought not to give effect to such dispositions of property, unless subject to the perpetual revision (after a certain interval has elapsed) of a fitting authority.

These are obvious limitations. But even the simplest exercise of the right of bequest, that of determining the person to whom property shall pass immediately on the death of the testator, has always been reckoned among the privileges which might be limited or varied, according to views of expediency. The limitations, hitherto, have been almost solely in favour of children. In England the right is in principle unlimited, almost the only impediment being that arising from a settlement by a former proprietor, in which case the holder for the time being cannot indeed bequeath his possessions, but only because there is nothing to bequeath, he having merely a life interest. By the Roman law, on which the civil legislation of the Continent of Europe is principally founded, bequest originally was not permitted at all, and even after it was introduced, a *legitima portio* was compulsorily reserved for each child; and such is still the law in some of the Continental nations. By the French law since the Revolution, the parent can only dispose by will, of a portion equal to the share of one child, each of the children taking an equal portion. This entail, as it may be called, of the bulk of every one's property upon the children collectively, seems to me as little defensible in principle as an entail in favour of one child, though it does not shock so directly the idea of justice. I cannot admit that parents should be compelled to leave to their children even that provision which, as children, I have contended that they have a moral claim to. Children may forfeit that claim by general unworthiness, or particular ill-conduct to the parents: they may have other resources or prospects: what has been previously done for them, in the way of education and advancement in life, may fully satisfy their moral claim; or others may have claims superior to theirs.

The extreme restriction of the power of bequest in French law was adopted as a democratic expedient, to break down the custom of primogeniture, and counteract the tendency of inherited property to collect in large masses. I agree in thinking these objects eminently desirable; but the means used are not, I think, the most judicious. Were I framing a code of laws according to what seems to me best in itself, without regard to existing opinions and sentiments, I should prefer to restrict, not what any one might bequeath, but what any one should be permitted to acquire, by bequest or inheritance. Each person should have power to dispose by will of his or her whole property; but not to lavish it in enriching some one individual, beyond a certain maximum, which should be fixed sufficiently high to afford the means of comfortable independence. The inequalities of property which arise from unequal industry, frugality, perseverance, talents, and to a certain extent even opportunities, are inseparable from the principle of private property, and if we accept the principle, we must bear with these consequences of it: but I see nothing objectionable in fixing a limit to what any one may acquire by the mere favour of others, without any exercise of his faculties, and in requiring that if he desires any further accession of fortune, he shall work for it.[2] I do not conceive that the degree

2. In the case of capital employed in the hands of the owner himself, in carrying on any of the operations of industry, there are strong grounds for leaving to him the power of bequeathing to one person the whole of the funds actually engaged in a single enterprise. It is well that he should be enabled to leave the enterprise under the control of whichever of his heirs he regards as best fitted to conduct it virtuously and efficiently; and the necessity (very frequent and inconvenient under the French law) would be obviated, of breaking up a manufacturing or commercial establishment at the death of its chief. In like manner, thus it should be allowed to a proprietor who leaves to one of his successors the moral burthen of keeping up an ancestral mansion and park or pleasure-ground, to bestow along with them as much other property as is required for their sufficient maintenance.

of limitation which this would impose on the right of bequest, would be felt as a burthensome restraint by any testator who estimated a large fortune at its true value, that of the pleasures and advantages that can be purchased with it: on even the most extravagant estimate of which, it must be apparent to every one, that the difference to the happiness of the possessor between a moderate independence and five times as much, is insignificant when weighed against the enjoyment that might be given, and the permanent benefits diffused, by some other disposal of the four-fifths. So long indeed as the opinion practically prevails, that the best thing which can be done for objects of affection is to heap on them to satiety those intrinsically worthless things on which large fortunes are mostly expended, there might be little use in enacting such a law, even if it were possible to get it passed, since if there were the inclination, there would generally be the power of evading it. The law would be unavailing unless the popular sentiment went energetically along with it; which (judging from the tenacious adherence of public opinion in France to the law of compulsory division) it would in some states of society and government be very likely to do, however much the contrary may be the fact in England and at the present time. If the restriction could be made practically effectual, the benefit would be great. Wealth which could no longer be employed in over-enriching a few, would either be devoted to objects of public usefulness, or if bestowed on individuals, would be distributed among a larger number. While those enormous fortunes which no one needs for any personal purpose but ostentation or improper power, would become much less numerous, there would be a great multiplication of persons in easy circumstances, with the advantages of leisure, and all the real enjoyments which wealth can give, except those of vanity; a class by whom the services which a nation having leisured classes is entitled to expect from them, either by their direct exertions or by the tone they give to the feelings and tastes of the public, would be rendered in a such more beneficial manner than at present. A large portion also of the accumulations of successful industry would probably be devoted to public uses, either by direct bequests to the State, or by the endowment of institutions; as is already done very largely in the United States, where the ideas and practice in the matter of inheritance seem to be unusually rational and beneficial.[3]

§5. The next point to be considered is, whether the reasons on which the institution of property rests, are applicable to all things in which a right of exclusive ownership is at present recognized; and if not, on what other grounds the recognition is defensible.

The essential principle of property being to assure to all persons what they have produced by their labour and accumulated by their abstinence, this principle cannot apply to what is not the produce of labour, the raw material of the earth. If the land derived its productive power wholly from nature, and not at all from industry, or if there were any means of discriminating what is derived from each source, it not only would not be necessary, but it would be the height of injustice, to let the gift of nature be engrossed by individuals. The use of the land in agriculture

3. 'Munificent bequests and donations for public purposes, whether charitable or educational, form a striking feature in the modern history of the United States, and especially of New England. Not only is it common for rich capitalists to leave by will a portion of their fortune towards the endowment of national institutions, but individuals during their lifetime make magnificent grants of money for the same objects. There is here no compulsory law for the equal partition of property among children, as in France, and on the other hand, no custom of entail or primogeniture, as in England, so that the affluent feel themselves at liberty to share their wealth between their kindred and the public; it being impossible to found a family, and parents having frequently the happiness of seeing all their children well provided for and independent long before their death. I have seen a list of bequests and donations made during the last thirty years for the benefit of religious, charitable, and literary institutions in the State of Massachusetts alone, and they amounted to no less a sum than six millions of dollars, or more than a million sterling.' – Lyell's *Travels in America,* Vol. I, p. 263.

In England, whoever leaves anything, beyond trifling legacies, for public or beneficent objects, when he has any near relatives living, does so at the risk of being declared insane by a jury after his death, or at the least, of having the property wasted in a Chancery suit to set aside the will.

must indeed, for the time being, be of necessity exclusive; the same person who has ploughed and sown must be permitted to reap: but the land might be occupied for one season only, as among the ancient Germans; or might be periodically redivided as population increased: or the State might be the universal landlord, and the cultivators tenants under it, either on lease or at will.

But though land is not the produce of industry, most of its valuable qualities are so. Labour is not only requisite for using, but almost equally so for fashioning the instrument. Considerable labour is often required at the commencement, to clear the land for cultivation. In many cases, even when cleared, its productiveness is wholly the effect of labour and art. The Bedford Level produced little or nothing until artificially drained. The bogs of Ireland, until the same thing is done to them, can produce little besides fuel. One of the barrenest soils in the world, composed of the material of the Goodwin Sands, the Pays de Waes in Flanders, has been so fertilized by industry, as to have become one of the most productive in Europe. Cultivation also requires buildings and fences, which are wholly the produce of labour. The fruits of this industry cannot be reaped in a short period. The labour and outlay are immediate, the benefit is spread over many years, perhaps over all future time. A holder will not incur this labour and outlay when strangers and not himself will be benefited by it. If he undertakes such improvements, he must have a sufficient period before him in which to profit by them; and he is in no way so sure of having always a sufficient period as when his tenure is perpetual.[4]

4. 'What endowed man with intelligence and perseverance in labour, what made him direct all his efforts towards an end useful to his race, was the sentiment of perpetuity. The lands which the streams have deposited along their course are always the most fertile, but are also those which they menace with their inundations or corrupt by marshes. Under the guarantee of perpetuity men undertook long and painful labours to give the marshes an outlet, to erect embankments against inundations, to distribute by irrigation-channels fertilizing waters over the same fields which the same waters had condemned to sterility. Under the same guarantee, man, no longer contenting himself with the annual products of the earth, distinguished among the wild vegetation the perennial plants, shrubs, and

§6. These are the reasons which form the justification, in an economical point of view, of property in land. It is seen that they are only valid, in so far as the proprietor of land is its improver. Whenever, in any country, the proprietor, generally speaking, ceases to be the improver, political economy has nothing to say in defence of landed property, as there established. In no sound theory of private property was it ever contemplated that the proprietor of land should be merely a sinecurist quartered on it.

In Great Britain, the landed proprietor is not unfrequently an improver. But it cannot be said that he is generally so. And in the majority of cases he grants the liberty of cultivation on such terms, as to prevent improvements from being made by any one else. In the southern parts of the island, as there are usually no leases, permanent improvements can scarcely be made except by the landlord's capital; accordingly the South, compared with the North of England, and with the Lowlands of Scotland, is still extremely backward in agricultural improvement. The truth is, that any very general improvement of land by the landlords, is hardly compatible with a law or custom of primogeniture. When the land goes wholly to the heir, it generally goes to him severed

---

trees which would be useful to him, improved them by culture, changed, it may almost be said, their very nature, and multiplied their amount. There are fruits which it required centuries of cultivation to bring to their present perfection, and others which have been introduced from the most remote regions. Men have opened the earth to a great depth to renew the soil, and fertilize it by the mixture of its parts and by contact with the air; they have fixed on the hillsides the soil which would have slid off, and have covered the face of the country with a vegetation everywhere abundant, and everywhere useful to the human race. Among their labours there are some of which the fruits can only be reaped at the end of ten or of twenty years; there are others by which their posterity will still benefit after several centuries. All have concurred in augmenting the productive force of nature, in giving to mankind a revenue infinitely more abundant, a revenue of which a considerable part is consumed by those who have no share in the ownership of the land, but who would not have found a maintenance but for that appropriation of the soil by which they seem, at first sight, to have been disinherited.' – Sismondi, *Studies in Political Economy*, Third Essay, on Territorial Wealth. [This quotation was in French in the 1871 edition: the translation given here is Mill's own from the People's edition of 1865.]

from the pecuniary resources which would enable him to improve it, the personal property being absorbed by the provision for younger children, and the land itself often heavily burthened for the same purpose. There is therefore but a small proportion of landlords who have the means of making expensive improvements, unless they do it with borrowed money, and by adding to the mortgages with which in most cases the land was already burthened when they received it. But the position of the owner of a deeply mortgaged estate is so precarious; economy is so unwelcome to one whose apparent fortune greatly exceeds his real means, and the vicissitudes of rent and price which only trench upon the margin of his income, are so formidable to one who can call little more than the margin his own; that it is no wonder if few landlords find themselves in a condition to make immediate sacrifices for the sake of future profit. Were they ever so much inclined, those alone can prudently do it, who have seriously studied the principles of scientific agriculture: and great landlords have seldom seriously studied anything. They might at least hold out inducements to the farmers to do what they will not or cannot do themselves; but even in granting leases, it is in England a general complaint that they tie up their tenants by covenants grounded on the practices of an obsolete and exploded agriculture: while most of them, by withholding leases altogether, and giving the farmer no guarantee of possession beyond a single harvest, keep the land on a footing little more favourable to improvement than in the time of our barbarous ancestors,

———— immetata quibus jugera liberas
Fruges et Cererem ferunt,
Nec cultura placet longior annuâ.

Landed property in England is thus very far from completely fulfilling the conditions which render its existence economically justifiable. But if insufficiently realized even in England, in Ireland those conditions are not complied with at all. With individual exceptions (some of them very honourable ones), the owners of Irish estates do nothing for the land but drain it of its produce. What has been epigrammatically said in the discussions on 'peculiar burthens' is literally true when applied to them; that the greatest 'burthen on land' is the landlords. Returning nothing to the soil, they consume its whole produce, minus the potatoes strictly necessary to keep the inhabitants from dying of famine: and when they have any purpose of improvement, the preparatory step usually consists in not leaving even this pittance, but turning out the people to beggary if not to starvation.[5] When landed property has placed itself upon this footing it ceases to be defensible, and the time has come for making some new arrangement of the matter.

When the 'sacredness of property' is talked of, it should always be remembered, that any such sacredness does not belong in the same degree to landed property. No man made the land. It is the original inheritance of the whole species. Its appropriation is wholly a question of general expediency. When private property in land is not expedient, it is unjust. It is no hardship to any one, to be excluded from what others have produced: they were not bound to produce it for his use, and he loses nothing by not sharing in what otherwise would not have existed at all. But it is some hardship to be born into the world and to find all nature's gifts previously engrossed, and no place left for the newcomer. To reconcile people to this, after they have once admitted into their minds the idea that any moral rights belong to them as human beings, it will always be necessary to convince them that the exclusive appropriation is good for mankind on the whole, themselves included. But this is what no sane human being could be persuaded of, if the relation between the landowner and the cultivator were the same everywhere as it has been in Ireland.

Landed property is felt even by those most tenacious of its rights, to be a different thing from other property; and where the bulk of the community have been disinherited of their share of it, and it has become the exclusive attribute of a small minority, men have generally tried to reconcile it, at least in

5. I must beg the reader to bear in mind that this paragraph was written eighteen years ago. So wonderful are the changes, both moral and economical, taking place in our age, that, without perpetually re-writing a work like the present, it is impossible to keep up with them.

theory, to their sense of justice, by endeavouring to attach duties to it, and erecting it into a sort of magistracy, either moral or legal. But if the state is at liberty to treat the possessors of land as public functionaries, it is only going one step further to say, that it is at liberty to discard them. The claim of the landowners to the land is altogether subordinate to the general policy of the state. The principle of property gives them no right to the land, but only a right to compensation for whatever portion of their interest in the land it may be the policy of the state to deprive them of. To that, their claim is indefeasible. It is due to landowners, and to owners of any property whatever, recognized as such by the state, that they should not be dispossessed of it without receiving its pecuniary value, or an annual income equal to what they derived from it. This is due on the general principles on which property rests. If the land was bought with the produce of the labour and abstinence of themselves or their ancestors, compensation is due to them on that ground; even if otherwise, it is still due on the ground of prescription. Nor can it ever be necessary for accomplishing an object by which the community altogether will gain, that a particular portion of the community should be immolated. When the property is of a kind to which peculiar affections attach themselves, the compensation ought to exceed a bare pecuniary equivalent. But, subject to this proviso, the state is at liberty to deal with landed property as the general interests of the community may require, even to the extent, if it so happen, of doing with the whole, what is done with a part whenever a bill is passed for a railroad or a new street. The community has too much at stake in the proper cultivation of the land, and in the conditions annexed to the occupancy of it, to leave these things to the discretion of a class of persons called landlords, when they have shown themselves unfit for the trust. The legislature, which if it pleased might convert the whole body of landlords into fund-holders or pensioners, might, à fortiori, commute the average receipts of Irish landowners into a fixed rent charge, and raise the tenants into proprietors; supposing always that the full market value of the land was tendered to the landlords, in case they preferred that to accepting the conditions proposed.

There will be another place for discussing the various modes of landed property and tenure, and the advantages and inconveniences of each; in this chapter our concern is with the right itself, the grounds which justify it, and (as a corollary from these) the conditions by which it should be limited. To me it seems almost an axiom that property in land should be interpreted strictly, and that the balance in all cases of doubt should incline against the proprietor. The reverse is the case with property in moveables, and in all things the product of labour: over these, the owner's power both of use and of exclusion should be absolute, except where positive evil to others would result from it; but in the case of land, no exclusive right should be permitted in any individual, which cannot be shown to be productive of positive good. To be allowed any exclusive right at all, over a portion of the common inheritance, while there are others who have no portion, is already a privilege. No quantity of moveable goods which a person can acquire by his labour, prevents others from acquiring the like by the same means; but from the very nature of the case, whoever owns land, keeps others out of the enjoyment of it. The privilege, or monopoly, is only defensible as a necessary evil; it becomes an injustice when carried to any point to which the compensating good does not follow it.

For instance, the exclusive right to the land for purposes of cultivation does not imply an exclusive right to it for purposes of access; and no such right ought to be recognized, except to the extent necessary to protect the produce against damage, and the owner's privacy against invasion. The pretension of two Dukes to shut up a part of the Highlands, and exclude the rest of mankind from many square miles of mountain scenery to prevent disturbance to wild animals, is an abuse; it exceeds the legitimate bounds of the right of landed property. When land is not intended to be cultivated, no good reason can in general be given for its being private property at all; and if any one is permitted to call it his, he ought to know that he holds it by sufferance of the community, and on an implied condition that his ownership, since it cannot possibly do them any good, at least shall not deprive them of any, which they could have derived from the land if it had been unappropriated. Even in the case of cultivated land, a man whom, though only one among millions, the law permits to hold thousands of acres as his single share, is not entitled to think that all this is given to him to use and abuse, and deal with as if it concerned nobody but himself. The rents or profits which he can obtain from it are at his sole disposal: but with regard to the land, in everything which he does with it, and in everything which he abstains from doing, he is morally bound, and should whenever the case admits be legally compelled, to make his interest and pleasure consistent with the public good. The species at large still retains, of its original claim to the soil of the planet which it inhabits, as much as is compatible with the purposes for which it has parted with the remainder.

§7. Besides property in the produce of labour, and property in land, there are other things which are or have been subjects of property, in which no proprietary rights ought to exist at all. But as the civilized world has in general made up its mind on most of these, there is no necessity for dwelling on them in this place. At the head of them, is property in human beings. It is almost superfluous to observe, that this institution can have no place in any society even pretending to be founded on justice, or on fellowship between human creatures. But, iniquitous as it is, yet when the state has expressly legalized it, and human beings, for generations, have been bought, sold, and inherited under sanction of law, it is another wrong, in abolishing the property, not to make full compensation. This wrong was avoided by the great measure of justice in 1833, one of the most virtuous acts, as well as the most practically beneficent, ever done collectively by a nation. Other examples of property which ought not to have been created, are properties in public trusts; such as judicial offices under the old French régime, and the heritable jurisdictions which, in countries not wholly emerged from feudality, pass with the land. Our own country affords, as cases in point, that of a commission in the army, and of an advowson, or right of nomination to an ecclesiastical benefice. A property is also sometimes created in a right of taxing the public; in a monopoly, for instance, or other exclusive privilege. These abuses prevail most in semibarbarous countries; but are not without example in the most civilized. In France there are several important trades and professions, including notaries, attorneys, brokers, appraisers, printers, and (until lately) bakers and butchers, of which the numbers are limited by law. The *brevet* or privilege of one of the permitted number consequently brings a high price in the market. When this is the case, compensation probably could not with justice be refused, on the abolition of the privilege. There are other cases in which this would be more doubtful. The question would turn upon what, in the peculiar circumstances, was sufficient to constitute prescription; and whether the legal recognition which the abuse had obtained, was sufficient to constitute it an institution, or amounted only to an occasional licence. It would be absurd to claim compensation for losses caused by changes in a tariff, a thing confessedly variable from year to year; or for monopolies like those granted to individuals by the Tudors, favours of a despotic authority, which the power that gave was competent at any time to recall.

MORE ABOUT PENGUINS, PELICANS
AND PUFFINS

For further information about books available from Penguins please write to Dept EP, Penguin Books Ltd, Harmondsworth, Middlesex UB7 0DA.

In the U.S.A.: For a complete list of books available from Penguins in the United States write to Dept DG, Penguin Books, 299 Murray Hill Parkway, East Rutherford, New Jersey 07073.

In Canada: For a complete list of books available from Penguins in Canada write to Penguin Books Canada Ltd, 2801 John Street, Markham, Ontario L3R 1B4.

In Australia: For a complete list of books available from Penguins in Australia write to the Marketing Department, Penguin Books Australia Ltd, P.O. Box 257, Ringwood, Victoria 3134.

In New Zealand: For a complete list of books available from Penguins in New Zealand write to the Marketing Department, Penguin Books (N.Z.) Ltd, Private Bag, Takapuna, Auckland 9.

In India: For a complete list of books available from Penguins in India write to Penguin Overseas Ltd, 706 Eros Apartments, 56 Nehru Place, New Delhi 110019.

A CHOICE OF PENGUINS

☐ **Small World** David Lodge   £2.50

A jet-propelled academic romance, sequel to *Changing Places*. 'A new comic débâcle on every page' – *The Times*. 'Here is everything one expects from Lodge but three times as entertaining as anything he has written before' – *Sunday Telegraph*

☐ **The Neverending Story** Michael Ende   £3.50

The international bestseller, now a major film: 'A tale of magical adventure, pursuit and delay, danger, suspense, triumph' – *The Times Literary Supplement*

☐ **The Sword of Honour Trilogy** Evelyn Waugh   £3.95

Containing *Men at Arms, Officers and Gentlemen* and *Unconditional Surrender*, the trilogy described by Cyril Connolly as 'unquestion-ably the finest novels to have come out of the war'.

☐ **The Honorary Consul** Graham Greene   £1.95

In a provincial Argentinian town, a group of revolutionaries kidnap the wrong man . . . 'The tension never relaxes and one reads hungri-ly from page to page, dreading the moment it will all end' – Auberon Waugh in the *Evening Standard*

☐ **The First Rumpole Omnibus** John Mortimer   £4.95

Containing *Rumpole of the Bailey*, *The Trials of Rumpole* and *Rumpole's Return*. 'A fruity, foxy masterpiece, defender of our wilting faith in mankind' – *Sunday Times*

☐ **Scandal** A. N. Wilson   £2.25

Sexual peccadillos, treason and blackmail are all ingredients on the boil in A. N. Wilson's new, *cordon noir* comedy. 'Drily witty, de-liciously nasty' – *Sunday Telegraph*

KING PENGUIN

☐ *Selected Poems* **Tony Harrison** £3.95

Poetry Book Society Recommendation. 'One of the few modern poets who actually has the gift of composing poetry' – James Fenton in the *Sunday Times*

☐ *The Book of Laughter and Forgetting*
Milan Kundera £3.95

'A whirling dance of a book . . . a masterpiece full of angels, terror, ostriches and love . . . No question about it. The most important novel published in Britain this year' – Salman Rushdie in the *Sunday Times*

☐ *The Sea of Fertility* **Yukio Mishima** £9.95

Containing *Spring Snow, Runaway Horses, The Temple of Dawn* and *The Decay of the Angel*: 'These four remarkable novels are the most complete vision we have of Japan in the twentieth century' – Paul Theroux

☐ *The Hawthorne Goddess* **Glyn Hughes** £2.95

Set in eighteenth century Yorkshire where 'the heroine, Anne Wylde, represents the doom of nature and the land . . . Hughes has an arresting style, both rich and abrupt' – *The Times*

☐ *A Confederacy of Dunces* **John Kennedy Toole** £3.95

In this Pulitzer Prize-winning novel, in the bulky figure of Ignatius J. Reilly an immortal comic character is born. 'I succumbed, stunned and seduced . . . it is a masterwork of comedy' – *The New York Times*

☐ *The Last of the Just* **André Schwartz-Bart** £3.50

The story of Ernie Levy, the last of the just, who was killed at Auschwitz in 1943: 'An outstanding achievement, of an altogether different order from even the best of earlier novels which have attempted this theme' – John Gross in the *Sunday Telegraph*

KING PENGUIN

☐ *The White Hotel* **D. M. Thomas** £3.50

'A major artist has once more appeared', declared the *Spectator* on the publication of this acclaimed, now famous novel which recreates the imagined case history of one of Freud's woman patients.

☐ *Dangerous Play: Poems 1974–1984*
Andrew Motion £2.50

Winner of the John Llewelyn Rhys Memorial Prize. Poems and an autobiographical prose piece, *Skating*, by the poet acclaimed in the *TLS* as 'a natural heir to the tradition of Edward Thomas and Ivor Gurney'.

☐ *A Time to Dance* **Bernard Mac Laverty** £2.50

Ten stories, including 'My Dear Palestrina' and 'Phonefun Limited', by the author of *Cal*: 'A writer who has a real affinity with the short story form' – *The Times Literary Supplement*

☐ *Keepers of the House* **Lisa St Aubin de Terán** £2.50

Seventeen-year-old Lydia Sinclair marries Don Diego Beltrán and goes to live on his family's vast, decaying Andean farm. This exotic and flamboyant first novel won the Somerset Maugham Award.

☐ *The Deptford Trilogy* **Robertson Davies** £5.95

'Who killed Boy Staunton?' – around this central mystery is woven an exhilarating and cunningly contrived trilogy of novels: *Fifth Business, The Manticore* and *World of Wonders*.

☐ *The Stories of William Trevor* £5.95

'Trevor packs into each separate five or six thousand words more richness, more laughter, more ache, more multifarious human-ness than many good writers manage to get into a whole novel' – *Punch*. 'Classics of the genre' – Auberon Waugh

PLAYS IN PENGUINS

PENGUIN BOOKS OF POETRY

CLASSICS IN TRANSLATION IN PENGUINS

☐ **Remembrance of Things Past** **Marcel Proust**

☐ Volume One: *Swann's Way, Within a Budding Grove*   £7.50
☐ Volume Two: *The Guermantes Way, Cities of the Plain*   £7.50
☐ Volume Three: *The Captive, The Fugitive, Time Regained*   £7.50

Terence Kilmartin's acclaimed revised version of C. K. Scott Moncrieff's original translation, published in paperback for the first time.

☐ **The Canterbury Tales** **Geoffrey Chaucer**   £2.50

'Every age is a Canterbury Pilgrimage . . . nor can a child be born who is not one of these characters of Chaucer' – William Blake

☐ **Gargantua & Pantagruel** **Rabelais**   £3.95

The fantastic adventures of two giants through which Rabelais (1495–1553) caricatured his life and times in a masterpiece of exuberance and glorious exaggeration.

☐ **The Brothers Karamazov** **Fyodor Dostoevsky**   £3.95

A detective story on many levels, profoundly involving the question of the existence of God, Dostoevsky's great drama of parricide and fraternal jealousy triumphantly fulfilled his aim: 'to find the man in man . . . [to] depict all the depths of the human soul.'

☐ **Fables of Aesop**   £1.95

This translation recovers all the old magic of fables in which, too often, the fox steps forward as the cynical hero and a lamb is an ass to lie down with a lion.

☐ **The Three Theban Plays** **Sophocles**   £2.95

A new translation, by Robert Fagles, of *Antigone, Oedipus the King* and *Oedipus at Colonus*, plays all based on the legend of the royal house of Thebes.

CLASSICS IN TRANSLATION
IN PENGUINS

☐ *The Treasure of the City of Ladies*
Christine de Pisan £2.95

This practical survival handbook for women (whether royal courtiers or prostitutes) paints a vivid picture of their lives and preoccupations in France, *c.* 1405. First English translation.

☐ *Berlin Alexanderplatz* **Alfred Döblin** £4.95

The picaresque tale of an ex-murderer's progress through underworld Berlin. 'One of the great experimental fictions . . . the German equivalent of *Ulysses* and Dos Passos' *U.S.A.*' – *Time Out*

☐ *Metamorphoses* **Ovid** £2.50

The whole of Western literature has found inspiration in Ovid's poem, a golden treasury of myths and legends that are linked by the theme of transformation.

☐ *Darkness at Noon* **Arthur Koestler** £1.95

'Koestler approaches the problem of ends and means, of love and truth and social organization, through the thoughts of an Old Bolshevik, Rubashov, as he awaits death in a G.P.U. prison' – *New Statesman*

☐ *War and Peace* **Leo Tolstoy** £4.95

'A complete picture of human life;' wrote one critic, 'a complete picture of the Russia of that day; a complete picture of everything in which people place their happiness and greatness, their grief and humiliation.'

☐ *The Divine Comedy: 1 Hell* **Dante** £2.25

A new translation by Mark Musa, in which the poet is conducted by the spirit of Virgil down through the twenty-four closely described circles of hell.

ENGLISH AND AMERICAN
LITERATURE IN PENGUINS

☐ *Emma* **Jane Austen** £1.10

'I am going to take a heroine whom no one but myself will much like,' declared Jane Austen of Emma, her most spirited and controversial heroine in a comedy of self-deceit and self-discovery.

☐ *Tender is the Night* **F. Scott Fitzgerald** £2.95

Fitzgerald worked on seventeen different versions of this novel, and its obsessions – idealism, beauty, dissipation, alcohol and insanity – were those that consumed his own marriage and his life.

☐ *The Life of Johnson* **James Boswell** £2.25

Full of gusto, imagination, conversation and wit, Boswell's immortal portrait of Johnson is as near a novel as a true biography can be, and still regarded by many as the finest 'life' ever written. This shortened version is based on the 1799 edition.

☐ *A House and its Head* **Ivy Compton-Burnett** £3.95

In a novel 'as trim and tidy as a hand-grenade' (as Pamela Hansford Johnson put it), Ivy Compton-Burnett penetrates the facade of a conventional, upper-class Victorian family to uncover a chasm of violent emotions – jealousy, pain, frustration and sexual passion.

☐ *The Trumpet Major* **Thomas Hardy** £1.25

Although a vein of unhappy unrequited love runs through this novel, Hardy also draws on his warmest sense of humour to portray Wessex village life at the time of the Napoleonic wars.

☐ *The Complete Poems of Hugh MacDiarmid*

☐ Volume One £8.95
☐ Volume Two £8.95

The definitive edition of work by the greatest Scottish poet since Robert Burns, edited by his son Michael Grieve, and W. R. Aitken.

ENGLISH AND AMERICAN
LITERATURE IN PENGUINS

☐ *Main Street* **Sinclair Lewis** £3.95

The novel that added an immortal chapter to the literature of America's Mid-West, *Main Street* contains the comic essence of Main Streets everywhere.

☐ *The Compleat Angler* **Izaak Walton** £2.50

A celebration of the countryside, and the superiority of those in 1653, as now, who love *quietnesse, vertue* and, above all, *Angling*. 'No fish, however coarse, could wish for a doughtier champion than Izaak Walton' – Lord Home

☐ *The Portrait of a Lady* **Henry James** £2.50

'One of the two most brilliant novels in the language', according to F. R. Leavis, James's masterpiece tells the story of a young American heiress, prey to fortune-hunters but not without a will of her own.

☐ *Hangover Square* **Patrick Hamilton** £3.50

Part love story, part thriller, and set in the publands of London's Earls Court, this novel caught the conversational tone of a whole generation in the uneasy months before the Second World War.

☐ *The Rainbow* **D. H. Lawrence** £2.50

Written between *Sons and Lovers* and *Women in Love*, *The Rainbow* covers three generations of Brangwens, a yeoman family living on the borders of Nottinghamshire.

☐ *Vindication of the Rights of Woman*
   Mary Wollstonecraft £2.95

Although Walpole once called her 'a hyena in petticoats', Mary Wollstonecraft's vision was such that modern feminists continue to go back and debate the arguments so powerfully set down here.

ENGLISH AND AMERICAN LITERATURE IN PENGUINS

☐ *Nostromo* **Joseph Conrad**   £1.95

In his most ambitious and successful novel Conrad created an entire imaginary republic in South America. As he said, 'you shall find there according to your deserts: encouragement, consolation, fear, charm – all you demand – and, perhaps, also that glimpse of truth for which you forgot to ask.'

☐ *A Passage to India* **E. M. Forster**   £2.50

Centred on the unsolved mystery at the Marabar Caves, Forster's masterpiece conveys, as no other novel has done, the troubled spirit of India during the Raj.

These books should be available at all good bookshops or newsagents, but if you live in the UK or the Republic of Ireland and have difficulty in getting to a bookshop, they can be ordered by post. Please indicate the titles required and fill in the form below.

NAME _____ BLOCK CAPITALS

ADDRESS _____

_____

_____

Enclose a cheque or postal order payable to The Penguin Bookshop to cover the total price of books ordered, plus 50p for postage. Readers in the Republic of Ireland should send £1R equivalent to the sterling prices, plus 67p for postage. Send to: The Penguin Bookshop, 54/56 Bridlesmith Gate, Nottingham, NG1 2GP.

You can also order by phoning (0602) 599295, and quoting your Barclaycard or Access number.

Every effort is made to ensure the accuracy of the price and availability of books at the time of going to press, but it is sometimes necessary to increase prices and in these circumstances retail prices may be shown on the covers of books which may differ from the prices shown in this list or elsewhere. This list is not an offer to supply any book.

This order service is only available to residents in the UK and the Republic of Ireland.

● ● ●